BASIC
REASONING

Edward MacKinnon
California State University
Hayward, California

PRENTICE-HALL, INC., *Englewood Cliffs, New Jersey 07632*

Library of Congress Cataloging in Publication Data

MACKINNON, EDWARD (date)
  Basic reasoning.

  Includes bibliographies and index.
  1. Reasoning. 2. Logic. I. Title.
BC177.M23 1985   160   84-26235
ISBN 0-13-068024-9

Editorial/production supervision and
  interior design by Alison Gnerre and Eva Jaunzems
Cover design by Ben Santora
Manufacturing buyer: Harry P. Baisley

Printed in the United States of America
10 9 8 7 6 5 4 3 2 1

ISBN 0-13-068024-9 01

Prentice-Hall International, Inc., *London*
Prentice-Hall of Australia Pty. Limited, *Sydney*
Editora Prentice-Hall do Brasil, Ltda., *Rio de Janeiro*
Prentice-Hall Canada Inc., *Toronto*
Prentice-Hall Hispanoamericana, S.A., *Mexico*
Prentice-Hall of India Private Limited, *New Delhi*
Prentice-Hall of Japan, Inc., *Tokyo*
Prentice-Hall of Southeast Asia Pte. Ltd., *Singapore*
Whitehall Books Limited, *Wellington, New Zealand*

To Barbara, Jennifer, and Kathleen

CONTENTS

PREFACE

In 1980 the Trustees of the California State College and University System instituted General Education requirements which included a course in "Critical Thinking." In doing this they were following, rather than setting, a trend. The need for an introductory level course on basic reasoning skills had long been recognized. Prior to the issuance of any formal decrees, Anita Silvers, Paul Bassen, and others had pioneered in establishing such courses. As chair of a philosophy department in the California State College and University System, I taught these courses and supervised others teaching them. This book is an outgrowth of that experience and of dissatisfaction with the texts currently available in this crucial area.

I am grateful to my fellow faculty members for their helpful discussions of the perils and problems of the present work. I owe a debt of gratitude to many successive classes of students who have served as an initial testing ground for the ideas developed in this book. I also wish to thank the editors of Prentice-Hall and some anonymous referees for their support and cooperation. I wish especially to thank the two people who contributed the most to purging this text of its more blatant errors and to contributing suggestions for improvement. They are Barbara, my wife and fellow philosopher, and Anita Silvers. Though they bear no blame for the shortcomings that remain, they do deserve credit for the absence of many shortcomings.

E.M.

INTRODUCTION

The recent proliferation of courses with titles like: "Critical Thinking," "Clear Thinking," "Basic Reasoning," "Practical Logic," and "Argumentation" manifests a response by educators to a real need of students. The variety of titles reflects the three different traditions that have contributed to the development of courses concerned with basic reasoning skills. This book draws on all three traditions. In this introduction I wish to indicate what I have drawn from each of these traditions and how this book may be adapted to fit courses that stress one or two of these traditions, rather than all three.

The first tradition, *Logic,* emphasizes formal rules that supply a basis for distinguishing valid from invalid arguments. A study of formal logic, the traditional argument goes, supplies basic skills needed to draw inferences, to reason to conclusions, and to distinguish good from bad arguments. The argument is, I believe, essentially correct, but often inappropriate. After some twenty years of teaching logic courses I have found, as have many others, that students in these course find it extremely difficult to relate the logic they learn to the arguments they encounter in daily life.

A reaction against the stress on formal logic led to the emergence of a new tradition stressing *Informal Analysis.* This tradition generally concentrates on detailed analyses of real-life arguments presented in articles, talks, speeches, or TV commercials, while minimizing the role of formal rules. Informal analysis, when properly developed, benefits from the advances made by the philosophical tradition commonly referred to as ordinary language analysis. With this new emphasis students can relate the skills they acquire to the arguments they encounter in their daily lives. It was soon realized, however, that one can only go so far in analyzing or diagramming given arguments. Any consideration of how strongly the premises support the conclusion or how good an argument is inevitably leads back to questions of logic.

The third general movement, *The Rhetorical Tradition,* developed rather independently. It grew out of the ancient tradition of rhetoric, the art and science of public speaking. Though this tradition generally faded in the nineteenth century, it was preserved in Jesuit colleges, universities, and seminaries. The rhetorical tradition was revived in modern times by professors of English, Speech, and Communications, and by those who created various forms of a new rhetoric. This tradition is like the informal analysis tradition in its stress on real-life arguments. It differs from the informal analysis approach primarily in its emphasis on adapting an argument to the audience being addressed.

This book includes more material than most students can cover in a term or a semester. I did this in order to allow room for selection. I will suggest some different tracks which more or less fit the different traditions considered. Each track should begin with the first four chapters. These focus on methods of analyzing the arguments students regularly encounter in their daily lives and in the readings they are expected to master. The treatment gradually moves from content analysis towards a concentration on the form of arguments. From this point on there is room for divergence.

Logical track.   The logic presented in this book is primarily traditional Aristotelian logic, supplemented by a brief introduction to symbolic logic. I have chosen this emphasis not because I consider Aristotelian logic superior to modern logic—it isn't—but because the older logic relates more directly to the ordinary language arguments considered. A course emphasizing logic should cover all of part II, skim chapter 8 and treat chapters 9 and 10 in detail. Chapter 9 treats some difficult and controversial material. The exercises are intended to supply a challenge for advanced students. The natural sequel to a course following this track would be a course in symbolic logic.

For those who wish to learn the elements of logic without getting involved in all the details, there are two possible subtracks. The first of these, *Minimal Logic,* introduces the student to some of the basic terms and ideas used in logic, but does not teach logic skills. The second, *Minor Logic,* gives an introduction to logical methods of drawing conclusions and appraising validity.

MINIMAL LOGIC	MINOR LOGIC
Chap. 5.1, 5.2	Chap. 5.1, 5.2, 5.3
6.1	6.1, 6.4
7.1, 7.2	7.1–7.5

Informal analysis track.   In following this track, focus on part 1, treat the sections included in the minimal or the minor logic subtracks, make a detailed study of chapter 8 and, if time permits, also include sections 2 and 3 of chapter 9, and chapter 10.

Rhetorical track.   The first draft of this book contained a chapter on rhetoric. I eliminated it from the final version because I found it impossible to treat this subject adequately without unduly enlarging the text. This book, however, may be used as a supplementary text in a course focusing on rhetoric, public speaking, or communication. In this case one should study the first four chapters of this book, to learn how arguments are developed and analyzed, before considering the further problems involved in the effective presentation of arguments to particular audiences.

In following any of these tracks, it will help to be aware of four other features of this book. First, the final chapter treats fallacies. Fallacies are not discussed earlier because there is no nonarbitrary way to distinguish them from good arguments until one has some norms for good arguments. Though I would suggest that each track conclude with a consideration of this chapter, it could feasibly be studied at any point in the course.

Each chapter that treats methods concludes with a *Summary* of the methods treated. Though these summaries are often oversimplified, they supply convenient references even for those who have not studied the material in detail. Thus a student who follows the minor logic subtrack could use the summary accounts to get a grasp of the material not covered in class.

Most chapters include three different types of exercises. The first type, A, involves questions about the material covered in the sections preceding the exercises. These are intended more as tests that students can use to gauge their progress than as assignments. Exercises of the second type, type B, are concerned with applying the skills learned to real-life arguments. Exercises of the third type, type M, are multiple choice questions. These are similar to, though not identical with, the questions in the computer-generated quizzes that accompany this course.

The final, rather minor, feature is a matter of punctuation. I have followed the currently accepted philosophical practice of using single quotes to highlight certain terms. This is illustrated by the following sentences. Boston is a city. 'Boston' has six letters. The train conductor bellowed, "Boston." The first sentence uses 'Boston' to refer to a city. The second sentence mentions 'Boston'; the reference is not to the city, but to the word. The third sentence quotes an expression involving 'Boston'.

Chapter 1

WHAT IS REASONING?

Suppose that you are at the bank of a river and have two jugs. One has a four-gallon capacity and the other has a nine-gallon capacity. Let's suppose further that, for some obscure reason, you need exactly six gallons of water, which you have to carry up a big hill. You have no measuring devices apart from the two jugs. How are you going to arrange to carry exactly six gallons? Before reading any further, stop and try to figure it out.

One point seems obvious. The six gallons has to end up in the big jug. But how to get exactly six gallons? Let's experiment. We could fill the nine-gallon jug and then use it to fill the small one. That would leave us with four gallons in the small jug and five gallons in the big jug. Or, we might keep filling the small jug and pouring the water from it into the large jug until the large jug is filled. That would leave us with nine gallons in the large jug and three in the small jug. Then we could dump the three gallons.

We still haven't achieved the goal—six gallons in the big jug. However, we seem to be taking some steps in the right direction. We now have three basic operations: filling a jug, pouring water from one jug to another, and dumping a jug. All of these operations can be performed verbally as well as physically. Since the verbal operations don't require jugs, water, and physical exertion, and don't get us wet, let's stick with them. The obvious thing to do now is to keep manipulating operations until we get the desired answer. To make what we are doing a bit clearer we will put it on a chart, using some obvious abbreviations: F—fill; P—pour; D—dump. If you experiment with different combinations, you will find there are various ways of coming to the desired answer—exactly six gallons in the big jug. Here's one:

Water Table

9 Gallon Jug		4 Gallon Jug	
OPERATION	AMOUNT	OPERATION	AMOUNT
F	9		0
P	5		4
		D	
	5		0
P	1		4
		D	
P	0		1
F	9		1
P	6		4

This simple example brings out some interesting features of reasoning. Sometimes we try to reason directly with things rather than with words. When an electrical toy ceases to work we often try to fix it by tugging a wire here, jiggling a switch there, or even pushing and banging it to see what happens. This method, as most of us learn by experience, rarely leads to useful results. More often, as with the water jugs, we reason with words rather than with things. This practice is, in fact, so familiar that we rarely reflect on its significance. It can only work if language supplies a basis for representing both physical reality and the operations we perform on this reality. In the present case the correspondence seems straightforward. The terms 'jug' and 'water' stand for things; numbers stand for gallons of water; while the terms 'fill', 'pour', and 'dump' stand for the operations named. Performance of the appropriate verbal operations parallels performance of the corresponding physical operations.

Let's examine this a bit more closely. Suppose we actually followed the series of steps indicated in the chart very carefully. Suppose we then carried the big jug to a measuring station and learned that it only contained five and one half gallons. How would we explain the discrepancy between the results based on verbal operations and the result based on physical operations? My first guess would be that some water was spilt in pouring or carrying, or that the jugs did not really hold the amount indicated. That is, I, and I think most other people as well, normally suppose that something went wrong with the physical operations rather than with the verbal reasoning.

Suppose that we could rule out the likelihood of such errors. The jugs were tested and found to hold exactly four and nine gallons. The pouring was done very carefully, using a large funnel to prevent any spilling. The jugs were then covered to prevent any loss of water through evaporation or spilling while carrying. In other words, let's assume that we can rule out any possibility of error due to physical operations. Yet a discrepancy remained. How would we explain it?

Let's explore another possibility. Sometimes reasoning fits reality. Sometimes it does not. Maybe this just happened to be one of the times when reasoning did not work. That is, we are assuming that all the operations were performed exactly as on the chart, that there were no physical difficulties due to water being spilt or evaporating or anything similar. Yet, the measured amount in the big jug turns out to be five and a half gallons, rather than six. So we try to explain the results by claiming that in this case reason and reality simply diverge.

Think this over for a few minutes. Are you willing to accept it, or even take it seriously? I think that few of us are, especially when we get out of a classroom situation and into real life. We have already learned enough about reasoning to know that if our starting point is true and our reasoning is correct, then the conclusion must be true. We may not be able to justify this belief—that's a very different problem. Yet, this is something we implicitly assume in the reasoning we do.

This is similar to the way we operate in other areas. We can know how to operate a radio, a TV set, a car, or even a computer, without understanding how they work. In such cases there are many things we can be sure of. If the radio is functioning properly and we turn the dial, then it will change stations. If the car is functioning properly and we press down on the brakes, then it will slow and stop the car. Yet, if we do not understand how these things work, then all that we can do with them is whatever the designer, manufacturer, or programmer intended us to do. If we wish to go beyond these preset limits, then we have to know how the machinery works. Reasoning is somewhat similar. It depends on structures implicit in, or accessible through, language; and it depends on rules.

All of us already know how to reason, or we never would have made it this far. Yet, if we wish to go beyond the reasoning abilities we assimilate simply by growing up, then we have to learn how the machinery of reasoning works.

In other words, we are supposing that all of us already know how to reason, at least in familiar situations. We are not supposing that any of you know how reasoning works. So what we intend to do is to examine why and how reasoning—the reasoning we already do—works, beginning with simple, familiar cases. If we make some of the rules and structures explicit, then we have some basis for extending these rules and structures to more difficult cases. This we will do in a step-by-step process, working from the relatively familiar towards the relatively unfamiliar. We hope thus to acquire skill in reasoning correctly, which we then apply even when working with difficult and unfamiliar material. We will *not* attempt to explain why reasoning fits reality as well as it does. We are not dismissing this as a false problem. It is a very real problem. But it is too deep and difficult a problem to be handled in an introductory course. In any case, no one can really treat the problem of *why* reasoning works until he or she understands *how* reasoning works. We will begin to study reasoning where reasoning itself begins, with language learning.

1.1 CONCEPTUAL STRUCTURES AND REASONING

An infant begins to learn language through simple word–object connections. 'Ma-ma', 'Da-da', 'ball', and 'juice' are associated with objects that are important in the baby's day and play. These are not yet names. As often as not, a cry of "Ma-ma" means: Find out what's wrong and do something about it—right now! Yet it's the mother who is being summoned to do something. The word–object association has begun. This limited starting point will be repeatedly reinforced, guided, and extended through the actions of parents, brothers and sisters, babysitters, teachers, and others who come to play a significant role in the life of the growing child.

Mature language use involves more than associations of words with objects or actions. To make meaningful sentences words must be combined according to syntactical rules. The growing baby, it seems,[1] begins with a simple syntactical structure, a thing-term coupled to an all-purpose operator: "Da-da all gone," "Juice all gone," "Cookie all gone," "More juice," "More swing," "More play," The degree to which a basis for assimilating a grammar is innate is a complex and sharply controversial issue. The point that concerns us, however, is noncontroversial. The growing child comes to assimilate our grammar and accommodate his or her usage to the accepted usage through an ongoing process of social interaction and reinforcement of correct response.

Through this process of language learning the growing child gradually assimilates a network of structural relations implicit in language. Here a simple example may be more helpful than a general statement. A little girl may have heard the term 'uncle' only when combined with her own uncles' first names—"Uncle Joe" and "Uncle Bill." As far as she is concerned, 'uncle' is part of a name and not a special title. Then her girlfriend informs her: "Uncle Frank is coming to visit." That doesn't sound right. 'Uncle' goes with 'Joe' or 'Bill', not with 'Frank'. In case of doubt—ask Mommy. Mommy informs her: "Frank is Susan's uncle because he's her Daddy's brother." Through such corrections and reinforcements the growing child assimilates the shared public meaning of the term 'uncle' and gradually accommodates her own usage to the common usage.

The shared public meaning this girl assimilates is easily explained. If we use the abbreviations, 'F', 'M', 'B', 'S', and 'H' to stand for 'father', 'mother', 'brother', 'sister', and 'husband', respectively, then we can say that Y is an uncle of X if Y fits into one of four categories:

$$\text{Y is an uncle of X if for X} \quad \begin{array}{rcl} FB & = & Y \\ MB & = & Y \\ FSH & = & Y \\ MSH & = & Y \end{array}$$

Here the first line, for example, means that Y is X's father's brother. What this very simple example brings out is that terms do not get meanings just through a relation to objects. Terms relate to other terms in different and varied ways. These relations supply a basis for inference. Thus, if someone becomes X's mother's sister's husband, then he becomes X's uncle, though he was not X's uncle before that. However, there can still be some loopholes or ambiguities. Should father's sister's ex-husband be called 'uncle'? How about her new live-in boyfriend? Such borderline cases are generally solved by convention of implicit social agreement.

This simple example illustrates a general principle: The language we speak has various sorts of structures and connections built into it. We assimilate these in learning to speak. Reasoning relies on such structures and relations. What we wish to do now is to learn how to use them more critically and effectively. As an initial approach to this, let's return to the water jug example and note three different sorts of things we did.

1. We broke the reasoning down into units like: fill, pour, and dump. We will be doing something similar in analyzing or constructing complex arguments. We will first learn how to handle simple arguments correctly. Then we will learn how to combine simple arguments into more complex ones and to break complex arguments down into simpler units.

2. We had a series of 'if . . . then' arguments. For example, *if* we fill the big jug and pour water from it into the little jug until the little jug is filled, *then* we will have four gallons in the small jug and five in the big jug. This illustrates a very common type of reasoning. We introduce an antecedent—the *if* part of the sentence. Next, we state a consequence—the *then* part of the sentence. This supplies a basis for a simple argument form. Consider the simple argument:

If it is raining, then the sidewalk is wet.
But, it is raining.
_____

So, the sidewalk is wet.

This argument is obviously valid. Let's consider another argument with the same form:

> If she is a surgeon, then she is a doctor.
> But, she is a surgeon.
> _____
> So, she is a doctor.

I think that we can see that what counts here is the form of the argument, rather than the meaning of the individual sentences. If we use (p) to stand for whatever proposition goes into the antecedent and use ⟨q⟩ for whatever proposition goes into the consequent, then the arguments considered all have the form

> If (p), then ⟨q⟩.
> But, (p).
> _____
> So, ⟨q⟩.

This argument form works every time, provided we are consistent in filling the brackets. We will examine such argument forms in more detail later. All that we need note now is that there are such forms and that we have implicitly learned a lot about them in learning how to use terms like 'if . . . then,' 'all', 'some', 'no', and 'or', and other logical connectives. For the time being we will rely on this implicit knowledge, correcting deficiencies when necessary.

3. Though some of the reasoning involved in this simple example can be reduced to formal rules, some can not. We took it for granted that if we add four gallons of water to four gallons of water the result is eight gallons. We made this assumption on the basis of a lesson taught in the second grade:

$$4 + 4 = 8.$$

It seems like a very straightforward application of a general rule to a particular case.

But is it? Suppose that I drew two lines inside the big jug to mark the four- and eight-gallon levels. Then I filled the big jug up to the four-gallon mark with irregularly shaped rocks and filled the small jug with fine sand. If I then emptied the small jug into the big one would the mixture still come up to the eight-gallon mark? The answer is obvious. Since much of the sand would slip between the rocks, the top of the mixture would be below the eight-gallon mark. Suppose that I substituted feathers for rocks and sand.

Four gallons of feathers added to four gallons of feathers would not come to the eight-gallon mark. The feathers at the bottom of the jug would be compressed by the feathers above them and take less room.

It is still true, even in these cases, that $4 + 4 = 8$. The problem is how the rule is to be applied. Quantitites of water add together in much the same way that numbers do. Sand and stones do not. Nor do feathers. The difference between these cases is not in the rules of arithmetic but in the material. Formal reasoning, as in the 'if . . . then' example, depends on rules whose validity is independent of content. Much of the reasoning we do is not formal in this sense. It is content-dependent reasoning. Usually, it is not possible to give general rules applicable to all cases of content-dependent reasoning. We knew that the sand added to the stones would be short of the eight-gallon mark, not because of some general rule of addition, but because we know how sand and stones generally behave. The best way to get at such content-dependent reasoning is to consider representative examples and try to see what patterns of reasoning and methods of analysis work.

The task facing us is becoming a bit clearer. First, we have to learn to distinguish reasoning from other things we do with language, such as describing, explaining, narrating, or complaining. Then we have to get familiar with some of the basic ingredients that go into reasoning. This is what we will do in the rest of this chapter. In later chapters we will learn some ways of analyzing arguments, of constructing arguments, and of distinguishing between good, mediocre, and bad arguments. After we have this general foundation, then we will focus on more specialized topics.

1.2 ARGUMENTS

The term 'argument' usually suggests a rather noisy emotional confrontation: a baseball coach screaming at an umpire, a clash at a political convention, or Archie Bunker castigating his wife. In treatises on reasoning and logic, however, the term 'argument' is given a more precise and sedate sense. An argument involves a conclusion and reasons supporting the conclusion. The reasons may be presented in one or more sentences. Arguments are divided into speculative ones and practical ones. A speculative argument is one in which the premises given support the *truth* of the conclusion. It need not involve a theory or any abstract reasoning. Consider this simple argument: All beagles are hunting dogs and Snoopy is a beagle; so Snoopy is a hunting dog. This is a speculative argument in our sense, because the reasons support the *truth* of the conclusion. A practical argument is one involving reasons supporting a conclusion that something *should be done,* rather than that something is true. For example: Gibbs is the best qualified candidate; so you should vote for him.

To see how an argument differs from narrating, describing, explaining, and other uses of language consider the following four examples. All are concerned with the dominant roles men play in society. Which authors are presenting an argument—either trying to get you to accept something as true, or trying to get you to do something?

1. Men are induced to labour for the maintenance and education of their children, by the persuasion that they are really their own; and therefore it is reasonable, and even necessary, to give them some security in this particular. This security cannot consist entirely in the imposing of severe punishments on any transgression of conjugal fidelity on the part of the wife; since these public punishments cannot be inflicted without legal proof, which it is difficult to meet with in this subject. What restraint, therefore, shall we impose on women in order to counterbalance so strong a temptation as they have to infidelity? There seems to be no restraint possible, but in the punishment of bad fame or reputation, a punishment which has a mighty influence on the human mind, and at the same time is inflicted by the world upon surmises and conjectures, and proofs that would never be received in any court of judicature. In order, therefore, to impose a due restraint on the female sex, we must attach a peculiar degree of shame to their infidelity, above what arises merely from its injustice, and must bestow proportionable praises on their chastity. . . .
   As to the obligation which the male sex lie under with regard to chastity, . . . It is contrary to the interest of civil society, that men should have an *entire* liberty of indulging their appetites in venereal enjoyment; but as this interest is weaker than in the case of the female sex, the moral obligation arising from it must be proportionably weaker. And to prove this we need only appeal to the practice and sentiments of all nations and ages.[2]

2. And yet he felt that, however he might revile and mock her image, his anger was also a form of homage. He had left the classroom in disdain that was not wholly sincere, feeling that perhaps the secret of her race lay behind those dark eyes upon which her long lashes flung a quick shadow. He had told himself bitterly as he walked through the streets that she was a figure of the womanhood of her country, a batlike soul waking to the consciousness of itself in darkness and secrecy and loneliness, tarrying awhile, loveless and sinless, with her mild lover and leaving him to whisper of innocent transgressions in the latticed ear of a priest.[3]

3. Male supremacy is a case of 'positive feedback', or what has been called 'deviant amplification'—the kind of process that leads to the head-splitting squeaks on public-address systems that pick up and then reamplify their own signals. The fiercer the males, the greater the amount of warfare, the more such males are needed. Also, the fiercer the males, the more sexually aggressive they become, the more exploited are the females, and the higher the incidence of polygyny—control over several wives by one man. Polygyny in turn intensifies the shortage of women, raising the level of frustration among the junior males, and increases the motivation for going to war. The amplification builds to an excruciating climax; females are held in contempt and killed in infancy, making it necessary for men to go to war to capture wives in order to rear additional numbers of aggressive men.[4]

4.   If women are to effect a significant amelioration in their condition it seems obvious that they must refuse to marry. No worker can be required to sign on for life: if he did, his employer could disregard all his attempts to gain better pay and conditions. In those places where an employer has the monopoly of employment this phenomenon can be observed. It should not be up to the employer to grant improvements out of the goodness of his heart: his workers must retain their pride by retaining their bargaining power. It might be argued that women are not signed up for life in the marriage contract because divorce is always possible, but as it stands divorce works in the male interest, not only because it was designed and instituted by men, but because divorce still depends on money and independent income. Married women seldom have either. Men argue that alimony laws can cripple them, and this is obviously true, but they have only themselves to blame for the fact that alimony is necessary, largely because of the pattern of granting custody of the children to the mother. The alimonized wife bringing up the children without father is no more free than she ever was. It makes even less sense to sign a life-long service contract which can be broken by the employer only. More bitter still is the reflection that the working wife has her income assessed as a part of her husband's, and he on the other hand is not even obliged to tell her how much he earns. If independence is a necessary concomitant of freedom, women must not marry.[5]

The first selection, from the eighteenth-century philosopher, David Hume, is an attempt to justify a double standard of morality. The basic conclusion is indicated by the 'therefore' in the first paragraph: We as a society must attach a peculiar degree of shame to female infidelity. Since this is something to be done, we have a practical argument. The reasons supporting this now unpalatable conclusion are a bit clearer if we project ourselves back to an earlier and harsher age, one that lacked effective means of contraception and reliable paternity tests. Hume begins with a laudable goal, that children receive adequate maintenance and education. Granted this, the other considerations form a chain leading to the conclusion. A man is generally unwilling to put in the time, money, and effort needed to raise children unless he is sure that they are his own. He can be sure of this only if there is a guarantee of wifely fidelity. The most effective guarantee is the harsh way in which society punishes the fact or even the suspicion of wifely infidelity. This is a typical practical argument in the way it relates the conclusion, a decision concerning what should be done, to a goal to be achieved by means of that decision. No consideration is given to the question of whether or not such a double standard of morality is unfair. This is not peculiar to Hume. It is a general characteristic of the age.

The second passage is concerned with the servile role James Joyce thought that women played in the Ireland of his youth. A woman can become conscious of herself as an individual, a responsible agent, only in secrecy, darkness, and loneliness. Society did not share or reward such aspirations. Joyce is not arguing for or against this position. He is simply narrating the stream of thought that is passing through the head of Stephan Dedalus. So, this passage is not an argument; it is a narration.

The third example is a bit more difficult. There is a conclusion: Male supremacy is a case of positive feedback. There are reasons supporting this. Male aggressiveness has a snowball effect leading to greater male aggressiveness. Nevertheless, what we have here is really not an argument. To see why, it is helpful to compare Harris with Hume. Hume is trying to get his readers to accept the conclusion that a double standard of morality should be accepted as reasonable. Harris is not doing that. He is an anthropologist attempting to *explain* how male supremacy evolved in some cultures. He is not asking the reader to accept this as right for our society, or even for alien societies. This is an explanation concerned with understanding, rather than an argument concerned with acceptance.

The fourth selection is another practical argument. It begins and ends with advice about what is to be done: Women should not marry. Two sorts of reasons are given in support of this conclusion. The first involves a comparison between the conditions of reasonable employment and the conditions of marriage. The second involves a consideration of the consequences of marriage for women: It tends to make them give up their freedom and become dependent on their husbands. The argument also treats and refutes an objection—the claim that the possibility of divorce allows women a reasonable measure of independence.

These examples also bring out one further aspect of argumentation. Simply giving reasons for the conclusion is not enough. If the reasons are not accepted as true, or the advice is not considered practical, then the argument need not convince anyone to accept the conclusion. In such cases one needs to give further arguments to support the truth of debatable premises. This is one reason why speculative and practical arguments tend to get mixed together. We will follow the practice of calling the overall argument speculative or practical depending on whether the overall conclusion is something to be accepted as true or something to be done.

EXERCISES

The exercises in this book are of three sections:

A.   This section involves questions about the material contained in the text. After completing a chapter or a section, you should attempt to answer all the questions in section A. If you are not sure of some of the answers, then go back over the text.

B.   This section involves exercises based on the text. The exercises require a knowledge of the material covered in the text and the ability to use this material. An * in front of a question indicates that the answer is given in the back of the book.

14   What Is Reasoning?

M. This section involves multiple choice questions. Here too an * indicates that the answer is given in the back. Some chapters omit section M of the exercises if the material covered in the chapter does not lend itself to multiple choice questions.

In this chapter, however, sections B and M have a different function. They supply an initial test of reasoning ability. They can help make clear which aspects of reasoning are fairly well known and which require further study.

A. 1. Is it possible to learn how to reason without taking a course in reasoning?
2. Are our spontaneous ways of reasoning always reliable?
3. Are our spontaneous ways of reasoning ever reliable?
4. What is meant by a syntactic structure?
5. What is the basic difference between formal inference and material inference?
6. Does the defense of a position always involve an argument?
7. What is an argument?
8. What is the difference between a speculative argument and a practical argument?

B. We are not yet analyzing arguments. That comes later. A preliminary task is to try to understand what an author is attempting to communicate in a particular paragraph. This does not involve any technical matters. It is basically a question of increased awareness and of paying attention. For each of the following selections try to answer the four questions:

a) Is the selection an argument, a description, a narration, an exhortation, or some-thing else?
b) What is the chief point being made?
c) How is that point supported?
d) Is the making of this point subordinate to some other goal?

* 1. The ultimate driving experience is when car and driver become one: the car provides the driver with accurate information as to what it is doing and what the road conditions are. The driver reacts in turn, by steering, accelerating, or braking. And the car responds—instantly, predictably, and precisely. This integration of car and driver reaches virtual perfection in the Porsche 928. Priced at more than $38,000, the 928 is the finest Porsche ever built.[6]

2. De Niro in *Taxi Driver*, Bronson in *Death Wish*, Hackman in *The Conversation*, Scheider in *The Seven-Ups*, Matthau and Dern in *The Laughing Policeman*, *Joe*, *Walking Tall*, the *Shaft* programmers, or the racist dragonade of the controversial *Fort Apache, the Bronx*,—these films, among others, in their differing ways, along with Eastwood's, represent a significant turning point in Hollywood's relation to low life, as well as a significant shift in leftist, and rightist sensibilities among the public. From *Dead End* to *Knock on Any Door*, *Detective Story* to *In Cold Blood*, roughly the four decades prior to the Seventies, there was always, more or less, an implicit sympathy for the plight of the disadvantaged—at the very least the extenuating circumstances of crime. An attitude so puissant it was amiably satirized in the Officer Krumpke number of *West Side Story*, the delinquents singing, "We're not responsible for our acts, social con-ditions are." By the time of Dirty Harry, though, a new dehumanization is apparent, with the criminals no longer considered even pathological, simply demonic. How can Dirty Harry be sure the Scorpio sniper will strike again? "Because," he replies, "he likes it." And of course Dirty Harry likes it too. "Nothing wrong with shooting, as long as the right people get shot."[7]

* 3. There is no substitute for excitement: not all the massage in the world will insure satisfaction, for it is a matter of psychosexual relief. Real satisfaction is not enshrined

in a tiny cluster of nerves but in the sexual involvement of the whole person. Women's continued high enjoyment of sex, which continues after orgasm, observed by men with wonder, is not based on the clitoris, which does not respond particularly well to continued stimulus, but in a general sensual response. If we localize female response in the clitoris we impose upon women the same limitation of sex which has stunted the male's response. The male sexual idea of virility without languor or amorousness is profoundly desolating: when the release is expressed in mechanical terms it is sought mechanically. Sex becomes masturbation in the vagina.[8]

4. Dramatic programs to stretch the carrying capacity of the earth by increasing food produion . . . will only provide a stay of execution unless they are accompanied by determined and successful efforts at population control. . . . As the most powerful nation in the world today, the United States cannot stand isolated.

   We (as enormous consumers of natural resources; are today involved in the events leading to famine; tomorrow we may be destroyed by the consequences . . .). The birth rate must be brought into line with the death rate or mankind will breed itself into oblivion.[9]

5. **Safety Belt Myths and Facts**

   MYTH: I don't want to be trapped by a seat belt. It's better to be thrown free in an accident.

   FACT: The chance of being killed is 25 times greater if you're ejected. A safety belt will keep you from plunging through the windshield; smashing into trees, rocks, or other cars; scraping along the ground; or getting run over by your own or another car. If you are wearing your belt, you're far more likely to be conscious after an accident to free yourself and other passengers.[10]

*6. Another point that helps to obscure the cultural crisis of our time. One need only glance beyond the boundaries of the high industrial heartland to see our science-based technics rolling across the globe like a mighty Juggernaut, obliterating every alternative style of life. It is difficult not to be flattered by our billions of envious imitators. Though they revile the rich white west, we nonetheless know that we are the very incarnation of the "development" they long for. And if all the world wants what we have got, must we not then be *right?* Are we not the standards for all that progress and modernity mean?

   But it is a pathetic self-deception to beguile the impotent and hungry with our power and opulence, and then seek the validation of our existence by virtue of all that is most wretched in them . . . their dire need, their ignorance of where our standard of development leads, their desperate convetousness. . . . Our job is to review the strange course that science and technique have travelled and the price we have paid for their cultural triumph. Here is the historical horizon to which we must rise.[11]

7. Because it is advantageous for males to mate with as many females as possible, behavioral ecologists argue that monogamy should evolve only when females space themselves in such a way that each male simply cannot control access to more than one mate, or when male parental care is essential for the offspring's survival. Most species of birds are monogamous, probably because both parents are needed to feed the clutch. In mammals, however, males have largely been freed from direct parental care, since lactation places the burden of feeding the young squarely on the female. Perhaps as a result, most mammalian species are polygynous.[12]

*8. Two conclusions can be drawn from these facts. In the first place the fact that some species are forbidden and others permitted is not attributed to the belief that the former have some intrinsic physical or mystic property which makes them harmful but to the concern to introduce a distinction between 'stressed' and 'unstressed' species (in the sense linguists give to these terms). Prohibiting some species is just one of several ways of singling them out as significant. . . . Eating prohibitions and obligations thus seem to be theoretically equivalent means of 'denoting significance' in a logical system some or all of whose elements are edible species.[13]

9. We have found — that is, we have been obliged to assume — that very powerful mental processes or ideas exist which can produce all the effects in mental life that ordinary ideas do, though they themselves do not become conscious. It is enough to say that at this point psychoanalytic theory steps in and asserts that the reasons why such ideas cannot become conscious is that a certain force opposes them, that otherwise they could become conscious, and that it would then be apparent how little they differ from other elements which are admittedly psychical. The fact that in the technique of psychoanalysis a means has been found by which the opposing force can be removed and the ideas in question made conscious renders this theory irrefutable.[14]

10. During the 1970's the United States passed through three stages with regard to the availability of legal abortion: until the middle of 1970 legal abortion was generally not available; from mid-1970 through early 1973 it was available in some regions; since 1973 it has generally been available throughout the nation. The number of reported legal abortions increased from approximately 22,000 in 1969 to over 1.5 million in 1980. Initially the increase in legal abortions was accompanied by a progressive decline in the estimated number of illegal abortions. Thus, most of the initial increase in legal abortions was due to a corresponding drop in illegal abortions.[15]

11. If the principle of utility be a right principle to be governed by, and that in all cases, it follows from what has just been observed, that whatever principle differs from it in any case must necessarily be a wrong one. The principle of asceticism (avoiding pleasure) is constantly opposed to the principle of utility.[16]

M.   *Inference:* An inference is a conclusion drawn from something accepted as true. Though we have not yet formally studied inferences, we have all been making inferences since we began to reason. This exercise is designed to test this acquired ability. Treat the material in the given paragraph as true. Following each paragraph are a series of further claims. The question is whether or not these should also be accepted as true *simply on the basis of the given paragraph.* In presenting your appraisal use the following code:

A. True
B. False
C. Probably true
D. Probably false
E. Truth or falsity cannot be determined on the basis of the evidence given

Furthermore, it is idle dreaming to think of black women simply caring for their homes and children like the middle-class white model. Most black women have to work to help house, feed, and clothe their families. Black women make up a substantial percentage of the black working force and this is true for the poorest black family as well as the so-called 'middle-class' family.[17]

1. More black women are generally obliged to work after marriage than white women.
2. The role of the black woman is almost identical with that of the middle-class white woman.
3. The majority of black women need paying jobs.
4. Black women have more musical talent than white women.
5. Black women are generally better trained for high technology jobs than white women.
6. Most black women have to work even after they have children.

One low tar cigarette continues to challenge higher tar smoking and win.

Latest research offers new evidence confirming MERIT as the proven taste alternative to higher tar smoking.

In impartial tests where brand identity was concealed, the overwhelming majority of smokers reported MERIT taste equal to — or better than — leading higher tar brands.

Moreover, when tar levels were revealed, 2 out of 3 chose the MERIT combination of low tar and good taste.

In a second part of the same study, smokers confirmed that MERIT taste is a major factor in completing their successful switch from higher tar brands.

> Warning: The Surgeon General Has Determined
> That Cigarette Smoking is Dangerous to Your Health

From an ad for MERIT cigarettes, April, 1982.

7. Smoking a pack of cigarettes a day is more harmful than working in an asbestos factory.
8. The higher the tar content of a cigarette, the more dangerous it is.
9. Cigar smoking is more of a health hazard than pipe smoking.
10. A large majority of the smokers tested indicated that MERIT tastes at least as good as high tar cigarettes.
11. MERIT tastes better than most other low tar cigarettes.
12. MERIT is completely free of harmful tars.
13. Smoking MERIT cigarettes presents no health problem at all.

CHICAGO — A cancer patient has been pain free for nearly a month because of morphine from a computerized device implanted in his body in what doctors say is the first such implant in a human.

The device, which is about the size of a hockey puck, was implanted March 19 by Dr. Richard D. Penn. The 69-year-old patient, a resident of Joliet, was not identified.

Penn, associate professor of neurological surgery at Rush-Presbyterian-St. Luke's Medical Center, said Friday the patient has had excellent pain relief without side effects.

"The device is working well and the patient is very pleased," Penn said. "The device has made it possible to care for the patient in the last stages of his illness."

The device, made by Medtronic Inc. of Minneapolis, was implanted in the patient's abdominal wall. It contains a refillable reservoir of morphine and injects the drug into the spinal cord by a catheter, Penn said.

By administering the drug directly to the nervous system in the painful area, Penn said, pain is relieved with one one-hundredth the amount of morphine usually required for debilitating lower back and pelvic pain.[18]

14. Dr. Penn is an associate professor of neurological surgery and a Presbyterian.
15. The new device successfully kills pain by injecting massive amounts of morphine into the painful area.
16. The new pain-killing device will prolong the life of the patient.
17. The success of the new pain-killing device depends on computer-controlled injections of morphine.
18. This new device will be helpful to other patients besides the one treated by Dr. Penn.
19. The patient in question was receiving morphine to alleviate pain before the device was implanted.

20. The treatment administered to the patient prior to the implantation of the new device produced no harmful side effects.

To survive on this earth, human beings require the stable, continuing existence of a suitable environment. Yet the evidence is overwhelming that the way in which we now live on the earth is driving its thin, life-supporting skin, and ourselves with it, to destruction. To understand this calamity, we need to begin with a close look at the nature of the environment itself. Most of us find this a difficult thing to do, for there is a kind of ambiguity in our relation to the environment. Biologically, human beings *participate* in the environmental system as subsidiary parts of the whole. Yet, human society is designed to *exploit* the environment as a whole, to produce wealth. The paradoxical role we play in the natural environment—at once participant and exploiter—distorts our perception of it.[19]

21. Environmental conditions are better now than when Commoner's book was written.
22. If we did not exploit our environment, then we would have an adequate understanding of how it functions.
23. If we continue to live in the future as we are living at present, our life-supporting environment will be destroyed.
24. Human society is designed to protect the environment as a whole.
25. Reptiles contribute more to an overall ecological balance than do mammals.
26. If our present environment were destroyed, a newer and better one would take its place in a reasonably short time.

Some women with small breasts assume that they will be less able to produce milk in sufficient quantity. There is probably little basis for this belief. When a woman is not pregnant and not nursing, the glandular tissue is quiescent and constitutes only a minor part of the breast. The greater part is composed of fat tissue, which is apparently concentrated there for purposes of beauty. The larger breast has more fat tissue; the smaller breast has less. As a woman's pregnancy progresses, secretions from the ovaries stimulate the glandular, milk-producing tissue to develop and enlarge. The arteries and veins that serve the glandular tissue enlarge, too, so that the veins become prominent on the surface of the breasts. Doctors who have cared for nursing mothers agree that even women who have unusually small breasts before pregnancy may produce copious amounts of milk.[20]

27. The basic point of Dr. Spock's argument is

a) A woman's ability to breast-feed her child does not depend on the size of her breasts.
b) Extra fatty tissue in the breasts is generally harmful.
c) Breast-feeding is better for a baby than bottle-feeding.
d) Women with small breasts can produce more milk than women with large breasts, because the fatty tissue in large breasts impedes glandular secretion.
e) Breast-feeding is outdated.

28. The major portion of this paragraph

a) is an argument encouraging women to breast-feed, rather than bottle-feed their babies.
b) is an attempt to refute conflicting scientific theories.
c) applies only to women with small breasts.

    d)   is a nontechnical account of the way the breasts of a pregnant woman develop the ability to produce milk.

    e)   encourages women to concentrate on developing more beautiful breasts.

29. This account of the way the breasts produce milk

    a)   indicates a dangerous enlargement of veins and arteries.

    b)   argues that breast-feeding improves a mother's health.

    c)   supports the claim that breast size does not determine milk-producing ability.

    d)   applies only to women having a first baby.

    e)   shows a tricky way of growing larger breasts.

30. The purpose of Doctor Spock's account is

    a)   to encourage all mothers to breast-feed their babies.

    b)   to correct a common misconception.

    c)   to discourage women from breast-feeding.

    d)   to encourage women to try to enlarge their breasts.

    e)   to counteract misleading advertising put out by baby food companies.

For the same reasons, I conclude that normative ethics is not a branch of any science. It deliberately deals with a type of disagreement that science deliberately avoids. Ethics is not psychology, for instance, for although psychologists may, of course, agree or disagree with one another in belief about attitudes, they need not, as psychologists, be concerned with whether they agree or disagree with one another *in* attitude. Insofar as normative ethics draws from the sciences, in order to change attitudes *via* changing people's beliefs, it *draws* from *all* the sciences; but a moralists's peculiar aim—that of *redirecting* attitudes—is a type of activity, rather than knowledge, and falls within no science. Science may study that activity, and may help indirectly to forward it; but it is not *identical* with that activity.[21]

31. The statement that normative ethics is not a branch of any science

    a)   is intended as a put-down to the egos of ethicians.

    b)   is a reason for asserting the superiority of science.

    c)   is part of a clarification of the nature of psychology

    d)   is a reason supporting the overall conclusion.

    e)   is the basic conclusion of the paragraph.

32. The statement, ''It deliberately deals with a type of disagreement science deliberately avoids''

    a)   is really irrelevant in this context.

    b)   is a reason supporting the claim that ethicians attempt to redirect beliefs.

    c)   is a conclusion flowing from the analysis of what psychology does.

    d)   is a conclusion flowing from the preceding sentence.

    e)   is a reason supporting the conclusion given in the preceding sentence.

33. The comparison between ethics and psychology

    a)   is intended to clarify the type fo reasoning proper to psychology.

    b)   is intended to illustrate the difference between the way disagreements are treated in ethics and in psychology.

    c)   is introduced to distract the reader from the point under discussion.

    d)   contributes nothing to the overall argument.

    e)   distinguishes psychology from every other type of science.

34. The discussion of attitudes

    a)   shows that prejudice plays a role even in science.

    b)   brings out a key difference between ethics and other disciplines.

    c)   is unscientific, because it is not based on an adequate survey of attitudes held by representative samples of the general population.

    d)   clarifies the special status of psychological investigations.

    e)   simply reflects the author's own prejudices.

35. The way the author distinguishes beliefs from attitudes

    a)   manifests his concern for improving people's beliefs.

    b)   is really a sneaky way of attacking religious beliefs.

    c)   indicates that he does not consider attitudes a part of knowledge.

    d)   indicates that attitudes are subordinate to beliefs.

    e)   indicates that beliefs are subordinate to attitudes.

REFERENCES

[1]Jill G. de Villiers and Peter A. deVilliers, *Language Acquisition* (Cambridge: Harvard University Press, 1978), especially pp. 69–94.

[2]David Hume, *A Treatise on Human Nature* (New York: Doubleday, 1961; originally published in 1740), p. 507.

[3]James Joyce, *A Portrait of the Artist as a Young Man* (New York: Viking Press, 1969; originally published in 1916), pp. 220–221. Copyright © 1916 by B. W. Huebsch, renewed copyright © 1944 by Nora Joyce, copyright © 1964 by the Estate of James Joyce. Reprinted by permision of Viking Penguin Inc. and The Society of Authors, London, as the literary representative of the Estate of James Joyce.

[4]Marvin Harris, *Cows, Pigs, Wars, and Witches: The Riddle of Culture* (New York: Random House, 1974), p. 87. Reprinted by permission of Random House, Inc.

[5]Germaine Greer, *The Female Eunuch* (New York: McGraw-Hall, 1971), pp. 340–341. Reprinted by permission of McGraw Hill Book Company and Granada Publishing, Ltd., London.

[6]From a Porsche ad in *Newsweek,* Feb. 22, 1982. Reprinted by permission of Porsche Cars of North America, Inc.

[7]From Robert Mazzocco, "The Supply Side Star," *The New York Review of Books,* April 1, 1982, p. 36. Reprinted with permission from *The New York Review of Books.* Copyright © 1982 Nyrev,Inc.

[8]Germaine Greer, *The Female Eunuch* (New York: McGraw-Hill, 1971), p. 37.

[9]Paul Ehrlich, *The Population Bomb* (New York: Ballentine Books, 1969), pp. 5–6.

[10]Jack Gillis, *The Car Book* (Washington, D.C.: Tilden Press, 1981), p. 26. Reprinted by permission of Tilden Press, Inc.

[11]Theodore Roszak, *Where the Wasteland Ends* (New York: Doubleday Anchor Books, 1973), p. 205. Copyright © 1972 by Theodore Roszak. Reprinted by permission of Doubleday & Co., Inc.

[12]Dorothy L. Cheney, review of Sarah Blaffer Hrdy, *The Woman That Never Evolved,* in *Science,* 215 (1982), pp. 1090–1091. Copyright © 1982 by the American Association for the Advancement of Science. Reprinted by permission of the publisher and author.

[13]Claude Levi-Strauss, *The Savage Mind* (Chicago: The University of Chicago Press, 1966), p. 91.

[14]Sigmund Freud, *The Ego and the Id,* trans. Joan Riviere, ed. James Strachey (New York: W. W. Norton & Co., 1960), p. 4. Copyright © 1960 by James Strachey. Reprinted by permission of W. W. Norton & Company, Inc. Permission to quote from *The Standard Edition of the Complete Psychological Works of Sigmund Freud,* trs. and ed. James Strachey, courtesy Sigmund Freud Copyrights, Ltd., The Institute of Psychoanalysis, and The Hogarth Press, Ltd., London.

[15]Willard Cates, Jr., "Legal Abortion: The Public Health Record," *Science,* 215 (1982), p. 1586. Copyright © 1982 by the American Association for the Advancement of Science. Reprinted by permission of the publisher and author.

[16]Jeremy Bentham, *An Introduction to the Principles of Morals and Legislation,* eds. J. H. Burns and H. L. A. Hart (London: Athlone, 1970; originally published in 1789), p. 17.

[17]Frances M. Beal, "Double Jeopardy; To Be Black and Female," in *Sisterhood Is Powerful,* ed. Robin Morgan (New York: Vintage Books, 1970), p. 342.

[18]From an article by F. N. D'Alessio, Associated Press, in the *Oakland Tribune,* April 18, 1982.

[19]Barry Commoner, *The Closing Circle* (New York: Knopf, 1972), p. 14. Reprinted by permission of Alfred A. Knopf, Inc.

[20]Dr. Benjamin Spock, *Baby and Child Care,* rev. ed. (New York: Pocket Books, 1972), p. 74. Copyright © 1945, 1946, 1957, 1968 by Benjamin Spock, M.D. Reprinted by permission of Pocket Books, a division of Simon & Schuster, Inc.

[21]Charles Stevenson, "Ethical Disagreements," cited in *Basic Philosophical Analysis,* ed. Charles Reid (Encino, Calif.: Dickenson, 1971), p. 384.

Chapter 2

ANALYZING ARGUMENTS

We have seen the basic difference between an argument and other forms of discourse. An argument involves a conclusion, together with reasons supporting the conclusion. There is, however, no standard form that arguments must take. The conclusion may be at the beginning, middle, or end. The reasons given may or may not supply adequate support for the conclusion. Even after we have distinguished arguments from other forms of discourse, many questions remain concerning the forms of arguments, the validity of arguments, and the effectiveness of arguments.

In this chapter and the next we are going to get at arguments by taking them apart and putting them back together. In the present chapter the emphasis will be on taking arguments apart. In the next chapter we will begin putting them back together again. The basic idea behind this is simple. Any argument, whether good or bad, must have some sort of structure. We will begin with the simplest structures. What we are doing here is descriptive, not normative. We are describing the structures arguments have, not prescribing the structures they should have. After considering some simple basic structures we shall examine the ways in which more complex arguments can be built up from simple ones.

This is similar to the method of learning we generally follow in other fields of practical learning. Young dancers do not first master the theory of tap dancing and then try to apply it. They begin by learning some simple basic steps: shuffle, tap, ball, heel. When they have these down, then they learn to put them together in more complex combinations. Similarly, one learning to play a musical instrument begins with individual notes—which finger goes on which key—and then moves on to chords. Even the solution of Rubik's cube is now broken down into sets of basic moves that can be combined in many different ways.

One point needs emphasis. Bad arguments have structures as well as good arguments. Diagramming an argument is not a sufficient basis for deciding whether an argument is good or bad, weak or strong. But it is a help in seeing how the parts hang together, how reasons relate to other reasons and to the conclusion. When we are familiar with this it is easier to construct arguments, to analyze arguments, to recognize arguments, and even to criticize arguments. The emphasis in this and the next chapter, accordingly, will be very much on practice and very little on theory. We will consider many arguments that people have actually presented in many different fields. Diagramming these arguments is one tool for coming to understand them. The important point is to study the different arguments and try to see how well they hang together.

2.1 INFERENCE INDICATORS

Consider something all of us were exposed to as children

> Now Goldilocks spied the porridge. "I am hungry," she said. So she tasted the porridge. The porridge in the big bowl was too hot. The porridge in the middle-sized bowl was too cold. The porridge in the wee little bowl was just right. So she ate it all up.

(2.1)

This, of course, is a narration, not an argument. But what it narrates is the argument Goldilocks used to convince herself that she should eat the porridge in the wee little bowl. Initially we all learned to reason by assimilating and imitating such simple examples. From the point of view of understanding how arguments function, the crucial word in that passage is the term 'so'. Goldilocks is using it to infer a conclusion. To do this one does *not* have to get exposed to a theory of inference. One does not even have to know that the word 'inference' means the process of drawing a conclusion from premises. But, one does have to learn by examples how the term 'so' is used in the beginning of a sentence to relate it to other sentences. Basically, it means that the sentence beginning with 'so' is inferred from one or more preceding sentences.

The term 'so' is an inference indicator, one of many terms we use to indicate that an inference is being drawn. Inference indicators do not always signal conclusions. Some indicate premises or reasons. Consider another argument which few, if any, of us were exposed to as children:

> Since the mind, in all its thoughts and reasonings, hath no other immediate object but its own ideas, which it alone does or can contemplate; it is evident that our knowledge is only conversant about them.[1]

(2.2)

Here the crucial inference indicator is the word 'since'. It goes with a reason to indicate that it is a reason. Here again, learning to use a term like 'since' properly is not a question of first learning a theory of inference and then applying it; it is a question of assimilating a practice. This is something all of us have already done, more or less satisfactorily. In learning to speak and to converse with others in an intelligible way, we have already learned much about the practice of argumentation. This is manifested especially in the way we use inference indicators. In the present chapter we are not attempting to reform the practices we have assimilated. We simply want to make them more explicit so we can get a better grasp on the way they work. Let's begin by listing a few familiar inference indicators.

INFERENCE INDICATORS

Premises	*Conclusions*
Because	Therefore
Since	So
For	It follows that
Whereas (legal documents)	Hence (science writing)
First	Accordingly
In the first place	I conclude that
Secondly	Consequently
In the eighteenth place	It follows that

(2.3)

These terms do not always function as inference indicators. 'For', 'since', and 'first', for example, have other familiar uses, as a preposition, a time indicator, and a counting term, respectively. Sometimes all inference indicators are omitted in an argument, especially when we can presume that our listeners can follow a particular argument without them. However, there is really no point in developing and presenting an argument if our audience does not realize that we are giving reasons to support a conclusion. Inference indicators are the simplest and surest way of doing this.

Before we begin analyzing arguments it will be helpful to clarify a few points of terminology. The first inference indicator we considered was used twice in our example in introducing sentences: "So she tasted the porridge"; "So she ate it all up." The 'since' in Locke's argument only goes with part of a sentence. As these examples show, we can not say that inference indicators always go with sentences. We will use the term 'proposition' for the unit that goes with an inference indicator. Philosophers and logicians have various, often competing, theories about what propositions are. These are not our concern. We will follow the example of Abraham Lincoln, who spoke of our forefathers founding a nation dedicated to the proposition that all men are created equal. A proposition is a sentence or clause that can be said to be either true or false. Thus, questions, commands, exclamations, and other locutions that are neither true nor false are not propositions. Inference indicators go with propositions, which are either sentences or clauses.

The terms 'premise' and 'conclusion' are relative terms. A premise is a proposition *from* which a conclusion is inferred. The conclusion may, in turn, serve as a premise for a further conclusion. Whether we call the results one long argument or two short arguments is often a matter of convenience. Thus, example (2.1), which has two separate conclusions, could be considered as reflecting two separate arguments. Tighter arguments, where an intermediate conclusion is simply a step towards an ultimate conclusion, will generally be treated as one argument.

2.2 ARGUMENT DIAGRAMS

In analyzing arguments we will use a diagramming technique introduced by Beardsley[2] and further developed by Thomas[3] and others. In its simplest form our adaption of this technique involves three steps:

1. Use angle brackets, ⟨ ⟩, to set off the propositions involved and number these consecutively by a number above or in front of the proposition.
2. Draw circles around the inference indicators.
3. Draw a structural diagram. In this diagram represent each proposition by its number and use arrows to represent the relation leading from a premise to a conclusion.

To see how this works, let's return to the example (2.2) from John Locke. The application of steps (1) and (2) yields:

(Since) ⟨the mind, in all its thoughts and reasonings, hath no other immediate object but its own ideas, which it alone does or can contemplate;⟩ ⟨it is evident that our knowledge is only conversant about them.⟩

The first proposition has a subordinate phrase, "in all its thoughts and reasonings," and a subordinate clause, "which it alone does or can contemplate." We are considering these as qualifications rather than as separate propositions. In this case the relation between the premise and the conclusion can be schematized as

$1 \rightarrow 2.$

This is the simplest argument diagram, one premise supporting one conclusion.

A straightforward extension of this is the *serial* (or chain) argument. A premise leads to a conclusion, which, in turn, serves as a premise for a further conclusion. This form is simple enough so that even Winnie the Pooh can use it:

> Pooh said to himself: The only reason for making a buzzing noise that I know of is because you're a bee. And the only reason for being a bee is to make honey. And the only reason for making honey is so that I can eat it.

The opening phrase, "Pooh said to himself," sets the stage for the argument carried on in the bear's mind. Winnie's inference indicator is a simple-minded use of the phrase, "the only reason for." Steps (1) and (2) of the diagramming method lead to:

> (1) ⟨The only reason for making a buzzing noise that I know of is because you're a bee.⟩ (2) ⟨And the only reason for being a bee is to make honey.⟩ (3) ⟨And the only reason for making honey is so that I can eat it.⟩

The diagram for this is

1 → 2 → 3.

The order of implication need not follow the order of the sentences. Thus, when Frankenstein's monster tells its creator, "Beware; for I am fearless, and therefore powerful," he intends an inferential connection which we may diagram:

> (1) ⟨You must beware;⟩ (2) ⟨I am fearless,⟩ and (therefore) (3) ⟨I am powerful.⟩

To put this in propositional form we had to amplify it slightly, changing "Beware" to "You must beware" and supplying the subject and predicate for the predicate adjective "powerful." This is a fairly standard procedure. The inference indicator "therefore" shows that the conclusion, "I am powerful," follows from the premise, "I am fearless." Because the monster is powerful, Frankenstein (which is the name of the doctor, not of the monster) should beware. Therefore, we have the argument diagram

2 → 3 → 1.

A more important extension of the simple argument form involves *coupled* premises. Consider the argument: (1) All sailors lead exciting lives and (2) Joe is a sailor. So, (3) Joe leads an exciting life. Sentence (3) is obviously the conclusion. However, neither premise, *by itself,* supports this conclusion. The two premises support the conclusion only when they are coupled together. We will indicate such coupling by a plus (+) sign. Thus, this argument is diagrammed as

$$\begin{array}{c} 1 \\ + \to 3 . \\ 2 \end{array}$$

This argument form is important, because it illustrates a general pattern. To draw particular conclusions from a general principle, such as a law of science or a law of government, one must couple a general principle to a particular fact or facts. Thus, in his *Third Rule for Reasoning in Philosophy,* Isaac Newton, the founder of modern physics, has:

> that abundance of bodies are hard, we learn by experience; and because the hardness of the whole arises from the hardness of the parts; we therefore justly infer the hardness of the undivided particles not only of the bodies we feel but of all others.[4]

The method of inferring the properties of atoms from the properties of the bodies we experience turned out to be much more complex and indirect than even Newton anticipated.[5] Nevertheless, he supplies a clear example of a pattern of reasoning that is as basic in science as it is in ordinary affairs. There is a particular fact—many bodies are hard, which is known by experience. There is a general principle—the properties of a whole are due to the properties of its parts. From the coupling of these two premises Newton infers the conclusion that the ultimate parts of matter must be hard.

Newton's example illustrates another point. When we use real-life examples, rather than cooked-up examples like the sailor argument, there are generally terms, phrases, or sentences, that do not fit into the argument pattern. Real-life arguments involve references to previously considered material, emotional appeals, stories, and sometimes material that is simply irrelevant. By working with particular examples we will gradually learn to recognize and isolate the propositions that are part of the argument.

There are two more simple argument forms that we should consider, *convergent* and *divergent* arguments. A convergent argument is one in which separate arguments support one and the same conclusion. It is well illustrated by the charges that the American *Declaration of Independence* brought against King George III of England:

> He has refused his assent to laws, the most wholesome and necessary for the public good.
> He has forbidden his Governors to pass laws of immediate and pressing

importance, unless suspended in their operation till his assent should be obtained; and when so suspended he has utterly neglected to attend to them.

He has kept among us in time of peace, standing armies without the consent of our legislatures.

He has affected to render the military independent of and superior to the civil power.

All together some thirty-three separate reasons are given to support the conclusion that the American colonies are justified in declaring themselves independent of British control.

Campaign speeches generally lack the grandeur, but follow the form, of the Declaration of Independence. They involve one conclusion—Vote for my candidate—supported by reasons geared to different groups. There are reasons geared to the rich and reasons geared to the poor, reasons for the conservatives, reasons for the middle-of-the-roaders, and reasons for the liberals. Convergent arguments differ from arguments that use coupled premises chiefly in the fact that in a convergent argument each reason can support the conclusion by itself. A convergent argument is symbolized

    1→]
    2→]→] 4 .
    3→]

This might be clearer if the arrows from 1, 2, and 3 all went directly to 4. However, we wish to use the same form here as in the computer generated quizzes. Since these depend on typewriters that draw horizontal lines, we have introduced square brackets to indicate parallel arguments, each of which supports the conclusion, 4.

Finally, there are divergent arguments, in which one premise supports different independent concusions. In a typical astrology column the faithful believers are informed:

If April 8 is your birthday you are a natural lover. People are attracted to you, feel turned on in your presence, and fantasize about you in your absence. You are drawn to human relations, teaching, service of others. You succeed in these pursuits because others naturally trust you, are willing and often eager to follow your lead. You are sensitive, caring, and a good judge of others. Libra, Leo, and Pisces people make your best partners in romantic affairs. But these are the very partners to avoid in business relations.

How all these genial conclusions flow from the one premise that April 8 is your birthday is not explained, or even indicated. Astrologers are not accustomed to supplying explanations or justifications. Whether this argument is sound or nonsensical, it illustrates the divergent form of one premise leading to many conclusions. It is schematized

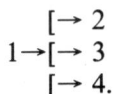

$$
\begin{array}{l}
\quad\; [\rightarrow 2 \\
1\rightarrow[\rightarrow 3 \\
\quad\; [\rightarrow 4.
\end{array}
$$

Here, as with convergent arguments, square brackets are used to indicate parallel conclusions each flowing from the one premise, 1.

2.3 ANALYZING GIVEN ARGUMENTS

The arguments we encounter in practice are rarely the bare-bones arguments of structural diagrams. Particular arguments are generally embedded in a larger context involving description, narration, stage-setting, witty asides, and other linguistic tidbits. The best way to learn how to separate the structure of an argument from such trappings is to begin with simple examples. We will do this, concentrating in this chapter on arguments that can be analyzed by diagrams. When an argument gets very long or very involved, other methods of analysis are often more helpful. These will be considered in the next chapter.

We will begin with a simple argument given by a recent recipient of a Nobel prize in physics:

> No signal can travel faster than the speed of light. So at any time we can only be affected by events occurring close enough so that a ray of light would have had time to reach us since the beginning of the universe.[6]

The first 'so' in the second sentence indicates a conclusion. The first sentence supplies a reason for this conclusion. Using 1 and 2 for the first and second sentences we have

$$1\rightarrow 2.$$

To avoid excessive repetition we will generally put brackets, numbers, and circles around inference indicators in the original argument.

Next, we will consider a slightly more complicated argument given by Benito Mussolini, the father of fascism:

> (1) ⟨Fascism does not, generally speaking, believe in the possibility or utility of perpetual peace.⟩ (2) ⟨War alone keys up human energies to their maximum tension and sets the seal of nobility on those people who have the courage to face it.⟩ (3) ⟨All other tests are substitutes which never place a man face to face

with himself before the alternatives of life and death.⟩ (4) (Therefore,) ⟨all doctrines which postulate peace at all costs are incompatible with fascism.⟩[7]

The 'therefore' of sentence (4) obviously indicates a conclusion. The question is: Is this the overall conclusion of the argument? Sentence (1) also
looks like a conclusion. So, we have to determine the relation between sentences (1) and (4). They might be interpreted as two different ways of saying
essentially the same thing. Yet, the argument is clearer if we interpret (4) as
a reason for (1). Because certain doctrines are incompatible with fascism,
therefore fascists should not believe them. Sentence (2) gives a reason for
sentence (4). Fascism, it must be remembered, was a very macho cult. It
glorified war, aggression, and the qualities of character that supported such
activities. Why does war *alone* key human energies to their maximum tension? Sentence (3) gives the reason for this. Putting these together we have
a neat chain argument

$$3 \rightarrow 2 \rightarrow 4 \rightarrow 1.$$

The next example is from Freud:

(1) ⟨When any situation that is desired by the pleasure principle is prolonged,
it only produces a feeling of mild contentment.⟩ (2) ⟨We are so made that we
can derive intense enjoyment only from a contrast and very little from a state
of things.⟩ (3) (Thus) ⟨our possibilities of happiness are already restricted by
our constitution.⟩[8]

The 'thus' of proposition (3) introduces a conclusion. There are no inference
indicators to show the interrelation between sentences (1) and (2). This must
be determined by the content, by what these sentences say. Sentence (1)
states, in Freudian terminology, what Freud takes to be a fact: our ability to
enjoy any situation is limited. Sentence (2) gives a general reason why this
is so. Should these be interpreted as coupled premises, or as part of a chain
argument? If we had coupled premises, then neither premise would support
the conclusion by itself. Premise (1) supports the conclusion by itself. Sentence (2) is intended to show that (1) is a particular illustration of a general
principle. This analysis leads to the argument diagram

$$2 \rightarrow 1 \rightarrow 3.$$

Next we will consider an argument given by Mao Tse-tung, the founding father of Chinese communism:

(1) ⟨The people's state is for the protection of the people.⟩ (2) ⟨Once they have
a people's state the people then have the possibility of applying democratic

methods on a nationwide and comprehensive scale to educate and reform themselves.⟩ (3) Thus ⟨the people can reform their bad habits and thoughts derived from the old society,⟩ (4) ⟨so that they will not take the wrong road pointed out to them by the reactionaries, but will continue to advance and develop towards a Socialist and then a Communist society.⟩[9]

There are two inference indicators in this passage: 'thus' and 'so that'. Each indicates a conclusion. The first conclusion, proposition (3), leads to the second conclusion, proposition (4). The first two propositions supply the reasons for (3). Proposition (1) is a general principle. Proposition (2) brings out one particular consequence of this general principle, the consequence needed to infer (3). This analysis supports the argument diagram

$$1 \rightarrow 2 \rightarrow 3 \rightarrow 4.$$

Finally, we will consider a more complicated example dealing with somewhat technical material. It is introduced primarily to show how an examination of inference indicators can be a help in coming to understand unfamiliar material.

(1) ⟨There are also three reasons why oxygen is unfavorable to the origin of life by natural processes.⟩ (2) ⟨Chemical evolution of the molecular building blocks from which living cells could be constructed depends on an adequate source of energy, of which the most likely is high-energy ultraviolet radiation.⟩ (3) ⟨Yet if as much as 1 percent of oxygen is present in the atmosphere, ozone forms in upper layers where it absorbs ultraviolet radiation of the intensity needed.⟩ (4) ⟨Any free oxygen present would rapidly degrade any large organic molecules that might have been produced by prior chemical evolution, causing them to be 'burned'—in the sense that they would combine with oxygen and become unavailable for further chemical evolution towards living forms.⟩ (5) ⟨If life did somehow manage to evolve despite such hazards, it would find the free oxygen in its atmosphere a lethal poison.⟩[10]

Anyone not familiar with arguments concerning the earth's atmosphere prior to the emergence of the first living beings might be inclined to quit here. Those who do not wish to quit can profit from the guides that the author himself supplies. The opening sentence says that there are three reasons why. . . . So, whatever follows the 'why' should be the overall conclusion. Further, one should expect to find three separate reasons supporting this conclusion. Since four rather than three sentences follow, one might guess that two of the sentences form a unit. Sentence (3) begins with 'Yet', suggesting that sentences (2) and (3) couple together as one reason and that sentences (4) and (5) are the other two independent reasons.

Now that we have a tentative outline, we can try to fill in the details. Sentence (2) tells us that evolution requires an energy source, ultraviolet radiation. This does not directly bear on the conclusion. The next sentence, however, tells us that oxygen in the atmosphere (ozone is a molecule made up of three oxygen atoms) would absorb the needed energy source. Therefore (2) and (3) combine to yield one reason. Sentence (4) informs us that oxygen would be dangerous to the organic molecules that precede the evolution of the first living beings. Sentence (5) adds the further consideration that oxygen would be a poison for the primitive life forms that would evolve first. If we put these together they suggest the diagram,

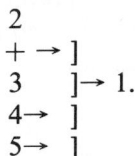

```
2
+ → ]
3    ]→ 1.
4→   ]
5→   ]
```

EXERCISES

A. 1. Must an argument always have inference indicators?
   2. Find two conclusion indicators and two reason indicators beyond those given in the text.
   3. What is a proposition, as the term is used in this text?
   4. Check the *Letters to the Editor* section of your newspaper and try to find examples of a serial argument and an argument with coupled premises.
   5. Must every sentence be either true or false?
   6. What advantage does a convergent argument have over an argument with coupled premises or an argument with serial premises? (Hint: Try to determine how each argument could go wrong.)

B.   In the following arguments put the propositions in angle brackets, number them, and circle the inference indicators. Then draw an argument diagram with numbers representing the propositions.
   1. For whether there is progress or not, at all events there is change; and the changed minds of each generation will require a difference in what has to satisfy their intellect. Hence there seems as much reason for new philosophy as there is for new poetry.[11]
 *2. The Shing could not be surprised; they were too self-absorbed, too egocentric.[12]
   3. Birds are given human Christian names in accordance with the species to which they belong more easily than are other zoological classes, because they can be permitted to resemble men for the very reason that they are so different.[13]
 *4. It is only Einstein's theory of gravitation which can explain both black holes and the origin of the master asymmetry. Hence, gravitation is the cause and the origin of asymmetry in nature. From it alone all the asymmetries in nature emerge. There is, therefore, no need to render black holes any special status in thermodynamics, in the physics of time asymmetries, or in any study about the origin of entropy growth, irreversibility, and asymmetries in nature.[14]
   5. There is also no way of explaining how a Monad can be altered or changed in its inner being by any other created thing, since there is no possibility of transposition within it, nor can we conceive of any internal movement which can be produced, directed, increased or diminished there within the substance, such as can take place within

composites where a change can occur among the parts. The Monads have no windows through which anything may come in or go out.[15]

6. As anthropologists have shown, women's sexual response is culturally conditioned; historically, women defer to whatever model of their sexuality is offered to them by men. So the sad thing for women is that they have participated in the destruction of their own eroticism. Women have helped make the vaginal orgasm into a status symbol in a male-dictated system of values. A woman would now perceive her preference for clitoral orgasm as a "secret shame," ignominious in the eyes of other women as well as those of men.[16]

*7. . . . the fractional increase in separation of these two galaxies (and hence of any other typical galaxies) during the light travel time is just the ratio of the galaxies' relative velocity to the speed of light. But as we have seen earlier, this same ratio also fixes the fractional increase in the wavelength of the lightwave during its journey. Thus, the wavelength of any ray of light simply increases in proportion to the separation between typical galaxies as the universe expands.[17]

8. The 1930's taught us a clear lesson. Aggressive conduct, if allowed to grow unchallenged, ultimately leads to war. This Nation is opposed to war. We are also true to our word. Our unswerving objective, therefore, must be to prevent the use of these missiles against this or any other country, and to secure their withdrawal or elimination from the Western Hemisphere.[18]

*9. If the motion of the carriage is now changed into a non-uniform motion, as for instance by a powerful application of the brakes, then the occupant of the carriage experiences a correspondingly powerful jerk forwards. The retarded motion is manifested in the mechanical behavior of bodies relative to the person in the railway carriage. The mechanical behavior is different from that of the case previously considered, and for this reason it would appear to be impossible that the same mechanical laws hold relatively to the non-uniformly moving carriage, as hold with reference to the carriage when at rest or in uniform motion.[19]

10. This gravitation of women's minds to the present, to the real, to actual fact, while in its exclusiveness is a source of error, is also a most useful counteractive to the contrary error. The principal and most characteristic aberration of speculative minds as such, consists precisely in the deficiency of this lively perception and ever-present sense of objective fact. Hardly anything can be of greater value to a man of theory and speculation than to carry on his speculation in the companionship, and under the criticism of a really superior woman. A woman seldom runs wild after an abstraction.[20]

11. The concept of perversion can hardly fail to be evaluative in some sense, for it appears to involve the notion of an ideal or at least adequate sexuality that the perversions in some way fail to achieve. So, if the concept is viable, the judgment that a person or practice or desire is perverted will constitute a sexual evaluation, implying that better sex, or a better specimen of sex, is possible.[21]

12. . . . both the magisterium of the Church (following a constant tradition) and the moral sense of the faithful have unhesitatingly asserted that masturbation is an intrinsically and seriously disordered act. The chief reason for this stand is that, whatever the motive, the deliberate use of the sexual faculty outside of normal conjugal relations essentially contradicts its finality. In such an act there is lacking the sexual relationship which the moral order requires, the kind of relationship in which "the whole meaning of mutual self-giving and human procreation" is made concretely real "in the context of true love." Only within such a relationship may the sexual powers be deliberately exercised.[22]

*13. WHEREAS it is common knowledge that women believe the condition of the marriage contract to be positive and reciprocal feelings between the two parties (known as "love and affection"); and

WHEREAS the marriage contract in fact legalizes and institutionalizes the rape of women and the bondage of women, both their internal (reproductive) and external (domestic labor) functions; and

WHEREAS the marriage contract, known as ''license,'' fails to list the terms of that contract, a failure which would automatically nullify the validity of any other important contract

THEREFORE, WE, THE FEMINISTS, do hereby charge the city of New York and all those offices and agents aiding and abetting the institution of marriage, such as the Marriage License Bureau, of fraud with malicious intent against the women of this city. (September 23, 1969)[23]

14. For the apparent irregular movement of the planets and their variable distances from the Earth — which cannot be understood as occurring in circles homocentric with the Earth — make it clear that the Earth is not the centre of their circular movements. Therefore, since there are many centres, it is not foolhardy to doubt whether the centre of gravity of the Earth rather than some other is the centre of the world.[24]

*15. To this war of every man, against every man, this also is consequent; that nothing can be unjust. The notions of right and wrong, justice and injustice have no place. Where there is no common power, there is no law: where no law, no injustice. Force, and fraud, are in war the two cardinal virtues. Justice, and injustice are none of the faculties neither of the body, nor mind. If they were, they might be in a man that were alone in the world, as well as his senses, and passions. They are qualities that relate to men in society, not in solitude.[25]

M.   Use the following diagrams as a basis for answering the first set of questions:

A.   1→ 2→ 3
B.   1→ 3→ 2
C.   2→ 3→ 1
D.   1
      +→ 3
      2
E.   2
      +→ 1
      3

Indicate which of the diagrams fits each of the arguments.

1. (1) If today is Tuesday, then this must be Belgium. (2) It is Tuesday. (3) So, this must be Belgium.
2. (1) He'll probably go to jail because (2) the jury is convinced that he stole the money; so (3) they'll find him guilty.
3. (1) The Red Socks have the pitching, but are weak in batting. (2) So, they probably won't win the division championship this year. (3) So, New York has a good chance.
*4. (1) All the girls in the Kappa Alpha Tau sorority are full-time students at the University. (2) I know that she is still a member in good standing of that sorority. (3) So, she must be a full-time student.
5. (1) He thinks that he's God's gift to the women of the world. (2) So, he doesn't believe me when I tell him that I'm leaving him for another man. (3) So, he's due to get the biggest surprise of his life.
6. (1) She's the best qualified person for that teaching position. (2) The position requires both a Ph.D. and at least five years teaching experience, and (3) she's the only candidate with both.

*7. (1) A tree was knocked over by the storm. (2) So, the power was cut off because (3) the tree knocked down a power line when it fell.

8. (1) He should win the seat because (2) he has the support of most of the workers in the district and (3) that support should give him the advantage he needs.

Use these argument diagrams for the next set of questions:

A.   1
     $+\to$ 3$\to$4
     2
B.   2
     $+\to$ 4$\to$ 1
     3
C.   1$\to$ 2
          $+\to$ 4
     3
D.   2$\to$ 3
          $+\to$ 1
     4
E.   2$\to$]
     3$\to$]$\to$ 1
     4$\to$]

Indicate which of these diagrams best fits each of the arguments.

9. (1) A major in computer math is the most practical course for me to take right now. (2) I've always liked mathematics. (3) I have a head start on computer programming. (4) And this gives me the best chance of getting a job when I graduate.

*10. (1) Many experts think that the Bay area is likely to get a major earthquake soon. (2) So, we should plan on the likelihood of an earthquake in the next few years. (3) Disaster insurance is one way to protect yourself and your prospects for the future in case of disaster. (4) Therefore, you owe it to yourself and your family to take our disaster insurance policy.

11. (1) Every student who took this course without having at least one year of calculus did very poorly. (2) Your transcript shows only one term of calculus. (3) So, you would probably have a hard time trying to get a decent mark. (4) Accordingly, I advise you to take more calculus now and take this course later.

12. (1) He has cancer that's too far gone to cure. (2) So, there is no way he will be able to finish out the term. (3) The governor knows that his own chances of re-election don't look very good. (4) So, I'm betting that the governor arranges to get the senate seat himself.

13. (1) This woman should be found guilty of shoplifting. (2) The saleswoman swore that she saw her slip the can of crab meat into her purse. (3) When she was stopped in the parking lot, the can of crab meat was still in her purse. (4) Even though she claims she bought it, she could not show a receipt.

14. (1) Keats was the greatest of the Romantic poets. (2) A great lyric poet must have exquisite sensitivity to the interrelatedness of sound and meaning, thought and emotion. (3) Keats certainly had that to a remarkable degree. (4) So, he must be judged better than the best of his contemporaries, Byron and Shelley.

*15. (1) The Audi is the most reliable performer in this price range. (2) It's been thoroughly tested under the most stringent conditions; (3) so there is no doubt about its reliability; (4) and the only other cars that are as reliable are in a higher price range.

16. (1) The negative results of the test cannot be attributed to any mistakes on the part of the investigator who performed the experiments. (2) Whenever the equipment and procedures are thoroughly checked and the experimenter is professionally competent, then you can have confidence in the reliability of the results. (3) Those conditions were clearly met in the present case. (4) So, we have to assume that the results are reliable.

2.4 REPEATED PREMISES
AND INFERENCE GAPS

When arguments get to be very long or very complex it is generally more helpful to reconstruct them than to diagram the given argument. This is what we will consider in the next chapter. What we wish to consider in concluding this chapter are some cases that fall between arguments that may simply be diagrammed and arguments that are best understood by reconstruction. These are generally of two types, one involving the repetition of propositions and one involving the omission of propositions or of inference indicators.

In developing an argument one often repeats the same proposition in more or less equivalent terms. Many of us, for example, have been exposed to high-school valedictorians who inform the graduating class: "The sea of life is rough, the waves are high, and the undertow is treacherous. But we must struggle, we must fight on, we must give it our best shot, we must never quit." The variations here are purely rhetorical, a rather shallow rhetoric. There is really only one premise—"Life is tough"; and only one conclusion—"We should try our best." In diagramming an argument like this, all the equivalent propositions should be assigned the same number.

In a complex argument it is often necessary to refer back to previous propositions. This may be done by using a referential term like 'that' or 'which', or by restating the gist of the propositions. As an example of the first method consider the simple argument: "The interest rates remain high. That is why the housing market remains sluggish." If the second sentence had been written: "Therefore, the housing market remains sluggish," then it would clearly be a conclusion following from the first sentence as a premise. The given argument has the same structure, except that it uses 'that' to refer back to the first sentence. In this case the method of diagramming would lead to

⟨The interest rates remain high.⟩ ⟨That is why⟩ ⟨the housing market remains sluggish.⟩

In simple cases, there is usually no need to treat referential terms as propositions and assign numbers to them. One would diagram any version of the given argument as

1→ 2.

In longer arguments, where referential terms may not refer to the immediately preceding sentence, it is important to assign referential terms the number of the proposition they refer to. Consider, for example, the way a lawyer might summarize the defense of his client.

> Ladies and gentlemen of the jury, my client is innocent of the charges brought against him. This is shown in a negative way by the fact that the prosecution has not produced even one witness who saw him present at the scene of the crime. He has a regular job and a fairly good income. This certainly indicates that he had no motive for stealing. Since he has become an adult he has never been convicted of stealing anything. This certainly must count strongly in favor of my claim that he is innocent. His wife attests to the truth of this claim. It is even supported by his competitors.

This rather artificial example was put in to supply an exercise in checking references. However, we don't check references quite the same way a bank or loan company does. The example begins with a claim: "My client is innocent of the charges brought against him." After that it uses a few terms, especially 'this' and 'it', which refer back to earlier propositions. The first temptation is to assume that they all refer back to the basic claim of the paragraph. We must resist this temptation and be a little more careful about checking references.

The 'this' in the second sentence clearly refers back to the preceding sentence. It should be assigned the same number. The next referential use of 'this' occurs in: "This certainly indicates. . . ." Here 'this' does not refer back to the original claim. It refers back to the immediately preceding sentence: "He has a regular job. . . ." There is nothing mysterious or complicated about such references. If there is any doubt, simply change the proposition into a question: "What certainly indicates that he had no motive for stealing?" Then the relation is rather obvious. Similarly, the next use of 'this' in "This certainly must count . . ." refers back to the immediately preceding sentence. Here again, if there is any doubt use the WHAT test. Substitute 'what' for 'this' and decide which proposition answers the 'what' question. The sentence ends with a reference to "my claim." This refers back to the original claim made: "My client is innocent." So does the next use of the term 'claim'. The use of 'it' refers back to this same claim.

Technically 'it' is a referring term; 'my claim' is not. The reason for that distinction is that 'it' is a pronoun whose function is to refer back. 'Claim' is a noun. It categorizes the type of assertion being made. However, 'my claim' effectively functions as a referring term. Here it is more helpful to consider sense than grammar. Instead of using a 'what' for clarification, we could use a 'that': "My claim *that* my client is innocent is. . . ." With these clarifications the argument given would be numbered and diagrammed as follows:

1
Ladies and gentlemen of the jury, ⟨my client is innocent of the charges brought
1
against him.⟩ ⟨This⟩ (is shown in a negative way by the fact that) ⟨the
2
prosecution has not produced even one witness who saw him present at the
3   3
scene of the crime.⟩ ⟨He has a regular job and a fairly good income.⟩ ⟨This⟩
4   5
(certainly indicates that) ⟨he had no motive for stealing.⟩ ⟨Since he has
5
become an adult he has never been convicted of stealing anything.⟩ ⟨This⟩
1
(certainly must count strongly in favor of my claim that) ⟨he is innocent.⟩
6   1   7
⟨His wife attests to the truth of this claim.⟩ ⟨It⟩ ⟨is even supported by his

competitors.⟩

```
      2→]
3→ 4→]
      5→]  →] 1
      6→]
      7→]
```

Besides using referential terms such as 'that' or 'which' to refer back, one may simply paraphrase a given proposition. As an example of this we may consider an argument contained in a recent *Scientific American* article, indicating the way two scientists reasoned from evidence to the dating of some fossilized footprints.

The Footprint Tuff was deposited over a short span, perhaps in a few weeks, near the end of the savanna dry season and extending into the early part of the rainy season. The excellent preservation of footprints and rainprints alike shows that the tuff layers must have been buried by fresh ash soon after the prints were made. Further evidence that the burial process was quick is provided by the continuity of layers, some only a few millimeters thick, over an area 70 square kilometers in extent.[26]

The opening sentence presents the conclusion: The layer with the fossilized footprints was deposited over a brief period of time, probably in the few weeks when the dry season was ending and the rainy season beginning.

The 'shows that' of the next sentence links evidence—excellent preservation caused by a layer of volcanic ash—to a restatement of the first proposition, the footprints were deposited in a brief period. The opening words of the next sentence, 'Further evidence', clearly indicates an independent reason for the conclusion, which is given one more paraphrase, 'the burial process was quick'. If we were to recast this argument in a form that fits our argument diagrams, then we would have

> (1) ⟨The footprints and rainprints preserved by the ash fall are in excellent condition.⟩ (2) ⟨Furthermore, there is a continuity of layers, some only a few millimeters thick, over an area 70 square kilometers in extent.⟩ (3) Therefore, ⟨the Footprint Tuff was deposited over a short span, perhaps in a few weeks, beginning near the end of the savanna dry season and extending into the rainy season.⟩

When the passage is reconstructed in this way, it clearly has the form of a convergent argument.

$$1\rightarrow]$$
$$\quad\quad]\rightarrow 3$$
$$2\rightarrow]$$

The reconstructed argument fits a diagram form more neatly than the original does. However, it does this by simplifying the way the evidence is interpreted and by using a rather stilted prose. Once we are clear on how terms referring to previous propositions fit into the process of argument development, it is not really necessary to rewrite an argument just to clarify some obvious references. Nor is it necessary, in obvious cases, to label referential expressions with the number of the proposition they are referring to. The argument diagram bringing out that relation suffices. Thus, the given argument could be numbered and diagrammed as follows;

> (1) ⟨The Footprint Tuff was deposited over a short span, perhaps in a few weeks, near the end of the savanna dry season and extending into the early part of the rainy season.⟩ (2) ⟨The excellent preservation of footprints and rainprints alike shows that the tuff layers must have been buried by fresh ash soon after the prints were made.⟩ (3) ⟨Further evidence that the burial process was quick is provided by the continuity of layers, some only a few millimeters thick, over an area 70 square kilometers in extent.⟩

$$2\rightarrow]$$
$$\quad\quad]\rightarrow 1$$
$$3\rightarrow]$$

Inference gaps are of various sorts. The most common simply leaves out the obvious on the grounds that it is obvious. This can apply to premises, conclusions, or inference indicators. Consider the argument: "All students are eligible for membership in the Co-op; so all sophomores are eligible for membership in the Co-op." This is incomplete as an argument unless one adds the further premise: "All sophomores are students." To add this, however, is to insult the intelligence of the audience. Explaining the obvious is the trademark of the bore. Even though one may omit obvious premises in *giving* an argument, one has to include them when *analyzing* an argument. We will indicate added premises by enclosing them in *square,* rather than angle brackets. Then the argument just given would be analyzed

(1) ⟨All students are eligible for membership in the Co-op.⟩
(2) [And all sophmores are students.] (3) So, ⟨all sophmores are eligible for membership in the Co-op.⟩

1
+ → 3
2

For a different sort of inference gap, consider the argument

He should be found guilty. There is no doubt about the fact that he committed the crime and all the evidence indicates that he was sane when he did it.

This argument lacks inference indicators. Here again, the obvious is omitted on the grounds that it is obvious. The second sentence gives two coupled reasons supporting the first. In this case it is hardly necessary to add inference indicators. When such an addition is necessary or helpful we will use square brackets to indicate that the inference indicators were added.

(1) ⟨He should be found guilty;⟩ [for] (2) ⟨there is no real doubt about the fact that he committed the crime⟩ and (3) ⟨all the evidence indicates that he was sane when he did it.⟩

2
+ → 1
3

Here the premises are interpreted as coupled, rather than separate, because both must be fulfilled together to fit the legal definition of murder.

When a conclusion is obvious, one may omit it just as one does with a premise. A more common trick, however, is to substitute one or more rhetorical questions for a conclusion. Thus, a political candidate might conclude a speech:

My opponent's record shows four years of waste, neglect, and corruption. Can this city afford another four years of waste, neglect and corruption? Should failure in office be rewarded by a return to office? Does my opponent really deserve your vote?

For the purpose of analyzing or diagramming an argument, these questions can be replaced by one proposition: My opponent does not deserve your vote.

There are more subtle ways of omitting conclusions than the substitution of rhetorical questions for propositions. Witty writers often use indirection as a means of hinting at a conclusion. Then the reader who draws the right conclusion is made to feel clever, and takes an active rather than a purely passive role in the process of argumentation. Bertrand Russell, one of the most famous philosophers of this century, was a master of this style of writing. Consider, for example, his rather thinly disguised argument on the morality of birth control.

> The commonest objection to birth control is that it is against "nature." (For some reason we are not allowed to say that celibacy is against nature; the only reason I can think of is that it is not new.) Malthus saw only three ways of keeping down the population: moral restraint, vice, and misery. Moral restraint, he admitted, was not likely to be practiced on a large scale. "Vice," i.e., birth control, he, as a clergyman, viewed with abhorrence. There remained misery. In his comfortable parsonage, he contemplated the misery of the great majority of mankind with equanimity, and pointed out the fallacies of the reformers who hoped to alleviate it.[27]

Russell does not explicitly draw the conclusion that the most humane method of limiting population is through birth control. Yet, he skillfully leads the reader to infer this. It may be necessary, for the sake of understanding the argument, to supply the conclusion and then diagram the argument. In the more complex cases to be considered in the next chapter it may be necessary to reconstruct the arguments. These, however, are just temporary expedients introduced to enable us to understand the structure of the argument. They are not ways of improving the original argument. In Russell's argument, to take a typical example, much of the persuasive force comes from the subtle indirect way the conclusion is suggested.

EXERCISES

A. 1. What is the difference between an ordinary question and a rhetorical question?
   2. Is it ever reasonable to present an argument and omit the conclusion?
   3. When is it reasonable to omit the premise in an argument?
   4. How might the omission of a part of an argument be more effective in getting audience involvement than inclusion of the omitted part?
   5. Why do so many advertisements involve inference gaps?

B. 1. Fill in what is needed to complete the following arguments.

   a)   9 out of 10 would do it again. Ford Escort.

b) The pleasure is back. Barclay.
c) It takes a Honda years to do what some cars do in a day. Depreciate.
d) You're not just moving in, you're moving up. Canadian Club.
e) It's time you stopped drinking ordinary scotch. Pinch 12-year-old scotch.
f) Because you enjoy going first class. Passport Scotch.
g) Does she or doesn't she? Only her hairdresser knows for sure. Breck's hair dye ad.
h) You see one nuclear war. You've seen them all.

2. The following slogans, premises in search of a conclusion, illustrate the use of humor in argumentation. Indicate what sort of conclusion each might support.

a) A Smith and Wesson beats four aces.
b) Anything enjoyable is either illegal, immoral, or fattening.
c) Never argue with a fool. An audience might not know the difference.
d) When in doubt, mumble; when in trouble, delegate.
e) The repairman will never have seen a model quite like yours before.
f) The race is not always to the swift nor the battle to the strong, but that's the way to bet.

3. Rewrite the following arguments by closing inference gaps or eliminating repetitions. Then diagram the resulting argument.

a) "Let us work without reasoning," said Martin, "it is the only way to make life endurable."[28] [The conclusion of Voltaire's *Candide*]
*b) "He's a businessman," the Don said blandly. "I'll make him an offer he can't refuse."[29]
c) Finally, altruism towards unrelated individuals should be most adaptive when directed towards those with the greatest likelihood of reciprocating effectively, thereby increasing the inclusive fitness of the altruist. Therefore preferred beneficiaries should have access to resources that they could subsequently bestow upon the altruist and/or his relatives: Money, promotions, etc.[30]
[Hint: 'thereby' refers back to a reason developed earlier in the book: Species acquire altruistic practices only when such practices increase the adaptive fitness of the species.]
*d) We repeat, the issue is not one of life or death. The issue is which kind of death, an agonized or peaceful one. Shall we meet death in personal integrity or in personal disintegration? Should there be a moral or a demoralized end to mortal life? Surely . . . we are not as persons of moral stature to be ruled by ruthless and unreasoning physiology, but rather by reason and self-control.[31]
e) All our cadres, whatever their rank, are servants of the people, and whatever we do is to serve the people. How then can we ever be reluctant to discard any of our bad traits?[32]
f) Wrong as we think slavery is we can yet afford to let it alone where it is, because that much is due to the necessity arising from its actual presence in the nation; but can we, while our votes will prevent it, allow it to spread into the national Territories, and to overrun us here in these free States? If our sense of duty forbids this, then let us stand by our duty fearlessly and effectively. Let us be directed by none of those sophisticated contrivances wherewith we are so industriously plied and belabored—contrivances such as groping for some middle ground between the right and the wrong, vain as the search for a man who should be neither a living man nor a dead man; such is a policy of "don't care" on a question about which all true men do care.[33]

g) Is it necessary for your liberty that you should abandon those great rights by the adoption of this system? Is the relinquishment of the trial by jury and the liberty of the press necessary for your liberty? Will the abandonment of your most sacred rights tend to the security of liberty?[34]

h) To behave like a ''blindfolded man catching sparrows,'' or ''a blind man groping for a fish,'' to be crude and careless, to indulge in verbiage, to rest content with a smattering of knowledge — such is the extremely bad style of work that still exists amøng many comrades in our Party, a style utterly opposed to the fundamental spirit of Marxism-Leninism. Marx, Engels, Lenin and Stalin have taught us that it is necessary to study conditions conscientiously and to proceed from objective reality and not from subjective wishes; but many of our comrades act in direct violation of this truth.[35]

*i) Are there not, also, poor devils who commit crimes in order to be sent to hard labor and thus to escape from the liberty which is more painful than confinement? A man's life is miserable, he has never, perhaps, been able to satisfy his hunger. He worked to death in order to enrich his master. In the convict prison his work will be less severe, less crushing. He will eat as much as he wants, better than he could ever have hoped to eat, had he remained free. On holidays he will have meat, and fine people will give him alms, and his evening's work will bring him in some money. And the society one meets with in the convict prison, is that to be counted for nothing? The new arrival can scarcely conceal the admiration he feels for his companions in labor. He has seen nothing like it before, and he will consider himself in the best company possible.[36]

REFERENCES

[1]John Locke, *An Essay Concerning Human Understanding,* bk. IV, chap. 1, sec. 1 (originally published in 1690).

[2]Monroe C. Beardsley, *Thinking Straight,* 4th ed. (Englewood Cliffs, N.J.: Prentice-Hall, Inc., 1975).

[3]Stephen N. Thomas, *Practical Reasoning in Natural Language,* 2nd ed. (Englewood Cliffs, N.J.: Prentice-Hall, Inc., 1980).

[4]Isaac Newton, *Principia Mathematica,* trans. A. Motte, rev. by F. Cajori (Berkeley: University of California Press, 1962), p. 398.

[5]The first three chapters of my *Scientific Explanation and Atomic Physics* (Chicago: University of Chicago Press, 1982) trace the complex historical process involved in going from the *suggestion* that bodies are composed of atoms to the reasonable scientific *conclusion* that atoms really exist. Such scientific inferences involve processes beyond those considered here.

[6]Steven Weinberg, *The First Three Minutes* (New York: Basic Books, 1977), p. 41.

[7]Benito Mussolini, *Fascism: Doctrines and Institutions,* cited in Henry Carroll et al., *The Development of Civilization,* vol. 2 (Chicago: Scott, Foresman, 1962), p. 417.

[8]Sigmund Freud, *Civilization and its Discontents,* trans. James Strachey (New York: W. W. Norton & Co., 1961) p. 23.

[9]Citation from Harry Carroll et al., eds. *The Development of Civilization* (Chicago: Scott, Foresman, 1962), vol 2. p. 497.

[10]Preston Cloud, *Cosmos, Earth, and Man* (New Haven: Yale University Press, 1978), p. 113. Reprinted by permission of Yale University Press.

[11]F. H. Bradley, *Appearance and Reality* (Oxford University Press, 1893), p. 5.

[12]Ursula K. LeGuin, *City of Illusions* (New York; Ace Books, 1967), p. 203.

[13]Claude Levi-Strauss, *The Savage Mind* (Chicago: The University of Chicago Press, 1966), p. 204.

[14]Benjamin Gal-Or, *Cosmology, Physics, and Philosophy* (New York: Springer-Verlag, 1981), p. 347.

[15]G. W. Leibniz, "Monadology," in *Leibniz: Basic Writings* (—:Open Court, 1902), pp. 251–252.

[16]Susan Lydon, "The Politics of Orgasm," in *Sisterhood Is Powerful,* ed. Robin Morgan (New York: Vintage Books, 1970), p. 203.

[17]Steven Weinberg, *The First Three Minutes* (New York: Basic Books, 1977), p. 31.

[18]President John F. Kennedy, "Quarantine of Cuba," address of Oct. 22, 1962, cited in the *Americana Annual, 1963* (The Americana Corporation, 1963), p. 160.

[19]Albert Einstein, *Relativity: The Special and General Theory,* Robert Lawson, trans., 17th ed. (New York: Crown Publishers, 1961), p. 62. Copyright © 1961 by the Estate of Albert Einstein. Used by permission of Crown Publishers, Inc. and Methuen & Company, Ltd., London.

[20]John Stuart Mill, *On The Subjection of Women* (Greenwich, Conn.: Fawcett, 1971; originally published in 1869), p. 79.

[21]Thomas Nagel, "Sexual Perversion," *The Journal of Philosophy,* 66 (1969), p. 16.

[22]"Declaration on Certain Questions Concerning Sexual Ethics," a document issued by the Sacred Congregation for the Doctrine of the Faith, approved by Pope Paul VI and released Jan. 15, 1976, cited in Thomas A. Mappes and Jane Zembaty, *Social Ethics* (New York: McGraw-Hill, 1982), p. 209.

[23]"The Feminists vs. The Marriage License Bureau of the City of New York," *Sisterhood Is Powerful,* ed. Robin Morgan (New York: Random House, 1970), p. 537. Copyright © 1970 by Robin Morgan. Reprinted with the permission of the author.

[24]Nicolaus Copernicus, *On the Revolutions of Celestial Bodies,* cited in Shmuel Sambursky, *Physical Thought from the Presocratics to the Quantum Physicists* (New York: Pica Press, 1975), p. 155.

[25]Thomas Hobbes, *Leviathan,* in *The English Works of Thomas Hobbes,* ed. Sir William Molesworth (London: John Bohn, 1839, originally published in 1651), vol. 3, p. 115.

[26]R. L. Jay and Mary Leakey, "The Fossil Footprints of Laetoli," *Scientific American,* 246 (Feb., 1982), 54.

[27]Bertrand Russell, *Unpopular Essays* (London: George Allen & Unwin Ltd., 1950), p. 100. Reprinted by permission of Simon & Schuster, Inc. and George Allen & Unwin, Ltd., London.

[28]Voltaire, *Candide.*

[29]Mario Puzo, *The Godfather* (New York: Fawcett Crest Books, 1969), p. 39. Copyright © 1969 by Mario Puzo. Reprinted by permission of the Putnam Publishing Group and Candida Donadio & Associates, Inc.

[30]David P. Barash, *Sociobiology and Behavior* (New York: Elsevier, 1977), p. 315.

[31]Joseph Fletcher, "Euthanasia," in *Personal Philosophy: Perspectives on Living,* ed. Burton Porter (New York: Harcourt Brace Jovanovich, 1976), p. 106.

[32]Mao Tse-Tung, *Little Red Book* (Peking: Foreign Language Press, 1950), p. 172.

[33]Abraham Lincoln, "The Cooper Institute Address," cited in *Abraham Lincoln: His Speeches and Writings,* ed. Roy P. Basler (New York: World, 1946), p. 536.

[34]Patrick Henry, "Against the Federal Constitution," in William Wirt Henry, *Patrick Henry: Life, Correspondence and Speeches* (New York: Burt Franklin, 1891), vol. 3, p. 435–436.

[35]Mao Tse-Tung, *Little Red Book* (Peking: Foreign Language Press, 1950), pp. 232–233.

[36]Fyodor Dostoevsky, *The House of the Dead,* trans. H. Sutherland Edwards (New York: Dutton, 1912), p. 60. Reprinted by permission of J. M. Dent & Sons, Ltd. (Everyman's Library), London.

Chapter 3

CONSTRUCTION
AND RECONSTRUCTION

The argument diagrams we have been studying provide a direct and simple way of representing the structure of an argument. It is certainly a helpful way to begin the study of argumentation. Yet the method of diagramming is a very limited tool. A consideration of three basic limitations in this method supplies the initial motivation in trying to go beyond it. The three limitations that we will consider are: firstly, actual arguments have many elements that do not fit into the structure of an argument diagram; secondly, in many cases diagrams conceal rather than reveal the way particular inference patterns function; and finally, in many arguments the basic difficulty is not with the logical structure diagrammed, but with the presuppositions underlying the premises. We will consider each of these in a bit more detail.

The first difficulty is one we have alluded to before. Since it is rather obvious it may be treated briefly. One generally finds pure arguments, arguments that fit the diagramatic forms, only in the manufactured examples proper to text books. The arguments we encounter in newspaper editorials, political speeches, syndicated columns, and even in normal discussions mix background information, stage setting, narration, description, personal asides, and even attempts at humor with the premises and conclusion. Any attempt to number and diagram all the sentences found in such an argument is likely to obscure more than it clarifies. However, there is generally no easy or automatic way of bracketing the sentences we think unessential and then diagramming the residue. Instead we have to construct a simpler argument that brings out the essential structure. This is the basic means of reconstructing the given argument. Construction and reconstruction go hand in hand.

The second difficulty involves a more serious limitation in the method of diagramming itself. Consider the three arguments:

(1) All baseball managers are argumentative.
(2) Billy is a baseball manager.
(3) So, Billy is argumentative.   (3.1)

(1) If Godzilla fights Mothra, then Tokyo will be demolished.
(2) Godzilla will fight Mothra.
(3) So, Tokyo will be demolished.   (3.2)

(1) In this course you either pass or fail.
(2) You didn't pass.
(3) So, you failed.   (3.3)

Each of these arguments is correctly represented by the diagram

$$\begin{array}{c} 1 \\ + \to 3. \\ 2 \end{array}$$

Yet the way in which proposition (2) couples with proposition (1) to imply the conclusion, (3), is different in each case. This difference is not brought out by the argument diagrams.

In example (3.1) the coupling is based on class inclusion. The first proposition says something about all members of a class, the class of baseball managers. Proposition (2) informs us that Billy happens to be a member of that class. In inferring the conclusion, (3), we are, whether implicitly or explicitly, relying on the principle that anything true of *all* members of a class is true of *any* member of the class.

Example (3.2) relies on a different principle of inference. The first proposition is a hypothetical one, an *if—then* relation between an antecedent (the 'if' clause) and a consequent (the 'then' clause). One principle governing such inferences is that, if the antecedent is true, then the consequent must be true. Proposition (2) affirms the antecedent. So, proposition (3) affirms the consequent.

Example (3.3) involves disjunctive reasoning. The first proposition informs us that one of two contraries must be true. The second proposition informs us that one of the two is not true. So, we conclude that the other must be true.

In principle we have already mastered the inference patterns just summarized. We did this, not by learning rules of logic, but by learning how to use such terms as 'all', 'some', 'none', 'if—then', and 'either—or'. However, this fundamental linguistic competence rarely means that we can handle all the details, combinations, and variations of these inference patterns. A systematic treatment of them will be given in part 3 of this book. It would be helpful to look through the summaries at the end of each of the chapters in part 3 and to use them in treating doubtful or complex cases.

The third difficulty we wish to consider is a limitation on any exclusive reliance on logical structures. To say that an argument is logically valid does not mean that the conclusion is true. It means that, *if* the premises are true, then the conclusion is also true. Arguments based on premises that are clearly false generally do not present much of a problem. The real difficulty comes with a rigorous looking argument whose premises rest on presuppositions that may be false.

To make this more concrete we will consider an argument taken from *Mein Kampf,* the book in which the young Hitler outlined his plans for the future of Germany and the world:

> (1) The state is a means to an end. (2) Its end lies in the preservation and advancement of a community of physically and psychically homogeneous creatures. (3) This preservation itself comprises, first of all, existence as a race and thereby (4) permits the free development of all the forces dormant in this race. (5) States which do not serve this purpose are misbegotten, monstrosities in fact. (6) Thus, the highest purpose of a folkish state is concern for the preservation of those original racial elements which bestow culture and create the beauty and dignity of a higher mankind. (7) If the German people in its historic development had possessed that herd unity which other people enjoyed, the German Reich today would doubtless be mistress of the globe. (8) World history would have taken a different course, based on the victorious sword of a master people, putting the world into the service of a higher culture.[1]

Logically, this is a fairly tight chain argument which can be diagrammed

```
1→ 2→ 3→4]
          ] →6]
       5]    ]→ 8.
       7]
```

Fanatics, like Hitler, often supply the clearest examples of chain arguments. Real fanatics usually select and interpret facts and events in terms of master visions. Whatever does not fit is either reinterpreted until it does fit, or else discarded. Then fanatics can prove to the satisfaction of themselves and of true believers that the plans they are implementing are decreed, not by them, but by nature, or God, or fate, or destiny, or sacred writings properly interpreted. The difficulty is rarely with the logic of the argument.

The real problem with Hitler's argument is not with the logic of the argument but with the propositions he *presupposes* as true. He is basing his argument on the presuppositions that the Aryans are a superior race; that nature itself has decreed that superior races should rule inferior races; and that Destiny, something he tended to personify, has chosen Hitler as the supreme leader of the master race.

There are rules for validity, some of which we will study later. There are no simple all-purpose rules for truth. What we need here is not a theory of truth but a more heightened awareness of which propositions or presuppositions are uncritically accepted as true. Reconstructing an argument is an aid both in getting at the basic structure implicit in an argument and in heightening our awareness of the role presuppositions play. This method builds on argument diagrams inasmuch as we reconstruct a given argument in a simpler version, one that easily fits an argument diagram. Once it is clear which premises play a critical role in supporting the conclusion, then we are in a better position to begin probing into their truth.

In this chapter we will consider the method of reconstruction, first for simple arguments and then for more complex ones. After that we will consider the role of presuppositions and some related issues. Here we also begin considering the question of the acceptability of propositions and presuppositions.

3.1 RECONSTRUCTING ARGUMENTS

The point of view taken here is that both construction and reconstruction involve essentially the same methods. The difference is that in a reconstruction we begin with an argument that is presented to us. As the first step in reconstruction we attempt to pick out the reasons supporting the main conclusion and present them in as simple a way as possible. After the basic structure of the argument is clear, then we can add on the further details, subtleties, or background information required. In constructing an argument of our own we should begin with a schematic outline showing the main reasons leading to the conclusion. The flesh is added on only after the skeleton is clearly formed.

Construction and reconstruction follow essentially the same path. Yet it seems better to begin with reconstruction for two reasons. First, reconstruction enables us to learn from the experience of others, to see what works and to criticize what doesn't work. Second, a study of many different arguments presents us with models and methods that we can use as guides in constructing arguments of our own. In this chapter and the following chapter we will intermix construction and reconstruction. The present chapter, however, will be primarily concerned with reconstructions, with developing methods, uncovering structures, and beginning critical appraisals.

In trying to analyze an argument by reconstruction we begin in exactly the same way we did earlier. Read the text and try to determine whether it is an argument, a description, a narration, or some other form of prose. If we decide that it is an argument, then we should circle the inference indicators and try to pick out the conclusion and the reasons supporting it. If this is straightforward, then nothing more is needed. We can simply diagram the argument as given.

What we wish to consider now, however, are the cases where such a straightforward method either doesn't work or leads to diagrams so complex that they seem more confusing than the original argument. These are the cases where reconstruction is helpful. Reconstruction is basically a three-step process.

Steps in Reconstruction

1. Replace the given argument by a simplified version. ˌᴏ do this first pick out the conclusion. Then find the reasons that directly support the conclusion. Present this in simple terms, even if this seems to oversimplify the precise meaning conveyed by more technical terms used.

2. Compare the simple reconstruction with the original. The key point of this comparison is to determine the role of the material present in the original but omitted in the reconstruction. If it is factual material or paraphrases of basic arguments, then this usually need not be included to clarify the structure of the argument. However, reasons supporting the premises are usually essential to the argument. Such reasons can be developed as a subargument. Through the development of such subarguments we build a second approximation to the original argument.

3. Replace subarguments by simplified versions. If steps 1 and 2 provide enough information to make the given argument clear, then no more is needed. If they do not show why the premises support the conclusion, then one should analyze the reasons supporting the premises that require further explanation.

4. Appraise the argument. When the basic logical structure is completed then one can ask: Are the reasons given adequate to support the conclusion?

In the present section we will be concentrating especially on steps 1 and 2. Steps 3 and 4 will be given more consideration in subsequent sections. In each case we will develop the method more by analyzing examples than by presenting a doctrine. One aspect of this development may seem a bit contradictory. We are presenting the method of reconstruction as one especially geared to long, complex arguments. Yet, we will begin with a couple of arguments short enough so that they can be handled by argument diagrams. This is done only for the purpose of illustration. We will begin with an argument from Charles Darwin.

(1) ⟨A struggle for existence inevitably follows from the high rate at which all organic beings tend to increase.⟩ (2) ⟨Every being, which during its natural lifetime produces several eggs or seeds, must suffer destruction during some period of its life, and during some season or occasional year.⟩ Otherwise, (3) ⟨on the principle of geometric increase, its numbers would quickly become so inordinately great that no country could support the product.⟩ Hence, (4) ⟨as more individuals are produced than can possibly survive,⟩ (5) ⟨there must in every case be a struggle for existence, either one individual with another of the same species, or with individuals of distinct species, or with the physical conditions of life.⟩[2]

Darwin, who writes quite well, makes our task easy by summarizing the basic argument in the opening sentence. This is a topic sentence, summarizing the content of the paragraph. We might rephrase it in the form of two sentences: "All organic beings tend to increase at a high rate"; and "Therefore there is a struggle for survival." The rest of the paragraph supplies the details needed to show why this premise leads to this conclusion. The next sentence in Darwin's argument contains a conclusion followed by a reason for the conclusion. The conclusion is necessary destruction. The reason is a geometric increase in population over generations (successive generations increase at a rate such as 2, 4, 8, 16, 32 . . .). In the next sentence this conclusion is restated in the form of a premise: "more individuals are produced than can possibly survive." The 'as' indicates that it is a premise. The 'hence' indicates that a new conclusion is being drawn: "there must . . . be a struggle for existence.

To a first approximation, propositions 2 and 4 are essentially the same. Both state the necessity of some destruction. So are propositions 1 and 5, which both state the necessity of a struggle for survival. Thus, to a first approximation we can replace Darwin's argument by a simplified version:

(10) ⟨The number of beings in every species tends to increase inordinately.⟩ (11) ⟨It is not possible for all these beings to survive.⟩ (12) ⟨Therefore, there must be a struggle for survival.⟩

10
+ → 12
11

When we compare this with the original we see that what are omitted are essentially reasons for proposition (11) and repetitions of the conclusion. We will not try adding these on since we are using this method to replace long, complex arguments by ones that are smaller and simpler.

The next selection is from Ernst Cassirer, a philosopher who speculated on the origins and nature of religion.

⟨Religion cannot be clear and rational.⟩ (2) ⟨What it relates is an obscure and somber story: the story of the sin and fall of man.⟩ (3) ⟨It reveals a fact of which no rational explanation is possible.⟩ (4) ⟨We cannot account for the sin of man;⟩ (for) (5) ⟨it is not produced or necessitated by any natural cause.⟩ (6) ⟨Nor can we account for man's salvation;⟩ (7) (for) ⟨this salvation depends on an inscrutable act of divine grace.⟩ (8) ⟨It is freely given and freely denied;⟩ (9) ⟨there is no human action and no human merit that can deserve it.⟩ (10) ⟨Religion, (therefore,) never pretends to clarify the mystery of man.⟩ (11) ⟨It confirms and deepens this mystery.[3]

The basic thrust of this argument is clear. Here, however, the first approximation is too weak. When we merely use the premises that directly support the conclusion we have

(11) ⟨Religion never clarifies the mystery of man⟩ because
(12) ⟨religion is concerned with sin and salvation.⟩

12→11

This reconstruction does not make it clear *why* this premise leads to this conclusion. In this case we need to move to a second approximation, reconstructing the reasons supporting the premise (12). This leads to the reconstructed argument

(11) ⟨Religion never clarifies the mystery of man⟩ because
(12) ⟨religion is concerned with sin and salvation.⟩
   (13) ⟨Sin can not be rationally explained,⟩
     (14) for ⟨it is not due to a necessary cause;⟩
   (15) Nor ⟨can salvation be rationally explained,⟩
     (16) ⟨for it is due to a free unmerited gift of divine
      grace.⟩

This is easily outlined

14→ 13→]
        ]→ 12→11.
16→ 15→]

When this is compared with the original argument, it is easily seen to be essentially the same. Proposition 1 of the original argument is a topic sentence. Proposition (12) summarizes proposition 2. Proposition 3 is a general proposition that is then broken down into two parts. We have presented the two parts as (13) and (15). Proposition (16) replaces three propositions, 7, 8, and 9, which differ only in theological nuances.

The essential sameness of these three propositions suggests a point that will be treated in more detail in the next section. The slight differences between the three depend on nuances of Christian theology. The discussion of sin, salvation, and grace is presented in terms derived from the Christian tradition. Yet, Cassirer is writing as a philosopher about the origins of religion in general. Is he implicitly presupposing that all religions teach essentially the same story? Or is he presupposing that the Christian doctrine presents the basic truth and that other religions are true to the degree that they have approximated Christian doctrine? If you study Cassirer, you will find that he is actually more subtle and complex than these questions suggest. However, the language of this passage does reflect accepted Christian terminology. It is this suggestion that raises the question of presuppositions.

3.2 EXTENDED ARGUMENTS

The technique of reconstruction is really geared to long arguments, especially arguments containing repetitions, paraphrases, and material incidental to the argument. If you strip away what is incidental to the argument and then express the result in your own terms, you are well on your way to understanding the argument and in a good position to appraise it. The proposed method should already be familiar. It is essentially what serious students do in attempting to understand difficult material. Instead of reading the same section over and over—usually a waste of time and effort—you should try to outline the material in your own words.

The first example we will consider is a fairly simple one. It was written in 1949, before the sexual revolution, and gives advice on the proper behavior for a single girl.

Love and the Single Woman

It cannot be established with scientific certainty that there is born within a woman an "instinct for marriage." But whether it is "instinct" or something else superimposed on emotional reactions by her early exposure to society and moral systems, escape it a woman cannot. Nothing in the training, background or education of single women has prepared them for sex indulgence; rather the conditioning has all been in other directions.

The girl or woman living at home with parents or in a small community cannot easily indulge in illicit affairs, for the simple reason that she will probably "get caught." Constantly she must wonder what she would do if her parents found out or if she were to become pregnant.

The woman under 30, at home or away, must also consider the value of her virtue. Most young men place high esteem on this asset when seeking a wife, however scornfully they may talk about it. And even more important, how will premarital sex affect chances for a happy marriage later? Is it necessary to sample physical compatability before going to the altar?

Physicians and psychologists both declare against it. Any young married couple, genuinely in earnest about making a go of marriage in every aspect, will work out a happy sex life unless physical or psychic impediments exist. If such do exist, they can usually be ironed out with medical advice and guidance. . . .

The shining goal for woman is a secure sense of being loved and wanted, rather than physical satisfaction. She must know that her relationship with a man will not be terminated by a whim or sudden change in circumstances. Never has she been fitted to cope with a shadowy, ephemeral love-substance. She wants to reach out and know that love is there, and that it will be there tomorrow, and the day after, and for all time.

There is no need for her to maintain a tense and rigid guard over virtue. Instead, she should accept chastity in her unmarried state as naturally as she accepts the rising sun. If she thus follows the dictate of common sense, she willl be a far happier and better adjusted woman–until the day comes when sex will go hand in hand with marriage.[4]

The main thrust of this argument is quite clear. To diagram the argument would add unnecessary complexity. The article from which this is excerpted argues that single women should not have sex before marriage. The section excerpted argues that a woman can not find happiness through sexual relations before marriage, but only in marriage. The opening paragraph states this, after countering the objection that there is no evidence supporting the claim that women have an "instinct" for marriage. The author contends that even without such an instinct, training produces the same result. The reasons fall into two groups.

A. Sex before marriage cannot bring happiness to the single girl.

1. She would constantly worry about being caught.
2. She must consider her virtue.
3. Sex experience is not required for a happy marriage.
5. Chastity before marriage is easy and natural for women.

B. Only marriage leads to lasting happiness.

4. She needs a secure love more than physical satisfaction.

The numbering reflects the article's order. Thus, reason 5 is in the last paragraph after reason 4. Most of these reasons require some sort of arguments to support them. Reason 2, for example, is supported by the consideration that men prize virtue, also known as virginity, in a bride.

Perhaps the most striking feature of this argument is its rather obvious datedness. This very datedness makes it a good pivot in turning from analyzing arguments to appraising arguments. For this purpose it helps to isolate the reasons and then try to decide whether they are true and how strongly they support the conclusion. In making such an appraisal we can consider the supporting reasons the author gives, but these may not be decisive for *our* appraisal.

Consider reason 1. A small town girl having an affair might be caught by parents or neighbors. This was important when being caught could lead to disgrace and rejection. This is no longer generally true. A couple who live together without benefit of a marriage ceremony are generally not ostracized today. One may still argue that premarital sex is immoral, but not that it inevitably produces unhappiness because of reason 1.

Next we will turn to a longer argument and show how this method is adapted.

THE FIRST STEP TO THE CEMETERY

MY TURN/KENNETH BERNARD

The prevailing vision of the good life in America has for some time included early retirement. Numerous voices speak in its behalf, from insurance companies to unions to government agencies. Quit while you're ahead, still healthy and young enough to enjoy a generous spread of the sunset years. Not only should you enjoy the fruit of your labors in this most bountiful of countries, say the many voices, but you should also give the young folk their chance to move up by exiting gracefully. There are, you are told, numerous benefits—tax, medical, recreational, psychological. It is not only foolish to overlook the opportunity; it is downright un-American. So why not do it? Why not? Because it will probably be the worst decision you have ever made. Here's why.

To begin, it is an immediate, and usually irrevocable, step into second-class citizenship. Once retired, you are one with blacks, Hispanics, the handicapped, homosexuals, jailbirds, the insane, the retarded, children and women: America's Third World hordes. America doesn't like old people, and retired people are old people, whether they are 45, 55 or 65. Old people clutter up the landscape. Their families don't want them. Their communities don't want them. They are a nightmare vision of everyone's future. They are of interest mainly to doctors and hospitals, real-estate brokers and travel agents—but not as people, rather as bodies from whom some final payments can still be exacted.

Colonies: In America you are primarily valued not for your good deeds or your good character. You are valued for the money you command. The more money you have, the better you are treated by everyone from your local cop to your congressman. If you doubt this, go to any store or social agency. Go, for example, to any urban clinic and see what it is like to be old, sick and poor. There is a living hell. You get neither kindness nor respect nor service. To voluntarily take a step toward that condition you have to be either blind or mad. For as your ability to command money decreases, so too does your stature as a human being. To doctors, you are less important than the forms they must process to get money for their services. To landlords, you are a barrier to higher rents. Small wonder that retirees band together in colonies, in clubs, homes and hospitals. They want to belong, and they can do so only with their own kind. Everywhere else, their money will be taken, but they will be shut out.

What are these colonies like? To be sure, just as there are decent people who respect old people, so too there are homes, hospitals and communities that are genuinely humanitarian, that perform genuine functions. But how many? Our public knowledge of old-age homes is that they are less clean and only slightly less efficient than slaughterhouses, dismal halfway houses to the grave: turnover is profit.

In some societies where people

live to be very old, it is observable that they, whatever their age, have useful, needed work to perform. In America, activities for old people are manufactured. People get degrees in how to occupy old people with busy work. But this has nothing to do with life; it is all meaningless filler. These people are out of it. Although everyone knows it, everyone lies about it and society conspires to keep them there. It is a not so genteel form of genocide. The old people know it, too; and, knowing it (and often being very gracious), they cooperate: they begin to die in spirit and then bodily. And no amount of shuffleboard, creative writing, canasta or sightseeing can hide the unpleasant truth. Society's message is: spend money, but stay out of the way, and make no demands.

Old people are besieged by indifference, loneliness and uselessness. They are also physically assaulted by toughs and criminals. They are, understandably, fearful. Often they are imprisoned in their own homes. Yes, the perpetrators are few in number, but the assaults could not take place without a climate of sentiment, a cast of mind, that allowed for them. Our society fears the natural extinction of life so much that it behaves grotesquely. After all, with luck we will all grow old someday. Thus the mistreatment of the old is a form of self-mutilation. Nevertheless, the cruelty persists.

Faced with such barbarism, why join the legions of the doomed and damned? All your life you maintain a certain schedule. You break that routine once or twice a year. You go on this way 30 or 40 years. Your heart, your bowels, your mind keep time with it. And then you stop. You leave your pleasures, your sorrows, your family, everything. You might as well run full speed into a brick wall. No body or mind was meant to stop like that. Things have to go wrong—your heart, your bowels, your mind. It is the first giant step to the cemetery. Why take it? What's the percentage? Why, indeed, do it younger and younger when people are living to be older and older? Would you invest money with the same logic? Does it make any sense? Perhaps it would if there were alternates (for example, working less) but there aren't any alternatives for most of us. It's out, totally out, out all the way, and don't try to get back in.

Don't Quit: In our society, life is useful work and continuing income. Even what seems like a large retirement income is to be regarded with deep suspicion in this day of inflation. Life and respect are work and money. It shouldn't be so, but it is.

There is something suicidal in retirement, just as there is something suicidal in society's callousness toward the old. So forget the young. You worked to get what you have. Keep it; enjoy it. They are young and strong; let them struggle. It isn't your problem, you shouldn't take the rap. Don't leave your job one minute before you have to—even if you hate it—unless you can't get out of bed. You have something to give. It isn't true that to be old is to be incompetent. Fight. Don't quit. Elect your own to legislative office. Band together: the old-age party, the life party. Don't let them convince you that the "golden years" await you. It's a lie. No one should go down without a struggle. Kick. Scream. Be heard all the way to Washington. You have nothing to lose but your dignity and your life.

Bernard, a playwright, teaches English at Long Island University.

The basic conclusion Bernard is drawing here is altogether clear. Don't choose early retirement, because such a choice is a drastic mistake. He gives a collection of separate reasons for this, each supported by its own argumentation. In our first approximation we leave out the reasons supporting premises and simply list the reasons directly supporting the conclusion.

Before doing this we should note the effective use of rhetorical amplification. Essentially the same conclusion is expressed in quite a few different ways: "Why not do it? Why not?"; "Why join the legions of the doomed and damned?"; Don't quit"; "Kick"; "Scream"; "Be heard all the way to Washington"; "No one should go down without a struggle", "To voluntarily take a step toward that condition you have to be either blind or mad." In terms of the logic of the argument these are all ways of asserting the same conclusion: Do not choose an early retirement. In terms of dramatic force—the author is a playwright as well as a professor—these variations are much more effective than simple repetition could ever be.

Argument Outline

Do not voluntarily choose early retirement because this would be the worst decision you could make.

1. It is a step into second-class citizenship.
2. Your social value drastically decreases.
3. In our society the old are given meaningless work.
4. You will be besieged by indifference, loneliness, and uselessness.
5. You are more likely to suffer physical assault.
6. Changing an established schedule causes physical and psychological damage.
7. The problems of the young are not your problems.

This first approximation brings out the basic structure of the argument very clearly. It is a convergent argument. There are many separate reasons, each supporting the same conclusion: It is foolish to choose an early retirement. When we compare this schematic outline with the original argument we notice two significant differences between the original and the outline. The first is the effective use of rhetorical amplification in the original, something totally lacking in the outline. The second is the collection of subarguments supporting the reasons. The best way to bring this out is by presenting each subargument as a separate argument having as a conclusion the reason supporting the main argument. We will illustrate this for the first two reasons.

Argument for Reason 1

Our second approximation involves reconstructing the subargument supporting a particular premise of the overall argument. We do this only for those parts of the first approximation that seem inadequate. We use the same method for analyzing subarguments that we used for main arguments. That is, we first outline only those reasons that directly support the conclusion. To avoid confusion between the main and the subargument we will use "one," "two," etc. for premises of the main argument that now function as conclusions. Then the subargument for premise one is reconstructed:

(one) Early retirement is a step towards second-class citizenship because

1. The old are in the second-class citizen group and
2. Retired persons are effectively old persons.

    1
    + →one
    2

To see what it means to call this an approximation we can compare it with a full reconstruction. This would take the form:

(one) Early retirement is a step toward second-class citizenship because

1. The old are in the second-class citizen group.
    2. America doesn't like old people.
        3. They clutter the landscape.
    4. Their families don't want them.
    5. Their communities don't want them.
        6. They are a nightmare vision of everyone's future.
        7. They are wanted only for exploitation, not as persons.
8. Retired persons are effectively old people.

This complete argument for premise one would be diagrammed

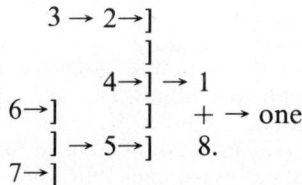

```
                  3 → 2→]
                       ]
                  4→] → 1
         6→]        ]    + → one
          ] → 5→]   8.
         7→]
```

Such a detailed analysis is generally needed or helpful only when the argument in question is difficult or obscure. The present one is not. To make this sort of detailed analysis for every subargument would defeat the purpose of making outlines, which is to make arguments simpler, not to make them more complex. In considering the subargument for premise two we will rely on a simple reconstruction.

Argument for Reason 2

1. In America people are valued primarily for their money. This is supported by illustrations and allegations.
2. To choose early retirement is to choose a poorer life. Therefore, when you choose early retirement your social value drastically decreases.

This simple sketch of the argument is sufficient to supply a point of departure of criticism. Is it really true that in America people are valued primarily for the money they command? The illustration of urban clinics and the allegation that doctors and landlords generally act out of base motives is not sufficient to establish this. Counterexamples could be found in abundance. In spite of this, the subargument does have some force, primarily because it is a subordinate part of an overall argument. The larger argument is a practical argument, one concerned with making a decision. People confronting the decision of whether to opt for early retirement do not have to prove that such treatment necessarily follows in every case. They simply have to be convinced that it could happen to them.

A more serious objection is that the author does not show any concern with the justice of the situation. He is simply concerned with preserving for himself the good life he has known as a university professor. Is this fair to others? To get a basis for appraising this it helps to see an opposing point of view. Fortunately, *Newsweek,* which printed Bernard's column, gave equal space to someone who argued that it is unjust for tenured professors to cling to their privileged positions and thereby prevent the young from having their fair chance.

THE OVERPROTECTED PROFESSORS
MY TURN/DUNCAN ROBERTSON

Let me introduce you to a lost generation. My friend Rob used to teach eighteenth-century French literature at a major university; he now builds redwood decks for California suburbanites. Ann, a linguist and a scholar, now works as a secretary in a computer firm. I followed a professional interest in medieval poetry and wound up cooking in a restaurant, for $4 and change an hour. Others of us drive taxis—the traditional occupation of exiles—or remain unemployed, dependent on spouses or family for support. We all have doctorates in the humanities. After spending a decade developing our careers, we are, on the whole, capable, hard-working people, with articles and books to our credit. Some of us are brilliant, some are less so. We have all been fired from universities that were unable to grant us tenure. We have lost not merely jobs, but whole livelihoods.

The tenure system means that after four or more years of graduate study and a six-year probation period, a university professor is either granted a lifetime contract or fired outright. There is no middle ground. The university must judge the performance of an individual in research and teaching over the first six years, and then make—or refuse to make—a salary commitment to him or her for the next 30. Small wonder that the decision is fraught with anxiety on all sides, and that mistakes are made: mediocrities are sometimes promoted, while productive people fall by the wayside.

Academic Freedom: The original purpose of tenure was to protect the faculty from political interference. Even today, no discussion of the system can take place without someone springing up to defend "academic freedom" against McCarthyism. Not that many professors have been out on the ideological battlefields of late. A lot else has changed since McCarthy's day. During the '60s, when funds were plentiful and teachers were scarce, eager administrators hired all candidates and promoted almost all to tenure. These people, now in their mid-40s, have populated the senior ranks of the universities for the last ten years; they will be with us for the next twenty, without fail.

In the meantime, we have seen an endless succession of budget cuts, and all expansion has stopped. No new positions are being created, whole programs and institutions are going under, yet tenure still protects the tenured—not from political interference, but from economic reality. In this time of widespread hardships, tenured faculty bear no share of the burdens. The truth is that the real value of their secure jobs has dramatically *increased.* Still they clamor for their customary raises and research subsidies. As far as I can tell, the dawn of any sense of responsibility is far away.

The university is now entering the second decade of what has been an unrelieved depression. This state of affairs does not merely reflect the fluctuations of the national economy. It is tempting to blame government and industry and the population trends and society at large, but the faculty

must also acknowledge their own failure of stewardship and of vision.

If there is now no visible future in English or history, it is because the recent research in these fields has opened no new pathways. The famous "grade inflation" is another symptom of bankruptcy: we no longer believe in the intrinsic worth of the subject we are teaching. True, undergraduate education is now largely given over to processing pragmatic youngsters on their way to business and medical schools. These kids can be taught to read Shakespeare, but only if you guarantee them an "A" in advance. The graduate students, those who wish to continue reading Shakespeare, are even more demoralizing to teach. Poorly advised to begin with, most have no prospects in academia, and they often stay on in degree programs simply because they are unable to face the "outside" world or make realistic career decisions. And still new Ph.D.'s are conferred each year, swelling the ranks of the lost generation.

A few will indeed find jobs. There are still some "tenure track" positions open to the inexperienced and industrious graduate, although the odds against one are usually higher than 100 to 1. Once miraculously hired, the young teacher will be kept busy with elementary instruction, advising and administrative chores. Six years later, with a few articles out and a book typically awaiting publication, this person will offer little resistance to being fired and replaced by a new beginner.

Victims: And if one is actually promoted, what awaits? Tenure used to be the springboard to continuing, intense production. The rewards included not merely an eventual full professorship, but also—more important—a movement to progressively better schools, brighter students and more brilliant colleagues. Now almost no one is moving, and tenure has become the whole objective, the end of all intellectual growth. It is well known that without pressure, positive or negative stimulus, many people fall silent, teach their six hours a week and putter with house repairs, cooking classes or racquetball for the rest of their days. But it is all too easy to denounce the deadwood lumber yard. These people are as much victims of the academic depression as the rest of us, and their number increases every year.

The teaching profession in the humanities is now gridlocked—"tenured in," as they say—up to 100 percent. Everybody concedes that this is a disaster. But so far, professors have refused to face the inevitable conclusion, which is that the tenure system itself is long overdue for reappraisal. The wholesale waste of intellectual resources must not simply be allowed to continue for the next twenty years, or until the present generation of senior faculty dies out or comes to its senses. At the present, difficult time, the professor's "academic freedom" from all job insecurity places an insupportable economic burden on the rest of us. There is a growing army of embittered, unemployable intellectuals in our midst. The whole phenomenon insults dearly held national values: can so much intelligence, hard work and dedication be so little valued today? It is time now to recognize the potential threat to society within this actual human tragedy and respond.

Robertson teaches French at the University of California, Santa Cruz.

This argument is typical of arguments found in newspapers, magazines, and speeches in one key feature. Over half the article is devoted to exposition. It begins with illustrations of the present academic situation. Many people trained in the humanities and quite well qualified to teach in universities are effectively being excluded from the academic profession. Most must find jobs that do not utilize the professional skills developed through a long, demanding process of graduate training.

Robertson sees the tenure system as one of the principal causes of this distressing situation. However, he can not presume that all readers of *Newsweek* understand how the tenure system functions and why it seemed to be an academic necessity some twenty years ago. The exposition required is tailored to the thrust of the argument. Robertson states that the original purpose of tenure was to protect the faculty from political interference. This protection provided a climate in which creative scholarship could flourish. At the present time, however, the tenure system really plays the role of protecting an entrenched mediocrity and thus depressing creative scholarship. The "grade inflation" found in most universities epitomizes the educational bankruptcy the present system produces.

The conclusion that Robertson is arguing for is that the present tenure system is overdue for reappraisal. The reasons supporting this are presented in the concluding paragraphs. These reasons, however, draw their strength from the preceding exposition. To bring this out we will restructure his argument as a convergent argument, many separate reasons supporting one conclusion.

Argument Outline

The present tenure system should be reappraised and changed because

1. It no longer achieves its intended purpose.
2. It supresses much creative scholarship.
3. It contributes to a lowering of academic standards.
4. It is unfair to untenured academics.
5. It produces an embittered army of unemployed professional humanists.
6. It insults dearly held national values.

The second step in our analysis through reconstruction is a comparison of the outline with the original. In the present case the most significant difference between the two is a logical one. The summary outline presents six separate reasons supporting one conclusion. The original argument brought out historical and causal interconnections between these reasons. Thus, the reason the army of the unemployed professional humanists is embittered is because they were treated unfairly. Similarly, the fact that creative scholarship is stifled contributes to a lowering of academic standards. This, however, does not significantly affect the strength of the argument. If we accept these six reasons as adequately established, then they give strong support to the conclusion.

The final step is appraisal. Though we do not intend to appraise this particular argument, we do wish to show how the method of reconstruction can contribute to such an appraisal. In an appraisal the basic questions that must be asked are

1. Should the premises be accepted as true?
   They can be rejected either as false or as resting on misleading presuppositions. If they are accepted as true then the next question is:
2. How strongly do the premises support the conclusion?

To illustrate the first question we will focus on the first premise. Is it really true that academic tenure no longer achieves its intended purpose?

Any attempt to answer this obviously involves distinctions. Are we talking about the purpose of the individual seeking tenure, of the university granting tenure, or of the institution of tenure as a feature of American academic life? Only the last really fits the argument given. In this case what is needed is a bit of historical scholarship. When and for what purpose was the American system of academic tenure introduced? A search for an answer to this should lead to the 1915 *Declaration of Principles* given by the first Committee on Academic Freedom and Academic Tenure established by the

American Association of University Professors. Their declaration concludes with three practical proposals. The final one is:

> To render the profession more attractive to men of high ability and strong personality by insuring the dignity, the independence, and the reasonable security of tenure, of the professional office.[5]

Thus, the institution of the tenure system was related to the purposes of academic freedom and creative scholarship, but it was not developed in the context of the McCarthy era. In answering the first question it is a help to have premises isolated in outline form. Then we can focus on the ones whose truth is questionable.

In answering the second question it is helpful to compare the outline with the original argument. Consider, for example, the final premise, the present tenure system insults dearly held national values. If this is considered in isolation it might seem to be patently untrue. A system that is intended to promote freedom from undue political pressure and to stimulate creative scholarship should fit in well with national values. This premise can only be meaningfully appraised in the context of the original argument. There Robertson is arguing that the tenure system now serves to protect entrenched mediocrity, to discriminate unfairly against the young, and that it fails to reward intelligence, hard work, and dedication. These results insult dearly held American values.

We will return to the methods of appraising arguments in the next section. Before doing that it is appropriate to practice the method of argument reconstruction.

EXERCISES

A. 1. Do argument diagrams bring out the way coupled premises imply a conclusion?
   2. What is the difference between constructing and reconstructing an agreement?
   3. Is it necessary to retain the original author's terminology in reconstructing an argument?
   4. Does one compare a reconstructed argument with the original to determine which of the two is better?
   5. Explain one significant difference between arguments and explanations.
   6. Is it ever possible to reconstruct a subargument the same way one reconstructs an argument?
   7. Should the reconstructed argument have the same conclusion as the original argument?

B.   Analyze the following arguments through the method of reconstruction. If the first approximation is not sufficient to make the original argument intelligible, then reconstruct whatever premises are needed to make the argument intelligible.

*1. The replacement for the surface ship is not yet in sight. Why? Because a maritime nation like the United States must transport large quantities of goods and raw materials to and from its shores, and for the forseeable future that must be done in surface ships. Neither submarines nor aircraft can deliver the volumes required. If we must utilize surface merchant ships, we must be able to protect them. Submarines can help protect shipping from attacks by surface ships and submarines but they are of little use against an attacking aircraft. Land-based aircraft can help, too, but not in situations like the Falkland Islands where no British base was close enough for land-based aircraft to be able to enforce the blockade in which the Sheffield was engaged.

We maintain military forces primarily to engage in wars overseas, surely not because of concerns with Canada and Mexico. We must, therefore, be able to move forces across oceans. We must also be able to base forces like aircraft carriers and amphibious forces on the seas when shore bases will not be available in a region of conflict. The British requirement to use force in as distant an area as the Falklands is one example, if an extreme one. Our limited capability to project military power into the Persian Gulf region today is another.

The lesson of the Sheffield is that because there is no substitute yet in sight we cannot dispense with surface ships like aircraft carriers, amphibious assault ships and destroyers even though they are vulnerable.[6]

2. How does it become a man to behave toward this American government today? I answer, that he cannot without disgrace be associated with it. I cannot for an instant recognize that political organization as *my* government which is the *slave's* government also.

All men recognize the right of revolution: that is, the right to refuse allegiance to, and to resist, the government, when its tyranny or its inefficiency are great and unendurable. But almost all say that such is not the case now. But such was the case, they think, in the Revolution of '75. If one were to tell me that this was a bad government because it taxed certain foreign commodities brought to its ports, it is most probable that I should not make an ado about it, for I can do without them. All machines have their friction; and possibly this does enough good to counterbalance the evil. At any rate, it is a great evil to make a stir about it. But when the friction comes to have its machine, and oppression and robbery are organized, I say, let us not have such a machine any longer. In other words, when a sixth of the population of a nation which has undertaken to be the refuge of liberty are slaves, and a whole country is unjustly overrun and conquered by a foreign army, and subjected to military law, I think that it is not too soon for honest men to rebel and revolutionize. What makes this duty the more urgent is the fact that the country so overrun is not our own, but ours is the invading army.[7]

3. The battle against censorship and for freedom of expression surely was a great battle to win, but has it not become a new straightjacket? The writers, both novelists and dramatists, "would rather hock their typewriters than turn in a manuscript without the obligatory scenes of unsparing anatomical documentation of their characters' sexual behavior. . . ." Our "dogmatic enlightenment" is self-defeating: it ends up destroying the very sexual passion it set out to protect. In the great tide of realistic chronicling, we forgot, on the stage and in the novel and even in psychotherapy, that imagination is the life-blood of eros, and that realism is neither sexual not erotic. Indeed, there is nothing *less* sexy than sheer nakedness, as a random hour at any nudist camp will prove. It requires the infusion of imagination (which I shall later call intentionality) to transmute physiology and anatomy into *interpersonal* experience—into art, into passion, into eros in a million forms which has the power to shake or charm us.

Could it not be that an "enlightenment" which reduces itself to sheer realistic detail is itself an escape from the anxiety involved in the relation of human imagination to erotic passion?[8]

*4. Today the Supreme Court and our entire federal court system are under attack. The new Right—aided and abetted by groups like the so-called Moral Majority— has launched a massive effort in Congress to curtail the power of the federal courts to protect our most basic constitutional liberties.

They call their plans for reining in the courts a "blueprint for judicial reform." But what the New Right is basically proposing to do is to destroy the independence of our federal courts simply because they don't like the way the courts have decided certain issues.

New Right critics of the Supreme Court's decisions on busing, abortion, and prayer in public schools have introduced nearly 30 bills in Congress that would, if passed, either invalidate the court's rulings on these issues or prohibit the courts from even considering cases in these areas.

With the publication of their "blueprint," New Right leaders acknowledge that "the battle lines are clearly drawn."

And so they are. Their legislative efforts are nothing short of a radical and unprincipled attack upon our constitutional system of government. And they have been given an influential boost by Attorney General William French Smith.

Mr. Smith recently leveled a broadside assault on decisions by the Supreme Court and lower federal courts. Although he stopped short of endorsing New Right efforts to overturn constitutional decisions by the Supreme Court, his failure to completely disassociate himself from those efforts is of deep concern. As head of the Justice Department, the Attorney General of the United States should be the ultimate guardian of the independence of our courts. He should be most concerned by attempts to "politicize" the judicial branch or to give legislators power to overturn constitutional decisions.

One does not have to agree with the Supreme Court's decisions on abortion, busing, or prayer in public schools to oppose New Right efforts to overturn those decisions. I, for example, have written critically of the abortion decision.

But if constitutional decisions are wrong, they should be changed by time and debate — or by a constitutional amendment approved by the people.

Congress should not redefine the Constitution nor strip the courts of their power to hear cases involving the issues of busing, abortion, and prayer in public schools.

For if bare majorities in Congress can prevent the Supreme Court from protecting *these* constitutional rights, bare majorities can deprive us of other fundamental liberties as well.

Consider, for example, an amendment offered by Sen. Jesse Helms (R–N.C.) to deprive the Supreme Court and all federal courts of jurisdiction to hear school prayer cases in the future.

Today, if a public school sponsors prayers, a parent can sue in the federal courts to enforce the Supreme Court's past decisions, based on the First Amendment, preventing such official sponsorship of religion. But the proposed legislation would prohibit such a suit from being brought into federal courts. And the Supreme Court would be prevented from hearing a state case on appeal.

Thus, Congress would render the Supreme Court powerless to hear a citizen's plea for the protection of First Amendment safeguards separating church and state.

Whether you agree in this particular case is not the point. If bare majorities in Congress can take away a citizen's right to appeal to the Supreme Court in this instance, then bare majorities in Congress can just as easily withdraw a citizen's right to freedom of speech, or political association, or the security of our homes or our persons, or any other basic constitutional liberties.

While those Members of Congress who want to strip the court of power may make a technical argument that they have that right, the present issue goes much deeper than technical arguments.

In the Roosevelt Court-packing fight of 1937, Congress had the technical right to increase the number of justices, but the plan was perceived for what it was — an assault upon our institutions.

Josiah W. Bailey, a *truly* conservative senator from North Carolina, opposed Roosevelt's scheme to pack the Supreme Court with six justices friendly to the New Deal. "Congress is mighty," Sen Bailey said, "but the Constitution is mightier . . . to weaken either is to weaken the foundations of our Republic; to destroy either is to destroy the Republic."

If the New right succeeds in the effort to establish congressional power to overturn Supreme Court decisions on constitutional issues, it will have found a way to impose its intolerance upon the nation.

In proposing the Bill of Rights, James Madison explained that the courts were to be the guardians of individual rights. He said the courts should be an "impenetrable bulwark" against every assumption of power in the legislative or executive branches.

The New Right "blueprint" is, in short, a politically expedient assumption of power. It is an assumption of power that would destroy the independence of our courts and lead to a breakdown in our system of government.

It merits nothing less than our determined opposition.[9]

5. The organization of Oil Exporting Countries has troubles, but in the industrialized world there are no wet eyes. The oil glut and falling oil prices are the kind of economic good news that has been all too rare.

But the good news will not continue unless the U.S. has the discipline to use this moment in history to make OPEC's troubles permanent.

Oil prices are falling because conservation has finally taken hold. U.S. oil imports are down 25 percent since they reached a peak in 1977. The world's 24 largest industrial countries are using 15 percent less oil than in 1979. OPEC has been forced to cut production by one-third in a failing effort to keep prices up.

OPEC can be forced to cut prices even more, however, if the U.S. has the discipline to undermine the cartel. By adopting policies that keep Americans conserving, U.S. oil imports can be further trimmed, putting more downward pressure on prices.

The best anti-OPEC instrument would be stiff taxes on imported oil. This would keep pump prices of oil products from falling and preserve Americans' incentive to conserve. Oil imports would continue to decline, OPEC would have to lower prices and the deficit-ridden Treasury would capture the gain for the benefit of the U.S. economy. OPEC's loss would be the United States' gain.

The U.S. had a similar opportunity to break OPEC in the middle of the last decade.

After the quadrupling of oil prices in 1973, there followed a period of falling real oil prices. But instead of battling OPEC, the U.S. fell into complacency.

Controls on domestic oil prices were continued, discouraging U.S. production and sending consumers the wrong signals about the real cost of imported oil. Americans even renewed their love affair with gas-guzzling cars.

Then the Iranian revolution shattered U.S. illusions, and oil prices soared again.

President Reagan took the first step toward a sane energy policy last year when he decontrolled oil prices.

But the effect of that move on Americans' appetite for imported oil is beginning to wear off. Already there are signs that Americans believe OPEC price rises to be a thing of the past.

They are not. An unlucky bullet in the Persian Gulf could send the region into chaos, disrupting production and putting the U.S. at the mercy of OPEC. By planned discipline now, the U.S. can avoid the discipline of crisis later on.

OPEC has never been shy about squeezing the U.S. whenever the opportunity arose. It is time for the U.S. to return the favor.[10]

*6. If the essence of the Comic be the contrast in the intellect between the idea and the false performance, there is a good reason why we should be affected by the exposure. We have no deeper interest than our integrity, and that we should be made aware by joke and by stroke of any lie we entertain. Besides, a perception of the Comic seems to be a balance-wheel in our metaphysical structure. It appears to be an essential element in a fine character. Wherever the intellect is constructive, it will be found. We feel the absence of it as a defect in the noblest and most oracular soul. The perception of the Comic is a tie of sympathy with other men, a pledge of sanity, and a protection from those perverse tendencies and gloomy insanities in which fine intellects sometimes lose themselves. A rogue alive to the ludicrous is still convertible. If that sense is lost, his fellow-men can do little for him.[11]

7. Thus, the wisdom of *philosophy* is set in opposition to the *common sense* of mankind. The first pretends to demonstrate, *a priori,* that there can be no such thing as a material world; that sun, moon, stars, and earth, vegetable and animal bodies, are, and can be nothing else, but sensations in the mind, or images of those sensations in the memory and imagination; that, like pain and joy, they can have no existence when they are not thought of. The last can conceive no otherwise of this opinion, than as a kind of metaphysical lunacy, and concludes that too much learning is apt to make men mad; and that the man who seriously entertains this belief, though in other respects he may be a very good man, as a man may be who believes that he is made of glass; yet, surely he hath a soft place in his understanding and hath been hurt by much thinking.

To what purpose is it for philosophy to decide against common sense in this or any other matter? The belief of a material world is older, and of more authority, than any principles of philosophy. It declines the tribunal of reason; and laughs at all the artillery of the logician. It retains its sovereign authority in spite of all the edicts of philosophy, and reason itself must stoop to its orders. Even those philosophers who have disowned the authority of our notions of an external material world, confess that they find themselves under a necessity of submitting to their power.

Methinks, therefore, it were better to make a virtue of necessity; and since we cannot get rid of the vulgar notion and belief of an external world, to reconcile our reason to it as well as we can; for, if Reason should stomach and fret ever so much at this yoke, she cannot throw it off; if she will not be the servant of Common Sense, she must be her slave.[12]

8. Loving, therefore, is a kind of growing. Love inspires one to live with at least one other person in mind. The circle of self-enjoyment grows into an ellipse in which the two poles are included. But, as Plato long ago reminded us, love is a suffering yearning for what one does not possess completely. The individual must refocus his mind and body, re-form his ideas and dreams, so that the good he wants for himself and for his sweetheart may be realized. Love means growth; it means work; it means moral progress. Thus love, *inclusive of sex, needs marriage to protect and nourish its values. And marriage, to be a most fruitful and inclusive experience which protects and nourishes the values of both love and sex, must be put to work in building a family and a society.* This is the inner progression of love.

Let the sexual act be the expression of the conscious desire and decision to become parents, and that act reaches its zenith in human feeling, inspiration and fulfillment. It is almost foolish to try to make this experience clear to those who have not known it. Words that receive their content from other levels of sex experience are quite inadequate for this. Let two persons extend their love for each other into the tender and responsible decision to have and care for children, and they will find the meaning of the sexual experience immeasurably enriched.

Sex, love, marriage, family, and social responsibility are human ventures all along the line. The question is: Which venture brings completeness, invites to growth in character and personality, enables the individual to feel that he has accepted the role that his abilities allow in the achievement of a dependable social order? It is our thesis that love, including sex love, is the more radiant and satisfying when it becomes a means of communicating one's concern for the wider range of values that purposeful living together makes possible. Sex without love, love without marriage, and marriage without creative commitments to children (or the equivalent) are in constant danger of vanishing away. Persons disregard the laws of growth and development in human nature only to find that they have forfeited their heritage.[13]

9. The fact, however, that the co-existence of sex and love may be desirable does not, to my mind, make it necessary. My reasons for this view are several:

1. Many individuals — including, even, many married couples — do find great satisfaction in having sex relations without love. I do not consider it fair to label these individuals as criminal just because they may be in the minority.

    Moreover, even if they are in the minority (as may well *not* be the case), I am sure that they number literally millions of men and women. If so, they constitute a sizeable subgroup of humans whose rights to sex satisfaction should be fully acknowledged and protected.

2. Even if we consider the supposed majority of individuals who find greater satisfaction in sex-love than in sex-sans-love relations, it is doubtful if all or most of them do so for *all* their lives. During much of their existence, especially their younger years, these people tend to find sex-without-love quite satisfying, and even to prefer it to affectional sex.

    When they become older, and their sex drives tend to wane, they may well emphasize coitus with rather than without affection. But why should we condemn them *while* they still prefer sex to sex-love affairs?

    Many individuals, especially females in our culture, who say that they only enjoy sex when it is accompanied by affection are actually being unthinkingly conformist and unconsciously hypocritical. If they were able to contemplate themselves objectively, and had the courage of their inner convictions, they would find sex without love eminently gratifying.

    This is not to say that they would only enjoy non-affectional coitus, nor that they would always find it more satisfying than affectional sex. But in the depths of their psyche and soma, they would deem sex without love pleasurable too.

    And why should they not? And why should we, by our puritanical know-nothingness, force these individuals to drive a considerable portion of their sex feelings and potential satisfactions underground?

    If, in other words, we view sexuo-amative relations as desirable rather than necessary, we sanction the innermost thoughts and drives of many of our fellowmen and fellowwomen to have sex *and* sex-love relations. If we take the opposing view, we hardly destroy these innermost thoughts and drives, but frequently tend to intensify them while denying them open and honest outlet. This, as Freud pointed out, is one of the main (though by no means the only) sources of rampant neurosis.[14]

3.3 PRESUPPOSITIONS AND PERSPECTIVES

Consider the statement, "John's wife is ill." Ordinarily we would say that this statement is true if she is ill, and false if she is not. Suppose, however, we learn that John does not have a wife. In that case should the statement be considered true or false? Some logicians would insist, for technical reasons, that all such statements be considered false. Most people, however, would insist that if John does not have a wife, then any statements about John's wife are neither true nor false. They are simply misguided.

This is what we will take as the technical sense of 'presupposition'. It is often called the semantic sense. A proposition, X, presupposes another proposition, Y, if both the truth and falsity of X presuppose the truth of Y. Thus, in the example above, X would be the proposition, "John's wife is ill," while Y would be the proposition, "John has a wife." It is easy to list similar examples.

X	presupposes	Y

X	Y
Joe's dog is dead	Joe had a dog
Her hair is bleached blonde	She is not a natural blonde
The Red Sox are winning	The Red Sox are playing

When presuppositions must be made explicit to clarify an argument, we will introduce the presuppositions and put square brackets around it to indicate that it is our proposition, not a part of the original argument. To illustrate this we will consider a recent letter in the syndicated *Dear Abby* column.

> *Dear Abby:* Why do you and other writers always refer to prostitution as "the oldest profession" when according to the Bible the oldest profession is sheepherding?
> Genesis: Chapter 4, Verse 2: "And again, she (Eve) bore his brother Abel. Now Abel was a keeper of sheep, and Cain was a tiller of the ground."
> —*Mary in Ellensburg, Wash.*
>
> *Dear Mary:* In typical sheeplike fashion, along with other writers, I bought the tale of the oldest profession. (No pun intended.) However, my Webster's New Collegiate Dictionary defines a profession as "a calling requiring specialized knowledge and often long and intensive academic preparation." So obviously neither prostitution nor sheepherding qualifies as a profession.[15]

If we were to reformulate the first paragraph of Mary's letter to make the implicit presupposition explicit we would have

(1)<You and others are wrong in referring to prostitution as "the oldest profession" because (2) <according to the Bible the oldest profession is sheepherding> and (3)[whatever the Bible says is true.]

$$\begin{array}{c} 2 \\ + \\ 3 \end{array} \rightarrow 1$$

Similarly Abby's reply involves two presuppositions. The first is that whatever the dictionary presents as the meaning of a term can be taken as authoritative. The second is that neither prostitution nor sheepherding require specialized knowledge nor long and intensive academic preparation. These may be perfectly reasonable presuppositions, depending on the audience, but they are presuppositions.

In addition to this technical sense of 'presupposition', there is also a broader and somewhat vaguer sense. Consider the proposition, "My suit is blue, but my tie is red." An eager student, who has just completed freshman physics, might wish to dispute such a claim by the following argument. The suit is not really blue. Being blue is not a characteristic of things like polyester (the suit is not really expensive either). What being blue really means is that the light waves reflected from the suit are in a certain frequency band. Color is really a property of light, not of material objects. He is claiming, in other words, that the statement in question presupposes a false theory of color.

This old chestnut of an argument is misleading. Ordinary color talk does not presuppose a theory of color. If it did then people who have not learned the theory could not speak the language correctly, just as someone who is not trained cannot correctly speak the language of econometrics, molecular biology, or quantum chromodynamics. What ordinary language color talk presupposes is ordinary language. We learn to use terms like 'blue' by associating them with the sky, blue paper, and blue suits. We would say that white paper seen under blue light, or through blue cellophane, looks blue. That means that it looks the way blue things look when seen under normal circumstances.

Such presuppositions can become problematic when we move out of an ordinary language context. These problems, however, are best deferred to a philosophy course. They are not our present concern. The point of the example is to indicate that a normal conversation rests on a network of presuppositions. Without such a network, conversation is impossible. Thus, we presuppose that others understand terms basically the same way we do, that they can know objects, persons, and places referred to. We often presuppose common background information or shared values.

How should the background presuppositions of an argument be treated? It would surely be impossible to isolate all of them and attempt to determine which ones are true. Even the attempt to do so rests on a misguided idea of how language functions, and how language should be analyzed. What we will follow here is a sort of common-sense approach, loosely based on the precedent set by legal reasoning.

In legal reasoning one speaks of 'presumptions'. Thus a person on trial is presumed innocent until proven guilty. This is not a judgment that the person really is innocent. It simply shows where the burden of proof is.

Unless the state can prove that the person is guilty, that person should not be found guilty. The defendant is not obliged to prove his or her innocence. Other presumptions are similarly related to the issue of who has the burden of proof. Thus, there is a presumption in favor of established institutions. If I am living in a house, paying my monthly mortgage to the bank, and acting as if I own the house, then I am presumed to be the owner. If you claim that the house is really yours, then the burden of proof is on you.

Any argument, any conversation for that matter, rests on a network of presuppositions. There is a strong presumption in favor of the truth (or reasonableness, or meaningfulness, depending on the type) of the presuppositions which are either commonly shared or shared by the participants in a conversation or argument. This is no guarantee of truth. It simply shows where the burden of proof lies. It lies with the person who denies or questions such shared presuppositions.

This does not mean that it is unreasonable to bring our implicit presuppositions into question or even to deny them. What it does mean, however, is that, as a general policy, shared presuppositions should not be questioned or doubted unless there is a *specific* reason for doubt. A reason that supplies a basis for doubting any and all presuppositions (There is no certain knowledge of anything; You can't believe anything you read in the papers; Don't trust anyone over thirty, etc.) is not a specific reason for doubt. To illustrate what we mean by a specific reason for doubt consider the following argument.

Destined for Greatness

Perhaps the most significant proof that the XL (XL for extra length) is well on its way to greatness is its market acceptance. In its first year of production, the XL accounted for more than half of the Piper's turboprop aircraft shipments.

So why is this particular airplane bound for glory? Let's consider, briefly, some of the factors the folks who are buying the XLs are considering.

First and foremost, the XL comes from one of the most respected turboprop families in aviation. Since Piper introduced its first Cheyenne (now the Cheyenne II) nearly 10 years ago the series has gained an unsurpassed reputation for performance, reliability and operating efficiency. What better proof of this claim could there be than resale value?[16]

The argument continues, with many and diverse reasons supporting the claim that the XL is destined for greatness. What specific reason is there for doubt? The inside cover contains a statement: "*Corporate Flight* is a quarterly magazine published by Johnson Hill Press, Inc. for the Piper Aircraft Corporation and its Corporate Aircraft Centers in the interest of business aviation." The argument that the new Piper XL is destined for greatness is presented in what is, in effect, a company magazine. This does not prove that the facts are misrepresented or that the arguments are invalid. There is, however, some ground for being suspicious of the presumption that the writer and the editor are objective in their judgments. The fact that both are working, directly or indirectly, for Piper Aircraft is a specific ground for doubt. This is a factor that must play a role in anyone's appraisal. If the same argument were found in, for example, *The New York Times* there would not be a specific reason for doubt. There might be generic reasons for doubt that cover both cases. Many new products have 'bugs' that are only discovered after the product has been on the market for a while. This is not a specific reason; it counts for any products whatever. But it could be a reason for doubt.

Perspectives.   Before considering particular types of presuppositions we should briefly consider a larger issue related to the question of presuppositions. People who share a culture or a subculture absorb ways of selecting and interpreting facts, methods of reasoning, guiding principles, and moral values. These supply a perspective in light of which particular arguments are carried out. Arguments that may seem cogent to those who share this perspective may seem to rest on a network of false presuppositions to those outside the culture or subculture. As an illustration consider the following argument given by an Indian native from Northwest Canada.

> We know what the animals do, what are the needs of the beaver, the bear, the salmon, and other creatures, because long ago men married them and acquired this knowledge from their animal wives. Today the priests say we lie, but we know better. The white man has been only a short time in this country and knows very little about the animals; we have lived here thousands of years and were taught long ago by the animals themselves. The white man writes everything down in a book so that it will not be forgotten; but our ancestors married the animals, learned all their ways, and passed on this knowledge from one generation to another.[17]

The typical 'white man', confronted with this argument, is likely to conclude that the argument is not merely wrong—it is patently absurd. Early Indians were no more capable of marrying beavers and salmon then are their present day descendants. Regardless of the relation they had, these animals could not communicate information. The interpretative principle that traditional folklore is a more reliable source of information than the scientific study of animal behavior seems ridiculous. Our typical 'white man' would, in effect, reject this argument's presuppositions concerning the sources of reliable information and the way the pertinent facts are selected and interpreted.

How might the typical native look at this difference in perspective? Let's try, as a thought experiment, to put ourselves in the native's place. Then we might reason something like this. The outsiders don't know any of the facts that really count: where the beavers build their dams in the fall season when the rivers have slowed their flow and fish is scarce; which caves the bears hibernate in during the winter; where and when it is easiest to catch the salmon when they are swimming upstream. These are the type of facts that are crucial for survival. We know them. The outsiders do not. We are the ones with the reliable knowledge. Our sources and methods are the ones to be counted on. The priests say we lie when we explain how the animals taught our ancestors. But they can't explain to us how God taught Abraham and Moses. At least we can see and hear the animals.

What this example illustrates in a simple way is a general doctrine called hermeneutics. In trying to understand arguments, stories, or explanations fashioned in a culture quite different from one's own, one cannot really understand the significance of any part until one has some understanding of the whole. Thus, it is impossible to come to responsible conclusions about accounts of ancestors marrying animals until one knows how myths function in a particular culture. However, one only gets to know a culture as an organized whole through an understanding of the parts that make it up. This leads to the method of the hermeneutic circle, beginning with a dim understanding of the whole, trying to understand the parts, from these getting a better understanding of the whole and then returning to the parts.

The problems presented by hermeneutics go far beyond the scope and purpose of this text. It has been introduced for one special reason. There is a problem intermediate between simply presupposing individual propositions in arguments developed within our own culture and trying to understand arguments developed in the perspective of an alien culture. Ours is a pluralistic society comprising many subcultures. Debates on national goals, public policy, and moral and social issues often involve arguments shaped within different subcultures, or by people who presuppose differing standards of reasonableness, different goals for public policy, different sources of truth, and different norms of morality.

A debate concerning laws to control the spread of pornography can pit a representative of the American Civil Liberties Union, whose arguments are concerned with preservation of freedom of speech and freedom of the press, against a leader of the Sodality of the Blessed Virgin, whose concern is with the way commercialized pornography corrupts purity of soul. Debates on the rights of homosexuals frequently involve leaders of the gay community—who argue from the principle that private behavior of consenting adults should not be controlled by law—and representative leaders of Evangelical Christianity—whose arguments are based on the Biblical condemnation of Sodom and Gomorrah. Legalized abortion, the rights of welfare recipients, overcrowding in prisons, crime in the streets, protection of the environment, prayer in public schools, the need for offshore drilling, and rights of animals: these are but a few of the issues that are privately argued and publicly debated by representatives of different subcultures.

How are we to handle the divergence in presuppositions that commonly characterize such discussions?

In attempting to answer this question, it is important to distinguish between two separate, though related, problems. The first is the problem of understanding a different subculture and the distinctively different works produced within it. Here, the methods of hermeneutics sketched above apply. The second problem concerns the requirements of public debate. One who intends to take part in public discussions should attempt to make his or her position intelligible, though not necessarily acceptable, to those who argue from a different perspective or on the basis of different principles. For this purpose it helps to be able to isolate and explicate any presuppositions or framework features that an argument requires. This is our concern.

Against this general background we may distinguish four different types of presuppositions, though only three of them will be treated in this chapter. These are presuppositions of fact; of principle; of value; and of policy. Presuppositions of policy will be deferred until the next chapter.

1. Presuppositions of fact.   Consider a letter to the editor of the *San Francisco Chronicle* published just after the Nov. 1982 elections.

> Editor—To read the Chronicle during the recent election coverage, one would believe that we have just a two-party system. Nations as small and diverse as Costa Rica and Thailand have no fewer than 15 major political parties, all of which receive fair and even press coverage. Although the Libertarians were given only the barest of mention during the campaign and they seated no candidates in California, they have captured the hearts and minds of California. No political party or newspaper has as accurately predicted the mood of the voters of this state and city, our positions from the bottle bill, nuclear freeze, gun control, water control—everything. We won.[18]

The author of the letter claims that Costa Rica and Thailand each have more than fifteen major political parties and that all of them receive fair and equal press coverage. How would such alleged facts be known? It would have to be based on information derived from people who read the native languages, collect all the local newspapers and then make a systematic study of the coverage each party receives. If the writer had such a study available, he would presumably cite it. He cannot simply assume that his readers are familiar with the way fifteen different parties are treated in newspapers written in Spanish or Thai.

He goes on to say that, though the Libertarian party did very poorly in the election, they have captured the hearts and minds of the people of California. Since most of the people derive their information about unfamiliar political parties from the newspapers and the TV stations and—as the author himself stresses—these ignored the Libertarian party, what is the basis for the claim that this party captured the hearts and minds of the people of California? Only the further claim that on some particular referenda the people supported the same position that the Libertarian party did. He cites four referendum issues, less than a fifth of those contained on the ballot. Such observations do not prove that the author was incorrect. But they do supply specific bases for doubt and for further investigation—at least for those who take the author's claims seriously.

Presuppositions of fact concern not only which alleged facts are presupposed as established. They also concern the way facts are collected and interpreted. As an illustration we might consider an excerpt from Herbert Spencer, the nineteenth-century leader of the movement known as Social Darwinism. The basic idea behind this movement was the theory that all cultures evolve in pretty much the same pattern. Cultures that are still in the state of savagery or barbarism correspond to what Europeans were like some thousands of years ago, before they developed their current refined sensibility. This perspective supplies a general framework for the selection and interpretation of facts about members of more primitive societies.

> According to Lichtenstein, the Bushman do not "appear to have any feeling of even the most striking changes in the temperature of the atmosphere." Gardiner says the Zulus "are perfect salamanders"—arranging the burning faggots with their feet and dipping their hands into the boiling contents of the cooking-vessels. The Abipones, again, are extremely tolerant of the inclemencies of the sky." So it is with the feelings caused by bodily injuries. Many travellers express surprise at the calmness with which men of inferior type undergo serious operations. Evidently the sufferings produced are much less than would be produced in men of higher types.[19]

Visitors are often amazed at the calmness with which native New Yorkers bear the noise of the subway trains or natives of Los Angeles adjust to the smog. Sooner or later most natives of any environment learn to adjust to the conditions they cannot change. Does this show that they are of an inferior type? Might the alleged facts simply indicate that natives of other cultures do not display emotions and reactions the same way we do or have different conditioning?

2. Presuppositions of principle.   There are many principles that are generally presupposed as obvious or as implicit in the meaning of the words we use. In learning terms like 'part', 'whole', and 'equal' we absorb the principles that the whole is greater than the part, and that things equal to the same thing are equal to each other. (The validity of such shared principles is not our present concern unless, in a particular context, there is some specific reason for doubting a principle presupposed.)

In addition to such generally shared principles, there are principles of reasoning assimilated by members of subgroups, usually as a result of training or indoctrination. Such principles need not be made explicit in arguments presented to fellow members of the same subgroup. However, if the same argument is presented to a larger group, it looses its force, and sometimes its intelligibility, unless the principles presupposed are made explicit. A couple of examples may illustrate this.

The first is from de Saussure, the founding father of the science of linguistics.

> The laws that govern the spread of linguistic phenomena are the same as those that govern any custom whatever, e.g., fashion. In every human collectivity two forces are always working simultaneously and in opposing directions: individualism or *provincialism* [*esprit de clocher*] on the one hand and *intercourse*—communication among men—on the other.[20]

What de Saussure presupposes is that the spread of any custom is governed by law. The problem then is one of determining which laws govern the spread of linguistic phenomena. De Saussure's presupposition is an assumption that seems natural enough to those trained in the social sciences. Yet it is an assumption that was simply not made in earlier times.

As a second example we will consider an excerpt from one of the most influential Catholic moral theologians of the past generation. In an article written for other theologians he reflected on Pope Pius XI's encyclical *Casti Cannubii* (Of Chaste Marriage) and its teaching on the immorality of birth control.

> ... to maintain that it could have been in the circumstances erroneous doctrine would seem to impugn the very providence of God with respect to His Church and her ordinary teaching mission. In a matter so serious and of such general concern—literally a matter of eternal life or death for millions—could God conceivably have allowed His vicar, even on one occasion, to misinform the faithful so outrageously? And is it not even more incredible, even to the point of being theologically impossible, that God could have permitted an entire tradition of such teaching to develop and to continue uninterruptedly and unopposed for centuries? Practical faith simply cannot reconcile error of this magnitude with any meaningful guarantee of divine assistance "usque ad consummationem saeculi" (even to the end of the world).[21]

When this article was written there was a debate among Catholic theologians between those advocating a change in the Church's teaching on the immorality of contraception and those opposing it. Earlier opposition had chiefly been based on the argument that contraception is wrong because it is against the natural law. Many Catholic theologians no longer found this persuasive. In the citation presented Lynch puts Catholic opposition to artificial contraception on a new basis. It must be wrong because the Catholic Church has always taught it is wrong. This doctrine played a basic role in Pope Paul VI's encyclical *Humanae Vitae* (Of Human Life) issued some two years after this article. The presupposition underlying the argument is the theological principle that the Pope is infallible, by virtue of divine protection, when he issues official pronouncements on matters of faith and morals. The force of Lynch's argument is to extend the scope of freedom from error from official *(ex cathedra)* papal pronouncements to ordinary papal teaching. The significance of this argument is not clear until this implicit principle is made explicit.

3. Presupposition of values.   Subgroups formed on the basis of voluntary associations, such as clubs, political parties, and to some degree, churches, are generally characterized by a set of shared values or goals. The direct mailing techniques that have become so widespread build directly on the assumption of shared values and goals. Such letters commonly begin by claiming, "We share the same values and goals." They conclude with a plea to send as much money as possible so that we, who share these goals, can help feed starving children, put a fellow Republican in the White House, spread the glad tidings of redemption, stop the corruption of Congress, or provide shelters for stray cats. Even those who do not accept such shared values or goals (though the *values* and *goals* are different, they play similar roles in argumentation) are generally able to understand what is being presupposed in an argument. Confusion arises only when one is presupposing values that are not widely recognized or are contrary to accepted values.

Consider, for example, one aspect of the life proper to the guardians in Plato's Republic:

> And on the young men, surely, who excel in war and other pursuits we must bestow honors and prizes, and, in particular, the opportunity for more frequent intercourse with the women, which will at the same time, be a plausible pretext for having them beget as many of the children as possible.
> Right.
> And the children thus born will be taken over by the officials appointed for this, men or women or both, since, I take it, the official posts too are common to women and men.
> Yes.
> The offspring of the good, I suppose, they will take to the pen or creche, to certain nurses who live apart in a quarter of the city, but the offspring of the inferior, and any of those of the other sort who are born defective, they will properly dispose of in secret, so that no one will know what has become of them.[22]

If we sidestep the disputed question of what Plato really intended in outlining the ideal republic and simply take the statement given above at its face value, it seems to involve various moral presuppositions. The first, and most obvious one, is that sexual promiscuity is permissable for the guardians of the state. The further discussion implicitly presupposes that the rearing of children is the duty and prerogative of the state, not of the parents, and that the state has the right to dispose of the unfit. These are all moral presuppositions and—as Plato fully realized—all are in need of justification.

4. Presupposition of policy.   This category of presupposition is included here for the sake of completeness. A more systematic treatment of presuppositions of policy will be given in the next chapter. The basic idea, however, is aptly illustrated by the disclosure of the Post Office's plans for mail delivery in the aftermath of a nuclear holocaust. Such planning presupposes that one policy is immutable: The mail must be delivered.

EXERCISES

A. 1. What is the basic test for determining whether one proposition presupposes another?
2. Pick a lead story or an editorial from today's newspaper and see if you can detect any basic presuppositions in the first two or three paragraphs.
3. Read the opening paragraph of the American Declaration of Independence and try to determine what facts or values it presupposes.
4. What value presuppositions are shared by boy scouts, or girl scouts?
5. What is the difference between a generic and a specific reason for doubt?
6. What is the difference between a culture and a subculture?
7. What significant differences do you note in the presuppositions underlying the moral judgments of your generation and your parents' generation?

B. 1. Try to match the propositions in I with the presuppositions in II. There may be items with no matching partners.

I	II
a) Joe's stepmother is nice.	m) Joe is married.
b) Joe's mother-in-law is mean.	n) Joe's mother is dead.
c) Joe's mother-in-law is a divorceé.	o) Joe is a bachelor.
d) Joe is the governor of our state.	p) Joe is a citizen of our state.
e) Jane's oldest boy is in the seventh grade.	q) Joe's father remarried.
	r) Jane has had sexual relations.
f) Jane is attending the orphans' picnic.	s) Jane has not had sexual relations.
	t) Jane is married.
g) Jane is pregnant.	u) Jane is a virgin.
h) Jane is not pregnant.	v) Jane could have children.
i) Jane is over thirty.	w) Jane's parents are dead.
j) Jane's husband is a lawyer.	

2. Not all of the following passages are arguments. Each, however, involves presuppositions that should occasion specific doubt. Try to identify the presupposition or presuppositions crucial to each passage. Identify the type of presupposition and comment on its reasonableness.

a) [The following exchange was occasioned by an eyewitness account of Israeli–PLO conflict, written up by Martin Peretz, editor of *The New Republic*.]
To the editors:
Martin Peretz is the liar. He was not an eyewitness of a *war*. Rather, he was a

tardy "witness" of parts of Lebanon. He mentions not one dead or mutilated body that he saw.

His numbers game with human lives is vomit-invoking. Would the Israelis really be less barbaric because they murdered 7,000 rather than 12,000 civilians? No one gives a doggone about an exact number. The magnitude is crystal clear: large!

Further, Mr. Peretz is either stupid or hopelessly ignorant. The idea that *Israeli* censored reports exaggerate and distort Israeli barbarity and callousness is patently absurd. Obviously, such Israeli censored reports grossly understate and distort Israel's destruction of human life and property.

Overall, Mr. Peretz's "eyewitness" account is as unconvincing and farcical as his cataloguing of Jewish journalists and labeling them as the only "trustworthy" ones in Lebanon.

[P_____ J_____, Washington, D.C.]

Mr. Peretz replies: Ms. J_____ assumes that the only journalists I cited as reliable are Jews. She is wrong: to my knowledge, only two of the seven are. Her false assumption is revealing. By the way, by far the worst and most tendentiously pro-PLO reporter from Lebanon during the war and long before it is a Jew, the Washington Post's Jonathan Randal.[23]

b) Editor — Your editorial comment November 14 on the condo controversy was right on.

May I also add another argument in favor of condos that the San Francisco, Berkeley, Santa Monica and other fatheads are unable to fathom. It is that every tenant (or owner-to-be) who buys a condo will leave a vacant rental property behind for some displaced tenant to occupy. So how does condo conversion exacerbate the housing crisis?[24]

*c) But we have arrived at the term or concept of the unconscious along another path, by considering certain experiences in which mental *dynamics* play a part. We have found — that is we have been obliged to assume — that very powerful mental processes or ideas exist (and here a quantitative or *economic* factor comes into question for the first time) which can produce all the effects in mental life that ordinary ideas do (including effects that can in their turn become conscious as ideas), though they themselves do not become conscious. It is unnecessary to repeat in detail here what has been explained so often before. It is enough to say that at this point psychoanalytic theory steps in and asserts that the reason why such ideas cannot become conscious is that a certain force opposes them, that otherwise they could become conscious, and that it would then be apparent how little they differ from other elements which are admittedly psychical. The fact that in the technique of psychoanalysis a means has been found by which the opposing forces can be removed and the ideas in question made conscious renders this theory irrefutable.[25]

d) But we must see how the words spoken by the Apostle, that not the woman but the man is the image of God, are not contrary to that which is written in Genesis: "God made man, to the image of God he made him; male and female he made them and blessed them." For he says that human nature itself, which is complete in both sexes, has been made to the image of God, and he does not exclude the woman from being understood as the image of God. For after he had said that God made man to the image of God, he went on to say: "He made him male and female," or at any rate (if we punctuate this passage differently) "male and female he made them." In what sense, therefore, are we to understand the Apostle, that the man is the image of God, and consequently is forbidden to cover his head, but the woman is not, and on this account is commanded to do so? The solution lies, I think, in what I already said when discussing the nature of the human mind, namely that the woman together with her husband is the image of God, so that the whole substance is one image. But when she is assigned as a help-mate, a function that pertains to her alone, then she is not the image of God; but as far as the man is concerned, he is by himself alone the image of God, just as fully and completely as when he and the woman are joined together into one.[26]

*e) With regard to the ''just so damn beautiful!'' $4 million Picasso painting just purchased by the Kimbell Art Museum (NEWS-MAKERS, Sept. 6), I beg to differ. Like a lot of Picasso's work, it isn't juvenile, but it certainly comes close. Just look at the man's idea of anatomy—if a real woman had legs like that she'd be in a hospital for surgery (or an autopsy). Michelangelo would have laughed—or cried—at it. Picasso has long been an example of the emperor's clothes syndrome.[27]

f) If, then we set aside what is not of the essence of the social contract, we shall find that it is reducible to the following terms: ''Each of us puts in common his person and his whole power under the supreme direction of the general will; and in return we receive every member as an indivisible part of the whole.''[28]

*g) There is, however, an obvious and essential proviso to be made. For the human particles to become really personalised under the creative influence of union, they must not—according to the preceding analysis—join up together anyhow. Since it is a question of achieving a synthesis of centres, it is centre to centre that they must make contract and *not otherwise.* Thus, amongst the various forms of psychic inter-activity animating the noosphere, the energies we must identify, harness and develop before all others are those of an ''intercentric'' nature, if we want to give effective help to the progress of evolution in ourselves.[29]

h) Editor—Those handguns bought to protect the home more often shoot another member of the family: a son sneaking home after lockup, a nagging husband/wife, one child by another. Or what more frequently happens to these guns is that they are stolen by thieves and end up on the streets, violating the civil rights of us honest citizens. The fewer handguns in the homes, the fewer guns will wind up in the hands of the vicious.[30]

3. The following arguments all depend on perspectives that differ to some degree from commonly shared perspectives, either because they are set in a different culture or because they presuppose particular value systems or religious views. Discuss the contribution of these perspectives to the overall force of the arguments and evaluate the degree to which these arguments might be acceptable even to those who do not share the particular perspective.

a) In almost all nations, whether of the ancient or the modern world, even amongst the Hottentots, property is inherited by the male descendants alone; it is only in Europe that a departure has taken place; but not amongst the nobility, however. That the property which has cost men long years of toil and effort, and been won with so much difficulty, should afterwards come into the hands of women, who then, in their lack of reason, squander it in a short time, or otherwise fool it away, is a grievance and a wrong, as serious as it is common, which should be prevented by limiting the right of women to inherit. In my opinion the best arrangement would be that by which women, whether widows or daughters, should never receive anything beyond the interest for life on property secured by mortgage, and in no case the property itself, or the capital, except where all male descendents fail. The people who make money are men, not women; and it follows from this that women are neither justified in having unconditional possession of it, nor fit persons to be entrusted with its administration.[31]

*b) Abraham's ''readiness'' to kill Isaac has absolutely nothing to do with infanticide. Abraham was unwilling to kill his son. He was, instead, carrying out an act of obedience to a command from God, and his action was a demonstration of his faith, which was being tested by God; it was not an act of fierce savagery.[32]

c)   The maxim, that the same cause in the same circumstances, will produce the same effect, is as true in the moral as in the natural world; the laws of mind, and the operation of moral causes, being just as uniform as the laws of matter. The Gospel, the greatest moral cause which ever operated in the world, is the same now as in the apostolic age; and the heart of man, civilized or uncivilized, is also the same. So that this great cause is operating now, in substantially the same circumstances as it did in the primitive age; —for the heart of man is the moral world, and is the same now as then. If there be a system of doctrines, then at the present time, whose effects are universally the same with those produced by the faith once delivered to the saints; that system, demonstrably, *is the faith* which was once delivered to the saints. Identity of moral effect proves identity of moral cause.[33]

d)   The advent of the Christian God, as the maximum god attained so far, was therefore accompanied by the maximum feeling of guilty indebtedness on earth . . .

In this psychical cruelty there resides a madness of the will which is absolutely unexampled: the *will* of man to find himself guilty and reprehensible to a degree that can never be atoned for; his *will* to infect and poison the fundamental ground of things with the problem of punishment and guilt so as to cut off once and for all his own exit from this labyrinth of "fixed ideas"; his *will* to erect an ideal— that of the "holy God"—and in the face of it to feel the palpable certainty of his own absolute unworthiness. Oh this insane, pathetic beast—man! What ideas he has, what unnaturalness, what paroxysms of nonsense, what *bestiality of thought* erupts as soon as he is prevented just a little from being a *beast in deed!*

All this is interesting, to excess but also of a gloomy, black, unnerving sadness, so that one must forcibly forbid oneself to gaze too long into these abysses. Here is *sickness,* beyond any doubt the most terrible sickness that has ever raged in man; and whoever can still bear to hear (but today one no longer has ears for this!) how in this night of torment and absurdity there has resounded the cry of *love,* will turn away, seized by invincible horror. —There is so much in man that is hideous! —Too long, the earth has been a madhouse! —[34]

*e)   When, therefore, the last judgment is completed, human nature will be entirely established in its goal. However, since everything bodily is somehow for the sake of man (as was shown in Book III), at that time, also, the entire bodily creation will be changed—and suitably—to be in harmony with the state of the man who then will be. And because men will then be incorruptible, the state of generation and corruption will then be taken away from the whole bodily creation. And this is what the Apostle says: "the creature also itself shall be delivered from the servitude of corruption, into the liberty of the glory of the children of God" (Epistle to the Romans, 8: 21).

Now, generation and corruption in inferior bodies are caused by the movement of the heavens. Therefore, that generation and corruption may come to a stop in the inferior bodies, the movement of the heavens must also come to a stop. And on this account the Apocalypse (Revelations 10:6) says "that time shall be no longer."[35]

REFERENCES

[1]Citation from H. Carroll et al., *The Development of Civilization* (Chicago: Scott, Foresman, 1962), vol. 2, p. 420.

[2]Charles Darwin, *The Origin of the Species,* in *Darwin: A Norton Critical Edition,* ed. Philip Appleman (New York: W.W. Norton), 1970, p. 117.

[3]Ernst Cassirer, *An Essay on Man* (New Haven: Yale University Press, 1944), p. 12.

[4]Janet Evans, "Love and the Single Woman," *Coronet* (April, 1949), pp. 177–178.

[5]"The 1915 Declaration of Principles" is reprinted as an appendix in *Academic Freedom and Tenure: A Handbook of the American Association of University Professors,* ed. Louis Joughin (Madison: The University of Wisconsin Press, 1967), pp. 155–176; citation from p. 174.

[6]Adm. Stansfield Turner, U.S. Navy, retired, in *Newsweek,* May 17, 1982, p. 45. [Note: In the Falklands war, HMS Sheffield was destroyed by a single missile.]

[7]Henry Thoreau, "Civil Disobedience," in *The Portable Thoreau,* ed. Carl Bode (New York: Viking, 1947), pp. 113–114.

[8]Rollo May, "Love and Will," cited in *Personal Philosophy,* ed. Burton Porter (New York: Harcourt Brace Jovanovich Inc., 1976), p. 141. Excerpt reprinted by permission of W. W. Norton & Company, Inc.

[9]Archibald Cox, "A New Right Blueprint for Destruction," *Common Cause,* Dec. 1981, p. 61. Reprinted by permission of Common Cause.

[10]"Squeeze OPEC," an editorial in the *Oakland Tribune,* March 15, 1982. Reprinted by permission of *The Tribune,* Oakland, California.

[11]Ralph Waldo Emerson, "The Comic," in *The Portable Emerson,* ed. Mark van Doren, (New York: Viking, 1946), p. 207.

[12]Thomas Reid, *Inquiry into the Human Mind on the Principles of Common Sense,* chap. V, sec. VII, 1764.

[13]Peter Bertocci, *The Human Venture in Sex, Love, and Marriage* (New York: Haddam, 1949), p. 52. Reprinted by permission of the author.

[14]Albert Ellis, "Sex without Guilt," in *Human Sexuality: Contemporary Perspectives,* ed. Morrison and Borosage (Palo Alto: National Press Books, Lyle Stuart Inc., 1973), p. 384. Reprinted by permission of Lyle Stuart Inc.

[15]From the *San Francisco Chronicle,* Nov. 28, 1982. Copyright © 1982 by Universal Press Syndicate. Reprinted by permission of Universal Press Syndicate.

[16]From *Corporate Flight,* (Spring, 1982), p. 4. Reprinted by permission of the Piper Aircraft Corporation.

[17]D. Jenness, "The Carrier Indians of the Bulkley River," *Bulletin no. 133, Bureau of American Ethnology,* Washington, D.C., 1943, cited in Claude Levi-Strauss, *The Savage Mind* (Chicago: The University of Chicago Press, 1966), p. 37.

[18]San Francisco Chronicle, Nov. 22, 1982.

[19]Herbert Spencer, *The Principles of Sociology* (New York: Appleton, 1896), vol. 1, part 1, p. 50.

[20]Ferdinand de Saussure, *Course in General Linguistics,* trans. Wade Baskin (New York: McGraw-Hill, 1959, p. 205.

[21]John J. Lynch, S. J., "The Contraceptive Issue: Moral and Pastoral Reflections," *Theological Studies,* XXVIII (1966), 258–259.

[22]*Plato's Republic,* trans. Paul Shorey in *Plato: The Collected Dialogues,* ed. Edith Hamilton and Huntington Cairns (New York: Pantheon, 1963), p. 699. Reprinted by permission of the publishers and the Loeb Classical Library from Plato's *Republic,* translated by Paul Shorey, Cambridge Mass.: Harvard University Press. 1930., 1935.

[23]*The New Republic,* Sept. 13, 1982, p. 4. Reprinted by permission of *The New Republic.*

[24]"Letters to the Editor," *San Francisco Chronicle,* Nov. 25, 1982.

[25]Sigmund Freud, *The Ego and the Id,* trans. Joan Riviere, ed. James Stracy (New York: W. W. Norton & Co., 1960), p. 4.

[26]St. Augustine, *On the Trinity,* Book 12, in the *Fathers of the Church* series, Washington, D.C., The Catholic University of America Press, vol. 45 (1963), p. 351–352.

[27]From "Letters to the Editor," *Newsweek,* Sept. 27, 1982. Reprinted by permission of Newsweek, Inc.

[28]Jean-Jacques Rousseau, *The Social Contract and Discourse on the Origins of Inequality,* ed. Lester G. Crocker (New York: Washington Square Books, 1967), pp. 18–19.

[29]Pierre Teilhard de Chardin, *The Phenomenon of Man,* trans. Bernard Wall (London: Wm Collins Sons & Co., 1959), p. 263. Reprinted by permission of Harper & Row, Publishers, Inc.

[30]"Letters to the Editor," *San Francisco Chronicle,* March 11, 1982.

[31]Arthur Schopenhauer, "On Women," in his *Studies in Pessimism,* trans. Thoms Bailey Sanders in *Complete Essays of Schopenhauer: Seven Books in One Volume,* Book 5 (New York: Wiley, 1942), p. 88.

[32]"Letters to the Editor," *Newsweek,* Sept. 20, 1982, p. 6. Reprinted by permission of Newsweek, Inc.

[33]Lyman Beecher, "The Faith Once Delivered to the Saints," a sermon delivered at Worcester, MA, 1823, cited in Ernest J. Wrage and Barnet Baskerville, *Contemporary American Forum* (New York: Harper & Row, 1946), p. 104.

[34]Friedrich Nietzsche, *On the Genealogy of Morals,* trans. Walter Kaufmann and R. J. Hollingdale (New York: Vintage Books, 1969), pp. 90, 93. Reprinted by permission of Random House, Inc.

[35]St. Thomas Aquinas, *On the Truth of the Catholic Faith: Summa Contra Gentiles. Book Four. Salvation,* trans. Charles J. O'Neil (Garden City, N.Y.: Doubleday Image Books, 1957), pp. 346–347.

Chapter 4

PRACTICAL REASONING

Practical reasoning is reasoning related to something to be done, or to something to be decided. In this it differs from speculative, or theoretical, reasoning, which is concerned with what is true, or what is the case. This simple and familiar distinction does not imply that one has to be a speculative theoretician to employ speculative reasoning. When I reason from black stains on the garage floor to the conclusion that my car is leaking oil, I am using speculative reasoning. When I reason from my desire to see a movie and my reading of reviews to the conclusion that I should see the film, *Sophie's Choice,* rather than the latest Cheech and Chong movie, then I am engaged in practical reasoning.

The arguments we have considered so far included both practical and speculative arguments. The reason for this is our chosen starting point. We began with the practices of reasoning we have already assimilated. Then we tried to refine, clarify, and systematize these practices. We did not begin with a theory of reasoning, though bits of theory were gradually introduced. Ordinary practice will still serve as our starting point. From now on, however, we will try to go beyond this starting point in a more systematic way. Thus, in considering practical reasoning we will build on what we have already considered and will focus on the features that distinguish practical reasoning from speculative reasoning and the problems they present.

An account of practical reasoning involves two rather different types of problems. Problems of the first type involve theoretical issues: to explain the role that reasons play in determining actions; to characterize the relation between the premises and conclusion of a practical argument; to clarify other issues involving intentions and structures. Problems of the second type are practical. We all have to make decisions. Most of us would like to make them more rationally. How can this be done? How can we improve our practice of practical reasoning? Though our concern here is basically with practical reasoning, the way in which this is treated depends, to some extent, on our understanding of its theoretical background. So, we will begin with a brief nontechnical survey of some of the theoretical problems concerning practical reasoning.

4.1 SPECULATIVE VS. PRACTICAL ARGUMENTS

Let's begin with a couple of simple examples that bring out some basic differences between speculative and practical reasoning.

> I want to preserve my health.
> Smoking is harmful to my health.
> ———————————————
> Therefore, I intend to stop smoking.   (4.1)
>
> All Pennsylvanians are Americans.
> All Philadelphians are Pennsylvanians.
> ———————————————
> So, all Philadelphians are Americans.   (4.2)

In each of these examples, the conclusion seems to follow from the premises in a very straightforward way. In example (4.2) there is simply no way in which the premises could be true and the conclusion be false. This is most clearly seen if we use diagrams (which will be considered more systematically later) with circles standing for the class of Pennsylvanians (Pn), Americans (Am) and Philadelphians (Pa).

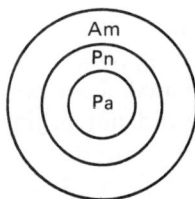

(4.3)

These circles represent classes, for example the class of all Americans. To hold the premises and yet deny the conclusion would be equivalent to claiming that something could be inside the innermost circle and yet not inside the outermost circle, a clear contradiction.

We cannot say the same about example (4.1). There are many people who are quite concerned with preserving their health, recognize that smoking is harmful to their health—and yet continue to smoke. This practice might be unreasonable. Yet, there is nothing contradictory about accepting the premises of argument (4.1) and yet not deciding to quite smoking. The connection between premises and conclusion in a practical argument cannot be quite the same as in a theoretical argument.

The basic reason for this divergence is that practical arguments involve, not just premises and conclusions, but persons as well. It is persons, not propositions, who have intentions and make decisions. Let's go back and examine (4.1) using this distinction. The first premise expresses an intention of a person, the intention of trying to realize some goal. The second premise expresses the belief that some particular action is necessary or helpful as a means of reaching that goal. What of the conclusion? First, we should distinguish two conclusions. The first is the conclusion of the *argument:* I should stop smoking. This follows from the premises. Yet, it may not really express the intention of the agent, her or his decision on what she or he intends to do. I personally drew that conclusion many times before I finally quit smoking. Most of us have had the experience of making resolutions on the basis of practical arguments and then failing to keep them.

Our concern here is with practical reasoning, not with the psychological problems of how a person reaches a decision, or why a person often fails to implement a decision, once it has been reached. Yet, we can not completely avoid the problem of persons, for it is persons, not propositions, who have intentions and reach conclusions. Different persons have different intentions. Whose should be considered?

In attempting to answer this it helps to be clear on what we are attempting to do here. It is not psychology, or sociology, or any other empirical study of how persons make decisions. It is a normative study of practical reasoning. We wish to set norms that distinguish good reasoning from bad. As the norm for practical reasoning we take the *reasonable person.* We cannot give any absolute definition of what it means to be a reasonable person. Here again, we use the ordinary notion of reasonableness as our starting point. To bring out its significance in the present context, we may return to example (4.1), which exemplifies a typical argument in practical reasoning.[1] In its essence it involves two premises, called the 'major' and the 'minor', and a conclusion. The typical structure is:

> *Major:*   a motivational premise—expresses the intention of realizing some goal.
> *Minor:*   expresses the belief that some particular means is helpful or necessary in achieving this goal.
> *Conclusion:*   expresses a practical judgment in choice of the means.

Here we have presented the major premise as the expression of an intention. Intentions do not stand alone. Ordinarily, the intention of attempting to realize some goal is connected with beliefs concerning the goodness, utility, or desirability of the goal. The precise way in which these interrelations are to be explained is a complex and disputed issue. For our purposes, however, we need only consider the role of intentions in practical arguments and not these further disputes.

It is possible for a person to have the intention expressed in the major and the belief expressed in the minor and yet not act on the decision expressed in the conclusion. This is possible, but not reasonable. What we are accepting as a minimal condition for reasonableness is intentional consistency. It is rationally inconsistent to intend a certain goal, believe that a certain available means is necessary to achieve that goal, and yet not choose the means. The obvious objection to this norm really supports it. The objection is that we—and other reasonable people—sometimes act contrary to this pattern. We do this, but we usually realize that in so doing we are being unreasonable. That is, we accept the standard of reasonableness and see ourselves as occasionally falling short of this standard.

In the movie that bears her name, Mary Poppins regularly introduces herself as a *practically perfect person.* Her final words in the movie explain what this means: "Practically perfect persons never allow sentiment to muddle their thinking." Since she never introduces herself as a speculatively perfect person, we must assume that the thinking she is referring to is practical reasoning. In this sense she may be taken as the symbol of the reasonable person—provided we ignore a few odd practices, such as her custom of flying through the air. The idea that sentiment should not muddle reason does not mean that sentiment or emotion should be excluded. They play an essential role in our desires and intentions. They can count as reasons, when we think it reasonable to follow our feelings. When reason and feeling are in conflict, however, the reasonable person decides on the basis of reason, rather than feeling.

The minor premise was presented as being concerned with the agent's belief about the facts, rather than with the facts as such. The signfcance of this can be seen by considering a celebrated example. When young Oedipus met an insolent stranger at the crossroads of Phocis, the two of them had a violent confrontation. Would it be reasonable to summarize Oedipus's resulting intention by the following argument?

> Oedipus intended to kill the insolent stranger.
> This stranger was really Oedipus's father, Laius.
> Therefore, Oedipus intended to kill his father.   (4.4)

The point and poignancy of Sophocles's tragedy stems from the fact that Oedipus never intended to kill his father. Oedipus's *action* can be described in the terms: "Oedipus killed his father." However, Oedipus's *intentions* can not be described in those terms, because he did not believe that the insolent stranger who confronted him was really the father he had never seen.

Our actions and decisions must, for better or worse, be based on the best information available to us, on what we believe to be the case. The actual facts may differ. Sometimes, this can be established fairly objectively. The referee calls the pass complete because he believes that the receiver had both feet in bounds when he caught it. An instant replay shows that one foot was out of bounds. The policeman shoots because he believes that the suspect is reaching for a gun. In the police review it becomes clear that the suspect did not possess any weapon. We judge these people in terms of how well they did on the basis of the information available to them, on the grounds of what it was reasonable for them to believe, not on the basis of facts they could not have known. This leads to the practical problem we will consider later: Many of our decisions have to be made on the basis of inadequate knowledge.

4.2 THE ORDER OF INTENTIONS

Around 300 B.C. Euclid published his *Elements of Geometry*. This work supplied the model deductive system for centuries to come. From a few propositions (eight general axioms and five axioms proper to geometry) Euclid developed all the basic theorems of geometry by means of a rigorous chain of arguments leading from the first axioms to the final conclusion. Practical reasoning involves something similar with the order of intentions. Ultimate intentions in practical reasoning are similar to basic axioms in speculative reasoning.

The easiest way to get at this is to begin by questioning a practical decision and then work backwards. I will present a model case by means of a dialogue between the devil's advocate (DA) and an imaginary freshman (IF). Each student should check this against his or her own responses to see if the process really works as sketched here.

DA: Let's go down to Clancy's tavern and chug-a-lug a few brews.
 IF: I can't; I have to study tonight.
DA: Why study tonight? We both need a night off.
 IF: If I don't study tonight I won't be ready for the physics quiz tomorrow.
DA: Big deal! What difference does one quiz make?
 IF: If I don't do well on these quizzes, I won't get a good mark for the course, and I won't master the physics I need for more advanced courses.
DA: So what! You can't drink good marks.
 IF: If I don't have good marks, I won't be able to get into a good graduate school.
DA: Why do you want to get into a graduate school anyway?
 IF: So I can get my Ph.D. in physics.
DA: What do you want that for?
 IF: So that I can get the type of job I want, doing research work in astrophysics.
DA: Why wait so long? We can both do research in beer and girls at Clancy's.

IF: Because I'd be happiest if I could spend my time doing research work in theoretical physics.

DA: Well, to each his own. You study; I'm splitting.

This string of intentions really supplies the basis for a chain argument. Unless our freshman intended to be an astrophysicist there would be no point in getting a Ph.D. in physics. Unless he intended to get a graduate degree in physics, there would be no point in working to get into such a graduate program. And so on. Both in discussions and in the debates we carry on with our own private devil's advocate, we do not usually make ultimate intentions explicit. Common or shared intentions are presupposed. We presuppose that people want to be happy, to succeed in their efforts, to get along with their friends, to make their families happy. From the point of view of an argument, such intentions can be treated the way other presuppositions are. We need only make explicit those presupposed intentions that occasion specific doubt. When a ballplayer loafs in the outfield and doesn't hustle to beat out a bunt we wonder if he really intends to win. When a student doesn't study for a crucial exam, we wonder if she really intends to succeed in school. When each does his or her best, we presuppose each really wants to succeed.

Pehaps the best way to clarify the distinction between intentions of agents and inferential chains in practical reasoning is for each student to lay out an eight-year plan. We pick eight years on the assumption that a freshman who hopes to go to graduate school, or to get established in business will need 3 more years to finish college and four more years to get further specialized training, whether in a university or on the job, and a year of on-the-job training. If this is not appropriate, pick the time when you would like to be established in your chosen career and then work backwards. Here we have a sample chart for our imaginary freshman who wishes to be an astrophysicist. The column on the right presents each successive stage towards the goal in a square bracket. The column on the left presents difficulties to be overcome in curly brackets. Your chart should have your own projected goals and anticipated obstacles.

Chart: Career Goals

OBSTACLES	STEPS TOWARDS GOAL
	[Be an astrophysicist]
{Stiff competition for positions}	
	[Acquire a Ph.D.]
{Grad. school difficult/grad. school expensive}	
	[Acceptance by grad. school]
{Hard to get in a first rate school}	

Chart: Career Goals (*Continued*)

OBSTACLES	STEPS TOWARDS GOAL
	[All prerequisites completed High grade-point average]
{Some prerequisites build on calculus}	
	[Need an A in calculus]
{Not ready for tomorrow's quiz}	
	[I should spend the evening studying calculus]

If this planning is to be done intelligently, then one should chart more than one goal. In each case the column at the right gives a strict chain argument: "If I want to be an astrophysicist, then I must have a Ph.D. If I want a Ph.D., then I must be accepted by a graduate school. . . . If I wish to pass the quiz tomorrow, then I must spend this evening studying calculus. Suppose that I have as an alternative goal: [Be a Rock Star!!!] That would ground a different chain of inferences leading, perhaps, to the conclusion that I should spend the evening practicing my guitar so I'll be ready for a show this weekend. Which of these chains expresses my intentions depends on which goal I choose. If I decide that I really want to be an astrophysicist, believe that I can overcome the anticipated difficulties, and believe that the connections on my chart really hold, then I should spend the evening studying calculus. I could conclude this—and then spend the evening practicing my guitar. Under the circumstances that would be an unreasonable choice. If Mary Poppins were in my place she would not shirk her studies. But there is no doubt about the fact that I could do it. The conclusion of my argument does not represent my choice until I actually choose it.

4.3 DECISIONS

Many, perhaps most, of the decisions we make are only indirectly related to rational arguments. We look over the restaurant menu and pick out the Beef Stroganoff, without going through any internal process of argumentation. A fast glance through the TV Guide leads to the decision to watch a football game, rather than a situation comedy or another cops and crooks series. If pressed we could give reasons. The Beef Stroganoff dinner represents a balance between what I like and what I can afford. I always choose football games over situation comedies.

We have intellectual habits, as well as practical ones, standard ways of doing things. When dealing with such habits, arguments are usually involved in changing fixed patterns, not in following them. There are two types of cases, however, where a process of reasoning plays a more direct role in decisionmaking. The first is the case of decisions involving conflicts, whether internal or external. An opportunity arises for a sexual adventure—but my religious code prohibits such adventures as immoral. I can get to school in time for the exam only if I do seventy miles an hour on the freeway—but this is prohibited by law. Should I or shouldn't I? The second type of case involves public decisionmaking. To win other members of the grammar school Garfield club or the state senate over to our point of view, we have to give arguments.

Arguments are related to decisions. But the conclusion of an argument does not automatically become a decision, for decisions depend on intentions as well as reasons. Again, we take as our norm the reasonable person. This might seem to make the resolution of conflicts a straightforward process. One can simply arrange the reasons for both sides in the form of an argument. Then the reasonable thing to do is to choose the side supported by the stronger arguments. A practically perfect person, like Mary Poppins, should have little trouble choosing.

It may seem straightforward. In practice it rarely is. What we wish to concentrate on, accordingly, are the complications involved in making decisions, two in particular. The first especially concerns public debates leading to public decisions. In such debates, even when there seems to be a clearcut conflict, the opposing sides are often arguing from different perspectives, presupposing different principles, and focusing on slightly different issues. The immediate problem, therefore, is one of getting the underlying conflict into a sharp enough focus so that we know which issues really count.

The second complication is one that concerns personal decisions more than public decisions. It often happens that even after we have considered the arguments for and against some proposal we are still not sure what is the reasonable thing to do. Yet we may have to make a decision whether or not we are certain that it is reasonable. This problem will be considered in the next section. In the rest of this section we will concentrate on methods of getting conflicts into focus. To make this more concrete we will consider the currently controversial issue whether or not abortion should be available on demand; that is, the issue of whether clinics subsidized by the government should provide abortions for women who request them, at little or no cost. I have often proposed this topic for class discussions and have had students write arguments for the position they support. Here, I will summarize the typical arguments presented.

PRO: ABORTION SHOULD BE AVAILABLE ON DEMAND.

1. A woman should have complete control over her own body.
2. If abortion is not available on demand, then only the rich can have abortions. This seems unfair to the poor.

3. An unwanted and illegitimate child can ruin a woman's chances for happiness and a career.
4. An unwanted child is usually an unhappy child. It would be better never to be born than to be born into a life of unhappiness.
5. Abortion is one means of controlling the very serious problem of excessive growth in population.

CON: ABORTION SHOULD NOT BE AVAILABLE ON DEMAND.

1. Abortion is murder.
2. An abortion violates the fetus's right to life.
3. Our tax money should not be used for immoral purposes. Killing an innocent unborn child is highly immoral.
4. There are many adequate means available to prevent conception without resorting to abortion.
5. A woman who does not want to raise an unwanted child can always give the child up for adoption.

It would be possible to present either side in the form of a coherent argument, which one could then develop and diagram. This, however, would not get us to the heart of the difficulty. The reasons listed above represent a fair summary of those presented by students in my classes. Advocates of either side are, typically, arguing from rather different perspectives. Those favoring abortion on demand usually focus on the individual woman faced with a choice and insist that the choice should be hers and hers alone. Whether the choice of abortion is moral or not is, advocates argue, for her to decide. In our pluralistic society with its traditional separation of church and state, it is not the task of the government to make moral choices for individuals or to impose the moral standards of one or another religious group.

For those opposing abortion the crucial issue is, almost invariably, the moral one. Consider reason 1. If a woman really believes that abortion is murder, then that settles the question of what is a reasonable choice *for her*. It does not, however, settle the issue as a matter of public debate. 'Murder' is not equivalent to 'kill'. 'Murder' is a legal term. The courts in our country have not declared abortion to be a form of murder. This lack of a declaration does not settle the moral issue. But it does clarify the status of the debate. One can not simply declare abortion to be murder and expect to have this accepted. One must give reasons to support the conclusion that abortion is murder.

Here, as in many debates on controversial issues, the initial problem is one of clarifying which issues are crucial and which are not. Reasons 3, 4, and 5 of the Pro argument and reasons 4 and 5 of the Con argument are not at the heart of the disagreement for the *public* issue, though some of these considerations may be crucial in making a *particular* choice. Here we will focus on the public issues. That still leaves two distinct issues: the morality of abortion and proper government policy. A comparison may be helpful. Orthodontic work for growing children is expensive, often prohibitively expensive for poor children in a large family. This seems unfair. Should orthodontics be available on demand? Here, there is no question about the morality of orthodontics. The only question is: Is it the government's job to supply such services? Similarly, one could argue that even if abortion is considered morally acceptable, it is not the proper role of government to supply abortions. *A fortiori,* if abortion is not morally acceptable, then it is certainly not the proper role of the government to provide abortion on demand.

This leads to the heart of the controversy. Is abortion morally acceptable or not? The answer to this depends, of course, on one's moral standards. However, the *way* of answering depends on arguments that have a distinctive structure. Earlier we considered coupled arguments. Arguments involving moral principles or legal principles usually involve a special type of coupling. Following Toulmin[2], we may call this the coupling of *grounds* and *warrant.* The warrant is the general principle. The grounds are the pertinent facts. The coupling is special in that the warrant effectively specifies which type of facts are pertinent.

In the present case the general principle is that deliberately killing another human being is morally wrong. Exceptions are often made in the case of self defense, a just war, and a legal execution. If we ignore these cases, since they are not pertinent to the present debate, then both sides would generally support this warrant. The grounds concern the status of the fetus. When does a growing fetus become a person, or a human being who is the subject of rights and obligations?

Once the crucial issue in the conflict has been isolated and clarified, then one can get at the reasons that really count. In the type of conflict being considered these reasons are usually of three sorts: the *truth* of the grounds; the *reasonableness* of the warrant; and *relation of grounds to warrant* in a particular case. In the present case there is little disagreement about the reasonableness of the warrant: directly and deliberately killing a person is morally wrong. There is some doubt about the truth of the grounds. Should the fetus be considered a person? In former times this was generally settled by theological considerations. The fetus becomes person when the soul is infused into the body. Though this consideration may be convincing for many individuals, it has no legal status in our pluralistic society. We have, however, no clear legal precedent on the issue of when the fetus is considered a person.

There may also be some doubt about the relation between the warrant and the grounds. Some have argued that even if the fetus is considered as a subject of rights, or has some status as a person, nevertheless an abortion is not a *direct* killing of a person. An indirect killing is illustrated by the bombardier who intends to destroy a missile site and in doing so kills the people working on the site. Similarly, some argue, the direct intention of an abortion is the termination of a pregnancy. The killing of the fetus is an indirect result.

We have no intention of attempting to settle these issues here. Our purpose is to show how a controversy can be clarified by separating out the different issues involved and then deciding which reasons are crucial in settling each issue. We focused on the issue of the morality of abortion. This still leaves the issues of what government policy should be, a further topic for public debate. Even if both of these issues were settled, there would still remain the private issue, a woman's decision whether she should have an abortion.

These questions may be good topics for good discussion. But here we will move on to another controversy, one where the reasonableness of the warrant emerges as a crucial issue. This is the issue of whether or not there should be federal laws restricting the private possession of handguns. Again, I will attempt to provide a fair sample of the reasons for each side proposed by students in my classes.

PRO: THERE SHOULD BE FEDERAL LAWS RESTRICTING PRIVATE POSSESSION OF HANDGUNS.

1. The proliferation of handguns represents a distinct threat to the security of every individual.
2. Homicide rates in the United States are far higher than in comparable countries, like England or Japan, where private possession of handguns is severely restricted by law. In 1979 there were 118 handgun deaths in Japan, 8 in Great Britain, and 10,728 in the United States.
3. Handguns figure prominently in many killings due to impulse or sudden passion.
4. Handguns are responsible for many accidental deaths, of children, for example, playing cops and robbers with Daddy's gun.
5. Possession of a handgun is as likely to be a source of danger as a means of protection. The thief, who only intended to rob you, may shoot you when you go for a gun.

CON: PRIVATE POSSESSION OF HANDGUNS SHOULD NOT BE RESTRICTED BY LAW.

1. Each citizen of the United States has a *constitutional* right to possess a gun.
2. If guns are outlawed, only outlaws will have guns.
3. The attempt to prohibit handguns, like the earlier attempt to prohibit alcoholic beverages, will be ineffective and will only result in producing contempt for the law.
4. I live in a very tough neighborhood. I am safe from burglars only if people know that I have a gun and am willing to use it.
5. Even if guns were outlawed, those who wanted to kill would find some other means of doing it.

Here the Pro argument is fairly straightforward. The basic warrant is given in reason 1 while the other reasons give grounds for the claim that the widespread proliferation of handguns constitutes a violation of the individual's right to security of person and possessions. The argument against restrictions represents more of a mixed bag. Reason 4, for example, essentially makes the point that I need a gun because others have guns. This is a matter of a personal choice in a difficult situation. It does not directly bear on long-range public policy. This could be interpreted as an argument for changing a bad situation. Reason 2 is a slogan more than an argument. If it is transformed from a bumper sticker to an argument, then it reduces to reason 3.

This still leaves us with two distinct issues. The first is the claim that restricting private possession of handguns is unconstitutional. The second is the more pragmatic claim that laws restricting private possession of handguns would not be effective either in limiting private possession or in decreasing homicides. Each requires separate consideration.

The contention that each citizen has a right to possess a gun is a general warrant. It is in apparent conflict with the basic warrant of the opposing position, that each individual has a right to be secure in his or her person and property. When warrants are challenged, then one has to look for the reasons supporting them. Since both claims concern constitutional rights of American citizens one should look to the Constitution of the United States for supporting reasons. The *Preamble* to the Constitution states:

> We the people of the United States, in order to form a more perfect Union, establish justice, insure domestic tranquility, provide for the common defense, promote the general welfare, and secure the blessings of liberty to ourselves and our posterity, do ordain and establish this Constitution for the United States of America.

The Constitution was written and enacted to ensure domestic tranquility and secure the blessings of liberty. There is no serious doubt about the claim that people should have a right to be secure in their persons and possessions. Much of the opposing argument implicitly grants this in contending that private handguns are needed as a guarantee of personal security.

What of the opposing warrant? The second amendment to the Constitution is:

Amendment 2
Right to Bear Arms

> A well-regulated militia, being necessary to the security of a free state, the right of the people to keep and bear arms shall not be infringed.

The wording of the amendment draws its significance from the debates leading to its acceptance. Champions of States' rights, like Patrick Henry, argued that the establishment of a strong central government should not prohibit individual states from having their own state militias. This amendment guarantees the individual states this right. In those days members of the militia were expected to supply their own arms. Today, members of state militias are prohibited from using their own private handguns on public duty. Should this amendment be given a broader intepretation, prohibiting the government from restricting private possession of handguns? In our tradition such questions are answered by the precedents set by the courts. There is no significant ruling by any major court supporting such a restriction of the powers of the federal government. There are rulings prohibiting local governments from issuing such restrictions. The people of San Francisco voted for gun restrictions in 1981. This ordinance was voided by a court, not on the grounds that it violated the Second Amendment, but on the grounds that such restrictions came under the control of the state government, rather than local governments.

If this analysis is accepted, then only the second general warrant remains as a significant basis for dispute. It aptly illustrates what is meant by the question "Is the warrant reasonable?" The general claim is that gun control laws would be so unenforceable that they would do more harm than good. Since this is a prediction about what is likely to happen if a proposal is accepted and implemented, one cannot judge it to be true or false. The pertinent question is: Does it seem reasonable to accept this evaluation? Such a question cannot be answered in the abstract. One would have to consider a particular law, the methods proposed for enforcing it, and the degree of cooperation anticipated from the general public. Once again, the analysis given here is not concerned with settling the substantive issue, but with methods of clarifying what the real issues are and what are the reasons that count for or against them.

4.4 REFUTATIONS

A *refutation* is a sort of antiargument, an attempt to nullify or weaken the force of an argument of the opposing side. We will only consider refutations in the context of practical arguments, where arguments are being presented for and against some proposal. The idea of a refutation is simple enough. The practice, however, often involves a certain amount of obscurity. The obscurity is effectively an offshoot of the difficulties noted in attempting to clarify the real points at issue in a public debate.

Suppose that we only consider an issue from our own perspective. In that case the opposing argument will probably be interpreted as being based on a denial of the grounds and/or warrant supporting our side. We oppose abortion as murder—so we say our opponents are in favor of murder. We support abortion as a woman's choice—so we say our opponents are against letting women have free choice. Similarly, we say that our opponents, on the gun-control issue, are not concerned with the security of individuals, or are siding with the outlaws.

This is what is known as the *straw man fallacy*. Instead of refuting the positions our opponents really hold, we build a mythical opponent and then treat it the way we would treat a tackling dummy at a football practice. The result is an easy victory, but a rather hollow one. It might be convincing to those who already share our views. If presented to an intelligent, informed, neutral audience, the straw man approach might do more harm than good. They might conclude that we are unable or unwilling to face up to the real arguments supporting the opposing view. Before passing on to a more honest approach, we must admit that the straw man fallacy is often effective in political campaigns. The best way to circumvent such reliance on a systematic misinterpretation of the opponent's position is to have public debates.

As a general rule, one does not really understand an issue unless one is able to explain the reasons for *both* sides. Before defending either side, one should attempt the type of clarification of issues previously considered. After this has been done, then the refutation of the opposing view generally takes one or more of the following lines.

1. The *grounds* supporting the opposing case are not what they are alleged to be. Thus, a prosecutor will attempt to prove that the alibi of the accused does not stand up. He was not fifty miles away from the scene of the crime, as he claims. He was seen in the vicinity of the crime just after the crime was committed. In more problematic cases one might contest an opponent's interpretation of the facts, such as whether the killing of a fetus is the killing of a person, or whether a certain voting record is really a sign of concern for the well-being of local voters.

2. The *warrant* supporting the opposing position may be attacked as being *incorrect, unreasonable, or inapplicable.* An appeal to the Constitution coupled with a misinterpretation of what it says is a clear case of an incorrect warrant. An unreasonable warrant is one pushed beyond reasonable limits. Thus, most people in our society will admit to and defend property rights. Yet, when we examine nineteenth-century arguments supporting slavery or opposing the right of labor to organize, we see property rights valued much more highly than basic human rights. I have a right to a reasonable security in my person and property. But this does not imply that the government has an obligation to protect me from earthquakes and hurricanes. In this context the warrant is inapplicable.

3. One may also refute an argument by showing that the warrant does not relate properly, or at all, to the grounds. The clearest example of this occurs in legal reasoning. Thus the law may supply the general warrant that

a public official is guilty of criminal negligence if and only if five conditions are met. Showing that an official was in fact negligent would not suffice to find him guilty of *criminal* negligence. The warrant specifies the pertinent grounds. All five conditions must be fulfilled.

EXERCISES

A. 1. What is the basic difference between speculative and practical reasoning?
   2. What is the relation between the conclusion of a practical argument and the decision of the person presenting the argument?
   3. Explain the typical structure of a practical syllogism.
   4. How reasonable must someone be to serve as a model for practical reasoning?
   5. What is the difference between an intention and a belief?
   6. Need our ultimate intentions always be clearly formulated?
   7. Should our routine decisions always be based on practical reasoning?
   8. What is the difference between a public and a private decision?
   9. What is the difference between grounds and warrant in a practical argument?
  10. Can the defense of a position involve more than one warrant?

B. 1. Make an eight-year (or whatever number seems appropriate) goal plan. As in the text, the plan should list the steps leading to the goal in one column and the obstacles to be overcome in another.
   2. Re-do the plan with an alternative goal or an alternative path to the same goal.
   3. Consider the following two letters both written to the *San Francisco Chronicle* in November, 1981, by men with military connections. Try to clarify the basic point of disagreement and then arrange each argument in terms of grounds, warrant, and claim. Finally, try to determine which arguments, if any, in each position may be taken as refutations of the opposing position.
   Editor — Maybe working in the healing arts has warped my perspective, but somehow Leonid Brezhnev's assessment of President Reagan's plans for limited European nuclear war as being ''madness'' appears quite appropriate. Doesn't Reagan know that the so-called tactical weapons for use against ''troops in the field'' are full-fledged atom bombs?
   These tactical weapons have been used only twice in battle; once at Hiroshima and once at Nagasaki. This very limited use produced hundreds of thousands of deaths by vaporization, incineration, and lingering radiation illness. To have as a military option the possibility of a first-use of atom bombs is madness. . . .
   We have so much in common with the Soviet Union, have never fought them in battle (as we have fought our allies, England, Germany, and Japan, in the past), and could potentially obtain many great achievements with them, if we worked in that direction (Remember Apollo-Soyuz?) . . .
   Must we continue with the present course of ''cowboys 'n Indians'' foreign policy? Radiation does have a proper use; in medicine and other useful fields, not for death and destruction.
   Editor — Secretary of State Haig evidently simply stated that at one time it had been suggested that the Western Alliance use a nuclear weapon as a ''demonstration'' to defer the Soviet Union from over-running Western Europe in a conventional war. . . . It is only logical that all options be considered in developing viable military plans. To not do this would be absurd and foolhardy.
   Isn't it a real possibility that had we used a ruse such as a demonstration of a

superior weapon to the North Vietnamese in the mid or late 1960's to show them our determination and will to win that war it might have ended then with the North Vietnamese suing for peace? If so South Vietnam would today be a democracy, thousands of American lives would have been saved, not to mention billions of dollars and the major divisive aspects of the Vietnamese conflict would not have materialized. Granted that such a measure would have brought initial world shock and condemnation, but it would have eventually been accepted and in the long run the United States secretly admired and respected for its action. . . . Perhaps the course of history might have changed and there would be no Communist intrusion in Africa and elsewhere.

4. Two reporters for *Common Cause*, Florence Graves and Julie Kosterlitz, set up a question and answer debate on the question: "Should we have a draft with a National Service Option?" The affirmative answer was defended by James Fallows, Washington editor of *The Atlantic* and author of *National Defense*. The negative answer was defended by Clifford Alexander, who was Secretary of the Army under President Carter. Excerpts from both sides are given. If necessary, clarify the issue and then arrange each side in terms of Grounds, Warrant, Claim, Refutation.

PRO: For the Draft with a National Service Option

Q. Should we have a draft with a national service option?

A. I think we should have some way of sharing the burden of military service more fairly than it is now, and I see no way of doing that other than some form of compulsion.

Now a draft would only work if it were perceived as being fair, and the best way to have a sense of fairness economically, racially, and between the genders is some sort of universal obligation.

[Also,] knowing that there is some proportion of people who profoundly object to military service, I think there needs to be some kind of alternative to avoid really tearing the social fabric.

Q. What's wrong with the Volunteer Army?

A. [It] conveys the idea that military service is just another job. Down through history that has not been true. What soldiers are finally called on to do is different from any other job. They can't be motivated properly if military service is conceived as a matter of punching in at nine and punching out at five, and you're motivated by fringe benefits and all the rest.

What it does to the country is probably worse than what it does to the military, because it destroys the bond of mutual trust and mutual respect between the military and the country if those who are serving are by and large people who don't have an economic choice, as is largely the case with the volunteer force now.

Q. You've noted that there are a higher percentage of blacks in the Army, . . . shouldn't you provide other outlets for career training, rather than just take away one of the few opportunities that exist for these people now?

A. This isn't taking anything away from anybody. If you had a plan here similar to the one in France or Switzerland or Sweden, where the people go in for a fairly short time and everybody does it, for six or nine months, probably still a much higher proportion of blacks than whites would choose to be career NCO's.

CON: Against a Draft with a National Service Option

Q. Should we have a draft with a national service option?

A. One shouldn't really confuse or link the two. Let's look at why you have a draft in the first place. It's to make up manpower shortages in the services. The fact is, it is not a necessity today. You don't have a shortage to fill.

If you want a national service, one should assume that it can stand on its own, and that there is some inherent need for it.

Q. Proponents of the draft/national service idea think all young people should serve their country. They see national service as an alternative for those who oppose serving in the military.

A. Let's not be lyrical about this. We're dealing with the lives of other people. If you do it the way the [Rep. Pete] McClosky legislation sets it up, [for example,] you are then creating a tax on the poor, by paying those people less than a minimum wage. It's fine for some millionaire's son or daughter to go off and "help the nation" for $1,000 a year; everybody allegedly feels good about the fact that they've helped. Now when the family needs the earnings of that 18- or 19-year old, you're having a profound effect on the income of the family.

Q. Critics of the Volunteer Army have said that it is made up of a disproportionately high number of poor people and minorities. Wouldn't the draft be fairer because people from all levels of society would be serving their country?

A. It isn't a question of fairness or unfairness. The question is, "Is there a necessity for the draft?" The main reason [Congress hasn't voted for a draft] is that it's not necessary. Another reason is that when you have people coming into the service by compulsion as opposed to coming in voluntarily, their attitude towards the service is quite different.[3]

*5 In 1973 the U.S. Supreme Court considered one more pornography case, the State of Georgia vs. the Paris Theater. The majority opinion, upholding the State, was written by Chief Justice Burger. The dissent, written by Justice Brennan, presents a contrary opinion. Both represent careful reasoning in a legal tradition. There are various issues at stake. Try to disentangle them and clarify the crucial point of disagreement. Then arrange each argument in terms of Grounds, Warrant, and Claim on the issue central to the dispute. To what extent does one argument refute the other on the central point of disagreement?

Paris Theater Case
Opinion by Chief Justice Burger

It should be clear from the outset that we do not undertake to tell the states what they must do, but rather to define the area in which they may chart their own course in dealing with obscene material.

We categorically disapprove the theory, apparently adopted by the trial judge, that obscene, pornographic films acquire constitutional immunity from state regulation simply because they are exhibited for consenting adults only.

Although we have often pointedly recognized the high importance of the state interest in regulating the exposure of obscene materials to juveniles and unconsenting adults, this Court has never declared these to be the only legitimate state interests permitting regulation of obscene material.

The states have a long-recognized legitimate interest in regulating the use of obscene material in local commerce and in all places of public accomodation, as long as these regulations do not run afoul of specific constitutional prohibitions.

In particular, we hold that there are legitimate state interests at stake in stemming the tide of commercialized obscenity, even assuming it is feasible to enforce effective safeguards against exposure to juveniles and to the passerby. Rights and interests "other than those of the advocates are involved." These include the interest of the public in the quality of life and the total community environment, the tone of commerce in the great city centers, and, possibly, the public safety itself.

Dissent by Justice Brennan

If, as the Court today assumes, "a state legislature may act on the assumption that commerce in obscene books, or public exhibitions focused on obscene conduct, have a tendency to exert a corrupting and debasing impact leading to antisocial behavior," then it is hard to see how state-ordered regimentation of our minds can ever be forestalled.

For if a state may, in an effort to maintain or create a particular moral tone, prescribe what its citizens cannot read or cannot see, then it would seem to follow that in pursuit of that same objective a state could decree that its citizens must read certain books or must view certain films.

However laudable its goal—and that is obviously a question on which reasonable minds may differ—the state cannot proceed by means that violate the Constitution.

Even a legitimate, sharply focused state concern for the morality of the community cannot, in other words, justify an assault on the protections of the First Amendment. Where the state interest in regulation of morality is vague and ill-defined, interference with the guarantees of the First Amendment is even more difficult to justify.

In short, while I cannot say that the interests of the state—apart from the question of juveniles and unconsenting adults—are trivial or nonexistent, I am compelled to conclude that these interests cannot justify the substantial damage to constitutional rights and to this nation's judicial machinery that inevitably results from state efforts to bar the distribution even of unprotected material to consenting adults.[4]

*6. This section contains excerpts from two speeches presenting opinions on proper government policy in times of high unemployment. Try to clarify the basic issues in the dispute and then with regard to these issues arrange each argument in the form of Grounds, Warrant, and Claim. In the present dispute it is important to bring out the presuppositions underlying each position.

The first excerpt is from an address by Edward Cornish, President of the World Future Society, to the Harvard Business Club, Washington, D.C. on Feb. 12, 1981.

If we are to avoid an economic calamity—that is, another great depression—what must be done?

First of all, we must recognize that an economic depression reduces a number of excesses or imbalances in the economy and thereby makes it possible for the economy once again to grow in a strong and healthy way. So perhaps we might begin by asking ourselves if there is some other way to accomplish the "work" of a depression without having to suffer its bad effects.

The "work" of a depression includes the elimination of the very heavy load of debt which weighs down economic activity. The debt load can be reduced through a massive wave of defaults or it can be reduced by a governmental inflation of the currency, which destroys the purchasing power represented by the original loan. Both procedures are painful, but the result is a freeing up of the economy for healthy growth.

Another task of a depression—a task which might be viewed by many tender-hearted people as unnecessary and even outrageous—is the disciplining of the work force. During a long period of good times, workers begin to take their jobs increasingly for granted and do not put forth the effort they exerted previously. At the end of the last Great Depression, workers gladly accepted long and unpleasant work at low wages, because they were glad just to have a job. They knew and accepted the fact that they could be fired for what today seems like minor infractions of petty rules.

After a spell of hard times, debt is reduced, workers are again taking their jobs very seriously, many of the economic dinosaurs have died off, and conditions are ready for new and healthy growth in the economy. Though there is probably no painless way to achieve these more favorable conditions, it is at least theoretically possible to revitalize our economy without a depression. Certainly, we should look for solutions.

The government could require that every American citizen who is not paying a certain minimum tax present himself for work in a work camp. Work at the camp would be hard, so that those who perform it would not want to go back; they would prefer to work somewhere else. Now such a program doubtless would provoke a lot of complaints because there are a lot of people who do not like to do any real work. But it is not fair to continue to tax the workers of the country to support the non-workers. The problem of unemployment in this country is not that there are not jobs for everyone who wants a job but rather that the country cannot possibly provide a high-paying, easy job for everyone who wants a job in just the place he wants it and with the exact hours that he wants to work. Real work requires that we sacrifice our personal desires in the interest of doing things for other people. This means that we have to perform tasks we don't like in places we don't like for people we don't like at times we don't like. Because we make the sacrifice of our personal desires, we are compensated in the form of money and other benefits. If we receive these benefits without having to make the sacrifices, required by most jobs, we naturally are not very enthusiastic about working. And that is what has happened in the United States. To put it bluntly, we have become a nation of loafers.[5]

The second excerpt is from an address given to the Council on Social Work Education Annual Program Meeting on March 8, 1981, by Vernon Jordan, President of the National Urban League.

I am sure you know the brutal facts of life for the third of America that is poor or near poor. You know of the pressures on families created by unemployment, by double-digit inflation, by impacted neighborhoods, poor health services, inadequate schools and the unavailability of resources to combat those problems.

And I hope too, that you are aware of the special disadvantages that continue to devastate the black community. Black people saw many of the gains of the 1960s erode. They suffer unemployment rates well over double the white rate; the twelve percent of Americans who are black provide a third of the poor, ghetto youth unemployment runs over sixty percent. In some cities more black kids drop out of high schools than graduate. And there is much more to be said about gross black disadvantage—in every area of life blacks lag far behind whites.

The budget calls for heavy cuts in vital social programs, some cuts in programs for the affluent that would be balanced by tax cuts, and vastly increased defense spending. Perhaps the best description of this budget comes from the Bible, which says:

"For unto everyone that hath shall be given,
and he shall have abundance
but from him that hath not shall be taken away
even that which he hath."

The ideal test of a budget should be whether it meets the needs of the nation while providing poor people with opportunities to join the mainstream. This budget fails the test. It even fails its own standard of keeping intact the safety net under the truly needy.

The so-called safety net programs left intact, programs like Social Security, Medicare, veterans' pensions, basic unemployment compensation, and others are primarily transfer payments to middle class people. The welfare programs included in the safety net amount to six percent of the total.

The real safety net for the needy—programs like food stamps, Medicaid, public service jobs, subsidized housing, and education—will be cut. Many of those cuts will be in the form of stricter eligibility requirements to exclude all but the—quote—truly needy—unquote.

Apparently the definition of the "truly needy" is the poverty line, a wildly inappropriate vehicle since it was originally intended to measure absolute destitution, not poverty. Millions of Americans, most of them working at hard jobs for low wages, fall just above that survival line we call the poverty line. They are the major victims of this budget. It is they who would lose their CETA jobs, be eliminated from Medicaid, and lose much else. For some, it would make more economic sense to quit their jobs and go on welfare.

An Administration that justifies its tax cut by stressing the need to provide incentives for the wealthy to work harder provides disincentives to the poor to work at all. An Administration that campaigned on a pro-family platform is suggesting new pressures on welfare families and the working poor that discourage familiy stability.[6]

4.5 POLICIES

We often encounter situations in both speculative and practical reasoning where the evidence seems insufficient to draw any conclusion. Yet, in practical reasoning it is often necessary to make a decision, regardless of whether or not we can be sure that it is a good decision. There are some obvious cases: the jury who has to reach a verdict; the executive who has to decide which person gets the promotion; the teacher who has to assign a grade to each student in the course. There are some less obvious cases. Think of the student trying to decide whether or not she should apply to graduate school and failing to make up her mind till the deadline for applications has passed. In such a case, not making a decision is, in effect, making a negative decision.

By *policies* we mean general guidelines for making decisions in the face of uncertainty. All of us acquire some sort of policies in the areas where we have to make decisions, though we may not recognize them as such. Consider, for example, the situation that the normal voter faces when he or she enters the voting booth. Usually the voter has already decided whom to vote for for the major offices—for president, governor, senator, mayor, or for congress. But the ballot also contains many minor offices and a list of candidates that the voter knows nothing about. Whom to vote for? Before reading any further, think what you would do or have done in such circumstances.

One method of resolving this problem is to choose, among the unknowns, whatever candidate belongs to my party. Another is to carry a list of recommendations given by a newspaper or organization I trust. Another method is to vote for whatever candidate is first on each list. This may not seem like a good policy. Yet studies of voting practices indicate that many people do follow such a policy. Reasonable or not, it is a policy. And it works. It supplies a basis for making decisions in the face of uncertainty.

Some forms of neurosis are characterized by a near paralysis when confronted with the problem of decision in the face of uncertainty. Apart from such extreme cases, we all develop policies to cover decisionmaking in the face of uncertainty. We do so, because it is a survival technique for life in a complex society. We have policies, but many of them have never been articulated or subjected to critical examination. This may lead to reliance on policies that are unreasonable or impractical. To consider a few famous examples. Scarlet O'Hara, of *Gone With The Wind,* had a standard policy for troublesome problems—procrastination: "I'll think about that tomorrow." The hero of John Updike's *Rabbit Run* had a standard policy for handling problems—he ran away. May West, sex star of an earlier generation, once explained her guiding policy: "When confronted with a choice of two evils, I always pick the one I haven't experienced before."

These are all policies. And they all work. Each supplies a method of making a decision in the face of uncertainty. Yet they are not good policies. They generally do not lead to reasonable decisions. What we wish to consider, accordingly, are methods of improving the policies we already have. Before getting down to particulars, two general points should be considered. The first is that there is no automatic or mechanical way of generating policies. In any particular field, it is chiefly a matter of learning from experience, or reflecting on what works and what fails and improving our practice.

The second general point is that policies for decisionmaking depend very much on goals and values. This is illustrated by the conversation Alice, lost in Wonderland, had with the Cheshire Cat.

"Would you tell me, please, which way I ought to go from here?
"That depends a good deal on where you want to get to," said the Cat.
"I don't much care where . . ." said Alice.
"Then it doesn't matter which way you go," said the Cat.
" . . . so long as I get somewhere," Alice added as an explanation.
"Oh, you're sure to do that," said the Cat, "if only you walk long enough."[7]

The same point is illustrated more strikingly by *The Spiritual Exercises* of St. Ignatius Loyola, which still supplies the principal source for the retreats given by Jesuits and others. St. Ignatius would have the retreatant spend the first week considering the ultimate purpose of life. After this sinks in, then the retreatant should be in a position to evaluate all his other decisions and policies to the degree that they lead to or away from that ultimate goal. Similarly for us, the first principle involved in getting policies straight is to get goals and values straight. The type of outline suggested earlier may be of help here.

Though it is not possible to give strict rules for developing and following policies, it is helpful to consider some models that may serve as guides. We will consider two. The first, legal reasoning, illustrates the way policies fit into a general structure of goals, values, and presumptions. The second, utility theory, is helpful when confronted with various alternatives, rather than a simple Yes-No situation.

Consider a standard legal situation, a case being presented to a jury. There is a clear-cut division of responsibility. There are usually two or more lawyers in a carefully structured adversary situation. They are opposing each other, not because they are enemies, but because that is their role. There is a judge who enforces the rules and determines the applicable law. Finally, there is the jury. The jury's official task is to determine the facts in accord with the general warrant, the law as interpreted by the judge.

The question of what precisely is to be decided is structured by presumptions. The term 'presumption' is used in law in two technical senses. First there are *imperative presumptions,* or presumptions that are not overcome by evidence that the actual facts are contrary to the presumption. Thus, there is an imperative presumption that someone is free from a debt after six years—the statute of limitations. This is not overcome by proof that the debt has not been paid.

Of more concern to us are *rebuttable presumptions.* These are the kind mentioned earlier. They do not represent a prejudgment of the facts. Rather they show where the burden of proof lies. Three standard rebuttable presumptions are: presumption in favor of an existing institution, for example, a marriage, a business, or parents' control over their children; presumption of innocence—a person is presumed innocent until proven guilty; and presumption against a paradox. If, for example, a defendant were to argue that the fire, which seems to have been caused by arson, was really caused by sunspots or by special magnetic rays beamed down from flying saucers, then that defendant is obliged to produce very strong evidence to support interpretations that are so contrary to common experience.

These presumptions can easily be interpreted as general policies that reflect the values of our society. Thus, because we set a high value on individual freedom, we have a general policy of not denying anyone freedom, which is the essence of a jail sentence, unless we are reasonably certain that that person is guilty. This is a policy in that it serves as a guide for the jury in making a decision. Unless they feel sure, *beyond a reasonable doubt,* that the defendant is guilty, then they should not find her guilty.

In addition to these general presumptions, which show where the burden of proof lies, the jury is given more detailed policies to guide their decisionmaking. If someone is being tried for a crime, then that person should be found innocent unless the evidence shows the defendant to be guilty beyond a reasonable doubt. If the case involves a tort (that is, if the case is a damage suit), then the evidence need not be so strong. Someone should be found guilty of damages only on the basis of clear and convincing arguments. Finally, if the case is simply an adjudication between two contenders, then the case should be decided on the basis of preponderance of evidence.

We will consider a couple of legal examples in the exercises. However, our basic concern here is with the model legal reasoning supplies, for our legal reasoning represents the collective practical wisdom that has evolved through hundreds of years of experience. The first obvious carry-over is the relation between presumption and burden of proof. Both individually and collectively, we have accepted ways of doing things. Suppose that you have guests for dinner. Consider the difference between a guest saying, "Please, pass the butter," and one saying, "PASS THE BUTTER!" The first is a simple request for butter; the second communicates hostility. Ordinarily, an experienced person would not make requests in this way unless he intended to communicate hostility. The presumption is that standard practices should be followed. If they are to be broken, then there should be a good reason for doing so. Here is where the burden of proof lies.

Consider a couple of practical examples. First, reflect on the situation of being confronted with a law that one does not wish to obey. It may be a simple traffic law, a sign forbidding a U-turn, or a more serious law, such as one requiring registration for the draft. Should the law be obeyed? The presumption is that it should. This is not an imperative assumption. The literature of civil disobedience argues persuasively that under certain conditions the moral thing to do is to disobey a law, seen as immoral, and face the consequences of such disobedience. However, the burden of proof clearly lies on the choice of breaking the law. This is the choice that must be defended by strong reasons. Unless they can be found, the presumption that the law should be obeyed remains the operative policy. Similarly, suppose that you are considering changing some aspect of your daily practice: your schedule, your diet, your exercise routine, your study habits, your dating practices. The presumption is in favor of the accepted way of doing things. A basic reason for this is economy. It takes too much mental energy to keep re-thinking routine decisions. So, the burden of proof lies on change. Keep to the accepted way unless there is a good reason for change.

The second basic point of comparison we can draw from the legal analogy comes from the coupling of values and strength of reasons. Because we place a high value on personal freedom we set a standard for the strength of proof required to overcome the presumption of innocence—guilty beyond a reasonable doubt. The presumption in favor of existing institutions is not as strong. Accordingly, the arguments requisite to overcome this presumption need not exclude all reasonable doubt, but they should be clear and convincing arguments. If there is no presumption for either side, then the case should be decided on the basis of preponderance of evidence.

Similarly, we have a presumption in favor of accepted practices and customs. How strong a reason should we have to overcome this presumption? A sort of rough general norm derives from the legal analogy. The more basic the custom, then the stronger the reasons should be to justify a break. How basic a custom or practice is can be determined in two ways: in terms of how basic a role it plays in our lives or our society; and in terms of the likely consequences of breaking with it. Thus, observance of laws is one of the supporting pillars of any society. A very strong reason is needed to overcome the presumption that laws should be obeyed. Suppose, at the other extreme, that we wish to change our regular TV viewing schedule. In this case the simple argument, "Why not?," might be sufficient. A consideration of anticipated consequences brings us to our second model.

The second model for policy formation comes from utility theory. Here we will merely skim over the technical ideas, by considering a simple example. Recently I received a card in the mail notifying me that I had assuredly won a prize—even though I had not entered any contest or drawing. However, the card did not reveal which of three prizes I had won. It was either a new Olds Cutlass, or $3000 in cash, or a small walkman radio. To collect the prize, both my wife and I, the card informed me, would have to travel to a new condominium site, about 125 miles from my home, listen to a talk by a salesman, and inspect sample condominiums. Then I could find out what prize I had won and pick it up—with no obligation to buy a condominium. Should my wife and I have made the trip to pick up the unknown prize?

Perhaps you, or your parents, have been confronted with similar decisions. What concerns us now is a reasonable method of making such decisions. The underlying principle here is summarized in the slogan: There's no such thing as a free lunch. I have to consider what I get and what I pay for it. Here the complication that serves as a come-on is that I don't know what I am going to get. There is always a chance that I might get a new car.

This is a simple problem in utility theory. One can think of the utility of a particular choice as the average value it would have for an indefinitely large number of people making the same choice. Since those offering the prizes are required by law to give some information on the chances of winning each prize, we have the information we need. The chance of winning the Olds Cutlass is .3%. Suppose that the Cutlass is worth $8000. Then the utility of the choice is the value of the prize times the chance of winning it. By using the rest of the information supplied we can construct a table.

PRIZE	VALUE (ESTIMATED)
Cutlass	$8000
$3000	$3000
Walkman	$40

CHANCE OF WINNING	UTILITY
.003	$24
.008	$24
.989	$39.56

The walkman radio is the least valuable prize. Yet it has the highest utility. This may seem surprising until we think in terms of large numbers.

If 1000 people were to receive prizes, then 3 would receive Cutlasses, worth a total of $24,000, 8 would receive checks for $3000, worth a total of $24,000, while 989 people would receive $40 Walkman radios, worth a total of $39,560. The average expected utility is determined by averaging the three utilities. It is $29.19. According to utility theory, this is a reasonable appraisal of the utility of a Sunday afternoon excursion to condo country. This, of course, is no guarantee of what we will get. But it is the most reasonable estimate based on the available evidence.

Now I know what I can expect—in the sense of average expectations—to get for my Sunday afternoon excursion. What price do I pay? If I do not make the trip, I would stay home and write this book. On the presumption that it will make some money I should value my time at $20/hour. Since my wife is also a philosopher and also writing a book, her time should also be valued at $20/hour. A four-hour trip costs $160. We should add in mileage costs of $.25/mile for a 250-mile round trip and $7 for a baby sitter. Altogether the trip cost $229.50.

Objectively, the trip costs about eight times what I can reasonably expect to get back. There may, however, be subjective factors that change this. Suppose that I had planned to inspect condos in that area, was feeling a bit stir-crazy, and wanted a walkman radio. Then the trip would make sense. As it happens, I have no intention of buying a condo and would never use a walkman radio even if I had a dozen of them. Yet, the overwhelming chance is that if I make the trip, I will receive the radio. In this case there was only one reasonable conclusion. I did not make the trip.

The case considered was a sort of accountant's dream. The expected profits and costs could be determined precisely and the two compared unambiguously. Few decisions are that clear cut. There can be much more uncertainty about the expected profits in drilling for oil, pushing a new dress style, or cutting a record. The costs may also be uncertain. In many cases precision in prediction is meaningless. Weather forecasters are sometimes advised: Always make your predictions precise; it will prove that you have a sense of humor. Nevertheless, even in difficult or obscure cases, policies for making decisions can be formulated. Once formulated they can be criticized, tested by practice, and improved.

The really complex cases go far beyond the scope of this book and involve disciplines like utility theory, game theory, and operations research. What we wish to do is to show how one can begin with actual practice and improve it partially through the guidance that these models suggest. Here is a general plan for working out policies when confronted with a decision in the face of uncertainty about different choices.

1. List the alternatives.
2. See if some can be eliminated because, for example, they are impossible dreams, or illegal, or immoral, or in conflict with ultimate goals.

3.   Put the remaining alternatives in a vertical column with three other columns for Value, Cost, and Net Utility. Sometimes this can be determined in dollars and cents as in the example given. More commonly, the measure is much more qualitative: degree of pleasure, pain, enrichment, boredom, personal growth, or community service. The only real requisite is that values and costs should be comparable. If one choice is clearly ahead of the others, then that is the reasonable choice.

4.   If none of the choices is clearly superior then ask: Must a choice be made now? If the answer is "No," then postpone a decision until the choice is clearer. If the answer is "Yes," then rely on a fall-back principle. A fall-back principle is any method of resolution. Examples are: pick the first candidate that clearly meets the requirements; close your eyes and point at a choice; pin the list to a wall and throw a dart at it. Arbitrary as this may seem, any way of resolving a conflict is generally superior to further procrastination.

Let's consider a simple very qualitative example, a girl shopping for a dress that she hopes to wear to a party coming up in three days. Let's suppose that she visits three boutiques, examines dresses in her size and picks out all the ones she likes. The next step is to eliminate some as being too expensive, or ones marked "dry clean only," or that are too flimsy, or too revealing. Let's suppose that this leaves nine candidates. When these are now ranked in terms of value and cost, money is no longer the key factor, because the ones that are too expensive have already been eliminated. All the remaining candidates are in the price range she can afford. Let's suppose that the basic value is appearance, how good she looks in it, while the basic cost concerns utility. The dresses that look the best wear the worst. To rank the candidates, accordingly, she has to get her priorities in order, the relative importances of appearance and durability.

Suppose that on this basis of relative utility she can eliminate two as being too flimsy, and three as being too plain, while the other four have about equal utility. The next question is: Must a choice be made? The answer is "Yes." The dress is needed for a party in a few days. So she should rely on a fall-back principle. She could ask the saleslady, "Which one do you think looks best," or pick the cheapest of the four, or the one she saw first. *Any* means of resolution is better than failing to make a choice.

4.6 DEVELOPING THE ARGUMENT

In the previous chapters we have been concerned with the way reasons support conclusions. In later chapters we will be treating inductive and deductive arguments more systematically. Now we are considering something slightly different, not how an *argument* fits together, but how an *individual* develops an argument. We can simplify this by considering two extremes. At one extreme is the situation of the individual who knows what she or he wants to say. It often happens that you have no doubt about what you want the conclusion of an argument to be. You want something to be accepted as true—"My client is innocent"—or something to be done—"Vote for Gildersleeve for governor." This extreme can be treated fairly briefly. We simply have to use the material we have already considered.

Usually the best way to do this is to begin with an outline or a diagram of the argument. Clarify the conclusion and the principal reasons supporting it, what we have been calling the first approximation. Then begin the second approximation. Which of the reasons need further support or justification? How do the reasons fit together? The answers to such questions should be developed in the form of an argument outline. Don't begin to write the argument yet.

The next step is to outline the argument for the opposing side, if there is one, through the same process of developing a first and second approximation. There are two reasons for this. The first is the one mentioned earlier: one does not really understand any disputed issue unless one is able to understand the arguments for both sides. The second is a more practical consideration. We are considering a situation in which you are confronting an audience that is not automatically on your side, that may have difficulties or objections, that may have been exposed to arguments for an opposing position. It is important to understand the nature and strength of the opposing arguments as clearly as possible. This is the first step in countering them effectively.

The opposite extreme occurs when you are in a situation where you must find reasons to support a given conclusion. This is a frequent occurrence in the life of a student. A professor announces that a term paper is required on a particular issue. Then it is your responsibility to search for information on this issue and often to develop arguments supporting a position. Something similar can happen in business or government. The chief executive has to make a decision by a certain date. So she asks her assistants to draw up position papers on different alternatives. A lawyer accepts a client and then must find reasons and develop arguments to support his client's case. An editorial writer is asked by his editor to prepare a column opposing a city ordinance, or supporting a rehabilitation project. A sales manager is given a new product and has to develop arguments that her salesmen can use to sell the product. An advertising concern takes on a new sponsor and must convince potential buyers that they need the sponsor's product.

There is no automatic procedure or set of rules for generating arguments. The reasons that count depend on the content and the topic. The best that can be done in terms of general guidelines is to give some search procedures that help to get started, or help when one doesn't even know where to begin.

Analyze the Conclusion

First determine the *type* of claim involved. Is it a statement of fact that you wish others to accept as true (My client is innocent); a matter of opinion (Jim Brown was the greatest runner in the history of pro football); a prediction (The interest rates will go back up two points and then stabilize); a matter of taste (Burgundy goes better with Chateaubriand than Pinot Noir wine); a conclusion about what should be done (Vote for me); or an ethical conclusion (even *de facto* segregation is immoral)? The nature of the conclusion determines the type of reasons needed.

Second, analyze the *status* of the conclusion. Is it obscure or puzzling (Schubert's music is more beautiful than Beethoven's but less sublime)? If so, you might have to begin by explaining the significance you are attaching to certain terms. Or you may use models and analogies as a step towards clarifying a technical claim. (Why does inflation depreciate the real value of money? Well, suppose you were running a hat-check stand and decided to give each customer a bigger ticket for each hat).

Find Arguments

When the significance and status of the conclusion is clarified, then one knows what type of arguments are needed. If the conclusion expresses a moral obligation (You *have* to marry me), then the reasons must couple moral principles to particular facts. If the conclusion is a call to action (Let's organize a boycott against any products this company sells), then some of the supporting reasons must couple motives or goals to contingent circumstances. If the conclusion is something to be believed (Russia is setting up concealed missile sites in Cuba), or accepted as true, then the argument must appeal to general reasons for believing the conclusion true. So the first thing to do is to determine the general type of argument or arguments needed to support the type of claim being made.

This initial analysis, however, just gives general guidelines. It indicates what type of arguments may be helpful. Something more is needed, particular arguments that support the particular conclusion you wish to draw. If such arguments are available, then the path is easy. However, suppose that you know the general type of argument needed but have difficulty finding or developing arguments of the type needed. What then? As a matter of last resort there are a few fall-back methods that may aid in finding or developing arguments.

Define and narrate.   This is not really argument; it is background information. Yet it is often necessary or at least helpful, before presenting arguments, to explain the significance you are attaching to crucial terms and to fill in pertinent background information. Suppose, for example, that you are speaking in behalf of an inexperienced mayoral candidate and can't think of anything special to say. You might start: "Let's consider what it means to be mayor of our city. What does the mayor do?" You list what the mayor is supposed to do and then argue that your candidate can do all these things well.

Compare.   One can often develop, or at least pad, an argument by finding examples that one can compare or contrast with the case in question. In the British and American legal traditions, one argues from cases that are similar to the present case—and so set precedents—or that are different from it in some crucial respects—and therefore cannot set precedents. Many arguments concerning moral issues proceed along similar lines. An analysis of such examples may lead to a clarification of the principles in terms of which they are decided. If these are discovered, then one has a good basis for developing an argument coupling the general principle to particular facts. Why should it be a crime to reveal secret computer passwords? Would you consider it a crime if a bank executive gave out passkeys to private safe-deposit boxes? Through a ploy like this the unfamiliar is related to, and sometimes replaced by, the more familiar.

Relate.   There are some established relations that play a general role in thinking: the relation between cause and effect, antecedent and consequent, principle and application. One effect, such as a high unemployment rate, may have many causes. One cause, assassinating a national leader, may produce many effects. Untangling and clarifying these relations can suggest reasons that can be developed into arguments. Similarly, principles implicit in applications may be transformed into reasons governing applications. These women are doing the same work that the men are. If they are doing the same work, then, one might argue, they should receive the same pay.

Circumstances.   Occasionally circumstances suggest an argument. If a course of action that sounds reasonable on general grounds (planning on being an airline pilot) seems impossible of fulfillment under particular circumstances (there is a long waiting list of much better qualified applicants for the few positions available), then this circumstance can serve as the core of a strong argument against the proposed action. More frequently, a consideration of circumstances does not supply an independent argument. It serves, rather to increase or decrease the strength of other arguments. Thus, arguments for raising or lowering the amount of money spent on national defense may be strengthened or weakened by particular circumstances, such as a crisis in a distant country, or a push for detente, a perceived threat to national security, or a recession.

Testimony.   Can experts or influential people be found supporting the claim in question? If I am arguing that some new trend represents a potential source of profit for an imaginative investor, then it would certainly help to find a statement in *The Wall Street Journal* supporting this analysis.

These are some approaches to explore or, in the terminology of an older rhetorical tradition, some common topics. Suppose that none of these approaches seems to lead anywhere and that no other approaches occur to me, what then? Ordinarily, the best thing for me to do under those circumstances is to abandon the topic or claim being considered and find something new.

EXERCISES

A. 1. What is the difference between a policy and a decision?
2. Is a policy the same thing as a habit or a custom?
3. Need policies always be explicit?
4. How do policies relate to goals?
5. Does the legal presumption of innocence mean that the judge or the jury must consider the defendent innocent?
6. What is the relation between presumption and burden of proof?
7. Is it ever possible to make a reasonable choice if one is not certain about the likely result of the choice?
8. How is the utility of an act defined?

B.   Most of the following questions are topics for discussions. They do not generally admit of any one right answer. The point of the exercises is to see how the doctrine developed in the chapter might serve as a guide in practical decisionmaking.

1. Reflect on your behavior, or the behavior of your friends, at a singles' dance. A boy for example, has a choice of asking a girl for a dance or not asking her. If he asks and is turned down, then he is embarrassed. If she accepts, he is rewarded. What are the policies that are implicit in your (or your friends') practices of selecting partners and requesting or declining invitations?
2. Suppose that you are the general manager of a pharmaceutical company and have to make a decision on whether the company should do research on "orphan drugs." These are drugs that may be helpful in the treatment of very rare diseases but, because of the rarity of the diseases, will never show a profit or even bring in enough money to cover the research program. What would be your guidelines in making a decision concerning company policy?
*3. You have $100,000, which you wish to invest, and have a choice of three possible investments.

 a)   Put the money in a bank that pays 8 percent interest and is insured against loss by the federal government.
 b)   Invest the money in stocks. The best information available is that the future of the stocks you're considering is crucially dependent on the success of a new product. The best estimate is that there is a 50 percent chance that the stocks will go down, in which case you will lose $20,000 and a 50 percent chance that they will go up, in which case you will gain $40,000.
 c)   Become a junior partner in a highly speculative oil-exploration scheme. The best estimate is that there is an 80 percent chance that the scheme will fail and you will lose everything. However, if it succeeds you stand to gain $1,000,000.

Situation I: You have just sold your home and retired from work. The $100,000 represents the only retirement money you and your wife have, apart from Social Security and a small pension.

Situation II: You are an investor for an insurance company. This is the type of routine decision you make about five times a day.

4. You are the director of the only hospital in a small, fairly isolated town during a blizzard that makes travel impossible. There are two kidney machines and five patients each likely to die of renal failure during the next few hours without the kidney machine. The data on the patients is:

PATIENT	SEX	MAR. STATUS	AGE	NO. OF CHILDREN	OCCUPATION
A	m	widower	72	5 (grown)	retired
B	f	single	38	0	librarian
C	m	married	45	3 (young)	thief
D	m	single	40	0	priest
E	f	divorced	32	2 (young)	prostitute

Which two patients would get the kidney machines? What are the policies guiding your decision? Would it seem reasonable to have the patients draw cards with the understanding that the ones with the two highest cards get the machines?

5. You are at the beginning of sophmore year and have still not settled on a major. However, you must make a choice before starting junior year. Some majors look interesting but are not likely to lead to jobs; others look more practical, but involve supressing your natural interests. Finally, there are fields that are both interesting and lucrative, but involve intense competition. List three or four majors and try to appraise them in terms of Value, Cost, and Net Utility. Since what counts here is the value or cost for you, it may be necessary to get your priorities in order.

6. You are a woman just finishing college with a degree in business administration. You have no immediate marriage plans, but wish to plot a course by evaluating the value, cost, and net utility (for you) of various possibilities.

a) Get married, have two or three children soon and postpone a career.
b) Get married, postpone having children, but subordinate a career to marriage.
c) Get married, postpone—perhaps indefinitely—having children, and focus on a career, even though this might jeopardize your marriage.
d) Concentrate on a career and substitute occasional affairs for a marriage.
e) Concentrate on a career and ignore romance.
f) Take things as they come and trust your female intuition when difficult decisions arise.

Try to make a table evaluating the utility for you of these different possibilities. This will require some appraisal of the values and goals behind your reasoning.

M. 1. Practical reasoning is

a) any reasoning done by practical people.
b) any reasoning not dependent on a scientific theory.
c) reasoning that is not related to the question of truth.
d) reasoning that is not related to any rules of inference.
e) reasoning that is ordered towards action.

Consider the following argument (or practical syllogism):
Major: I intend to maximize my take-home pay for the coming year.

Minor: Investing money in a real-estate deal that allows a tax write-off seems to be the best way of doing this.
Conclusion: So I should invest my surplus money in this deal.

*2. The major premise of this argument

    a)   will be proven false if I don't succeed.
    b)   is an expression of my present intention.
    c)   is one whose truth can only be appraised by psychologists.
    d)   is false, if I don't understand economics.
    e)   is too particular to serve as a premise in any argument.

3. The minor premise of this argument

    a)   is false, since money-market funds represent a better investment.
    b)   is true, because real estate always increases in value
    c)   expresses my present beliefs concerning the pertinent facts.
    d)   cannot be treated as true until the year is over and all the facts are known.
    e)   can only be judged on the basis of probability theory.

4. The conclusion of this argument

    a)   is essentially a prediction concerning the future.
    b)   necessarily expresses what I intend to do.
    c)   uses ``should'' to indicate that it expresses moral values.
    d)   is totally unrelated to whatever decisions I make.
    e)   is a practical conclusion that should serve as a reasonable guide in decisionmaking.

Consider the following moral argument:
(A) Whenever we can prevent great harm from happening without sacrificing something of comparable moral importance we should do it. (B) We are rich and resourceful enough to prevent famine. (C) Famine causes many people to die through starvation. (D) Famine weakens and worsens living conditions for a large number of people. (E) Even when we give enough to prevent famine our basic welfare does not suffer. (F) Therefore, we ought to give extensive famine relief aid.

5. The word indicating that a conclusion is being drawn is

    a)   Therefore
    b)   Even
    c)   Whenever
    d)   Causes
    e)   Ought

*6. The basic claim being argued is

    a)   A
    b)   B
    c)   F
    d)   C
    e)   D

7. The basic warrant, or moral principle, by which this claim is inferred is

    a)   A
    b)   F

   c) C
   d) D
   e   E

*8. The grounds for this claim are

   a) A, F, and B
   b) F, C, and E
   c) A, D, E, and F
   d) A, C, D, and F
   e) B, C, D, and E

Consider the following internal debate: (A) I am now majoring in Engligh Literature (henceforth *EL*). (B) However, I don't see much of a financial future in EL. (C) I would like to make a good living. (D) People working in Computer Mathematics (henceforth *CM*) generally make a good living. (E) they also do interesting work. (F) However, I personally like EL much better than CM. (G) I should switch my major from EL to CM. (H) However, if I do that I will have to spend an extra year in college to get a degree. (I) I will probably lose whatever chance I now have of becoming a decent poet. (J) I might have to move to Silicon Valley, where housing is crowded and expensive.

   Try to arrange this argument in terms of the decision being considered, and the reasons for and against it. Then answer the following questions.

9. The conclusion (or potential decision) being considered is

   a) A
   b) J
   c) C
   d) G
   e) F

10. The reasons supporting this decision are

   a) A, B, C, D, E
   b) F, H, I, J,
   c) A, B, G, J
   d) G, F, H, J
   e) A, B, G

*11. The reasons opposing this decision are

   a) A, B, C, D, E
   b) F, H, I, J,
   c) A, B, G, J
   d) G, F, H, J
   e) A, B, G

Consider the following situation:
(A) Bill Jones, an executive in Applied Engineering, Inc., consults Spike Smith, a representative of Pineapple Computers, about a new computer system. (B) After analyzing the problems Applied Engineering is facing, Spike declares that the Pineapple 527 system is adequate to the task of controlling the automated assembly line, keeping records of all spare parts, figuring the payroll, and making out the monthly bills. (C) This system is installed and soon proves inadequate. (D) A competing system, Wong G13 would have been adequate to these tasks. (E) Furthermore, Jones learns that

Smith knew the capacity of both systems, and (F) that Pineapple wanted to unload the few remaining 527 models before bringing out their new 613 system, which is competitive with the Wong G13. (G) Furthermore, Smith's sister-in-law played a key role in designing the Pineapple 527. (H) Jones takes Smith to court charging deceit and claiming that his company suffered a $750,000 loss because of the deceit. (I) He also claims that there are further pertinent considerations. (J) Both he and Smith are members of the same Rotary Club. (K) Smith knew the system was inadequate from the beginning. (L) One should not lie to a Rotary brother.

Smith counters that: (M) his analysis indicated this system to be adequate, though not optimal; (N) that he had not discussed this with his sister-in-law; (O) that he had no intention of deceiving; (P) and that he had just resigned from the Rotary Club.

The judge instructs the jury that a defendant (Df) is liable for damages on the grounds of deceit only if:

Df made a false statement; and

Df knew it to be false; and

the statement was made with the intention of inducing the victim (Vm) to act or refrain from acting; and

that Vm justifiably relied on Df's misrepresentation in his subsequent actions; and

that Vm suffered damages because of this reliance.

*12. The burden of proof in this case

    a)   is determined by the judge.
    b)   rests on Jones.
    c)   is determined by the jury.
    d)   rests on Smith.
    e)   is equally divided between Smith and Jones.

13. The presumption that Smith is not liable for damages

    a)   manifests prejudice on the judge's part.
    b)   represents the starting point for the proceedings.
    c)   represents a moral evaluation.
    d)   unfairly stacks the deck in Jones's favor.
    e)   represents the judge's opinion on the verdict the jury should reach.

14. Since Jones is suing for damages he needs to establish his case

    a)   by clear and convincing arguments.
    b)   beyond a reasonable doubt.
    c)   by a preponderance of the evidence.
    d)   well enough to win over the judge.
    e)   well enough to convince opposing lawyers.

15. In accord with the instructions given the jury the *pertinent* grounds supporting the damage claim are

    a)   A through L.
    b)   A, C, D, E, F, and G.
    c)   A, B, C, D, G, J, K, and L.
    d)   B, C, E, F, G, J, K, and L.
    e)   A, B, C, D, E, F, and K.

16. In accord with the judge's instructions, the *pertinent* grounds refuting this charge are

    a) M, N, O, and P.
    b) M and O.
    c) N, O, and P.
    d) M, O, and P.
    e) M, N, and P.

*17. Smith's refutation

    a) disputes the grounds of Jones's claim.
    b) attacks Jones's honesty.
    c) denies the court's jurisdiction over electronic computers.
    d) claims Jones is lying.
    e) is based on a reinterpretation of the law.

REFERENCES

[1] The distinction between speculative and practical reasoning stems from Aristotle. A good contemporary survey of the problem may be found in Robert Audi, "A Theory of Practical Reasoning," *American Philosophical Quarterly* 19(1982), 25–37. See also Gilbert Harman, "Practical Reasoning." *Review of Metaphysics,* 29(1976), 431–463.

[2] Stephen Toulmin, Richard Rieke, and Allan Janik, *An Introduction to Reasoning* (New York: Macmillan, 1979). I attribute the pattern to Toulmin because he used it in earlier writings.

[3] From *Common Cause,* Feb. 1982, pp. 30, 31. Reprinted by permission of Common Cause.

[4] From *The New York Times,* June 22, 1973.

[5] From *Vital Speeches,* 48 (April 1981), pp. 373–374.

[6] From *Vital Speeches,* 48 (May, 1981), p. 421.

Chapter 5

A CLASSY LANGUAGE

As we saw in earlier chapters, most reasoning depends on structures that are implicit in, or somehow accessible through, language. This is not true, or at least not so obviously true, for such mental activities as judging that someone is lying, getting the point of a joke, or discovering a new scientific law. There are no set rules to determine whether a poker player is bluffing by the way he squints or squirms. One might make rules for jokes, but that would certainly ruin the jokes. If there were rules for scientific discovery, then anyone could make discoveries just by following the rules. Francis Bacon tried to present such rules in the seventeenth century. Many others have since. It never worked.

Our concern now is with reasoning that depends on shared structures and shared rules. This can be taught and learned. We will begin with the simplest structure that can supply a basis for reasoning. It is simple in the special sense that we can focus on the structure, rather than on the content.

5.1 CLASSES

Around the turn of the present century the term 'class' (or 'set', the difference need not concern us) came into use in treating foundational issues in mathematics. By 'class' we mean any collection of things, in the broadest possible sense of the word 'thing'. Usually we class together things that seem to belong together. Flowers form a class. So do men. So too do one-armed paper hangers. We already have available in the language we use an indefinitely large number of class terms: 'horses', 'petunias', 'extinct reptiles', 'prime numbers between ten and thirty,' 'red objects', or 'beautiful people'. Since we wish to develop the notion of class in a way that is independent of content, we are willing to count as a class any items of any sort that are associated together for any reason, or even for no discernible reason, provided we treat the items as belonging to a class. Thus, I can simply postulate a class whose members are buxom blond movie stars, five-legged dogs and $\sqrt{-17}$. The movie stars are real. Five-legged dogs do not exist. The number is imaginary. Yet, these items form a class, simply because I wish to consider them a class.

People concerned with the foundation of mathematics have many difficulties with classes, especially with the way in which classes with an infinite number of members are defined. These problems, serious as they are, have little bearing on the type of practical reasoning we are concerned with. So we'll ignore them. However, we will borrow one idea that these logicians have introduced. It is called the *principle of extensionality*. According to this principle a class is determined only by its members, rather than by any special properties the members may or may not have. If two classes include exactly the same members, then they should be counted as one class. Consider, for example, the two class labels:

Class A: All odd numbers between 2 and 8.
Class B: All prime numbers between 2 and 8.

We will generally use curly brackets to indicate a class. Here Class A has the members {3,5,7} So does Class B. A and B are, accordingly, one and the same class.

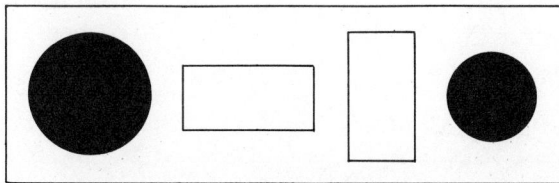

(5.1)

For a slightly different example we will let the large outside rectangle in Fig. 5.1 represent our *universe of discourse,* all the things we are talking about. Within this very limited universe we seem to have four classes: circles, rectangles, dark-colored objects, and light-colored objects. However, the class of circles and the class of dark objects have exactly the same members. By the principle of extensionality these two members constitute one class, regardless of whether it is labeled 'circles' or 'dark objects'. Similarly, 'rectangle' and 'light' do not have the same meaning. Yet, they denote the same class in this highly limited universe of discourse.

Class Relations

Suppose we have two classes, A and B. We can represent each by a circle, sometimes called an Euler diagram after the Swiss scientist, Leonard Euler (1707–1783). All the members of Class A are inside circle A. All the members of class B are inside circle B. What are the possible relations between class A and class B? The Euler diagrams show only three types of relations:

INCLUSION

All A's and B's, or
If anything is in A it is also in B.
Similarly, all B's are A's

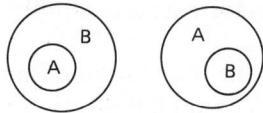

(5.2)

EXCLUSION

No A's are B's, or
There is nothing that is in both
A and B

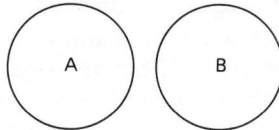

(5.3)

OVERLAP

Here the geometry is clear, the
interpretation is not. This could
be interpreted as showing: Some A's
are B's; or Some A's are not B's; or
Some B's are not A's.

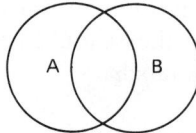

(5.4)

To eliminate this sort of ambiguity we will use an X to stand for 'some'. Then the overlap diagram can be given a more definite interpretation:

Some A's are B's, or
Something is both an A and a B

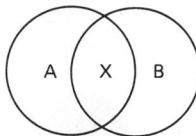

(5.5)

Some A's are not B's, or
Something is an A but not a B

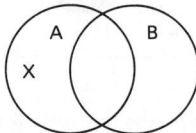

(5.6)

These new diagrams are called Venn diagrams (after John Venn, a nineteenth-century British logician). The relation depicted in Figure (5.5) is called *partial inclusion;* that in Figure (5.6) is called *partial exclusion.*

To see how these simple class relations can supply a basis for reasoning, let's begin with a simple system of class terms already available in our language. This is the classification of living beings into *natural kinds*. For the most part we will rely on familiar animal names, rather than scientific terms. Some simple examples of the class relations discussed are:

INCLUSION	All dogs are mammals.
EXCLUSION	No cats are dogs.
PARTIAL INCLUSION	Some mammals are lions.
PARTIAL EXCLUSION	Some mammals are not lions.

Some class relations do not seem to fit into this simple scheme. Suppose that we have an example like

All *panthera leos* are lions.

This seems to have the form of an inclusion relation. However, *panthera leo* is simply a scientific term used to designate lions. So we also have

All lions are *panthera leos.*

How can one class both include and be included in another? Here the two classes are identical. We can treat identity as a limiting case of class inclusion. In this limit the class of lions is included in the class of *leo pantheras,* while the class of *leo pantheras* is included in the class of lions. Though this is not the usual use of the word 'include', it does not lead to any difficulty.

The class relations of inclusion, exclusion, and overlap supply about the simplest structure that can serve as a vehicle for reasoning. It is rather amazing how much can be accomplished with this simple structure. Before going on, however, we have to consider a basic difficulty. The structures we are working with are simple and explicit. Two classes are related by inclusion, exclusion, or overlap. Ordinary language does not generally conform to the principle of extensionality. Thus, terms like 'tall' or 'rich' denote classes that have fuzzy borders, a topic which will be considered much later. The logical structures implicit in ordinary language are much more subtle and complex than the simple class relations of inclusion, exclusion, and overlap. What we do here, accordingly, is to simplify ordinary language. We cut and stretch, squeeze, and trim to make it fit our simple structural mold. The result is a simple, but precise basis for reasoning.

Classes and Propositions

In chapter 2 we defined a proposition as a sentence that is either true or false. Sentences come in many forms. The class relations we are considering come in only the four forms previously listed. Our first task, accordingly, is to show how a sentence can be transformed into one of these four forms. To do this both the subject and the predicate must be class terms and they must be connected by the verb *to be*. We will consider what this means first for the subject and then for the predicate.

Subjects of propositions.   If the subject is a class term, then the sentence can be about all members of the class, some members of the class, or no members of the class. A sentence about all members of the class is exemplified by the standard form: "All A's are B's."

Ordinary English, however, allows many variants of this standard form. The differences are not merely stylistic. As Zeno Vendler has shown,[1] terms like 'all', 'every', 'each', and 'any' have subtle, but significant, differences in meaning and implication. These subtle differences, and the inferences they sanction, are lost when we transform these sentences into relations between class terms. This is the price we pay to get the precision that pure logical forms allow. As long as we are aware of this, we may use our classy language when the subtle differences are not the issue.

There are a few standard simplifications that may be used to transform ordinary English sentences into a relation between two class terms.

Universals.   'Each', 'every', and 'any' are all replaced by 'all'.

Predicates.   We are considering sentences that have the form of attributing a predicate to a subject. If the predicate is an adjective, or anything except a class term, then it must be changed into a class term. This may be done by adding an all-purpose class term to the adjective. Thus

ORDINARY ENGLISH	CLASSY LANGUAGE
Roses are red.	All roses are red things.
Sharks are dangerous.	All sharks are dangerous things.
Every sophomore is eligible.	All sophomores are eligible persons.

Ordinarily, nothing hinges on the choice of a class term used to fill out the predicate. One may use 'thing', 'object', or even 'thingamajig' when explicit class terms are needed.

Verbs.   These must be replaced by the verb 'to be' plus an appropriate class term.

ORDINARY ENGLISH	CLASSY LANGUAGE
Fish swim.	All fish are swimmers.
Cats chase mice.	All cats are mice chasers.
Any doctor will tell you.	All doctors are persons who will tell you.

Some.   Just as we regimented universals till they all fit into the standard form: "All A's are B's," so we must also regiment particulars until they have the form of the class relations pictured in figures (5.5) or (5.6). This presents another case of achieving syntactical precision through semantical impoverishment. We sacrifice subtle inferences based on the connotation of 'some' to get the precision of class relations.

Suppose that a knowledgeable person informs you: "Some politicians take bribes." What would you infer about the others? I think that we would usually infer that most politicians do *not* take bribes. This is why we use an expression that picks out *some* politicians, rather than all, or most politicians. Suppose, however, that we interpret "Some A's are B's" as a pure class relation:

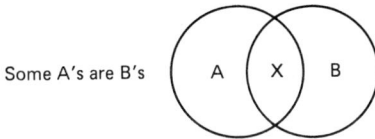

Some A's are B's (A X B)

(5.7)

The diagram captures the class relations. All that it tells us is that there is at least one thing that is in the A class and also in the B class. It does not give us any information about whether all A's are B's or whether some A's are not B's.

Consider the sentence,

Some dogs are mammals.

By ordinary standards, this would be considered a peculiar use of "some." *All* dogs are mammals; not just some. In our classy language, however, this sentence is perfectly appropriate. It does not imply "All dogs are mammals," which is true. Nor does it imply "Some dogs are not mammals," which is false. Here, what you see is what you get. What we see is an X in the intersection of the two class circles. What we get is the conclusion that at least one thing is both an A and a B. And this is *all* we get. Any further implications must be based on further information.

Individuals.   Suppose we have a sentence like

Joe Green is mean.

Since this concerns one person, rather than all persons, it might seem to be a particular, rather than a universal. Yet, that way of treating the sentence doesn't work very well. We're not really claiming that just some of Joe Green is mean, his scowl, his tongue, and his fingernails, while some of him is not, his hair, toes, and belly-button. What we are asserting is that he is a mean man.

To handle such cases we will treat individuals as classes with just one member. In this approach individuals are effectively treated as universals. The language may be stilted, but the logic is straightforward.

ORDINARY ENGLISH	CLASSY LANGUAGE
Joe Green is mean.	All individuals identical with Joe Green are mean persons.

EXERCISES

A. 1. What is a class?
   2. What does the principle of extensionality mean?
   3. What are the different relations that can obtain between classes?
   4. How should class identity be treated?
   5. What is the standard form of a categorical proposition in class language?
   6. What sort of implications might an ordinary language universal have that its classy language equivalent universal lacks?
   7. How is a predicate adjective expressed in classy language?
   8. How is an active verb expressed in classy language?
   9. How is a proposition about an individual treated in classy language?
   10. What is the basic difference between the ordinary use of *some* and its use in classy language?
   11. What is an exclusive proposition?

B. 1. Name two classes that each have exactly ten numbers
   2. If class A is {a,b,c}, while class B is {a,b,c,d,e}, how is the relation between them described?
   *3. If class A is {a,b,g}, while class B is known to include g, what is the relation between them?
   4. Write the classy equivalents of the following propositions:

      a) Dogs chase cats.
      *b) I never trust anyone over thirty.
      c) Each student who applied was accepted.
      d) Not all doctors are rich.
      e) The only real losers are those who stop trying.
      f) Percival Snodgrass wins the *Mr. Universe* contest.

   5. Write out three *questions* involving 'each', where 'every' is not an acceptable substitute; and then three questions involving 'every' where 'each' is not an adequate substitute.
   6. Write down a declarative sentence where either 'any' or 'every' could be used. Then test which terms are appropriate for the corresponding questions.

M.   The following codes should be used in answering questions 1 through 5:

      A. Inclusion
      B. Exclusion
      C. No relation.
      D. Partial inclusion
      E. Partial exclusion.

*1. Class F is {a,b,c}; class G is {a,b,c,d,e}. What is the relation of F to G?

2. Class F is {x,y,z}; class G is known to include z. What is the relation of G to F?

3. Class F is {a,b,c}; class G is {x,y,z}. What is the relation between them?

4. Class F is {x,y,z}; class G is known not to possess y. What is the relation of F to G?

5. Class F is {a,b,c,d}; class G is {c,d,e}. What is the relation of either class to the other?

*6. Given the proposition, "Not all physicians are paupers," the classy equivalent is:

    a)   No physicians are paupers.

    b)   Most physicians are not paupers.

    c)   Some physicians are paupers.

    d)   Physicians are not all paupers.

    e)   Some physicians are not paupers.

7. Which one of the following propositions is *not* expressed by the classy proposition: All people admitted are Marine officers.

    a)   All Marine officers are admitted.

    b)   Only Marine officers are admitted.

    c)   The only people admitted are Marine officers.

    d)   Marine officers are the only ones admitted.

    e)   None but Marine officers are admitted.

8. Which one of the following is *not* in classy language?

    a)   All but the extreme conservatives voted Aye.

    b)   Some legislators are not lawyers.

    c)   All nuclear weapons are dangerous devices.

    d)   Some movies are not money makers.

    e)   No actor is a play producer.

5.2 ARGUMENTS

The basic ideas on arguments that we have already considered carry over to formal arguments, or arguments formulated in a classy language. An argument is a set of propositions including a conclusion and premises that support the conclusion. Inference indicators supply a basis for determining which proposition is the conclusion and which propositions are the premises.

Now, however, our emphasis will be switched from functioning arguments to *argument forms*. The significance of this can be seen by considering a few examples. First consider

> All San Franciscans are Californians.
> All Californians are Americans.
> _____
>
> Therefore, all San Franciscans are Americans.   (5.8a)

Here and later, the horizontal line separates premises from conclusion. This is not only a valid argument; it is also an example of a valid argument form.

To bring out the form we will rewrite (5.8a) with S, C, and A as terms

All S are C.
All C are A.
_____

Therefore, all S are C.   (5.8b)

Since we are dealing with extensional concepts, we can use circles to delimit the entire extension of each class. All San Franciscans are, symbolically speaking, inside the S circle. Anyone outside this circle is not a San Franciscan. Thus, we would not count as a member of S anyone who left his heart in San Francisco, if his body is elsewhere.

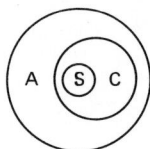

(5.9)

As the diagram clearly shows there is no way in which anything could be inside the S circle (and so be a San Franciscan) without at the same time being inside the A circle (and so being an American).

What these circles actually schematize is a simple argument form. It should fit any other argument based on the same inclusion relations. Thus, we can let

S— stand for Dalmatians.
C— stand for dogs.
A— stand for mammals.

With this interpretation the circles schematize the argument

All Dalmatians are dogs.
All dogs are mammals.
_____

Therefore, all Dalmatians are mammals.   (5.10)

This is not the same argument as (5.8). It has different premises and a different conclusion. Yet, arguments (5.8) and (5.10) both have the same logical form. It might seem that if argument (5.8) works and argument (5.10) works, then any other argument having the same logical form should work just as well. But does it? Let's try a bizarre example having the same form

S— stand for squares.
C— stand for circles.
A— stand for triangles.

This interpretation of our symbols yields the argument

All squares are circles.
All circles are triangles.

Therefore, all squares are triangles.   (5.11)

Here reliance on what we took to be a good logical form seems to have led to a ridiculous conclusion. The conclusion is absurd. But the fault is not with the form. Computer programmers have coined the anacronym, GIGO, to stand for "Garbage In, Garbage Out." Argument forms, like computers, produce garbage when fed garbage. The form of argument (5.11) is perfectly good. The conclusion is false because the premises are false. If the premises had been true, then the conclusion would have been true.

To make this point explicit we should note the contrast between two sets of terms:

True vs. false—These apply to propositions.
Valid vs. invalid—These apply to arguments or argument forms.

A *valid* argument form is one in which the truth of the premises supports the truth of the conclusion. The manner and strength with which this support is given depends on the type of argument involved. An invalid argument form is a form that leads from true premises to a conclusion that may be false.

Argument (5.11), like arguments (5.8) and (5.10), is based on a valid argument form. In argument (5.11), however, the premises are not true. We would call this argument *unsound.* Arguments (5.8) and (5.10) have both true premises and a valid argument form. This combination makes them sound arguments.

Not let's consider an argument that seems, at least at first glance, to be a simple variant of argument (5.8):

All Californians are Americans.
All San Franciscans are Americans.

Therefore, all San Franciscans are Californians.   (5.12)

In this argument the premises are true and the conclusion is true. Yet this is *not* a valid argument, for the form is not valid. This is shown by the fact that it is possible to have arguments with exactly this form in which the premises are true and the conclusion is false. For example,

All dogs are mammals.
All cats are mammals.

So all cats are dogs.   (5.13)

A valid deductive argument form is one in which the truth of the premises *guarantees* the truth of the conclusion. Here again, since we are dealing with classy concepts, we may use circles to symbolize classes. Let's begin by putting in the first premise of argument (5.12).

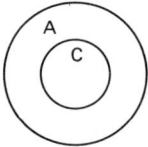

(5.14)

To represent the second proposition we have to put the S circle inside the A circle. But where? There are four possibilities, which can be represented as

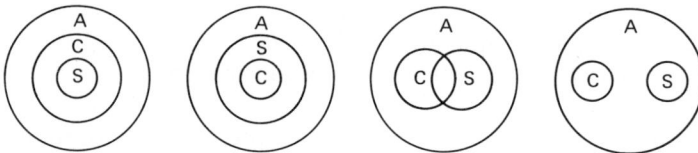

(5.15)

The first diagram, an inclusion relation, represents the relation between San Franciscans and Californians. The fourth diagram, an exclusion relation, represents the relation between cats and dogs. We do not know this, however, on the basis of the argument given, but on the basis of supplementary information.

In the earlier chapters, where we concentrated on arguments people actually used, we tried to find examples that were stimulating, interesting, or informative. In this and the next two chapters we will be concentrating on argument forms, rather than on arguments encountered in literature. For the most part, we will present examples that are artificial, banal, or trivial. Arguments that are stimulating, interesting, or informative tend to draw attention away from the form to the content. The more banal the content, the easier it is to focus on argument forms.

Earlier we made a distinction between speculative and practical arguments, depending on whether the argument involved a decision or determination of the truth of a conclusion. Now we are primarily concerned with speculative arguments. There is further distinction between *deductive* and *inductive* arguments. Older logic books often explained deduction as an argument that goes from the general to the less general, and induction as an inference from particular to general. This explanation does not fit the practice of modern logic. Following contemporary usage we will call a valid deductive argument one in which the truth of the premises *guarantees* the truth of the conclusion. In a valid deductive argument, such as (5.10), it is not possible to have true premises and a false conclusion.

There are many arguments in which the truth of the premises *supports* the truth of the conclusion, without guaranteeing the truth of the conclusion. Consider the argument

> Tom must be aggressive, because he is an offensive lineman for the Steelers. All the offensive linemen I've ever met are aggressive.

This is not a deductively valid argument. The premises could be true: Tom is an offensive lineman, and all the offensive linemen I've met are aggressive. Yet the conclusion could be false. Tom could be the exception to the rule and not be aggressive. The truth of the premises does not guarantee the truth of the conclusion. Yet, it does support the truth of the conclusion. If this is all the information I had to go on I would be justified in drawing the conclusion that Tom is probably aggressive.

It is usually possible to reconstruct a given argument in either a deductive or an inductive form. A simple example may bring out the advantages and limitations of each type of reconstruction. A student looks through a catalog and plans her schedule for the next semester. After considering one particular course she reasons: "This is an upper-division math course; so it will be difficult." We will give this inference two simple reconstructions:

Deductive

All upper-division math courses are difficult.
This is an upper-division math course.
_____

So, it is a difficult course.

Inductive

Most upper-division math courses are difficult.
This is an upper-division math course.
_____

So, it is probably a difficult course.

In the deductive reconstruction the truth of the premises guarantees the truth of the conclusion. This is not so in the inductive reconstruction, something indicated by the 'probably' in the conclusion. Inductive reasoning is the natural pattern of reasoning when we are concerned with the relation between evidence (here an upper-division course number) and the implications of the evidence (the difficulty of the course). In the deductive reconstruction the problem of interpreting evidence is changed into a problem of the truth of the first premise. Are *all* upper-division math courses difficult? This is something that would generally be settled by inductive reasoning from examples.

In our habitual reasoning, deduction and induction are mixed together. In reconstructing arguments, however, there is a difference. Deductive argument forms do not presuppose inductive reasoning. Inductive inferences do presuppose deductive forms. For this reason we will treat deduction before induction and concentrate on valid argument forms. When the emphasis is on content rather than form, inductive reasoning is generally more appropriate.

EXERCISES

A. 1. Explain the difference between 'true', 'valid', and 'sound' as these terms are used in logic.
2. What is the essential characteristic of a valid deductive argument?
3. Is a deductive reconstruction always better than an inductive reconstruction of an argument?
4. What is the difference between a valid argument and a valid argument form?
5. Is it ever possible to have a deductive argument with a valid form and a false conclusion?

B.   For each of the following arguments:

   A.   Underline the conclusion
   B.   Circle the inference indicators.
   C.   Indicate whether the argument is deductive or inductive.

1. She is a Republican senator from the sunbelt. So, she must be a conservative, because all Republican subelt senators are conservative.
2. All Congressmen are citizens, and all elected officials are citizens. Therefore all Congressmen are elected officials.
3. All seven-legged horses are thoroughbreds, because all Shetlands are thoroughbreds and all seven-legged horses are Shetlands.
4. Seventy three percent of the people sampled preferred Axlegrease mouthwash over Lonely Petunia mouthwash. This sample represents the population with a sampling error of plus or minus five percent. Therefore, I conclude that approximately three fourths of the people prefer Axlegrease mouthwash to Lonely Petunia mouthwash.

M. 1. An argument, as the term is used in logic, signifies

   a)   Any ordered collection of propositions.
   b)   A collection of propositions including reasons and a conclusion supported by these reasons.
   c)   A squabble.
   d)   A discussion involving emotion as well as reason.
   e)   A confrontation between two disputants.

2. Which one of the following terms is *not* used to introduce a premise in an argument?

   a)   Because
   b)   Since
   c)   In the first place
   d)   In the third place
   e)   Therefore

3. Which one of the following terms is *not* used to indicate the conclusion of an argument?

   a) On the grounds that
   b) Accordingly
   c) Therefore
   d) It follows that
   e) Hence.

4. Which of the following could be called an argument (or at least a mini-argument)?

   a) Genes used to be considered the unit of inheritance and mutation. Recent advances, however, have shown that the situation is more complex than anticipated.
   b) I know that goodness always triumphs, at least in soap operas.
   c) He must be the guilty one, because no one else could have done it.
   d) The square of the hypotenuse is equal to the sum of the squares of the other two sides.
   e) It's been more than three months since you left and I am beginning to get lonely.

5. An argument is considered valid if

   a) The premises support the conclusion.
   b) The conclusion is true.
   c) The premises are true.
   d) Both the premises and the conclusion are true.
   e) The conclusion is consistent with the premises.

6. To call a deductive argument valid means

   a) It is not possible for the premises to be true and the conclusion to be false.
   b) The conclusion must be true.
   c) It is formulated in the correct logical notation.
   d) The person advancing the argument has mastered the rules of logic.
   e) The truth of the premises is no guarantee that the conclusion is true.

5.3 THE SQUARE OF OPPOSITION

The basic question we are considering is: When may a conclusion be validly inferred from premises? We will call such inferences 'immediate' if drawn from just one premise, 'mediate' if drawn from more than one premise. In the remainder of this chapter we will treat immediate inference. Mediate inferences will be considered in the next two chapters.

Immediate inferences are of two general sorts. The first concerns the interrelation of the different types of inclusion, exclusion, and overlap relations we have schematized. The second involves manipulating the forms of sentences. In this section we will consider the first type of immediate inference.

When a categorical (or simple declarative sentence) type of proposition is expressed in a classy language it has the general form: X is Y. Here 'X' and 'Y' are both class terms. These may be classified in terms of: *quantity*—all, some, or none; and in terms of *quality*—affirmative or negative. This classification leads to the traditional designations:

A—Universal Affirmative	All L is N.
E—Universal Negative	No L is N.
I—Particular Affirmative	Some L is N.
O—Particular Negative	Some L is not N.

The letters used are taken from the vowels in the Latin terms, *Affirmo*—I affirm, and N*ego*—I deny. The letters 'L' and 'N' are general class terms. Here they indicate that we are working with propositional forms, rather than with propositions. This is done so that we may concentrate on establishing valid deductive forms. When we substitute meaningful terms for 'L' and 'N', then we have a proposition that may be either true or false. Accordingly, we will use propositions, with terms substituted for 'L' and 'N', as illustrations.

Contradictories.   Consider the *A* proposition

A   All tigers are carnivores.

Suppose that we learn that the local zoo has a tiger, Alphonse, who never eats meat. Alphonse survives on a diet of carrots, soy beans, and yogurt. This one exception would suffice to falsify our universal proposition asserting that all tigers are carnivores. It might not suffice to falsify the looser universal forms such as, "Tigers are carnivores," or "Any tiger is a carnivore." Now, however, we are taking 'all' in the strict categorical sense. Any exception makes it false.

We are also taking 'some' in the strict sense of meaning 'at least one'. When we use this strict sense, then the proposition, "Some politicians are honest," does not imply "Some politicians are not honest." Now consider the two propositions

A   All tigers are carnivores.
O   Some tigers are not carnivores.

If *A* is true, then *O* must be false. Suppose that *A* is false. This could only happen if *O* were true. More concisely, the two propositions are *contradictories.* The truth of one implies the falsity of the other and vice versa.

This can be shown graphically by means of Venn diagrams. These diagrams symbolize our classy language because they are based on the principle of extensionality: A class is determined only by its members. Propositions in this classy language connect L, standing for the subject class, with N, standing for the predicate class, by the verb *to be* plus terms indicating quantity and quality (all, no, some, not). We will symbolize such propositions by two intersection circles, one labeled L, the other labeled N.

We need one further notion, the complement of a class. This is the collection of things that are *not* members of the class. It will be symbolized by a prime over the class term. Thus if L stands for tigers, then L′ stands for non-tigers. If Q stands for artists, then Q′ stands for non-artists. When it is important to limit our universe of discourse, we will have a box around the circles to symbolize our universe of discourse. Thus our classy propositions have the general representation illustrated in Figure (5.16).

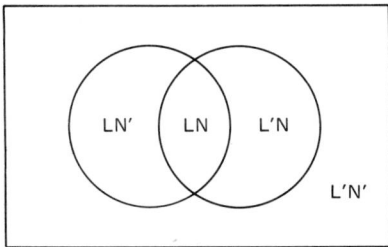

(5.16)

For our present purposes we will not need the box. Now we adopt two conventions.

1. Shading an area signifies that it is empty, or has no members.
2. An *X* stands for 'some'. The part of the class with an X in it has at least one member.

With these conventions the two propositions we have been considering have the representations:

A   All L is N

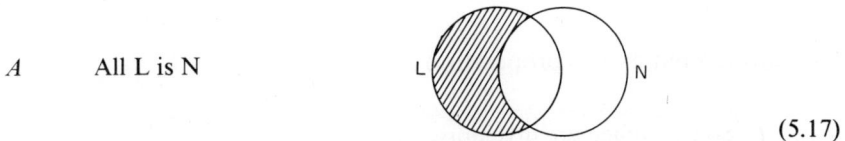

(5.17)

O   Some L is not N.

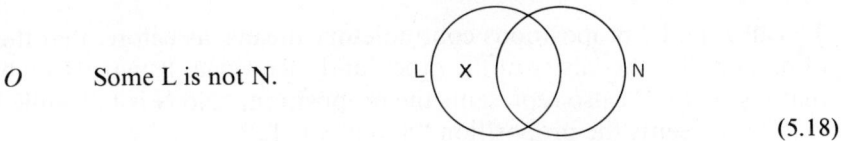

(5.18)

A   All N is L.

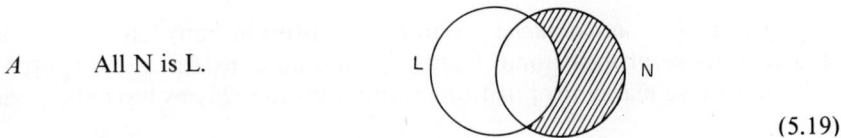

(5.19)

O   Some N is not L.

(5.20)

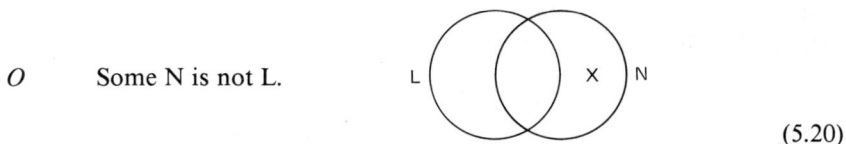

If we compare these with Figure (5.16), then we can see that this *A* proposition tells us that the class of things that are L's and non-N's (LN′) is empty. The *O* proposition tells us that it is not empty. The two propositions are contradictory. Neither proposition gives us any information about the things that are N's but non-L's (L′N). Hence, we are not authorized to infer anything about this class.

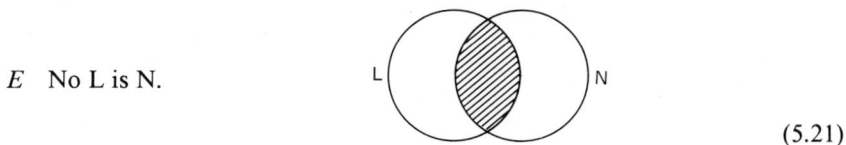

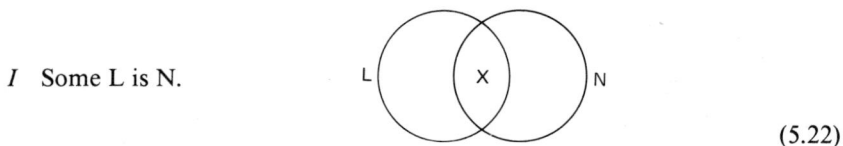

E   No L is N.

(5.21)

I   Some L is N.

(5.22)

There are also contradictory. If we compare the diagrams with Figure (5.16) we can see that the *E* proposition informs us that the class of all things that are both L and N (L N) is empty. The *I* proposition tells us that it has at least one member. Thus the proposition

E   No women are inventors

is contradicted by the proposition

I   Some women are inventors.

To call *E* and *I* propositions contradictory means, as before, that the truth of one implies the falsity of the other, and vice versa. It may easily be seen that Figure (5.21) also represents the proposition, "No N is L," while Figure (5.22) represents the proposition "Some N is L."

Existential assumptions. Before examining any further relations between these propositional forms, we should consider one disputed issue: whether these classy propositions imply that the classes have members. On this point ordinary usage is a somewhat ambiguous guide. Thus, consider the frequently posted sign:

All trespassers will be prosecuted.

This could be true in the sense that it is strictly enforced. Yet the 'all' does not imply that there are trespassers. The sign is posted in the hope of preventing anyone from being a trespasser. Similarly, "All centaurs have four legs" would be accepted as true while "All centaurs have seven legs" would be considered false, even though we do not believe in the real existence of centaurs.

Statements about empty classes are often used as a part of scientific reasoning. Thus physicists, interested in determining whether or not there are tachyons, particles that travel faster than the speed of light, formulate the properties that such particles would have in propositions like

All tachyons have imaginary mass.

The idea of imaginary mass is unfamiliar. Yet, the purpose of the assertion is clear. If particles with imaginary mass are never found, then there is a strong reason for believing that there are no tachyons. However, no one would even know what to look for unless it were possible to say something meaningful about the (probably empty) class of all tachyons. Similar considerations apply to X-mesons, super-viruses, extra-terrestial intelligences, and other postulated theoretical entities. Unless we can say something meaningful about these classes, which may be empty, we do not even know how to determine whether or not they have members.

'All' can allow empty classes in meaningful statements. In some usages, however, it does not do so. Sentences of the form, "All the . . . " are not used for empty classes. Consider "All the children are sick" or "All the missing sailors are accounted for." We would not use such sentences unless we were discussing real children or real sailors.

'Some' generally seems to presuppose existence. Compare "All trespassers will be prosecuted" with "Some trespassers are in jail." We would never use the latter unless we were discussing actual trespassers. Yet, 'some' does not invariably imply real existence. Suppose that, in developing a theory of tachyons, I conclude that if there are tachyons, then they must come in two different kinds, bosons and fermions. It would then seem appropriate to say

Some tachyons are fermions.

This use of 'some' does not presuppose the real existence of tachyons any more than the 'all' statement does.

To get a less technical example, we might compare Japanese monster movies with medieval European legends and their cinematic extensions. The Japanese movies extend the Oriental mythological tradition of friendly dragons. Godzilla is kind to children. In Western mythology (Walt Disney movies excepted) dragons are always hostile. In comparing the two I might claim

Some dragons are friendly.

In this case 'some' does not imply the real existence of dragons.

Our classy language is a regimented language. We can, accordingly, resolve the ambiguity by regimentation, by adopting a convention. The convention we adopt is one that extends and regularizes ordinary usage, and also fits the use of 'all' and 'some' in modern logic.

Universal propositions do not entail existential assumptions. That is, we do not presuppose that the classes involved have real members unless this is either explicitly stated, or is clear from the context. Thus, propositions about all people, all dogs, and other classes familiar from our experiences with members of the class, will be assumed to be about classes that have members. However, when we use argument *forms,* we will not automatically assume that the classes involved have members.

Particular propositions are treated as having existential assumptions. Thus, no proposition of the form "Some L is N" will be accepted as true unless there are L's.

With these conventions we may now return to further immediate inferences about *A*, *E*, *I*, and *O* propositions. We will do this first on the assumption that the classes being considered *do* have members.

Contraries.   Consider the propositions

A   All men are wealthy.

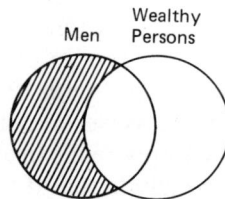

(5.23)

E   No men are wealthy.

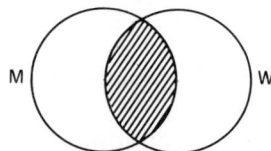

(5.24)

If one of these propositions is true, then the other must be false. Notice, however, that this relation only obtains on the assumption that there are men. Some part of the M circle must be members. Contraries are like contradictories in that the truth of one implies the falsity of the other. However, the falsity of one does not imply that the other is true. Both of the above propositions happen to be false of the world we live in, a world in which some men are wealthy but most are not. This is the distinguishing characteristic of contraries. It is not possible for both to be true at the same time. It is possible for both to be false at the same time.

Subcontraries.   Consider the propositions

I Some women are business executives.

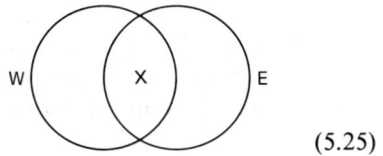

(5.25)

O Some women are not business executives.

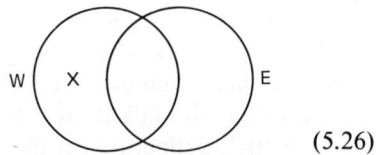

(5.26)

Both propositions are, as a matter of fact, true. Suppose, however, that these propositions were uttered during some less enlightened era, one in which the *I* proposition was false. It could be false only if no women were business executives. Since there are women, but the W E part of the circle, signifying the class of all women executives, is empty, there must be members in the W E' part of the circle. That is, regardless of which group of women we were discussing during this benighted era, we could truly say of them "Some women are not business executives." Thus, subcontraries represent a reversal of contraries. Two subcontraries can both be true at the same time, but both cannot be false. The falsity of one implies the truth of the other.

Subalternation.   Consider the propositions

A   All dolphins are intelligent.

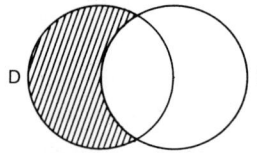

(5.27)

I   Some dolphins are intelligent.

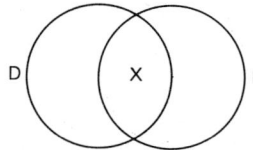

(5.28)

If the *A* proposition is true, then the *I* proposition must be true. No matter which group of dolphins we select we can say that they are intelligent. Suppose, however, that the *A* proposition is false. It could be false in two different ways. If some dolphins were intelligent and some were not, then it would be false. It would also be false if no dolphins were intelligent. The falsity of the *A* proposition, accordingly, does not supply a basis for inferring either the truth or falsity of the corresponding *I* proposition.

For similar reasons, the affirmation of the *I* proposition does not supply a basis for inferring the truth or falsity of the *A* proposition. It is not that easy to go from 'some' to 'all'. However, if the proposition "Some dolphins are intelligent" is false, then there is no way in which the proposition "All dolphins are intelligent" can be true. From the falsity of the *I* proposition we can infer the falsity of the *A* proposition.

A little reflection on the propositions

E   No women are bank presidents

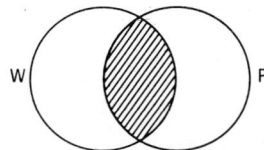

(5.29)

O   Some women are not bank presidents

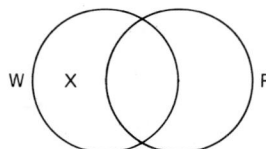

(5.30)

shows that the same type of relation obtains. If the universal is true, then the particular must be true. If the particular is false, then the universal must be false. Nothing follows, however, from denying the universal or affirming the particular.

Deviant forms.   Consider the following propositions:

1. Not all baseball players chew tobacco.
2. Popes are all males.
3. Only those who pass the physical exam are candidates for flight training.
4. None but the brave deserve the fair.

The general procedure here is to interpret such sentences as relations between the class expressed by the subject term and the class expressed by the predicate term. Then try to determine which of the four standard forms best fits the given sentences in the sense of being true of the same class relations. Thus sentence 1 has both 'not' and 'all'. Yet it cannot be interpreted as an *E* proposition. It must be the *O* form: "Some baseball players do not chew tobacco." In sentence 2 'all' goes with 'male'. Yet the sentence must be interpreted as claiming "All popes are males," rather than "All males are popes." Such a predicate 'all' is really a subject 'all', displaced for the sake of emphasis.

The next sentences are *exclusive* forms. The subject is expressed in a way that excludes those not having the specified qualification. Such an exclusive has the effect of converting the logical form. Thus sentence 3 cannot be intepreted as claiming that *all* who pass the physical exam are candidates for flight training. Those who pass the physical yet fail the academic exams are not candidates. However, all candidates are persons who have passed the physical exam. Similarly, in courtly lore, being brave is a necessary condition for deserving the fair. But it is not sufficient. One should also be honest, have lofty ideals, and perhaps slay a dragon or two. Sentence 4, accordingly, is best interpreted as claiming: "All deservers of the fair are brave."

In case of doubt, a simple technique may prove helpful. If you are not sure which of two interpretations is correct, then draw diagrams for each interpretation. In each case try to read off from the diagram *all* the possibilities the diagram allows. If any of them are incompatible with the given sentence, then the interpretation is incorrect. Thus, we might try to represent sentence 3 by the interpretation, "All who passed are candidates." This has the diagram (with P for pass and C for candidate)

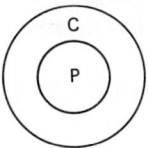

(5.31)

This tells us that everyone who passed the physical is a candidate. It also tells us that anyone who is not a candidate did not pass the physical. Neither claim is compatible with 3.

Now we diagram the interpretation, "Everyone who is a candidate passed the physical."

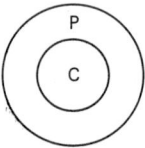

P

C

(5.32)

Since everything outside the P circle is also outside the C circle, only those who passed the physycal are candidates. This interpretation catches the significance of 'only' in sentence 3. This must be the interpretation we need.

The relations we have been considering are graphically summarized in a diagram traditionally referred to as The Square of Opposition.

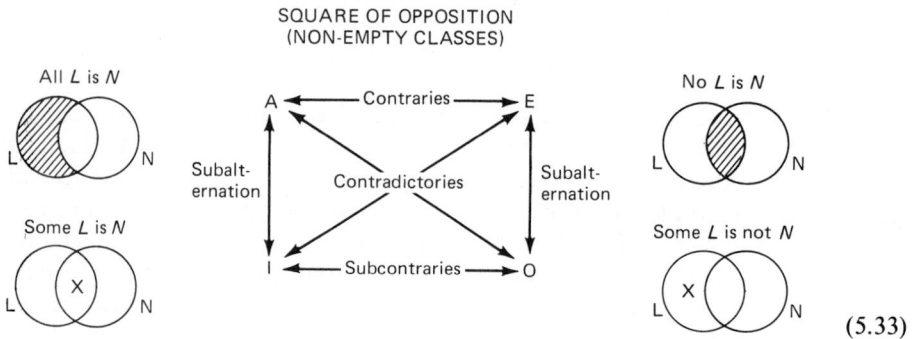

SQUARE OF OPPOSITION
(NON-EMPTY CLASSES)

All L is N

L N

Some L is N

L x N

A ← Contraries → E

Subalternation   Contradictories   Subalternation

I ← Subcontraries → O

No L is N

L N

Some L is not N

L x N

(5.33)

The maxim here is: Truth flows downwards; falsity seeps upwards. If either of the top propositions is true, then the truth values (that is, the truth or falsity) of all the other propositions are determined. Also, if the falsity of either of the bottom propositions is determined, then the truth values of all the other propositions are determined. Suppose that A is true. Then its contradictory, O, must be false. Look at the Venn diagrams (5.23) and (5.26). The A tells us that LN' has *no* members; the O proposition tells us that this region has at least *one* member. We are presupposing that there are L's. If LN' is empty, then LN must have members. Or, the E proposition, which shows LN as having no members, must be false. Similarly, the I proposition, which tells us that LN has at least one member, must be true. In summary, the truth of A implies that I is true, and that E and O are false.

Suppose A is false. Then its contradictory, O must be true. Or the region LN' must have members. This, however, does not tell us whether LN has members (which the *I* proposition affirms) or has no members (which the *E* proposition affirms). Thus, from the falsity of *A* all that we can validly deduce is the truth of *O*. The truth of *E* and *I* remains undetermined.

Suppose that *O* is false. Then *A* must be true. As we have already seen, the truth of *A* implies the truth of *I* and the falsity of *E*. This is what was meant by the aphorism, "Falsity seeps upwards." If either bottom proposition is false, then the truth value of all the other propositions is determined.

Suppose that *O* is true. Then *A* must be false. As we have already seen, this leaves the truth values of the *E* and *I* propositions undetermined. It is easy to show, either on the basis of the relations that we have already established or by examining the Venn diagrams, that these further relations also obtain:

> *E* true implies *O* true, *A* false, and *I* false.
> *E* false implies *I* true and leaves *A* and *O* undetermined.
> *I* true implies *E* false and leaves *A* and *O* undetermined.
> *I* false implies *A* false, *E* true, and *O* true.

Empty classes.   Suppose that we are not sure whether or not there are L's. Then we may be talking about empty classes. In this case it is not obvious what relations obtain. However, if we accept the convention discussed earlier, that universal propositions do not imply existential commitments but particular propositions do, then the situation is completely determined. Here again, it helps to study the Venn diagrams used in the square of opposition.

Suppose that an *A* proposition is true of a class that may be empty

> *A*   All invading starships are hostile.

In the speculative realm that is now our universe of discourse LN' is empty. It represents the class of invading *non*-hostile starships. The corresponding *O* proposition, which says that this class has members, must be false. But we cannot infer that LN, the class of hostile starships, has members, as the *I* proposition asserts. Nor can we infer that it does not have members, as the *E* proposition asserts. If we do not know whether or not there are alien ships capable of traveling interstellar distances, then our inferences should not hinge on implying or denying the real existence of such ships.

When we are discussing classes that may or may not have members, then only one type of inference is justified. From the truth of one proposition we may validly infer the falsity of its contradictory, and vice versa. This relation of contradiction is the only one we can count on.

EXERCISES

A. 1. What is a categorical proposition?
   2. What are the four basic forms of categorical propositions?
   3. What is the difference between contradictories and contraries?
   4. Can a universal proposition be true of a class that has no members?
   5. Can one validly argue from the truth of an *I* proposition to the truth of the corresponding *A* proposition?
   6. Can one argue from the falsity of an *E* proposition to the falsity of the corresponding *O* proposition?
   7. Which of the square of opposition relations hold good when we are discussing classes that may be empty?

B.   For the next four questions:

   A.   Write out the three propositions related to the given proposition by the square of proposition;
   B.   Assuming that the given proposition is true, indicate which of the related propositions are true, false, and undetermined;
   C.   Repeat (b) on the assumption that the given proposition is false:
   D.   Draw the Venn diagram proper to the given proposition.

   1. No statesmen worthy of that proud name are collaborationists.
   2. All men who take up the sword are men who perish by the sword.
   3. Some sophomores are better students than many juniors.
 *4. Some tumors are not malignant.

M.   The multiple-choice questions in this section present a proposition labeled with a capital letter and five related propositions. The questions concern the relation of propositions labeled A . . . E to the given proposition.

   I. "All things that are ineffable are sublime truths."   S
       Code:

       A.   No thing that is ineffable is a sublime truth.
       B.   Some things that are ineffable are not sublime truths.
       C.   All sublime truths are ineffable.
       D.   Some things that are ineffable are sublime truths.
       E.   There are no sublime truths.

   1. The contradictory of S is
   2. The contrary of S is
   3. The subaltern of S is
   4. If S is false, then a proposition that is true is
   5. If S is true then a proposition that is also true is

   II. "No green salads without dressing are fattening foods."   G
       Code:

       A.   Some green salads without dressing are fattening foods.
       B.   All green salads without dressing are fattening foods.
       C.   Nothing lacking dressing is fattening.
       D.   Some green salads without dressing are not fattening foods.
       E.   None of the above.

6. If G is true, then another proposition known to be true is
7. The contradictory of G is
8. The subcontrary of G is
9. If G is false, then a proposition known to be true is
10. The contrary of G is

III. ``Some students are juniors.''   J
Code:

    A.   Some students are not juniors.
    B.   No students are juniors.
    C.   All students are juniors.
    D.   Some students are seniors.
    E.   None of the above.

11. The contrary of J is
12. If J is true, then a proposition that is false is
13. The contradictory of J is
14. If J is false, then a proposition that is also false is
15. The subcontrary of J is

IV. ``Some flowers are not roses.''   F
Code:

    A.   No flowers are roses.
    B.   Some flowers are roses.
    C.   All petunias are flowers.
    D.   All flowers are roses.
    E.   None of the above.

16. The subcontrary of F is
17. If F is true, then a proposition that is false is
18. The contrary of F is
19. If F is false, then a proposition that is also false is
20. The contradictory of F is

V. Suppose that the F circle stands for financiers, the R circle stands for Republicans, and that we have the code:

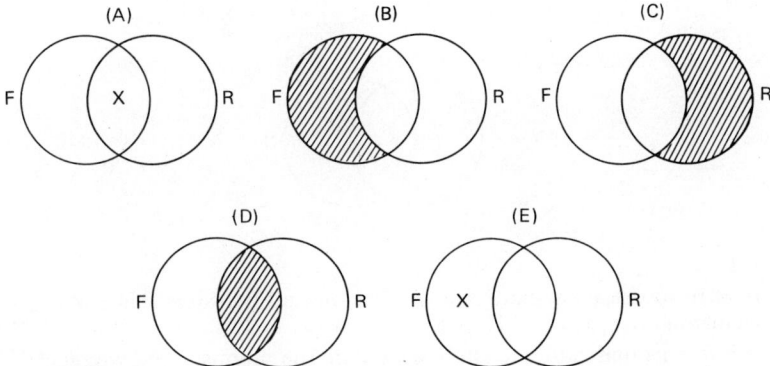

21. "All Republicans are financiers" is represented by
22. "Some financiers are not Republicans" is represented by
23. "Some Republicans are financiers" is represented by
24. "No financiers are Republicans" is represented by
25. "All financiers are Republicans" is represented by

SUMMARY

CLASSES:

are any collection of things, in the broadest possible sense of 'thing'.
are determined exclusively by their members (principle of extensionality).
have as their complements all nonmembers of the class.

PROPOSITIONS, CATEGORICAL:

are sentences that are either true or false.
can be expressed in classy language by "S is P" plus terms for quantity and quality, where 'S' and 'P' are both class terms.
are divided into four basic types.

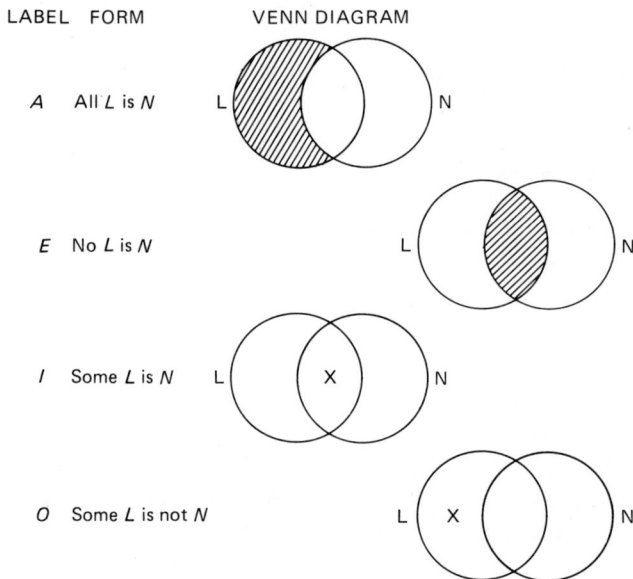

LABEL	FORM	VENN DIAGRAM
A	All L is N	
E	No L is N	
I	Some L is N	
O	Some L is not N	

ARGUMENTS:

are collections of propositions including a conclusion and premises that support the conclusion.
generally have inference indicators to show which are the premises and which is the conclusion.

Are deductively valid only if the truth of the premises guarantees the truth of the conclusion.

involve inferences.

INFERENCES:

Mediate: depend on more than one premise.

Immediate:

Square of Opposition:	A	E
(for non-empty classes)	I	O

Contradictories (A—O; E—I): the truth of one implies the falsity of the other and vice versa.

Contraries (A—E): the truth of one imples the falsity of the other.

Subcontraries (I—O): the falsity of one implies the truth of the other.

Subalternation (A—I; E—O): the truth of the universal implies the truth of the particular; the falsity of the particular implies the falsity of the universal. These relations hold only for nonempty classes.

REFERENCES

[1]Zeno Vendler, *Linguistics in Philosophy* (Ithaca, N.Y.: Cornell University Press, 1967), pp. 70–96.

Chapter 6

CATEGORICAL SYLLOGISMS

The immediate inferences considered in the last chapter do not really yield any new information. If we know that some students are freshman, we shouldn't be surprised to learn that it is false that no students are freshmen. Immediate inference is a useful, but very limited, tool for reasoning.

The first step beyond immediate inference is the syllogism. A syllogism is a set of three propositions, two being premises and the third the conclusion. A syllogism also has just three terms, each occurring in two different propositions. The term that occurs in both premises, but not in the conclusion, is called the *middle term* and will generally be denoted by an M, while L and N will be used for the *subject and predicate of the conclusion,* respectively. Aristotle, the ancient Greek philosopher whom many still consider the greatest philosopher of all time, made the first systematic study of syllogisms. He used something like the classy language used in the last chapter, in that he spoke of one term being included in another term. However, he was not altogether clear on such linguistic issues. Later philosophers distinguished between terms, their meanings, and their extensions (or the class of things they applied to). For present purposes it is best to stick with the classy language that considers only extensions.

A simple syllogism was smuggled into the last chapter. Now we will alter it slightly to put it in a more standard form:

All Californians are Americans.
All San Franciscans are Californians.

All San Franciscans are Americans.   (6.1)

The horizontal line stands for 'Therefore' and signals a conclusion. Inclusion circles capture the class relation involved.

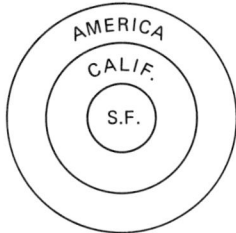

(6.2)

This example makes syllogisms seem so simple and obvious that one wonders why a theory is necessary. The role such a theory plays is a bit clearer when we switch from propositions to propositional forms. If we replace "Californians" by "M," "Americans" by "N" and "San Franciscans" by "L," Then (6.1) has the form

Major	M—N	A
Minor	L—M	A
Conclusion	L—N	A.

(6.3)

This syllogism is written in standard form: the major premise comes first; then the minor. Even if it does not come first, the major premise is always the one that links the middle term to the predicate of the conclusion. In (6.3) the middle term is subject of the major premise and predicate of the minor premise. Other arrangements are possible. There are, in fact, four possible arrangements, which are traditionally called *the four figures*.

Syllogistic Figures

1	2	3	4
M—N	N—M	M—N	N—M
L—M	L—M	M—L	M—L
L—N	L—N	L—N	L—N

(6.4)

Perhaps the easiest way to remember this arrangement, in which the middle term is crucial, is to remember that, when the four figures are together, then the M terms have the shape of a wing collar, the type of old-fashioned collar that goes with a bow tie and a tuxedo.

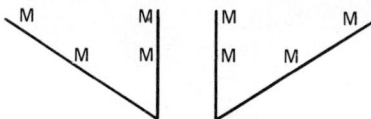

(6.5)

If we look at the first premise of the first figure in Table (6.4), we can see that M—N is really a blank form. We could plug into this form an A

proposition, as in the original example, or an *E*, or an *I*, or an *O* proposition. Suppose we pick the *A* form, then the minor could be an *A*, *E*, *I*, or *O* form. This would be the same for any of the four choices for the major. This gives 4 × 4, or 16, possible combinations of premises. The conclusion could also be any one of the four proposition types. This gives 4 × 16, or 64 possible combinations for the first figure. Each of the other figures has 64 possible forms, yielding a grand total of 256 possible syllogistic forms.

Which of these forms are valid? It is here that a theory is needed. What we wish to do is to determine in a systematic, though not too rigorous, way which of these 256 possible forms are valid. Here, as earlier, a valid deductive form is one in which the truth of the premises guarantees the truth of the conclusion. We will work this out by diagrams for figure 1, and then treat the other figures more briefly.

6.1 FIGURE ONE

As we saw in the last chapter, propositions in a classy language express relations of inclusion, exclusion, partial inclusion, and partial exclusion. We will start with a simple case where the major expresses an inclusion relation and represent this relation by means of a Euler diagram, or membership circle.

All mammals are nursing animals.

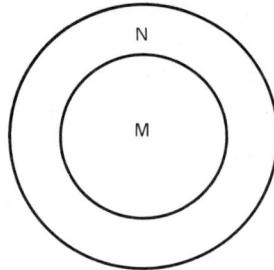

(6.6)

The size of these circles has no significance provided that, for an inclusion relation, the smaller one is totally inside the larger one. However, we have drawn the circles so that a dime will fit inside the M circle. We can let this dime stand for L, the class of all lions. By sliding the dime around Figure (6.6) we can see what sorts of relations M, the middle term, mediates between L and N. If the dime is totally inside M, then it must be totally inside N. This yields the form we considered earlier

All M is N.   *A*
All L is M.   *A*
_____
All L is N.   *A*.   (6.7)

Now, slide the dime so that it is partially inside M and partially outside. In this case we can say nothing about *all* L. All that we know is that they are inside the L circle, but we don't know where. They could all be inside N as in (6.8) (temporarily ignoring the X), or they could be partially inside N and partially outside N, as indicated by (6.9).

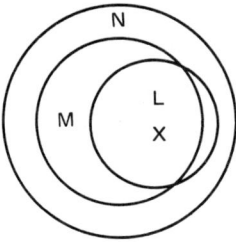

(6.8)

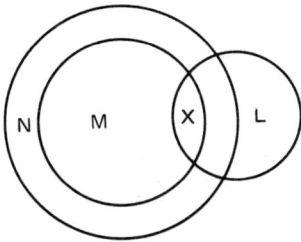

(6.9)

If, however, we have a *partial* inclusion relation, "Some L is M," this would be indicated by the X in (6.8) or (6.9). Since this X is inside the M circle, it would have to be inside the N circle. We have, in other words, established a second valid form for figure 1:

All M is N.   *A*
Some L is M.   *I*
_____
Some L is N.   *I*.   (6.10)

Now try sliding the dime around Figure (6.6) to see if there is any other way in which M can mediate a relation between L and N. If anything looks promising, trace a circle by running a pencil around the dime and/or putting an X somewhere different from the X in (6.8) or (6.9). I feel secure in the claim that no other valid forms will be found to fit (6.6), with one partial exception, which will be discussed later.

Instead of (6.6) we could have started with an exclusion relation:

No males are nursing animals   *E.*

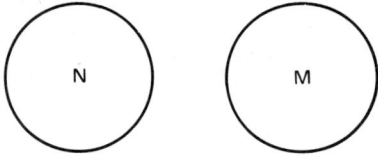

(6.11)

Now use a dime to stand for lectors, people who read the Scriptures in church ceremonies. This used to be exclusively male domain. First put the dime totally inside M. This shows that all L is M and no L is N. Next have the dime partially inside M, so that, for example, the LIB in the word LIBERTY on the face of the dime is inside the M circle. Then this part of the dime must be outside the N circle. We have just discovered two more valid figure 1 forms:

No M is N.   *E*
All L is M.   *A*

No L is N.   *E*

(6.12)

and

No M is N.   *E*
Some L is M.   *I*

Some L is not N. *O*

(6.13)

These valid forms have *mood* names, which are simply the letters standing for the type of proposition. We have discovered four valid moods for figure 1: *AAA, EAE, AII,* and *EIO.* What we have not shown is that these are the only generally valid forms for figure 1. It is difficult to do this through Euler circles. In his original treatment Euler established the valid forms, but did not prove that these are the only valid forms.[1] For this reason we will now turn to a method that is more systematic.

Venn Diagrams

The basic idea here is rather simple. We have three intersecting circles (or rectangles) representing the three terms in the syllogism, L, M, and N. If we can feed in the premises and then read out the conclusion, we have a valid form. If we cannot read out any definite conclusion, then we do not have a valid form. To develop this more systematically we show two forms of Venn diagrams for syllogisms. The first (6.14a) is the standard representation of syllogisms in a Venn diagram. Figure (6.14b) is the type of diagram that a computer printout can give. We include this type of diagram here and later for the sake of those who will encounter such printouts.

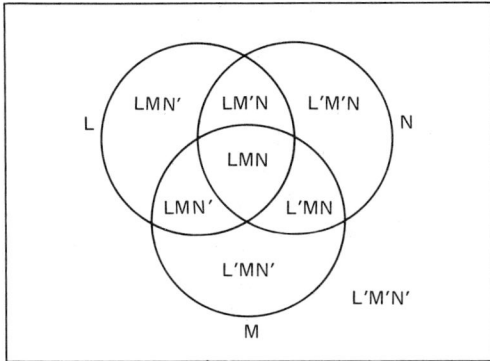

(6.14a)

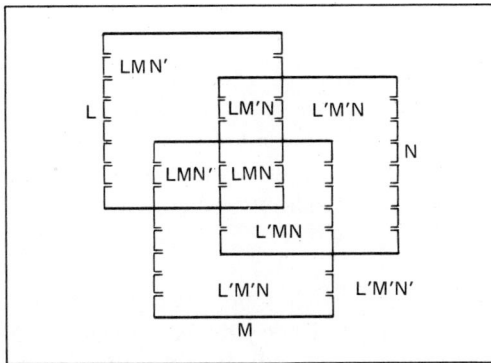

(6.14b)

These two diagrams are, in mathematical terms, topologically equivalent. Both express exactly the same class relations of three classes L, M, and N and their complements, L', M', and N'. Thus LM'N' is the class of all things that are L but are not M or N. To indicate that a region is empty we shade it in with diagonal lines. Thus the proposition, "All M is N" has the obverse, "No M is N' (MN' = O)." For *A* propositions the Venn diagram really represents this obverse. This fits the convention adopted earlier that universal propositions do not have existential commitments. In feeding this information into (6.15) we simply ignore the L circle.

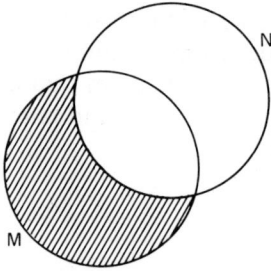

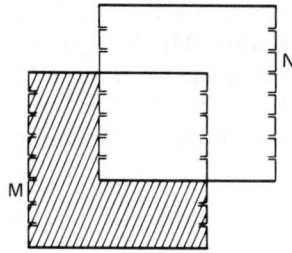

(6.15)

Similarly, to express "All L is M (LM′ = O)" we fill in all of the L circle outside M. When we put this together with (6.15) we have the net result

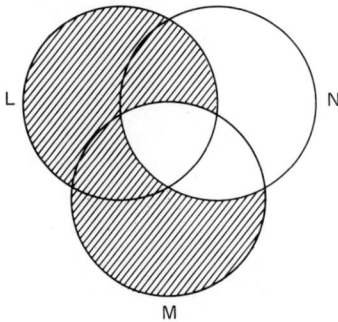

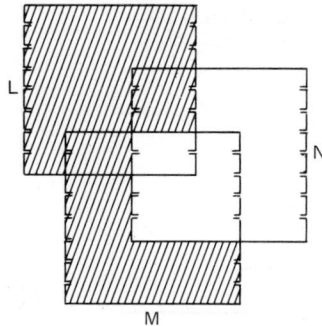

(6.16)

Now that we have fed in the two premises we try to read out the conclusion, the relation between L and N. Figure (6.16) clearly shows that all L outside N is empty (LN′ = O). Thus the diagram clearly shows the conclusion

All L is N.

As a next step we will consider the mood already tested *(EAE)* and a plausible variant *(AEE)*. For purposes of clarity we will show the two premises separately and then the conclusion.

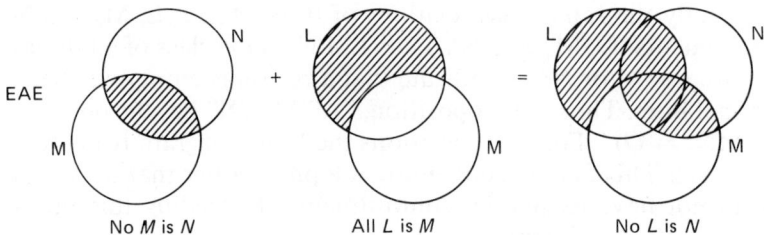

EAE

No *M* is *N*   All *L* is *M*   No *L* is *N*   (6.17)

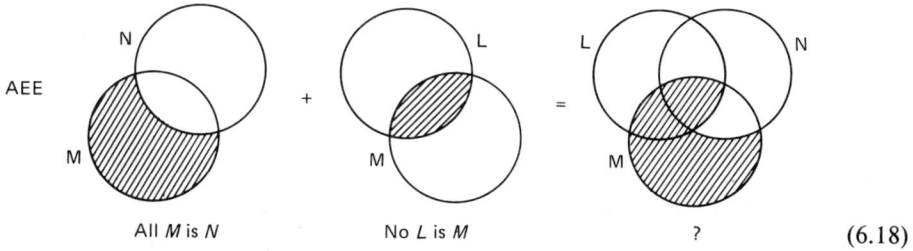

AEE

All *M* is *N*   No *L* is *M*   ?   (6.18)

Figure (6.17) supports the same conclusion we drew on the basis of the Euler diagrams and shows that *EAE* is a valid form. Figure (6.18), on the other hand, does not establish any definite relation between L and N. We cannot say that all L is N, because the region LM'N' is not shaded in. It could contain things that are L but not N. Nor can we say that no L is N, for the top part of the intersection of L and N, the region LM'N is not shaded in. The diagram contains no X to indicate a particular conclusion. There is, in short, no way in which (6.18) can be interpreted as expressing an *A*, *E*, *I*, or *O* proposition concerning the relation of L and N. The form *AEE* is, accordingly, *not* a valid form.

To claim that the form is not valid does not mean that it can never yield a true conclusion from true premises. It merely means that it is possible to have true premises and a false conclusion. To see this let's consider two simple animal examples that both have figure 1, *AEE* forms and true premises.

All seagulls are fisheaters.   *A*
No canaries are seagulls.   *E*
_____
No canaries are fisheaters. *E*   (6.19)

All lions are dangerous.   *A*
No tigers are lions.   *E*
_____   (6.20)
No tigers are dangerous.   *E*

All that is required to prove a deductive form invalid is one counterexample. In (6.20) the premises are true, while the conclusion is false. This shows that for this form the truth of the premises does not guarantee the truth of the conclusion. Example (6.19) has exactly the same form, and all the propositions in it are true. Yet we cannot properly call the final proposition a *conclusion* drawn from the premises. It is really just a third proposition that happens to be true.

The mood *AII* brings out a different aspect of Venn diagrams. It does not matter what order the premises are fed into a Venn diagram. Suppose we have premises

All mouse catchers are nocturnal animals.   *A*
Some lynxes are mouse catchers.   *I*

If, in a standard Venn diagram, we wish to put in the second premise first, we would put an X in the intersection of L and M. But should it be inside or outside the N circle? The proposition itself does not answer that question. In the face of such uncertainty we choose a political solution. Like many politicians confronted with difficult choices, we will straddle the fence. A symbol, X   X, should be interpreted as an either–or X. In (6.21) it indicates that there is something that is both an L and an M and that may or may not be an N. If one of these either–or X's happens to be a region that is empty, then it is wiped out by the shading.

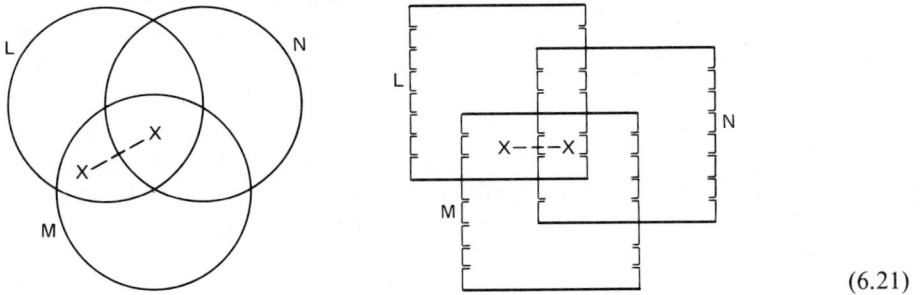

(6.21)

If we assemble this Venn diagram as we did the earlier ones we have

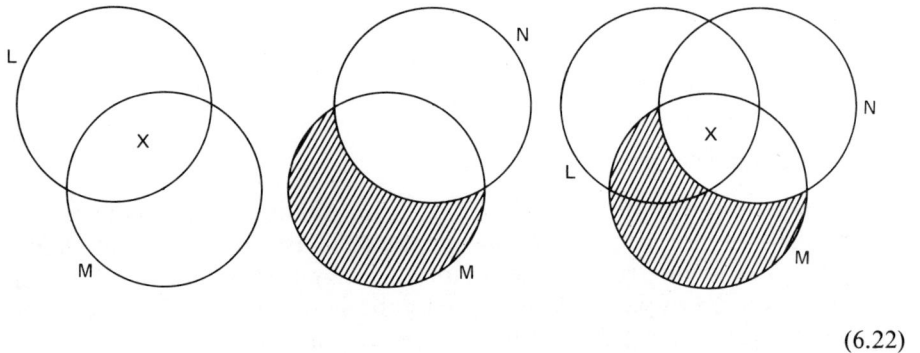

(6.22)

This supports the conclusion, "Some L is N."

There is one further type of example that requires special consideration. Suppose that a theoretical physicist is speculating about the properties of particles called *leptoquarks*. This is a class of particles postulated on theoretical grounds, but not yet observed. His speculation might take this form:

All mesons are non-stable.	*A*
All leptoquarks are mesons.	*A*

Some leptoquarks are non-stable.   *I*

(6.23)

If (6.23) is accepted as valid, then it might seem that elementary logic has solved a problem that the most advanced theoretical physics is not yet able to solve. It has established the real existence of leptoquarks, since the 'some' in the conclusion of (6.23) carries existential commitment. However, before we start panting after a Nobel prize, it would be well to check the Venn diagram proper to (6.23).

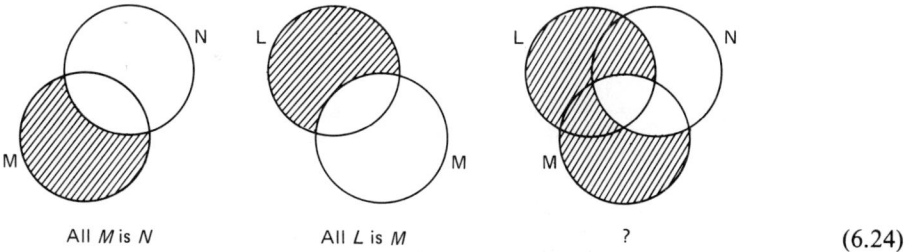

All *M* is *N*   All *L* is *M*   ?   (6.24)

The Venn diagram for "Some L is N" has an X in the intersection of L and N. The conclusion of (6.24) does not. If we make the further assumption that there are leptoquarks, then the X in the L circle would have to be in the region LMN, since the rest of this circle is empty. In this case, however, we did not establish the existence of leptoquarks. We simply assumed it. Such assumptions hardly merit Nobel prizes.

What we have in (6.23) is an example of a *weakened* syllogism. If a syllogism supports a universal conclusion, then it also supports the corresponding particular conclusion, provided that we assume that the subject term represents a class that is not empty. Such weakened syllogisms need not be listed or treated further, for they fall under the general square of opposition rule that *A* implies *I* and *E* implies *O*, when we are discussing non-empty classes.

6.2 THE OTHER FIGURES

When we are using Venn diagrams as a means of drawing conclusions, we can ignore the question of what figure a syllogism has. We simply fill in the premises and try to read out the conclusion. To rely exclusively on the method, however, we would have to test out all of the 256 possible syllogistic forms mentioned earlier, a tedious and unnecessary task. The results have been known for centuries. What we will do, accordingly, is to list the valid forms for each figure and then comment on some of them. This will give us two means of checking valid argument forms, the Venn diagram method and the scorecard method. Since we wish the table to be complete, we will include weakened forms.

Valid Syllogistic Forms

FIG. 1	FIG. 2	FIG. 3	FIG. 4	
M—N	N—M	M—N	N—M	
L—M	L—M	M—L	M—L	
L—N	L—N	L—N	L—N	
AAA	EAE	IAI	AEE	
EAE	AEE	AII	IAI	:PRESUPPOSITIONS
AII	EIO	OAO	EIO	:REQUIRED
EIO	AOO	EIO		:
AAI*	AEO*		AEO*	; L's exist.
EAO*	EAO*			;
		AAI*	EAO*	; M's exist.
		EAO*		:
			AAI*	; N's exist.

(6.25)

An asterisk (*) in Table (6.25) indicates that the conclusion follows only if one makes the existential assumption listed in the column at the right. We will first consider the Venn diagram method and then the scorecard method. This is the easiest method to use. It is postponed until the end because it does not supply a justification of the forms as valid or not valid.

Venn Diagram Method

In the preceding section we constructed Venn diagrams by a three-step process: premise 1, premise 2 → readout of the conclusion. This splitting was only for pedagogical purposes. From now on we will simply feed the premises into the three-ring diagram, using any convenient letters for the terms. As an example we will consider the *AEE* mood of figure 2. This mood was shown to be invalid in figure 1. Yet it is listed among the valid forms for figure 2. As an example we have the premises

All gamblers are superstitious people.   *A*
No rationalists are superstitious people.   *E*   (6.26)

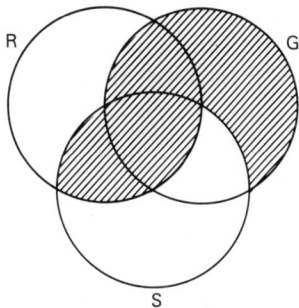

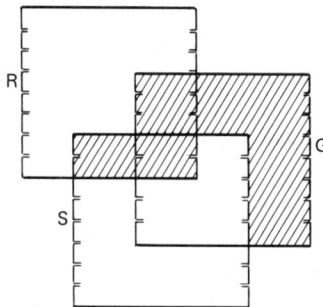

(6.27)   (6.27)

The intersection of R and G is totally shaded in, indicating that

No rationalists are gamblers.   *E*

As an example of figure 3 we may examine *AAI** (and illustrate the significance of the *). Consider the premises

All dictators are authoritarians.   *A*
All dictators are insecure.   *A*

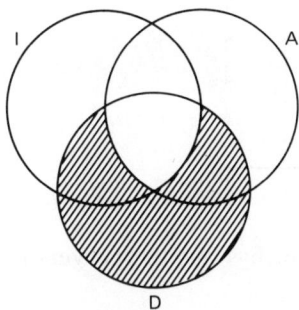

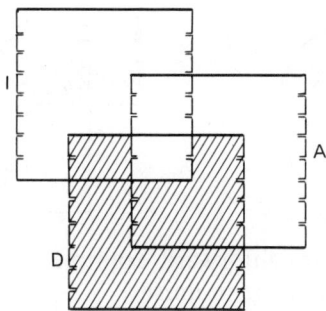

(6.28)

No conclusion seems to follow, for the *I* and *A* relation exhibited in (6.28) does not resemble any of the four acceptable propositional forms. If, however, there are dictators, then they must be in the only part of the D circle left unshaded, in IDA. If we put an X there to indicate that there are dictators, then by virtue of this assumption we establish the conclusion

Some insecure people are authoritarian.   *I*

The asterisk (*) in Table (6.25) goes with the presupposition in the right column: M's exist. The conclusion follows only if we presuppose that the middle term is not empty. In some of the other cases with asterisks we must presuppose that the subject term, L, or the predicate term, N, is not empty.

It should be noted that *AAI** in figure 3 is not a weakened syllogism, like *AAI* in figure 1. It is the strongest conclusion that can be drawn from the given premises rather than a weakened form of an allowed stronger conclusion.

Figure 4 is rather perverse. It has the subject of the conclusion as the predicate of a premise and the predicate of the conclusion as the subject of a premise. Aristotle and many later logicians ignored this figure, presumably on the grounds that any valid figure 4 form can always be reduced to figures 1, 2, or 3 (in Aristotle's treatment all other figures were reduced to figure 1) by conversion of a premise or by other tricks that we need not consider. In spite of such semantic perversity, the Venn diagram method works as well here as in any of the other figures. Thus suppose that we have the premises

No bankers are paupers.   *E*
Some paupers are educators. *I*   (6.29)

Since 'paupers' is in both premises, it must be the middle term. Accordingly, (6.29) is a figure 4 form.

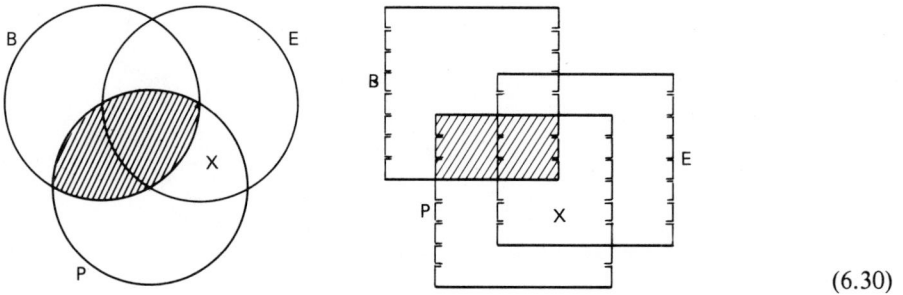

(6.30)

For a less straighforward example, one that brings out the perversity of figure 4, consider the premises

All rioters are lawbreakers.   *A*
All lawbreakers are punishable.   *A*   (6.31)

This has the Venn diagram

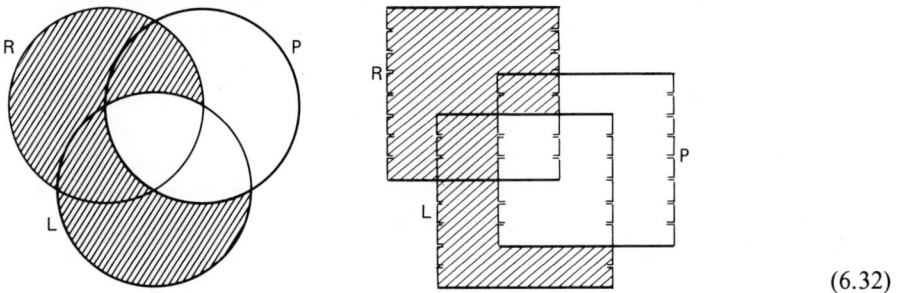

(6.32)

which has the conclusion

All rioters are punishable.   *A*

This conclusion also follows if we change the order of the premises in (6.31) and then interpret it as figure 1 (*AAA*). If, however, we wish to treat this as a figure 4 form, then 'punishable people' must be the subject of the conclusion. It is in the minor premise in (6.31). From (6.32) we see that if there are rioters, then the only place they can be is in RLP. The rest of the R circle is empty. This establishes the conclusion

Some punishable people are rioters.   *I*

Since this conclusion depends on an existential presupposition ("There are rioters"), it is marked with an * in Table (6.25). Though a syllogism with this conclusion would be a weakened syllogism in figure 1, it is not in figure 4.

EXERCISES

A. 1. Does any set of three categorical propositions count as a syllogism?
   2. How is the figure of a syllogism determined?
   3. How is the mood of a syllogism determined?
   4. What figure does not admit of any universal conclusions?
   5. What figure does not admit of any affirmative conclusions?
   6. Name a weakened syllogism besides figure 1, *AAI*.
   7. How many counterexamples are needed to disprove the validity of a syllogistic form?
   8. If an argument form admits of counterexamples, does a Venn diagram of its premises supply a readout of its conclusion?

B. I. For the given premises:

   A. draw a Venn diagram;
   B. indicate what conclusion, if any, validly follows,
   C. indicate any existential assumptions needed to draw this conclusion.

   1. All presidents of the United States are males.
      No presidents of the D.A.R. are males.
  *2. All asteroids are in Keplerian orbits.
      All asteroids are rocky formations.
   3. All mules are sterile, and some injured animals are sterile.
   4. No heavy smokers are good insurance risks.
      All good insurance risks are people with lower monthly payments.
   5. All puppies are friendly animals, and all kittens are friendly animals.

   II. Use the Venn diagram method to test the validity of the following arguments. Any existential assumptions needed to draw a valid conclusion should be noted.
   1. Some members of the Tax Committee are not members of the Ways and Means Committee, because some members of the Tax Committee are Republicans, and no Republicans are members of the Ways and Means Committee.

*2. All accountants are people who handle large sums of money. So some accountants are wealthy, because all wealthy people are people who handle large sums of money.
3. All science-fiction monsters in the movies are just mechanical contraptions. But some mechanical contraptions are sure scary. So some of these movie monsters are scary.
4. No investor who has a net loss for the year is an income taxpayer. But some investors with a net loss are actually quite well paid. So some persons who are well paid are not taxpayers.
5. All black holes are energy sinks. So some collapsed stars are energy sinks, because all black holes are collapsed stars.

III. Establish counterexamples to show that the following forms are invalid.
1. Figure 1, *IAI*
2. Figure 2, *AAA*
*3. Figure 3, *AAA*
4. Figure 3, *EAE*
5. Figure 4, *OAO*

M. I. Use the following code in specifying the conclusion to the arguments given:

A.   Some H is not F.
B.   No F is H.
C.   No conclusion follows.
D.   Some H is F.
E.   All H is F.

*1. All F is G, but some F is H.
2. All F is G, and all H is G.
3. No F is G. Some G is H.
*4. All F is G. No H is G.
5. All F is G, and all H is F.
6. No F is G, and no H is F.
7. No G is F, but some H is G.
*8. Some G is F, and some H is G.

II. Use this code to specify which Venn diagrams represent the given premises.

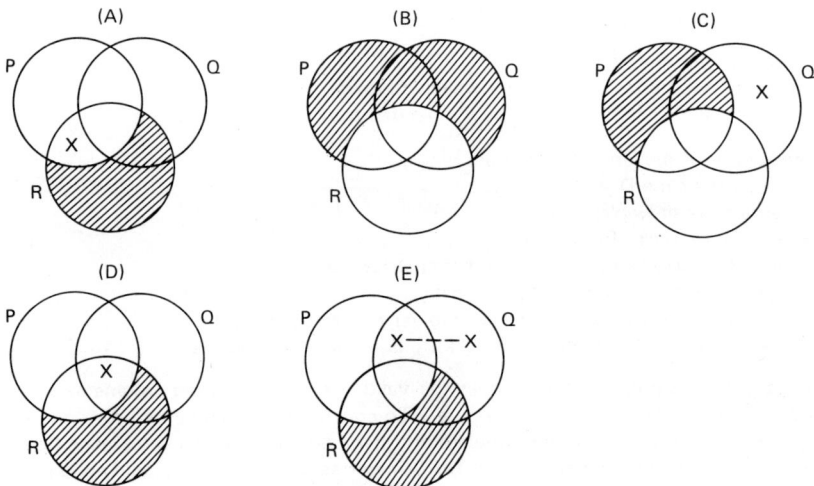

(A) (B) (C)

(D) (E)

9. Some R is not Q, and all R is P.
*10. All R is P, and some Q is not R.
11. All Q is R, and all P is R.
12. All R is P, and some R is Q.
*13. All P is R, and some Q is not R.
14. Some Q is R, and all R is P.

III. Use this code to specify which Venn diagrams represent the given premises.

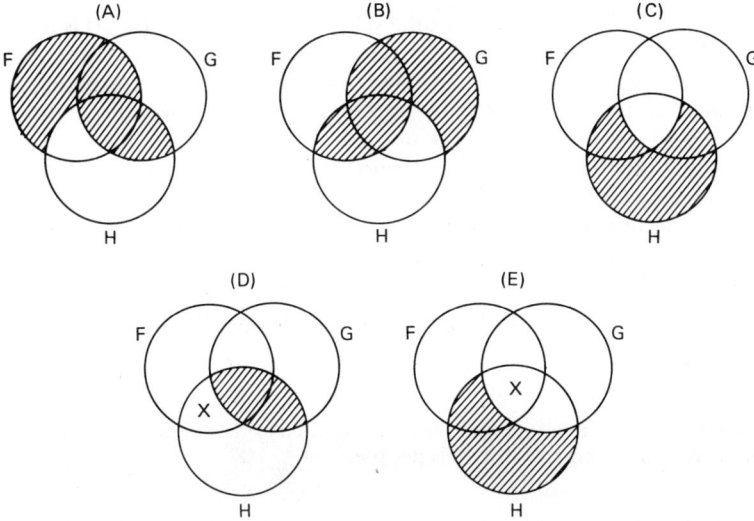

(A)   (B)   (C)

(D)   (E)

15. No H is G, and some H is F.
16. All H is G, and some H is F.
17. All G is H, and no H is F.
18. All H is G, and all H is F.
19. All G is H, and no F is H.
20. No G is H, and all F is H.

6.3 THE SCORECARD METHOD

Table (6.25) lists all the valid syllogistic forms. It is something like the official scorecard for a baseball team. A player whose name is not on the official scorecard is not on the team, regardless of how good he may look. Similarly, any syllogism in Table (6.25) is a member of the team Valid Syllogisms. Any syllogism not on the table is not valid. Accordingly, to test the validity of a given syllogism, or to determine what conclusion, if any, follows from two categorical premises having three terms, one simply reduces it to standard form and then checks the result against the official list. If it is on the list it is valid, otherwise it is not. This is the simplest method of testing validity.

But it cannot be considered the most basic, for it does not show why a conclusion follows.

The application of this method to a given syllogism is essentially a six-step process (all baby steps):

1. *Find the conclusion:* Inference indicators guide this search.
2. *Find the major premise:* This is the premise that contains the predicate of the conclusion. (In standard form it is listed first.)
3. *Find the minor premise:* This contains the subject of the conclusion. (It is listed second in standard form.)
4. *Determine the figure:* When the major and minor are written in order, or, a better procedure, are schematized by appropriate letters, then the figure is determined by the arrangement of the middle term.
5. *Determine the mood:* This is done by labeling the proposition as *A, E, I,* or *O.*
6. *Determine validity by checking the results of steps 4 and 5 against Table (6.25).* If the mood determined in Step 5 is found under the figure determined in 4, then the syllogism is valid. Otherwise it is not valid.

As an example of this method, let us attempt to test the validity of the following argument:

> Some alcoholics are not sick people, because all heavy drinkers are alcoholics, and some heavy drinkers are not sick people.

The 'because' indicates reasons or premises. The proposition before the 'because', which is supported by these reasons, is the conclusion. Its predicate, 'sick people', occurs in the last proposition. So this must be the major and the other one the minor. If we put the propositions in this order and use some obvious symbols, we have

$$H—S \quad O$$
$$\underline{H—Al \quad A}$$
$$Al—S \quad O.$$

Since H, the middle term, is the subject of both premises, we have a figure 3 form. Table (6.25) shows that the mood *OAO* is valid in figure 3. Therefore the given argument is valid.

As a second example, consider the following argument, which echoes a type of political rhetoric that used to be fairly common:

> All anarchists are subversives. So some anarchists are communists, since all communists are subversives.

Here 'so' signals a conclusion, while 'since' indicates a premise. The remaining proposition must also be a premise. Since the final proposition contains 'communist', the predicate of the conclusion, it must be the major premise. Accordingly, reduction to standard form yields

$$
\begin{array}{ll}
\text{C—S} & A \\
\underline{\text{An—S}} & A \\
\text{An—C} & I.
\end{array}
$$

Since the middle term, S, is predicate in both premises, this is a figure 2 form. Table (6.25) does not have AAI under figure 2. Therefore the argument is invalid.

This scorecard method does not always work quite as automatically when one is trying to determine what conclusion, if any, follows from given premises. Thus, suppose that you were confronted with the premises

No advocates of liberalized abortion laws are candidates we will support.
Some members of Congress are advocates of liberalized abortion laws.

This is rather easily reduced to the form

$$
\begin{array}{ll}
\text{Adv.—Can} & E \\
\text{M. C.—Adv} & I.
\end{array}
$$

From the arrangement of the middle term, this should be a figure 1 form. Then the chart indicates the conclusion

$$
\begin{array}{ll}
\text{M. C.—Can.} & O
\end{array}
$$

or "Some members of Congress are not candidates we will support." In this case the method applied automatically.

Now consider the premises that are wandering about in search of a conclusion

All garlic and cucumber salads are hard to digest. But some garlic and cucumber salads are not expensive.

This easily reduces to the form

$$
\begin{array}{ll}
\text{GC—HD} & A \\
\text{GC—E} & O.
\end{array}
$$

This is a figure 3 form. Table (6.25) does not list any valid *AO* form under figure 3. However, it does list the form *OAO*. To make this into a valid argument, accordingly, we should treat the second premise as our major. Then it is the first premise that contains the subject of the conclusion. Thus the conclusion that follows from these premises is: "Some hard-to-digest foods are not expensive." It will be left as an exercise to the reader to show that a Venn diagram yields the same conclusion.

EXERCISES

A. 1. In using the scorecard method, does it matter in what order the premises occur?
  2. What is the distinguishing characteristic of the major premise?
  3. If the conclusion of an ordinary argument is not the last proposition, how is it known to be the conclusion?
  4. What is the difference between the figure and the mood of a syllogism?
  5. Can there be a valid syllogism without a unviersal premise?
  6. Give an example of an equivocal term besides 'man'.

B. 1. Give an example of two valid syllogisms in different figures that have the same Venn diagram.
  2. Why does no syllogistic figure have a valid *IE* form, though each has an *EI* form?
  3. Determine the validity of the following arguments by reduction to standard form. Indicate any existential assumptions needed.

   a) All humans are mortal, and all Greeks are human. So all Greeks are mortal.
   b) No metals are insulators, because all metals are good conductors of heat and no insulators are good conductors of heat.
   c) All term papers are time-consuming projects. All time-consuming projects are interferences in a student's social life. So all term papers are interferences in a student's social life.
   d) All unicorns are mythical animals. All unicorns are also guardians of virgins. So, some guardians of virgins are mythical animals.
   e) No Vietnam veterans are satisfied with government benefits, and some of these veterans are not combat veterans. So, even some combat veterans are not satisfied with government benefits.
   f) All Stoic philosophers are people who believe that virtue is the supreme good. It follows that no Epicureans are Stoics, for no Epicureans are people who believe that virtue is the supreme good.
   g) No movies with messages are works of lasting value, because all message movies are dated by their social commentaries, and no art works of lasting value are so dated.
   h) Some congressional junkets are not worth their cost, and all congressional junkets are burdens on the taxpayer. So some things not worth their cost are burdens on the taxpayer.
   i) No irrational number is expressible as the ratio of two integers. So all irrational numbers are transcendental, for no transcendental number is expressible as the ratio of two integers.
   j) All switch hitters are difficult to pitch to. No switch hitters are pitchers. So some hitters who are difficult to pitch to are not pitchers.

4. By using reduction to standard form, determine what conclusions come from the following premises. It may be necessary to transform some of the premises.

   a) None but the toughest are Marines, and these men are all Marines.
   b) A thing of beauty is a joy forever. But all punk rock is ugly.
   c) Some racehorses are not winners, but racehorses are all thoroughbreds.
   d) All wasps are unfriendly, and only friendly creatures are welcome.
   e) Not all nuclei are unstable against radioactive decay. But only radioactively unstable nuclei are fissionable.
   f) No overweight animals run well, but some greyhouds run well.
   g) All gatecrashers are uninvited guests. Only invited guests are welcome.
   h) No misers are unselfish. None but misers save eggshells.

M. I. Consider the argument

   A. All sorority sisters are club members:
   B. So, all pledges are sorority sisters,
   C. Because all pledges are club members.

1. The major of this syllogism is
2. The minor of this syllogism is
3. The conclusion of this syllogism is
4. The figure of this syllogism is:

   a) Figure 1.
   b) Figure 2.
   c) Figure 3.
   d) Figure 4.
   e) None of the above.

5. This syllogism is

   a) Valid.
   b) Invalid.
   c) Valid only if one assumes the middle term has members.
   d) Valid only if one assumes the subject of the conclusion has members.
   e) Valid only if one assumes the predicate of the conclusion has members.

II. Consider the argument

   A. Some social beings are language users:
   B. because all intelligent aliens are social beings,
   C. and all intelligent aliens are language users.

*6. The major premise of this syllogism is
 7. The minor premise of this syllogism is
*8. The conclusion of this syllogism is
 9. The figure of this syllogism is (coded as 24)
*10. The syllogism is (coded as 25).

III. Consider the argument

   A. No dogs are cats.
   B. All five-foot tall spaniels are dogs.
   C. So, some five-foot tall spaniels are not cats.

11. The major premise of this syllogism is
12. The minor premise of this syllogism is
13. The conclusion of this syllogism is
14. The figure of this syllogism is (coded as 24)
*15. The syllogism is (coded as 25).

IV. Consider the premises

All P is Q, and some R is Q.

16. These premises imply

    a)   some P is R.
    b)   some R is P.
    c)   some P is not R.
    d)   some R is not P.
    e)   no valid conclusion.

V. consider the premises

No Q is P, but some Q is R.

17. These premises imply (coded as 36)

VI. Consider the premises

Some R is not Q, and all Q is P.

18. These premises imply (coded as 36).

SUMMARY

SYLLOGISM:

has three unequivocal terms and three propositions
    middle term (M) is in both premises.
    major premise: contains predicate of conclusion (N).
    minor premise: contains subject of conclusion (L).
figure determined by arrangement of M.
mood determined by forms of propositions.
valid forms given in table (6.25).

REDUCTION TO STANDARD FORM:

identify
    conclusion through inference indicators.
    major premise through predicate of conclusion.
    minor premise through subject of conclusion.

symbolize terms by letters and arrange propositions
    Major   Propositional type
    Minor   Propositional type
    Conclusion   Propositional type.
identify
    figure by arrangement of middle term.
    mood by pattern of *A, E, I, O.*
check results with table (6.25)—
    valid argument if this mood is found under this figure.
    invalid if not so found.

VENN DIAGRAMS:

use three intersecting circles.

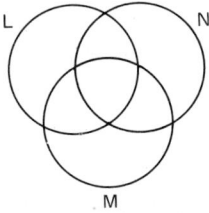

feed in premises by
    shading in an empty region.
    putting an X for some
        (use an either–or X to straddle any lines in this area X   X).
read out conclusion—
    any X wiped out by shading doesn't count.
    conclusion must be interpretable as

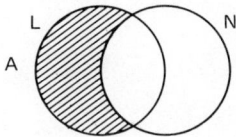

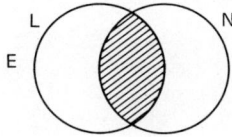

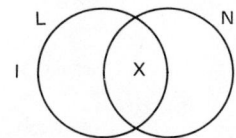

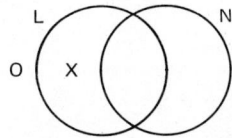

existential assumptions
   needed to derive particular conclusions from universal premises.
   should be explicitly indicated.

REFERENCES

[1]L. Euler, "Letters à une Princesse d'Allemagne," in *Leonhardi Euleri Opera Omnia* (Basle: Swiss Society of Natural Sciences, 1960), *Ser. Tertia,* Vol. XI, pp. 233–56. This collection of letters, presenting a general survey of learning, was one of the most influential works of the Enlightenment era.

Chapter 7

OTHER SYLLOGISTIC FORMS

We have defined deductive inferences as inferences in which the truth of the premises guarantees the truth of the conclusion. In the last chapter we considered deductive inferences based on categorical (L is N) propositions. Now we wish to consider two more basic forms: deductive inferences based on *hypotheticals* (or various types of *If . . . then* connections); and deductive inferences based on *disjunctives* (or various types of *or* connections. Long chains of deductive reasoning—at least reasoning not involving mathematical deduction—are usually made up of combinations of these basic units.

7.1 HYPOTHETICAL INFERENCES

Consider the simple argument

> If Towser is a dog, then Towser is a mammal.
> Towser is a dog.
> _____
>
> So, Towser is a mammal. (7.1a)

It seems obvious that the conclusion must be true, if both premises are true. Compare it with the simple categorical form,

> All dogs are mammals.
> Towser is a dog.
> _____
>
> So, Towser is a mammal. (7.1b)

This is not quite a categorical syllogism, since 'Towser' is not a class term. Yet the comparison suggests that the major premise in each version of (7.1) can be represented by an inclusion relation,

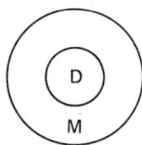

(7.2)

We can represent the minor by putting a T—or simply the tip of a pencil— inside the D circle.

Now consider the simple shift

If Towser is a dog, then Towser is a mammal.
Towser is a mammal.
_____

So Towser is a dog.   (7.3)

If the premises of (7.3) are true then the conclusion *might* be true. But, it need not be. Towser could be a horse, a cat, or an elephant. The inclusion diagram for (7.3) could be either

(7.4)

Since (7.3) represents an argument form in which the premises can be true while the conclusion is false, it cannot be a valid deductive form.

Here we wish to clarify the valid forms of hypothetical inference and to focus on the way they function in the language we speak. This leads to a consideration of two aspects of hypotheticals. The first is the sentence that expresses the hypothesis. The question here is how the 'if' part of a conditional sentence relates to the 'then' part. What sorts of connections are allowed? The second question is: Which forms of 'if . . . then' arguments are valid?

In treating the first question it helps to have a consistent terminology. An 'if . . . then' sentence is a conditional sentence. The clause or proposition that goes with the 'if' part is called the 'antecedent'; the clause or proposition that goes with the 'then' part is called the 'consequent'. The question we wish to consider is: What sorts of relations between antecedent and consequent are expressed by the use of 'if . . . then' constructions in English? Let's consider some examples:

If he is a bachelor, then he is unmarried. (7.5)

If the beast is a cat, then it is a mammal. (7.6)

If the button is pushed, then the bomb will explode. (7.7)

If there is insufficient oxygen, then the fire will go out. (7.8)

If she is the governor of Idaho, then she must be a citizen of Idaho. (7.9)

If X is greater than 20, then X is greater than 15. (7.10)

If the killing was done with malice aforethought, then it is
first-degree murder.
(7.11)

The connection between the antecedent and the consequent is somewhat different in each of these cases. In (7.5) the relation is based on synonomy (or near synonomy) of meaning. In its most familiar usage the term 'bachelor' means 'unmarried man'. In (7.6) the conditional expresses a relation of class inclusion. The next sentence, (7.7), expresses a causal relation. Sentences (7.8) and (7.9) represent two different types of conditions, necessary and sufficient, respectively. These will be treated in more detail later. Now we merely wish to show that both are expressed by conditional sentences. The if–then link in sentence (7.10) is a simple ordering relation. In the final sentence, (7.11), the antecedent and consequent are related by legal stipulation, or by the way 'first-degree murder' is defined in law.

We will consider some of these differences later. What we wish to consider now is one simple feature that all of these examples have in common. Regardless of the nature of the connection between the antecedent and the consequent, there is no case of an acceptable conditional sentence in which the antecedent is true and the consequent is false. In some cases, such as the first two examples, this relation is rather obvious. In some other cases, such as the final example, the relation may not be so obvious. We should examine such nonobvious cases by considering the type of situations in which the sentence in question is normally used. Sentence (7.11) would be used in a jury deliberation. If the members of the jury have already reached agreement on all other factors pertaining to a murder, then it is not possible, within the guidelines of the operative law, for them to affirm that there was malice aforethought and yet deny that the crime is a first-degree murder.

This common logical structure is the only aspect of hypothetical reasoning that we shall consider in the present chapter. A conditional statement cannot be true if the antecedent is true while the consequent is false. On this basis we will be concerned in the present chapter with drawing inferences *from* conditional statements. Reasoning *about* the hypotheses expressed by the conditional will be considered in the next chapter. This limits us rather sharply. There are really only three kinds of things we can do: affirm, deny, and build chains. We will consider each of these.

7.2 TRUTH TABLES

The easiest way to demonstrate the inferences proper to both hypotheticals and disjunctives is through *truth tables*. The idea of truth-table definitions of logical connectives originated in logic. Now these definitions are routinely incorporated in such computer languages as BASIC, FORTRAN, PASCAL, and others. The basic idea behind truth tables is a straightforward extension of the classy language we have been considering. In deductive logic we assume that all propositions are either true or false. To call a proposition 'undetermined' does not mean that it has some value intermediate between true and false; it simply means that we do not know whether it is true or false.

One proposition, p, can have two values, T and F. Two propositions, p and q, can have four values. Three propositions, p, q, and r, can have eight possible values (combinations of T and F). This is most easily seen by putting these combinations in tables, generally referred to as *truth tables*.

P ~P		p q		p q r
T F		T T		T T T
F T		T F		T T F
		F T		T F T
		F F		T F F
				F T T
				F T F
				F F T
				F F F (7.12)

The first truth shows the two values that p can have, T and F. If we let '~p' stand for "It is not the case that p" then we can use the truth table to *define* ~p. ~p is false when p is true; and true when p is false. The next two tables show all the possible combinations of truth values for two variables, p and q, and then for three variables, p, q, and r. The easiest way to get these right is to start in the right column and write T–F combinations one at a time. In the next column write them two at a time, then four. We will not have to go any higher than this. However, the general rule is that n variables require 2^n rows.

The table with two columns can be used to define the meaning that regimented logical connectives have in our classy language. Thus if we use '&' to stand for 'and,' and ' $\supset$ ' to stand for "implies," then we can define the logical connectives

p q	(p & q)	(p $\supset$ q)
T T	T	T
T F	F	F
F T	F	T
F F	F	T

(7.13)

The definition of "p & q" corresponds to the meaning that we usually assign to *and*. We would not consider a compound sentence like, "Today is Tuesday and it is raining," true unless both clauses are true: it *is* Tuesday and it *is* raining. The same truth-table definition would also fit: "Today is Tuesday, but it is raining"; or "Today is Tuesday; nevertheless it is raining." The subtle differences between 'and', which doesn't suggest a surprise, and 'nevertheless', which does, are lost in the truth-table definition. For this reason one should not interpret this table as defining the meaning 'and' has in English. It defines the meaning '&' has in logic.

The truth-table definition of 'p $\supset$ q' may seem a bit unnatural. Think of p as standing for 'it is raining' and q for 'the ground is wet.' Then the first two rows of our definition seem OK. We would consider the conditional sentence, "If it is raining, then the ground is wet," true if it is raining and the ground is wet, but false if it is raining and the ground in question is dry. But suppose it is not raining? Then the table assigns T to the conditional both when the ground is wet and when the ground is dry.

Here again, it is helpful to remember that we are not trying to define the meaning that 'if . . . then' has in English. As we have seen this combination fits a variety of different connections between the antecedent and consequent. We are trying to define the meaning that ' $\supset$ ' has in logic. It is an essential part of a theory of deductive inference. Deductive forms are considered valid only if they meet one essential requirement: the truth of the premises guarantees the truth of the conclusion. If it is not raining then it might be perfectly reasonable to consider the sentence, "If it is raining, then the ground is wet," to be true. It is not yet tested. If we were to assign this the value F, then we couldn't tell whether a false conclusion is due to the false premise or to an invalid argument form. If we assign it the value T, then we have a basis for defining a valid form.

7.3 DIRECT INFERENCE

Direct inference is the most straightforward use of hypothetical reasoning. Given a conditional sentence that we accept as true, then affirming the antecedent entitles us to affirm the consequent. Thus, in example (7.1) the first premise gives the link between antecedent and consequent. The second premise tells us that the antecedent is true, that Towser is a dog. We conclude that the consequent must also be true, that Towser is a mammal. This simple argument is an instance of a simple widely used argument form, which can be represented by a Venn diagram.

If p, then q.
p.
_____

Therefore, q.

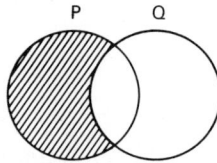

(7.14)

What the Venn diagram represents is the major premise. It has essentially the same form as an *A* proposition. This is not surprising when we compare "If Towser is a dog, then Towser is a mammal" with "All dogs are mammals." Earlier we said that in logic universal propositions are not treated as having existential implications. This is much clearer in the conditional form. The inclusion relation comes from the fact that dogs are a subclass of mammals. But affirming this does not entail affirming either that Towser exists or that Towser is a dog. Compare this with the sentence, "If anyone born in the sixteenth century is still alive, then he or she is much older than I am." This is certainly true, though no one from that era is still alive.

The minor premise affirms p. As earlier, we can symoblize this by putting a letter—or simply the tip of a pencil—inside the *available* (or nonempty) part of the p circle. We will use this to indicate that p is true. Then the same convention, a pencil tip inside the circle, also indicates that q is true. Traditionally this argument form is called *modus ponens,* which is really short for *modus ponendo ponens,* the method of positing the conclusion by means of positing the antecedent. Rather than worry about Latin gerundive constructions, we will simply call it 'direct inference'.

A simpler, though perhaps not so familiar, way to get the same conclusion is to read it off the truth-table definition of "⊃". We are accepting the antecedent, p, as true, and the conditional, p ⊃ q, as true. Only the first row of the truth-table definition fits these assignments, and in this row q has T. It is easy to see that it fits all the examples, (7.5) through (7.11). Thus if "Joe is a bachelor" is true, then we can infer from (7.5) that Joe is unmarried. Since 30 is greater than 20, we can infer from (7.10) that 30 is greater than 15.

Now suppose that we try turning the process around, as we did with the Towser example. In each of the sentences (7.5) through (7.11) we will affirm the consequent and see if this entitles us to affirm the antecedent. Since we are turning things around, we can begin with the last example: "This is a case of first degree murder." So, by virtue of (7.11) we conclude, "Therefore, there was malice aforethought." This seems reasonable enough. Let's try another example. Suppose that we say of Morris the cat, "He's a mammal." Can we reasonably infer, by virtue of (7.6), "Therefore, he is a dog"? If Morris were not so lazy, he might scratch our eyes out for drawing such an inference.

The reason that this backward reasoning seemed to work in the murder example will be clarified when we consider necessary and sufficient conditions. The point to be noted now is that it does not work all the time. A deductively valid argument form is one that *always* works. The reason why may be seen by returning to the Venn diagram in (7.12). We symbolize affirming the consequent by putting the pencil tip inside the q circle. Is it also inside the p circle? It may be or it may not. This can also be read off the truth-table definition, (7.13). We are assuming that the consequent, q, is true, and that the conditional, $p \supset q$, is true. This assignment fits row 1, where p is T, and row 3, where p is F. This form of inference occurs often enough that it is given a label: the *fallacy* of affirming the consequent.

7.4 INDIRECT INFERENCE

Let's return to example (8.1) and again assume that the antecedent is true. Suppose we also know that Towser is not a mammal. Then it is certain that Towser is not a dog. In the Venn diagram for (7.12) we symbolize the denial of the consequent by putting the pencil tip outside q. Then it cannot be inside any available (nonshaded) part of p. The truth-table definition yields the same conclusion. We are assuming that the consequent, q, is F and that the conditional, $p \supset q$, is T. This assignment only fits the fourth row, which has p as T. Now we have a second valid argument form for hypothetical reasoning with the general form

If p, then q.
It is not the case that q.

Therefore, it is not the case that p.   (7.15)

The phrase "It is not the case that p" is a bit awkward. We will generally abbreviate it to "not-p." This form is used to indicate that what we are denying is the whole proposition, q. In ordinary English this is usually done by putting a "not" before the predicate (A snake is not a mammal) or before the verb (Jones is not running for mayor). This argument form is traditionally referred to as *modus tollens,* short for *modus tollendo tollens,* the method of denying the antecedent by means of denying the consequent. We will refer to it as *indirect inference.*

As with direct inference, there is a fallacy that resembles the valid form. Consider the general form

If p, then q.
Not-p.
_____

Therefore, not-q.   (7.16)

A brief consideration of the examples already treated shows that this form can easily lead from true premises to a false conclusion. Thus, "If Mary is a Nun, then she is a woman. But Mary is not a Nun. So . . . ?" Return again to the Venn diagram. We symbolize "It is not the case that p" by putting the pencil tip outside the p circle. It may or may not be outside the q circle. In this case we can see the advantage of filling the gaps in the truth-table definition of ' ⊃ ' with T. The assignment of F to p and T to p ⊃ q fits both the third row of the definition (where q is T) and also the fourth row (where q is F). Since a true conditional with a false premise can fit either value of q, we cannot validly infer that it is either T or F. Form (7.16) is traditionally referred to as the fallacy of denying the antecedent.

7.5 HYPOTHETICAL SYLLOGISMS

The two types of valid hypothetical inferences just considered depend on affirming or denying part of the hypothesis. We may not always do that. Consider the general form

If p, then q.
If q, then r.
_____

So, if p then r.   (7.17)

The conclusion does not tell us either that p is true or that r is false. What it tells us is that, *if* p is true, then r is also true. This is generally called a *hypothetical syllogism,* or, sometimes, a chain argument. We have used inclusion circles, rather than Venn diagrams, to represent it for two reasons. First, we are not going to put our pencil tips anywhere to represent true premises. Second, we want to be be able to extend this to long chains, something best symbolized by inclusion circles.

We can begin extending this by noting that what we have here is a special case of a general form of reasoning that we have already assimilated in learning to use terms like 'older than', 'heavier than', 'taller than'. These all have the form

If Jules is older (taller, heavier . . .) than Jim,
and Jim is older (taller, heavier . . .) than Catherine,

then Jules is older (taller, heavier . . .) than Catherine.   (7.18)

This is a very general form that fits any chain based on relational terms that have certain simple properties. The relational terms used must *connect* the items in some domain. We rank people or animals by age, but not sand pebbles or water drops. The relation must be *asymmetrical*. A symmetrical relation works both ways. If Jules is as tall as Jim, then Jim is as tall as Jules. An asymmetrical relation works only one way. If Jules is older than Jim, then Jim can not be older than Jules. Finally, the relation must be transitive, one that is passed along. Compare (7.16) with

Jules loves Catherine,
and Catherine loves Jim.

Therefore, ???   (7.19)

One would hesitate to conclude from (7.19) that Jules loves Jim—though the Jules and Jim of the movie remained friends in spite of Catherine's switches.

It may seem that the 'if . . . then' forms we have been considering need not exhibit the properties of connectedness, asymmetry, and transitivity. That they do so, however, is clearer if we replace 'if p, then q' by 'p implies q', or by $p \supset q$. Then all the relational terms we have been considering have the same form. If we let '$>$' stand for any relational term that is connected, asymmetrical, and transitive, we have

$p > q.$
$q > r.$
$\cdot \cdot \cdot \cdot \cdot \cdot$
$\cdot \cdot \cdot \cdot \cdot \cdot$
$y > z.$

Therefore, $p > z$.   (7.20)

The general rule governing such chain arguments is that any term not in the conclusion must occur both as antecedent and as consequent. This rule allows us to avoid fallacious arguments of the form

Lassie is larger than Benji.
King Kong is larger than Benji.

So, Lassie is larger than King Kong.   (7.21)

EXERCISES

A. 1. Give three example of "if . . . then" sentences involving different types of connections between the antecedent and the consequent.
   2. Direct inference involves a premise positing the truth of one part of a conditional sentence. Which part is it?
   3. Does affirming the consequent always lead to a false conclusion?
   4. Indirect inference involves a premise positing the truth of one part of a conditional sentence. Which part is it?
   5. Does the fallacy of denying the antecedent always lead to a false conclusion?
   6. What terms in an extended hypothetical syllogism (or chain argument) do not function as both antecedent and consequent in a premise?

B.   For each of the following arguments:

      A.   determine whether it is valid or invalid;
      B.   label the type of argument or fallacy involved.

   1. If it is Tuesday, then this is Belgium. It is Tuesday. So, this is Belgium.
  *2. If it's a nice day, then we'll go swimming. It's not a nice day. It follows that we won't go swimming.
   3. The unemployment rates will rise if the interest rates stay high. But the interest rates will not stay high. So, the unemployment rates will not rise.
  *4. If the inmates are running the asylum, then everything is in chaos. The asylum sure is peaceful. So, the inmates can't be running it.
   5. If the ultimate felicity of man does not consist in external things, which are called goods of fortune, nor in goods of the body, nor in the goods of the soul according to its sensitive part, nor as regards the intellective part according to the activity of the moral virtues, nor according to the intellectual virtues that are concerned with action, that is, art and prudence—we are left with the conclusion that the ultimate felicity of man lies in the contemplation of truth. But the ultimate felicity of man does not consist in external things, nor in goods of the body or soul, as has been shown. So, man's ultimate felicity must lie in the contemplation of truth.[1]
   6. I am certain that the issues will be settled, for both sides have too much to lose in a strike. If both sides have too much to lose in a strike, they settle issues.
   7. She can't be sick for she came to work. If she's sick, then she doesn't come to work.
  *8. If it's Borden's, then it's got to be good. This candy sure is good. So, it must be Borden's.
   9. If the President does not veto the bill, then it will become law. But the President will veto it. So, it won't become law.
  10. The Yankees will win the series if Johnson gets out of his batting slump. But Johnson is not getting out of his slump. So, the Yankees won't win.
  11. If the lead soprano does not show up, then the opera does not go on. The opera is going on. So she must have come.
  12. McGuinness will win the election if she wins the primary. So, she's going to win the election, because she is sure to win the primary.

*13. If it is a squirrel, then it is in the genus Tamiasciurus. If it is in the genus Tamiasciurus, then it is in the family, Sciuridae. If it is in the family, Sciuridae, then it is in the order, Rodentia. If it is in the order Rodentia, then it is in the class, Mammalia. If it is in the class, Mammalia, then it is in the phylum, Chordata. If it is in the phylum, Chordata, then it is in the kingdom, Animalia. So, if it's a squirrel, then it is in the kingdom, Animalia.

14. If it is a trump, then it beats the king of spades. If it is the ace of spades, then it beats the king of spades. So, if it is a trump, then it beats the ace of spades.

*15. If the player down field was a tight end, then he was an eligible pass receiver. If he was an eligible pass receiver, then the penalty was wrong. So, if the penalty was not wrong, then he was not a tight end.

M. For questions 1 through 10 use the code:

A. Not really an argument.
B. Valid argument: direct inference.
C. Valid argument: indirect inference.
D. Invalid argument: fallacy of denying the antecedent.
E. Invalid argument: fallacy of affirming the consequent.

*1. If the movie has enough sex appeal, then it will make money. With both Bo and Susan in it it certainly has enough sex appeal. So, it will make money.

2. Jones wins the race if Smith is disqualified. So, Jones wins the race because Smith is disqualified.

*3. I'll have my steak medium rare, if you please. Then it will taste right. Mmm, this steak tastes just right. It must be medium rare.

4. If a plane's wings are too short, then it cannot fly at high altitudes. The new plane that the Russians have developed flies at very high altitudes. So, it can't have short wings.

5. If you use a gun to commit a crime, then you'll go to jail. Though Wharton committed a crime, he did not use a gun. So, he won't go to jail.

6. If the salmon are running, then we'll have a fish fry. I guess that we'll have a fish fry, because the salmon are running.

7. If the computer program is not working, then the monthly payroll cannot be determined. Fortunately, the program is now working. So, the payroll can be determined.

8. It seems that beggars can't ride, because wishes are not horses. If wishes were horses, then beggars would ride.

*9. If Saudi Arabia will not go along with the price hike, then the OPEC nations will not raise oil prices. Since the OPEC nations are not raising prices it seems clear that Saudi Arabia did not go along with the price hike.

10. If Francis Bacon was the real author of the plays attributed to Shakespeare, then some of the mystery concerning Shakespeare's education would be cleared up. But this mystery is not cleared up, because Francis Bacon did not write these plays.

7.6 VARIANT FORMS

In the last chapter we noted that ordinary English has a variety of forms corresponding to the regimented use of 'all' and 'some'. We also noted that these forms are distinguished by subtle differences that standard logic does not capture. Something similar is true of 'if . . . then'. Ordinary English certainly uses this. It also uses variant forms, which have a similar logical force, though they differ in wording, emphasis, or proper usage. We will list some forms often used for hypothetical reasoning in English and discuss the way in which these relate to the forms we have considered.

We can begin with the simplest and least problematic variants, those that simply change the order of the terms. Consider, for example:

> The game will be postponed if it rains.   (7.22)

This does not differ in any significant way from

> If it rains, then the game will be postponed.   (7.23)

Now consider

> The concert will be a money maker, provided that the Stones show up
> in time.   (7.24)

In ordinary usage 'provided that' is a bit more specific than 'if'. It generally signals a condition, while 'if' is an all-purpose connective. Such considerations, however, only concern the appropriateness of the term in ordinary usage. They do not require any modification of the logic. This also applies to such similar terms as 'on condition that'.

Other variants have slightly different uses. There is the story of the rugged old miner who came into the town tavern on a busy Saturday night. He barged through the crowd till he got to the front, then pounded his big fist on the bar and bellowed, "When MacDougal drinks, everybody drinks." After everyone in the tavern had a drink MacDougal put one dollar on the bar and said, "When MacDougal pays, everyone pays." Then he stomped out before anyone could stop him.

The other drinkers did not interpret 'when' the same way that Mac-Dougal did. They thought of it as a promise to buy a round of drinks. He intended a simple conditional. 'When', in MacDougal's sense, is equivalent to 'if'; it does not depend on any specific connection between the antecedent and the consequent. Logically, this is quite defensible. From a more practical perspective, no student should imitate MacDougal's precedent unless he is very big or very fast—or both. As far as the logic is concerned we will treat 'when ... then' or 'whenever ... then' as equivalent to 'if ... then'. Thus, when the stockbroker announces

> When everyone else is selling, then I buy   (7.25)

he is presenting a conditional affirmation. One can validly draw a conclusion from it only if one can either affirm the antecedent or deny the consequent.

Now consider the sentence

It is a racehorse *only if* it is a thoroughbred.   (7.26)

What (7.26) really means is that if it is not a thoroughbred then it is not a racehorse, and if it is a racehorse, then it is a thoroughbred. Thus, (7.26) has the *logical* form

If it is a racehorse, then it is a thoroughbred.   (7.27)

Denying the antecedent of (7.27) entitles us, by indirect inference, to deny the antecedent. Similarly, affirming the antecedent of (7.27) entitles us to affirm the consequent. The general rule here—"p, *only if* q"—should be interpreted as "if p, then q." This is quite similar to the use of 'only' in categorical statements. "Only thoroughbreds are racehorses" is interpreted as having the *logical* form, "All racehorses are thoroughbreds."

Necessary and sufficient conditions.   The specification of necessary, or sufficient, or necessary and sufficient conditions plays a role in many contexts from legal requirements to mathematical proofs. The nature of these conditions is context dependent. A mathematical condition is quite different from a legal condition. However, the *logic* of conditional affirmations is not context dependent. It is essentially the same in all these different fields. Thus to say that

X is a necessary condition for Y   (7.28)

means that unless something is an X it cannot be a Y. Thus we have the legal requirement that being over thirty-five years of age is a necessary condition for being President of the United States. Similarly, in a social context one might have: An income of at least $100,000 is a necessary condition for membership in Country Club El Snobbo. One need not have such a stilted formulation. The same information could be communicated by a notice: Only those whose income is greater than $100,000 per year are eligible for membership. In mathematics, however, people tend to express conditions formally; for example, being a subgroup is a necessary condition for being an ideal.

Suppose that we tried to express (7.28) and the other examples by the formulation

If X, then Y.   (7.29)

This clearly does not fit any of the examples given. It is not true that if someone is over thirty-five, then she or he is President; that if one's income is over \$100,000, then one is a member of the club El Snobbo; or that if something is a subgroup, then it is an ideal.

Let's try turning (7.29) around:

If Y, then X.   (7.30)

This fits all our examples. If someone is President then she (the day will come) must be over thirty-five. If someone is accepted as a member of club El Snobbo, then his annual income must be over \$100,000; if a mathematical entity is an ideal, then it is a subgroup. The form (7.30) catches the *logic* of necessary conditions. But it does not give the *grounds* of this necessity. This is hardly surprising, since the grounds of the necessity is context dependent. In the examples given it varies from legal requirements, to social agreements, to mathematical definitions. The form (7.30) simply captures the minimum antecedent–consequent connection that these different forms share.

Sufficient conditions can be thought of as a reversal of necessary conditions. Thus, to say that

A is a sufficient condition for B   (7.31)

is, as far as the logic is concerned, equivalent to saying

If A, then B.   (7.32)

Thus, being a circle is a sufficient (though not necessary) condition for being a plane geometric figure; having five dimes is a sufficient condition for having fifty cents.

Now we can put both of these together and say:

R is a necessary and sufficient condition for S.   (7.33)

From the discussion of necessary conditions it follows that "R is a necessary condition for S" is expressed by

If S, then R.   (7.34)

The earlier discussion of 'only if' shows us that (7.34) could also be written in the form

$$S, \text{ only if } R. \tag{7.35}$$

Similarly, the statement "R is a sufficient condition for S" could be written as

$$S, \text{ if } R. \tag{7.36}$$

If we put together (7.34) and (7.35), we have the standard way of expressing necessary and sufficient conditions:

$$S, \text{ if and only if } R. \tag{7.37}$$

The formulation (7.37) is the way that necessary and sufficient conditions are generally expressed in definitions or legal stipulations. Mathematicians use this form so often that they have developed a standard abbreviation:

Q, iff R.

Logicians express (7.35) by using a new symbol, $\equiv$, which is defined by a truth table:

p	q	p $\equiv$ q
T	T	T
T	F	F
F	T	F
F	F	T

(7.38)

Anyone interested in playing with truth tables should be able to show that: $(p \equiv q) \equiv [(p \supset q) \,\&\, (q \supset p)]$.

Unless.   When we considered universal propositions in the last chapter we noted that exceptives require special treatment. This carries over to conditionals because of the parallel between "All A is B" and "If something is an A, then it is a B." The complicating factor here is that 'unless' has slightly different uses in English, so that there is no automatic way of replacing a proposition containing an 'unless' by its classy-language equivalent. One must consider what is meant by the particular usage.

Suppose that you have a dinner guest who claims to be a wine expert and that during dinner you serve him a glass of chablis. After sniffing and sipping it he declares, "This is a good sauterne; not a great sauterne, but a good sauterne." I think that you would conclude that he is not an expert on the grounds:

> No one is a wine expert unless he can distinguish chablis from sauterne.
>
> (7.39)

In (7.39) 'unless' has the force of 'if . . . not'. It could be rewritten as

> No one is a wine expert if he cannot distinguish chablis from sauterne.
>
> (7.40)

This is the form of 'unless' that is generally presumed in logic. Then the logic of (7.39) and (7.40) is standard. If one affirms the antecedent (which happens to contain a negative term)—the guest cannot distinguish the two wine varietals, then one affirms the consequent (which also contains a negative term)—so, he is not a wine expert. However, the ability to distinguish these two varietals is not sufficient to constitute anyone as a wine expert. Thus, (7.39) expresses a necessary condition.

Now, suppose that the class is planning a picnic and I promise:

> I will go to the picnic unless it rains.   (7.41)

It does rain, but I show up anyway. Have I broken my promise? Let's consider two different ways of translating (7.41) into classy language:

> I will go to the picnic if it does not rain.   (7.42)

> I will not go to the picnic if it does rain.   (7.43)

Here sentence (7.42) unpacks (7.41) the same way that (7.40) unpacked (7.39). In both cases the term *unless* is replaced by an antecedent of the form 'if . . . not'. Then in (7.42) one could affirm the antecedent—it is not raining—and so affirm the consequent—so I go to the picnic. However, if one denies the antecedent—it does rain—then nothing follows. If this construal is correct, then I have not broken my promise (7.41) by going to the rainy picnic. However, I believe that most people hearing this promise, (7.41), would interpret the 'unless' as equivalent to *if and only if . . . not,* or (7.42) + (7.43). In this stronger sense of 'unless' as expressing necessary and sufficient conditions (7.41) should be unpacked as

> I will go to the picnic if and only if it does not rain.   (7.44)

Sometimes a context makes it clear that this stronger sense is intended. Suppose, for example, I go to the rainy picnic and in a discussion inform a student:

I will give you an F, unless you do well on the final.   (7.45)

She does well on the final; but I'm in a mean mood and give her an F anyway. When she arranges for a hearing before a university fairness committee I explain that by (7.45) I meant

I will give you an F if you do not do well on the final.   (7.46)

Then I explain to them that for her to claim "I did well on the final (or it is not the case that I did not do well), so I should not get an F" involves the fallacy of denying the antecedent. However, she has learned her logic. She counters by saying that (7.45) should be interpreted as also including:

I will not give you an F if you do well on the final.   (7.47)

What should the fairness committee decide?

In this case I think that they would have to decide in favor of the student. The promise made in (7.45) includes both (7.46) and (7.47). Or, doing well on the final is a necessary and sufficient condition for not getting an F.

'Unless' had the strong sense of expressing necessary and sufficient conditions in these examples, not so much because of the logic of 'unless', but because of the logic of promises. This strong sense should not be presumed, unless there is some special reason for so presuming. That is, "p, unless q" always implies "if not-q, then p." Whether or not it also implies "if q, then not-p" is context dependent. Since logic is concerned with forms detached from contexts, it uses the weaker sense of 'unless'.

EXERCISES

A. 1. If a necessary condition is fulfilled, does the consequent always follow?
   2. If a sufficient condition is fulfilled, does the consequent always follow?
   3. Consider the statement: "I will agree, provided that he also agrees." Should this 'provided that' be interpreted as meaning 'if' or 'if and only if'?
   4. If A is a necessary condition for B, what can be said of B as a condition for A?
   5. If A is a necessary and sufficient condition for B, what can be said of B as a condition of A?
   6. State whether the item on the left is a necessary condition for the item on the right, a sufficient condition, or both:

being female	being a mother
First Lady	wife of current President

having ten dimes	having 25 cents
having 25 cents	having twenty-five pennies
well coordinated	trapeze artist
winning Pulitzer prize	a successful writer
triangle	plane geometric figure
Pope	Roman Catholic

B.   For the following arguments:

    A. determine whether each is valid or invalid;

    B. give a reason for validity or invalidity.

* 1. Superman will escape the fiendish plot only if he can remove the debilitating kryptonite in time. He will remove the kryptonite in time. So, he will escape the plot.

* 2. Triangles M and N are congruent if and only if two sides and the included angle of M are equal to two sides and the included angle of N. M and N are congruent triangles. Therefore, two sides and the included angle of M are equal to two sides and the included angle of N.

3. Passing the state bar exam is a necessary condition for practicing law in this state. John did not pass the bar exam. So, he cannot practice law in this state.

4. Being the star of a hit TV series is certainly a sufficient condition for being a celebrity. Brooke is not the star of any TV series. So, she can't be a celebrity.

* 5. A person is guilty of first degree murder if and only if that person did commit a murder and did so with malice aforethought. Henry was judged not guilty of first-degree murder. So, he can't be a killer.

6. If Senator Gillis introduces a gun-control bill, then her chance of being selected as the vice-presidential candidate is significantly decreased. So, she doesn't really desire to be a vice-presidential candidate if she introduces a gun-control bill.

M.   For questions 1–10 use the code:

    A. Valid agreement: direct inference.

    B. Invalid argument: fallacy of denying the antecedent.

    C. Valid argument: indirect inference.

    D. Invalid argument: fallacy of affirming the consequent.

    E. Valid argument: hypothetical syllogism.

* 1. I will accept the position, provided that there is a guarantee of job security. I'll have to move my family if I accept the position. So, if there is a guarantee of job security, then I will have to move my family.

* 2. Winning a tournament is a necessary condition for being a seeded tennis player. Virginia has won a tournament. So, she must be a seeded tennis player.

3. Winning a Nobel prize in chemistry is a sufficient condition for being listed in *Who's Who among American Scientists*. Bernstein is not listed in that *Who's Who*. So, he couldn't have won the Nobel prize in chemistry.

* 4. Not having a felony conviction is a necessary condition for admission to the police academy. Smith has a felony conviction. So, he can't be admitted to the police academy.

5. The TV set will work only if it's plugged in. If you'll look under the couch, you'll see that this set is plugged in. So, it will work.

6. A chemical may be included in the food processing only if it is not a known carcinogen. The chemical you are referring to is known to be a carcinogen. So, it cannot be included in the food processing.

7. No one can be considered a real sailor unless he or she has ridden out a storm at sea. Joe has never ridden out a storm at sea. So, he can't be considered a real sailor.
8. A person is a member of the Assembly if and only if he or she is duly elected and takes the oath of office. Sellars was duly elected. Yet, she never became a member of the Assembly. So, she must have declined to take the oath of office.
*9. A student becomes a member of Sigma Alpha Phi fraternity if and only if he is voted in by a majority of the members. If a student becomes a member of SAP then he is welcome at SAP beer blasts. So, if a student is voted into SAP by a majority of the members, then he is welcome at SAP beer blasts.
10. A new automobile is satisfactory only if all the parts are as advertised. This automobile is clearly unsatisfactory. So, all the parts cannot be as advertised.

7.7 ALTERNATION AND DISJUNCTION

The Kennedy family slogan was reputed to have been: Second best is a loser. This could be expressed in the form

One is either a winner or a loser.   (7.48)

Here the term 'or' certainly indicates an exclusive relation. One cannot be both a winner and a loser. The same holds true for such familiar dichotomies as: alive or dead, with us or against us, part of the solution or part of the problem, in or out. In each case one is presented with a pair of opposing terms. Being a member of one half of the pair excludes being a member of the other.

The word 'or' does not always function that way. Suppose that you take out an insurance policy that stipulates that benefits will be paid if you are sick or disabled. You come down with a severe case of the hepatitis and then break your leg in an automobile accident on the way to the hospital. You contact your insurance agent to being collecting payments. After he listens to your case he explains with a genial smile, "Sorry, but you are not eligible for benefit payments. The contract specifies that benefits will be paid if you are sick *or* disabled. Since you are both sick and disabled, you don't fulfill the conditions of the contract." Have you been cheated?

You sure have. The 'or' in this contract should be interpreted as being *inclusive,* rather than exclusive. In real contracts, not the artificial one just discussed, this is often indicated by replacing 'or' with 'and/or'. When used in this inclusive sense "either A or B" means that either A is true, or B is true, or both are true. In logical contexts the term 'or' is always taken in the inclusive sense and is symbolized by '∨'. In many computer languages the exclusive 'or' is symbolized by 'xor'. Disjunction is a related notion. To express disjunction in English we use, "Not both p and q." In logic this would be expressed by "p|q." Before discussing the way these three interrelated terms are used we will present their truth tables.

P	Q	(P ∨ Q)	(P XOR Q)	(P|Q)	
T	T	T	F	F	
T	F	T	T	T	
T	T	T	T	T	
F	F	F	F	T	(7.49)

Inclusive or ∨ *:* The pattern is:

Either p or q.	Either p or q.	
Not p.	Not q.	
Therefore, q.	Therefore, p.	(7.50)

The major of this alternative syllogism informs us that at least one of the two propositions, p or q, is true. The minor tells us that one of them is not true. So the conclusion affirms that the other one is true. This can be read off the truth table for (p ∨ q). The only row which has F for p and T for (p ∨ q) has T for q; the only row which has F for q and T for (p ∨ q) has T for p. It may easily be seen that alternative syllogisms are equivalent to the hypothetical inferences just considered. Compare (7.50) with:

Direct inference	*Indirect inference*	
If not-p, then q.	If not-p, then q.	
Not-p.	Not-q.	
Therefore, q.	Therefore not not-p (or p).	(7.51)

Disjunction is illustrated by the case of the state governor who wishes to take over a U.S. Senate seat that has just been vacated. Before being appointed a senator, he must first resign as governor. The law is clear: One can not be both a governor and a senator simultaneously. The inference pattern here is:

Not both p and q.	Not both p and q.	
p.	q.	
Therefore, not-q.	Therefore, not-p.	(7.52)

This inference pattern differs from (7.50) in two respects. First, in (7.52) one *affirms* one disjunct and then, as a consequence, denies the other. Alternative inference involves a denial in the minor and an affirmation in the conclusion. Second, the major premise of a disjunctive syllogism asserts that both disjuncts cannot be true simultaneously. However, both may be false. Most of us spend our lives being neither a governor nor a senator. In the truth table (7.49) (p|q) is given the value T when p and q are both F. The contrast between disjunctives and alternatives is very much like the contrast between contraries and subcontraries considered in the last chapter.

When disjunctives are given in ordinary English, rather than in logic, the fact that they are disjunctives is usually indicated explicitly. We will list some standard forms used to express disjunctives and the equivalent hypotheticals:

Disjunctives	Hypotheticals	
Not both p and q.	p, only if not-q.	
Not p and also q.	If p, then not-q.	
Either not-p or not-q.	q, only if not-p.	(7.53)

Thus: "A girl cannot be both a lady wrestler and a prima ballerina"; "A man cannot be a saint and also a scoundrel."

Exclusive "or" (xor) was placed between the alternative and disjunctive forms on the truth table to indicate that it combines aspects of both patterns. In English it can be expressed explicitly by the form

Either p or q, but not both p and q.   (7.54)

However, the exclusive clause "but not both p and q" is not needed when it is clear from the meaning of the terms used that one excludes the other. Thus: dead or alive, a winner or a loser, safe or sorry, guilty or innocent, with us or against us, part of the solution or part of the problem. One can combine (7.54) with an alternative pattern or reasoning to get:

p xor q.	p xor q.	
Not-p.	Not-q.	
Therefore, q.	Therefore, p.	(7.55)

Or, one can combine (7.54) with the disjunctive pattern:

p xor q.	p xor q.	
p.	q.	
Therefore, not-q.	Therefore, not-p.	(7.56)

Ordinary English (and some text books on informal reasoning) does not always make a clear distinction between disjunctive and exclusive or forms. However, when precision is desired these are some standard forms for expressing the exclusive 'or' in English together with their equivalent hypotheticals:

Either p or q, but not both.   If p, then not-q and if not-p,
p or q (when p and q are   then q.
mutually incompatible).   p is equivalent to not-q.   (7.57)

Anyone who wishes to study these forms and their interrelations in more detail should consult a book on symbolic logic. Then you would find, for example, that (p xor q) is equivalent to $\sim$(p $\equiv$ q).

EXERCISES

A. 1. Find two examples of alternative propositions, different from those given in the text, which clearly involve the inclusive sense of 'or'.
  2. Find two examples, different from those given in the text, of sentences using the exclusive sense of 'or'.
  3. Would it be correct to express a disjunction by the form: "At least one of these two, p or q, is false"?
  4. What pattern of reasoning, if any, governs "Neither p nor q"?
  5. Can you cite any language that has different terms for the inclusive and exclusive senses of 'or'?

B.   For each of the following arguments:

  A.   indicate whether or not it is valid;
  B.   indicate what pattern is followed (for valid inferences) or violated (for invalid inferences).

 *1. It is not possible to be both a gourmet and a vegetarian. Ellie must be a vegetarian, because she sure is no gourmet.
  2. The leading actor in this play has to be either handsome or quite athletic. Tom got the lead role, and he's no athlete. So, he must be handsome.
  3. A girl is either intelligent or beautiful. Marie is beautiful. So, she can't be intelligent.
  4. Either it is raining or it is not raining. It is not raining. Therefore, it is raining.
 *5. No one can be a drinker and, at the same time, a member in good standing of Dubuque teetotalers club. Joe is a member of the club in good standing. So, he can't be a drinker.
  6. Either we get rain within the next two weeks or the crops will be ruined. The weather reports assure us that there will be no rain. So, the crops will be ruined.
  7. Hamlet could not have both believed his father's ghost and also doubted his uncle's guilt. He seemed, at least initially, doubtful of his uncle's guilt. So, he could not have believed his father's ghost.
  8. It is not possible to be both a world class runner and also a cigarette smoker. Josephine is no longer a smoker. So, now she must be a world class runner.
  9. That overenthusiastic handshake I just received must signal either a politician or a salesman. Oh, I recognize the guy now; he's a used-car salesman. So, he can't be a politician.
 *10. Either the blouse and skirt have compatible colors, or your outfit looks tacky. Since you have just finished a seminar on color coordination, you should no longer have incompatible colors in your blouse and skirt combinations. So, you should not look tacky any more.

M.   In answering the following questions use the code:

A.   Valid: alternative argument.
B.   Valid: disjunctive argument.
C.   Invalid: neither alternative denied.
D.   Invalid: neither disjunct affirmed.
E.   Invalid: consequence goes beyond premises.

1.   Since Julie is collecting her health insurance, she must be either sick or disabled. She's obviously not disabled. So, she must have hepatitis.
*2.   It is not possible to be a timid person and also a successful salesman. Herman is as timid as any man I've ever seen. So, Herman cannot be a successful salesman.
3.   There is no way you can continue your present life style and not have further heart problems. In spite of this warning you insist that you will not change your life style. So, my friend, you are going to have heart problems.
4.   Linda can't be both over fifty years of age and also be pregnant. The tests show that she is not pregnant. So, she must be over fifty.
*5.   Either he was temporarily insane or he's guilty of first-degree murder. The psychiatric tests conclusively show that he was not insane at the time of the crime. Therefore, he is guilty of first-degree murder.
6.   She's someone famous, either a movie star or a TV celebrity. Now I remember her. She had the lead role in the movie, *Ordinary People.* So, she can't be a TV celebrity.
7.   There is no way that you can continue to flunk math courses and yet succeed as a theoretical physicist. However, your recent report card shows that you did not flunk math last semester. So, you are sure to succeed as a theoretical physicist.
8.   No one can neglect his health and also be a first-rate athlete. John has been neglecting his health. So, I conclude that he won't try out for the team.
*9.   It seems clear that we will either have to sell the house or borrow a lot of money. I've tried every bank and financial company in town and found that no one is willing to lend us any more money. So, we have no choice left. We'll have to sell the house.
10.   Congresswoman Greene was chair of the committee that approved the fraudulent contract. She must be either incompetent or dishonest. From past experience I know that she is incompetent. So, it seems clear that she can't be dishonest.

Truth Tables for Logical Connectives

p	q	(p & q)	(p ⊃ q)	(p ≡ q)	(p ∨ q)	(p xor q)	(p | q)
T	T	T	T	T	T	F	F
T	F	F	F	F	T	T	T
F	T	F	T	F	T	T	T
F	F	F	T	T	F	F	T

SUMMARY

HYPOTHETICAL INFERENCE:

Major premise: If p then q.
Three valid argument patterns
Direct inference: p. Therefore q.

Indirect inference: Not-q. Therefore, not-p.

Chain argument: If q, then r. So, if p, then r.

Two common fallacies (†—conclusion not validly inferred):

Denying the antecedent: not-p. †Therefore, not q.

Affirming the consequent: q. †Therefore p.

Variant forms:

English expression	*Standard form*
q, if p.	If p, then q.
q, provided that p.	
p is a sufficient condition for q.	
Whenever p, then q.	
p only if q.	
p is a necessary condition for q.	If q, then p.
p, if and only if (iff) q.	If p then q, and if q then p.
p, unless q.	(standard) If not-q, then p.
	(strong form) p, if and only if not-q.

Alternation and disjunction:

Alternation (valid for any use of 'or')

Either p or q.	Either p or q.
Not-p.	Not-q.

Therefore, q.

Therefore, p.

Disjunction

Not both p and q.	Not both p and q.
p.	q.

Therefore, not-q.

Therefore, not-p.

Exclusive 'or' (xor)

This supports both alternative and disjunctive argument patterns.

REFERENCES

[1]St. Thomas Aquinas, *Summa Contra Gentiles,* trans. Vernon Bourke (New York: Doubleday, 1956). bk. III, p. 123.

Chapter 8

THE EVIDENCE
AND THE EXPERTS

In chapter 5 we considered the basic differences between deductive and inductive reasoning considered as *patterns of argumentation.* We did not consider any theory of induction; we simply reflected on some ways of reasoning we already use. Informal inductive reasoning was seen to be characterized by two distinctive features. First, the truth of the premises does *not* guarantee the truth of the conclusion. It makes it more or less probable. Second, inductive reasoning is the natural pattern of reasoning when the point at issue is the relation between the evidence and the conclusion the evidence points to. In this chapter we wish to explore inductive reasoning in more detail. We will begin with the *practice* of inductive reasoning and try to clarify some significant features. There are conflicting theories of induction, each of which has its own difficulties. Fortunately, a description of the practice of inductive reasoning is only minimally dependent on theories of induction.

8.1 ARGUING FROM EVIDENCE

Let's begin with a manufactured example, but one that reflects a problem that an increasing number of parents confront. Joe and Sally Griesbach each work an eight-hour day. They have one daughter, Maureen, who is sixteen. Maureen generally takes the bus home from high school, and lets herself in with her own key. She usually spends the afternoon doing homework—so she'll be free in the evening, and then preparing dinner—for which she gets paid a weekly allowance.

One Friday afternoon Sally returned home at 5:45 to find the house empty. Maureen was not there and dinner was not ready. After putting a steak in the microwave oven to defrost, Sally began calling Maureen's friends. The results were inconclusive. No one knew where Maureen was; but some of her friends could not be reached. By the time Joe arrived home at 6:15 Sally was getting worried. Joe, whose relations with Maureen were already strained, muttered a few profane remarks about her new boyfriend and then said: "Let's eat without her; I can't be late for my bowling match tonight."

When Joe returned from his bowling match around 11:30 Sally was quite distraught. There was still no sign of Maureen. A suitcase was gone, along with much of Maureen's clothes and personal belongings. All of her friends had been contacted, except her new boyfriend, and no one knew anything. Maureen had been very secretive about her new boyfriend, because she knew her father would disapprove of him. All that her parents knew for sure was that she seemed to have an interest in someone named Chico. He was not a student, but Joe and Sally did not know what sort of work, if any, he did.

Eventually Joe and Sally contacted the police, the local hospitals, and even the morgue. Nothing turned up. There seemed to be only three possibilities left: Maureen had moved in with Chico, or she was a runaway, or she was kidnapped. Kidnapping for ransom was not likely, since Joe and Sally were not rich and no ransom note had been received. It was hardly likely that any kidnapper would have had her pack her clothes before leaving. Young girls, however, are sometimes kidnapped for purposes other than ransom and sometimes cooperate with abductors who promise them the world.

Sally talked the situation over with her pastor and finally got Joe, who was not a church-goer, to attend a counseling session. Joe's usual reserve broke down. He admitted that he felt uptight, even somewhat threatened, in Maureen's presence because of her precocious sexuality. He covered up his feelings and warded off temptation by being cold and harsh with her, and by being jealous of any boy she went out with. Sally, who felt the tension between them, was also harsh with Maureen. However, she encouraged Maureen to go out with boys and dropped some taunting remarks about the fact that she herself had become a real woman by the time she was Maureen's age. The three of them decided that Maureen had probably run away from home. The best they could think of was to wait for Maureen to contact them and then try to convince her that her home situation would be better if she returned.

Instead of stretching out this sorrowful saga we will go back over it and reflect on the reasoning employed. The starting point was an anomaly, something different from what was expected. The anomaly in this case was the fact that Maureen was absent when her parents expected her to be home. In this case, as with most anomalies, there is no direct inference from the puzzle to the solution. The process of reasoning involved is one referred to as *hypothetical–deductive*. We will first explain it schematically and then fill in the details.

The first two steps in hypothetical–deductive inference are:

1.   There is an anomaly (A), or puzzling fact;
2.   If a certain hypothesis, (H), were true, then the anomaly would be explained.

The fact that a certain hypothesis would explain the anomaly is *not* a sufficient reason for considering the hypothesis to be true. If (H1) Maureen had been teleported out of the galaxy by aliens from an invisible spaceship, then her absence would be explained. An indefinite number of such hypotheses could be developed. Each could explain the anomaly; that is the reason why it was introduced. So, we move on to step three:

3.   Test the truth of H.

We can make an initial distinction between two different types of tests, direct and indirect. Sally's initial hypothesis (H2) was that Maureen was in her room. She tested this by looking in her room. Her next few hypotheses were that she was visiting Mary (H3), Jenny (H4), or some other girl friend (H5) . . . Calling Mary and asking whether or not Maureen is there is a fairly direct test of H3. It involves some presuppostions, for example, that Mary is not lying. But these are routine presuppositions.

The next hypothesis is a bit deceptive: (H6) Maureen is in a hospital. In terms of testing, this must be considered a disjunction. Maureen is in hospital A, or hospital B, or . . . , until all the hospitals have been listed. This hypothesis is a generalization, but a very limited generalization. One can check it by testing to see if she is in hospital A or hospital B, and so on until the list has been exhausted.

The next two hypotheses considered were: (H7) Maureen was kidnapped, and (H8) Maureen ran away. Under the circumstances, neither one of these can be tested directly. One cannot look up "Kidnappers" in the telephone Yellow pages and keep calling until the right one is reached. Nor is there any standard sanctuary where run-away children can be located. This is where the hypothetical-*deductive* aspect of the inference pattern emerges. If Maureen were kidnapped, then she would be missing. H7 implies A. But it implies more than A. If Maureen were kidnapped for ransome, then the kidnappers would send a ransom note. If she were kidnapped or abducted, then she would not have a chance to pack her belongings in her own suitcase. Since no note was received and her clothes were taken, this hypothesis seems to be eliminated.

The only plausible hypothesis left is that Maureen ran away. This fits all the evidence including the assessment of Maureen's motives. This hypothesis does not have any implications that supply a decisive test. The best that Joe and Sally could do was to assume that *if* Maureen ran away, then she would probably send a note sooner or later, informing them that she is well—or that she has changed her mind and wants to come back.

This is a pattern of reasoning that is common in daily life and even more common in science. To explain an anomaly, A, one introduces a hypothesis, H. The inference pattern is: if H then A. This, by itself, does not mean much. One already knows that A is true. The problem is to determine whether or not H is true. Hence, one tries to find other things that H implies. In the next section we will illustrate how such reasoning is used in science through a detailed examination of one historical incident. Before doing that we wish to consider the logic involved in more detail.

To make the logic more concrete we will focus on a particular example. Look at a globe of the world. You can see that if Africa were pushed over, then Africa and South America would fit together like two pieces in a jig-saw puzzle. I will consider this surprizing fact the anomaly to be explained, A. Now to explain it I will entertain the hypothesis (H) that Africa and South America were once joined together and have since drifted apart. The fact that if H is true, then A follows, is hardly an adequate reason for believing A. So I try to see what other conclusions (C) follow from H. A few come rather quickly. If the two continents were once together and have since drifted apart, then (C1) rock formations on the west coast of Africa should match rock formations on the east coast of South America. Also (C2) plant life on the west coast of Africa should match plant life on the east coast of South America. Animal life might not match, because animals are more mobile. Finally, if the continents are drifting apart, then (C3) there must be some force responsible for pushing them apart.

Suppose I test C1, C2, and C3, and find them all true. Does that suffice to establish the truth of H? Not by the logic given in the last chapter. In each case we have the inference pattern: if H then C. We test C and find that it is true. To conclude on this ground that H is true would seem to be a very clear case of the *fallacy* of affirming the consequent. It does not matter, from the point of view of logic, how many consequences are tested and found to be true. None of them individually or collectively would seem to be able to establish the truth of H.

Here the practice of science seems to contradict the teaching of logic. There is usually no other way to test a hypothesis besides testing the consequences that flow from it. If these test out, then scientists usually consider this a good reason for believing the hypothesis. For example, the hypothesis just discussed was a simplified version of the continental-drift hypothesis introduced by the German meteorologist Alfred Wegener in 1915. It won little acceptance for fifty years, because no plausible mechanism was introduced to explain the forces responsible for continental drift. After a mechanism for explaining this drift was developed (the continents ride on huge underground plates that float on molten rock) and other implications of the hypothesis checked out, then most scientists accepted the continental-drift hypothesis.

In this case, as in the disappearance case, the practice of reasoning does not really contradict logic. There are further considerations involved. We can get at these in a schematic form. Suppose that two hypotheses, H1 and H2, have been introduced to explain some anomaly, A. In each case we have the inference pattern, if H then A. We look for further consequences. Suppose we were to find that H1 implies that C is true while H2 implies that C is false. This gives us two further inference patterns: if H1 then C; if H2 then not-C. Suppose we test and find that C is true. We cannot directly infer H1 without the fallacy of affirming the consequent. However, we can use *indirect inference* to infer that if C is true then H2 is false. If H1 and H2 are the only hypotheses that can explain C and H2 is false then, by disjunctive inference, H1 must be true.

In practice we rarely get a case where there are only two competing hypotheses. More often, an indefinite number are possible. What is usually done here is to grade them in levels of plausibility. Let's return to the disappearance example. On the first level of plausibility Maureen's parents assumed that her absence could be explained in terms of her normal behavior patterns. This led to a finite number of hypotheses. Maureen might be at Mary's house, or Jane's house, or at the house of her new boyfriend, if she really has such a boyfriend. Some of these possibilities were eliminated by telephone calls. Others were effectively eliminated by presuming normal behavior patterns. If she stayed overnight at a girlfriend's house, she would not go two days without notifying her parents. Thus, all the girlfriend hypotheses were eliminated.

On the next level of plausibility were hypotheses of the nature: something awful has happened. When her parents learned that Maureen was not in jail, or in a hospital, or in the morgue, some of these hypotheses were eliminated. Eventually, only three hypotheses remained on this level of plausibility. She was kidnapped, she ran away from home, or she ran off with her new boyfriend. The facts that she took a suitcase full of clothes, her jewelry, and the teddy bear she sleeps with, and that no ransom note was received would seem to eliminate the kidnapping hypothesis. The only reasonable hypothesis remaining is that she ran away from home, either by herself or to be with her new boyfriend.

This hypothesis might be wrong. If Maureen were discovered in a hospital in another town then the run-away hypothesis would be falsified. As long as it is not falsified, it seems to be the most reasonable hypothesis to accept. One can, of course, postulate higher levels of plausibility (or implausibility). Maureen's disappearance would be explained if she had been teleported out of the solar system, if she entered a time warp and emerged in the far future, if she shrunk to submicroscopic size, of if she had been transformed into a bat. Though all of these hypotheses have been treated in films, none of them would be taken seriously as possible explanations of Maureen's disappearance.

There is no automatic pattern of reasoning or set of rules of inference leading from anomalies to the hypotheses that might explain them. There are, however, some guidelines. In stating them we are merely making explicit what is implicit in ordinary practice. The examples so far considered suggest two guidelines for introducing hypotheses.

The first guideline is the *conservative* principle. It is reasonable to start by assuming ordinary patterns of behavior, ordinary cause effect relations, and similar principles of everyday life. The initial group of hypotheses, the most plausible ones, are the ones that accord with already accepted principles and facts. Only if these are eliminated does one move on to intrinsically implausible hypotheses.

The *pragmatic* principle is the second guideline for introducing hypotheses. If all the hypotheses on a certain level of plausibility have been eliminated except one, and the existing evidence supports that one, then it is reasonable to act on the assumption that this hypothesis is true. This is not an instance of the logical fallacy of affirming the consequent. At issue here is the type of practical reasoning considered in chapter 4. Acting on the basis of a highly plausible hypothesis is usually a much more reasonable policy than suspending action until the hypothesis is conclusively proven.

In the rest of this section we will consider some examples of inductive arguments based on the relation between evidence and hypotheses introduced to explain anomalies. The first example illustrates the way competing hypotheses are introduced and judged. The second, developed in more detail, illustrates how attempts to explain anomalies lead to chains of inferences.

1. The disappearance of the dinosaurs.   As archeologists study the fossil records, they try to trace the proliferation and evolution of plant and animal species. They have discovered that there have also been mass destructions. The evidence seems to indicate that at least three times in the past 570 million years there have been widespread and more or less simultaneous (the evidence on this point is difficult to interpret) extinctions of large numbers of species of animals and plants. The most puzzling of these extinctions occurred about 65 million years ago. Before that time dinosaurs roamed and ruled the earth. They represented the culmination of reptilian life forms that had dominated life on land for about 160 million years. There is no trace of dinosaurs after this period. They did not die alone. Most other species of large animals were extinguished around the same time. The sketchy evidence available suggests that almost every species of land animal whose mature members weighed more than twenty five pounds was extinguished. This is the anomaly we wish to consider, the great dinosaur die-out.

The first point to note is that the nature of the anomaly puts constraints on the type of hypotheses that are likely to explain it. The effect was sudden, by geological standards, worldwide, and somewhat selective. Some small animals, such as the protomammals from which later mammals evolved, survived. Large land-based reptilian forms were wiped out. The cause had to be some sort of worldwide catastrophe. Yet the catastrophe could not have been total, or nothing could have survived. A number of hypotheses have been introduced. Each explains the great dinosaur die-out, since each was introduced for this purpose. So they are generally tested by the further consequences of the hypotheses. We will summarize the leading hypotheses and the consequences that serve to test them.

H1: A stagnant Arctic Ocean. As mentioned earlier, the continents seem to be drifting. H1 assumes that about 70 to 80 million years ago the drifting made the Arctic Ocean into a large lake isolated from the other oceans. Because of the rain draining into it, it became less salty than the other oceans, and rather brackish. When, after some millions of years, further drifting opened the Arctic Ocean, the relatively light fresh water gradually spread out in the form of a chilly brackish layer covering the salt water. This could have lowered the surface temperature of the world's oceans by as much as 60 degrees centigrade. Such a drop in temperature would have drastically reduced the amount of water absorbed into the atmosphere, causing worldwide droughts. Extinction of plants would lead to the extinction of plant-eating animals and of the carnivores that prey on them. This is a plausible hypothesis. If it were true, then there should be evidence, especially in the ocean bottom underneath the Arctic, of such a fresh-water period. No such evidence has been found.

H2: Male Sterility. There is evidence contradicting H1. Deep seacores drilled around the world indicate that the ocean waters, and presumably the atmosphere as well, grew warmer some 65 million years ago. This suggested a new hypothesis. The larger an animal is the smaller is the ratio of its body size to its surface area. With relatively less skin area, it is harder to get rid of excess body heat. Elephants, for example, have gradually developed large ears and saggy, baggy skin to increase their skin area. If the worldwide temperature gradually increased, larger species, whose surface-to-volume ratio is low, would find it difficult to get rid of excess body heat. High temperatures tend to kill sperm. As an adaptive mechanism, a male's testicles descend when the body is heated, and snuggle closer to the body under cold conditions. The dinosaurs, which lacked such adaptive mechanisms, might have died out because the males became sterile. H2 would explain the great dinosaur die-out. However, it leads to the prediction that the large reptilian species would have died out while the smaller ones, presumably more efficient in getting rid of body heat, would have survived. The evidence seems to indicate that both types disappeared at about the same time.

H3: Cosmic Collisions. Most of the asteroids, or tiny planets, in our Solar System are in a ring between Mars and Jupiter. Some of them are in eccentric orbits that pass through the earth's orbit. When a tiny asteriod hits the earth's atmosphere, it burns up through frictional heating and is seen on earth as a shooting star. When a larger asteroid hits, much of its surface is evaporated, but the core can survive and hit the ground. In 1980 the team of physicist Luis Alvarez, his son, geologist Walter Alvarez, F. Asaro, and H. Michel proposed that 65 million years ago an asteroid about 6 miles in diameter collided with the earth. Because of its high velocity it would have dug a crater about 100 miles across. The dust and debris from this crater would have been thrown into the stratosphere and spread out by prevailing winds. There would have been enough dust to block the sunlight for an extended period. This would have killed the plants, the animals that live off the plants, and the large predators that live off those animals. The ancestors of mammals were small rodent-like forms. A dead dinosaur would supply months of food for even a large family of rodents. So this hypothesis explains both the extinction of the dinosaurs and the survival of the protomammals.

This hypothesis explains both the die-out and the selective nature of the extinction. It also has supporting evidence. For technical reasons it is assumed that the asteroid collision would have thrown relatively large amounts of the rare element, iridium, into the atmosphere. Relatively large traces of it have been found in layers of earth associated with this period. The discovery of this iridium layer, in fact, suggested the collision hypothesis. However, evidence from Hell Creek in Montana indicates that the dinosaurs in this area were wiped out long before the event that deposited the iridium. This finding does not conclusively falsify the collision hypothesis, but it does weaken its support.

H4: Massive Drug Overdose. This was suggested by Ronald Siegel, a psychiatrist from UCLA. Flowering pants evolved late in the dinosaur era. Many of them produced alkaloids, which are psychoactive drugs. Most mammals avoid them because they taste bitter. Also, the livers of most mammals have the ability to detoxify these drugs. If the dinosaurs lacked the capacity to detect bitter taste and also lacked livers capable of detoxifying alkaloid drugs, then the herbivores could have died of massive drug overdoses. The carnivores would then have perished with their vanishing prey. This hypothesis, unfortunately, cannot explain the simultaneous extinction of such creatures as ammonites and ocean plankton. There is no evidential support for the hypotheses that dinosaurs lacked the capacities to taste bitter alkaloids or to detoxify them.

H5: The Multiple Cause Hypothesis. Sooner or later, extinction is the normal end of every species. The age of the dinosaurs could not have lasted indefinitely. They might have been on their way to extinction due to multiple causes. A catastrophe, such as collision with an asteroid or an immense volcanic explosion, could have sped up an extinction that was already in progress. This hypothesis is hard to test directly, since it is general enough to accommodate almost any evidence. It does accommodate the evidence of some dinosaur extinction occurring before the catastrophe that deposited the iridium layer. However, it does not fit well with more recent evidence indicating that the dinosaur population was thriving until the great die-out.

H6: A Death Star. This hypothesis was introduced by Alvarez and some associates in 1984. Fossil records indicate periodic extinction events, occurring about every 28 million years. Another major extinction event occurred about 250 million years ago. The layer of earth that corresponds with this date also shows relatively high amounts of iridium. To account for this periodicity it is postulated that the sun has a companion star, a dark star with about one tenth of the sun's mass. This star travels in a highly elliptical orbit ranging from 14 trillion miles to 3 trillion and takes about 28 million years to complete one revolution. When this star is closest to the sun it passes through a region known as the Oort comet cloud, where more than 100 billion comets are traveling in rather circular orbits. The dark star could disrupt the orbits of a billion or so comets, putting some into highly elliptical orbits. This could cause some 20 to 30 comets, including some big ones, to strike the earth during a relatively short, by astronomical standards, interval. This hypothesis would explain the periodicity of mass extinctions, and their association with an iridium layer. It also leads to clear predictions. If such a death star exists it could be detected by putting an infrared telescope in orbit and observing the star.

The anomaly of the great dinosaur die-out has not yet been adequately explained. However, it seems most probable that further efforts will follow the pattern sketched above. New hypotheses will be introduced. For these and for the earlier hypotheses that still seem viable it will be necessary to work out the further consequences of each hypothesis. Such working out supplies a basis for determining what should count as confirming or refuting evidence. If the time ever comes when all plausible hypotheses except one have been effectively refuted and the surviving hypothesis is in accord with all the evidence, then it would be reasonable to accept this hypothesis as the explanation of the great dinosaur die-out.

2. Snow on cholera. The patterns of inductive and hypothetical-deductive reasoning we have been considering have played, and continue to play, a significant role in the advancement of science. It is for this reason that a detailed examination of incidents from the history of science supplies the clearest illustrations for the way these patterns of reasoning actually function. Contemporary science, unfortunately, tends to be too complex to supply examples suitable for an introductory account. The inductive reasoning reflected in technical articles and reports generally presupposes a detailed familiarity both with background theories and also with highly developed methods of scientific procedure. For our purposes it is better to consider cases from the more formative stages of scientific development.

John Snow's analysis of the causes and treatment of cholera is a good example of the way inductive reasoning is actually practiced for two reasons. First, it represents a significant step in the advancement of medicine, but a step that can be understood by people with no background in medicine. Second, Snow has supplied a very detailed account of the reasoning processes he actually followed. The summary that follows is based on his account.[1]

Plagues are widespread epidemics of contagious diseases. In ancient times they were thought of as forms of divine punishment. After the "black death," the bubonic plague that devastated much of Europe in the fourteenth century, people began to classify plagues into different types involving differing symptoms. In the nineteenth century a new plague appeared, cholera. The disease spread northwards and eastwards from India. In England cholera epidemics occurred between 1831 and 1832, 1848 and 1849, and 1853 and 1854. The victims were afflicted by watery diarrhea, vomiting, and cramps, often followed by collapse and death.

Cholera epidemics had one peculiar feature. They invariably struck the poor much more severely than the rich. Originally, many interpreted this as evidence that cholera was sent as a divine punishment against indolence, just as syphilis was interpreted as divine retribution against moral depravity. The working poor, however, suffered at least as much as the nonworking poor. The group that suffered the most, miners, included some of the hardest working people in England.

Many people contributed to an understanding of the cause and treatment of cholera, but the decisive role was played by John Snow (1813–1858). He got at the manner of communication of the disease by tracing the way in which it spreads. We will summarize his presentation of his reasoning.

> There are certain circumstances . . . connected with the progress of cholera, which may be stated in a general way. It travels along the great tracks of human intercourse, never going faster than people travel, and generally much more slowly. In extending to a fresh island or continent, it always appears first at a sea-port. It never attacks the crews of ships going from a country free from cholera, to one where the disease is prevailing, till they have entered port, or had intercourse with the shore. Its exact progress from town to town cannot always be traced; but it has never appeared except where there has been ample opportunity for it to be conveyed by human intercourse. [p. 2]

The conclusion Snow drew from these facts is that cholera is transmitted from the sick to the healthy. This still left the problem of determining *how* it is transmitted. Though the germ theory of disease had not yet been developed, it was known that different contagious diseases were transmitted in different manners: syphillis by sexual contact; the "itch" by physical contact with some one who had it. Other diseases, like typhoid and cholera, could be communciated without such physical contact. The prevailing hypothesis was that the diseased person gave off some sort of effluvia, or disease vapor.

Snow tested the effluvia hypothesis by examining its consequences. If the hypothesis were correct, then anyone in the vicinity of a cholera victim had an equal chance of contracting the disease. Yet the disease did not seem to spread that way. Members of the victim's families often contracted the disease. Members of the medical profession who attended the victim almost never contracted the disease. This was true even of those who performed post-mortem examinations. Any acceptable hypothesis had to account for this difference.

From an analysis of the progress of the disease, Snow concluded that cholera always begins with an infection of the alimentary canal. Those who contract the disease must swallow some morbid matter, matter too small to be seen under a microscope. Snow saw one way of accounting for the fact that members of the victim's family might inadvertently swallow some morbid matter, while members of the medical profession were not likely to do so.

> Nothing has been found to favour the extension of cholera more than want of personal cleanliness, whether arising from habit or scarcity of water, although the circumstances till lately remained unexplained. The bed linen nearly always becomes wetted by the cholera evacuations, and as those are devoid of the usual colour and odour, the hands of persons waiting on the patient become soiled without their knowing it; and unless these persons are scrupulously clean in their habits, and wash their hands before taking food, they must accidentally swallow some of the excretion, and leave some on the food they handle or prepare, which has to be eaten by the rest of the family, who, among the working classes, often have to take their meals in the sick room; hence the thousands of instances in which, amongst this class of the population, a case of cholera in one member of the family is followed by other cases; whilst medical men and others, who merely visit the patients, generally escape. The *post mortem* inspection of the bodies of cholera patients has hardly ever been followed by the disease that I am aware, this being a duty that is necessarily followed by careful washing of the hands; and it is not the habit of medical men to be taking food on such an occasion. [p. 17]

This hypothesis explained why the poor, who lived in crowded and unsanitary conditions and lacked a tradition of personal cleanliness, suffered from cholera more than the rich. It even explained why some professions were peculiarly vulnerable.

> The mining population of Great Britain have suffered more from cholera than persons in any other occupation, a circumstance which I believe can only be explained by the mode of communication of the malady above pointed out.

Pitmen are differently situated from every other class of workmen in many important particulars. There are no privies in the coal-pits, or, as I believe, in other mines. The workmen stay so long in the mines that they are obliged to take a supply of food with them, which they eat invariably with unwashed hands, and without knife and fork. [p. 19]

This hypothesis explained how cholera was transmitted from a victim to others who had contact with a victim. Yet, it did not explain the transmission of cholera to those who did not have any direct contact with a cholera victim. Snow introduced an auxiliary hypothesis to account for this: "but there is often a way open for it to extend itself more widely, and to reach the well-to-do classes of the community; I allude to the mixture of the cholera evacuations with the water used for drinking and culinary purposes, either by permeating the grounds and getting into wells, or by running along channels and sewers into the rivers from which entire towns are sometimes supplied with water." [p. 23]

The direct way to test this auxiliary hypothesis would be through a controlled experiment, giving one group of people drinking water thought to be contaminated with cholera material while giving a control group pure water. This however, would be highly unethical. Snow would not expose people to contaminated water. However, he did try to determine whether such an experiment had already been performed inadvertently. He found many cases of well water, or stream water used for drinking, that had been contaminated, chiefly by washing of the bed linen of cholera victims. Cholera was transmitted to people who used this contaminated water. This supported the auxiliary hypothesis. Yet the evidence was not conclusive.

Snow began a systematic examination of the correlation between the water supplied to different districts of London and the cholera rate. Much of the evidence was ambiguous. Two districts that differed in their water supply and also differed in their poverty levels might have different cholera rates. But it was not clear which factor was responsible for the difference in disease rates, the difference in the water supply or the difference in the standard of living. However, Snow found one district of South London where water was supplied by two different companies. One of these companies, the Lambeth Company, drew its water from waterworks upstream from London. The other, the Southwark and Vauxhall Company, drew its water from downstream, from areas contaminated by London sewage and refuse. This was the control experiment he had been seeking:

The experiment, too, was on the grandest scale. No fewer than three hundred thousand people of both sexes, of every age and occupation, and of every rank and station, from gentlefolks down to the very poor, were divided into two groups without their choice, and, in most cases, without their knowledge; one group being supplied with water containing the sewage of London, and amongst it, whatever might have come from cholera patients, the other group having water quite free from such impurity. [p. 75]

Snow began to examine the correlation between water supplies and cholera deaths during the previous cholera epidemic. While he was engaged in this investigation cholera returned to London. He switched his attention to the new cases. His results confirmed his hypothesis. For the then current epidemic he found: "There were forty-four deaths in these sub-districts down to 12th August, and I found that thirty-eight of the houses in which these deaths occurred were supplied with water by the Southwark and Vauxhall Company, four houses were supplied by the Lambeth Company, and two had pump-wells on the premises and no supply from either of the Companies." [pp. 76–77]

He returned to his systematic study of the correlations between cholera deaths and water supply during the epidemic of 1853. The results strongly supported his hypothesis.

> According to a return which was made to Parliament, the Southwark and Vauxhall Company supplied 40,046 houses from January 1st to December 31st, 1853, and the Lambeth Company supplied 26,107 houses during the same period; consequently, as 286 fatal attacks of cholera took place, in the first four weeks of the epidemic, in houses supplied by the former company, and only 14 in houses supplied by the latter, the proportion of fatal attacks to each 10,000 houses was as follows. Southwark and Vauxhall 71. Lambeth 5. The cholera was therefore fourteen times as fatal at this period, amongst persons having the impure water of the Southwark and Vauxhall Company, as amongst those having the purer water from Thames Ditton. [p. 80; The Lambeth company had moved its waterworks to Thames Ditton, above London, in 1852.]

Snow considered this to be conclusive evidence that his auxiliary hypothesis was correct. When he published his results he concluded his report with very specific suggestions for preventing the spread of cholera. The suggestions, not surprisingly, centered on personal cleanliness and public sanitation. It took a generation for these suggestions to be implemented in Europe and North America. In poorer countries, where there are not adequate sewage treatment facilities and where sewage and drinking water mix together, cholera epidemics perdured. It was not until 1968 that an effective and inexpensive method of treating cholera—victims drink copious amounts of water with glucose and salt added—was devised.

8.2 PATTERNS OF INFERENCE

We have been attempting to get at patterns of inductive reasoning inductively, beginning with examples rather than general rules. Now we wish to pull together what we have learned by indicating some general patterns of probabilistic inference. We will present the four basic steps and then comment on each.[2]

1. *The Anomaly:* A puzzling fact requiring explanation.
2. *Abduction:* Introducing explanatory hypotheses.
3. *Deduction:* Determining the consequences.
4. *Testing:* To see if these consequences obtain.

1. The Anomaly.   Something emerges as an anomaly because it is different from what we expect: Maureen's disappearance, the great dinosaur die-out, an epidemic of sudden deaths. What counts as an anomaly, accordingly, is relative to our expectations. There are many expectations that most of us share. These are based on the common-sense view of reality implicit in ordinary language. We expect behavior, whether of people, animals, or of nature, to manifest an underlying consistency and regularity. When the sun rises in the morning, the alarm clock goes off, the baby wants breakfast, the paper is delivered, the automatic coffee-maker produces coffee, there is heavy rush-hour traffic, the factory whistle blows at nine, the school day begins with the pledge of allegiance to the flag, people are normally dressed, the sun's in its heaven, and all's well with the world, then we hardly advert to such things. Our fundamental relationship to the lived world is one of activity. We use things to achieve purposes, individual and collective goals. Our habitual understanding of things is functional. We understand a hammer by hammering with it, a bus by riding on it. The world is encountered more as a workshop and toolbox than as an object of study.[3]

Things or events emerge as objects to be studied, rather than simply used, only when there is a breakdown, the hammer that does not work, the bus that does not go, the person who manifests erratic behavior. These are the anomalies that generally trouble us. The attempt to come to understand these anomalies is basically an attempt to fit them into our network of accepted facts and principles.

In addition to this common-sense framework that, in varying degrees, we all share, there are also specialized frameworks. Each profession and specialization tends to develop a characteristic terminology, an extension of ordinary language reflecting a battery of shared presuppositions and criteria of judgment. The clearest case of this is the use of a scientific theory. Some facts emerge as puzzling because they are not what is expected on the basis of accepted scientific theories or general laws. When the motion of a planet does not fit Kepler's laws of planetary motion, when a person diagnosed as schizophrenic does not experience hallucinations, when a disease does not respond to standard treatment, in such and similar cases a scientist spots an anomaly.

It may even happen that regular behavior is an anomaly, when a theory predicts irregular behavior. One of the great discoveries of modern astronomy is cosmic black-body radiation, a remnant of the big bang in which the universe originated. Scientists were initially gratified to note that, with suitable corrections for the motion of our galaxy, the radiation coming from all parts of space is uniform. Gradually, the very uniformity emerged as an anomaly. Standard big-bang models plus the theory of special relativity lead to the conclusion that spectral distributions should be more chaotic. At the time of this writing there is no adequate explanation of this anomaly. There is, however, a widely shared agreement that the way around this impasse is through a modification of the standard big-bang accounts of the first few milliseconds of the universe's history, not through any modification of the theory of special relativity.[4]

2. *Abduction.*   The term 'abduction' comes from C. S. Pierce, the founder of American pragmatism. It refers to the leap from an anomaly to an hypothesis that might explain it. There are no strict rules governing such leaps; they are a matter of discovery, of creative imagination. There are, however, some guidelines. The first involves a peculiar blending of daring and caution. It takes daring to introduce a novel explanatory hypothesis. One takes a chance of being shown wrong, perhaps of looking foolish. Yet, when confronted with an anomaly, some daring is needed. Any hypothesis, no matter how wild, is preferable to having no explanatory hypothesis at all. A false hypothesis leads to testable consequences and often to suggestions for revisions and adaptions. The lack of any explanatory hypothesis leads to conceptual chaos. Error, as Francis Bacon noted long ago, is much more productive of progress than confusion. If no good hypothesis occurs to you, then try a wild one. Run it up the flagpole, to adopt Madison Avenue jargon, and see if anyone salutes.

An interval of caution follows a moment of daring. The initial test of a new hypothesis concerns its *plausibility,* not its truth. At this stage one adopts the *conservative principle* mentioned earlier. Explanation is generally a matter of finding some way of fitting an anomaly into an accepted framework of facts and principles, of laws and regularities. The initial presumption is in favor of the hypothesis that involves the least change in our accepted framework.

3. *Deduction.*   The inital hypothesis is often one of a class of competing hypothesis. Often a novel hypothesis is nebulous about some details. Maureen's parents assumed that she ran away, but did not know where or with whom. Wegener assumed that the continents were drifting, without knowing a force that could explain that drift. Snow assumed the cause of cholera to be something too small to be seen under any microscope then available, yet something that preserved its structure in water rather than being diluted as a chemical would be. He could not offer any plausible account of what that something might be.

Hypotheses are initially judged in terms of plausibility, not truth. Testing begins in a similar vein. Initially, one is often concerned with the question, not of which hypotheses are true, but of which hypotheses can be eliminated. This is generally done by showing that some hypotheses lead to consequences that are at variance with the facts, or with accepted general principles. This is a matter of deduction, of showing that if a certain hypothesis were true then certain consequences would follow. With these hypotheses eliminated, one is then in a position to concentrate on the one, or few, hypotheses that remain plausible. The question then is how well each of these hypotheses is supported by the evidence.

4. Testing.   In some segments of *Sesame Street* the detective Sherlock Hemlock imitates his famous namesake by ceaselessly searching for clues. Unfortunately for him, there are no such things as clues pure and simple. Clues are a form of evidence, and evidence is only evidence relative to an hypothesis and a problem. An hypothesis, in fact, generally determines what sorts of things would count as evidence for or against the hypothesis. When Snow introduced the hypothesis that the morbid matter causing cholera is transmitted through drinking water, then it was important to investigate the correlation between different sources of drinking water and cholera rates. This evidence would have no significance in testing the hypothesis that cholera is transmitted by some effluvia in the air, or that it is transmitted only by contact with cholera victims.

Evidence is relative to an hypothesis. More as a matter of convenience than of precision, we can divide hypotheses into two types, particular and general. By a 'particular hypothesis' we mean an assumption that some particular fact obtains or that some particular event happened; that, for example, Maureen ran away, that a big meteor hit the earth 65 million years ago, that Richard Nixon personally produced the famous eighteen-and-a-half minute gap in the Watergate tapes. By a 'general hypothesis' we mean an assumption concerning a general correlation such as an empirical law (all planets travel in elliptical orbits; all metals conduct electricity), or a causal connection (cholera is caused by a submicroscopic entity that preserves its structure in water; an unbalanced federal budget produces inflation). In the next chapter we will investigate some systematic methods of serching for and testing general connections. Here we will treat the relation of evidence to particular hypotheses.

Let's begin by considering the way evidence supports a few hypotheses. The *National Enquirer* ran a feature story with the headline:

Noted UFO Expert Declares: Millions of Pets Are Really Space Aliens

The noted expert was introduced as "noted alien researcher and author Brad Steiger." His hypothesis was "One out of five dogs and cats are space pets—descendents of original alien creatures that were 'seeded' on earth 50,000 years ago." The evidence for this hypothesis was that roughly one out of every five dogs or cats have very charismatic personalities, extremely protective natures, very compelling eyes, and healing powers. The sure sign that a particular dog or cat is descended from aliens is when someone dreams about her or his dog or cat in a remote and alien landscape. Confirming evidence for this hypothesis came from the agreement of three more UFO-ologists cited in the article.[5]

This argument seems to parallel the argument presented earlier attributing the great dinosaur die-out to the impact of a big meteor. Both argue from present evidence (fossil remains, peculiar behavior of some pets) to an event in the prehistoric past. Let's examine the parallel a bit more closely.

The hypothesis of meteor impact would, if true, explain the dinosaur die-out. It was introduced for this purpose. But the hypothesis also has a certain intrinsic plausibility. Asteroids of the postulated size pass within the earth's orbit. Though the chance of a collision on any particular orbit is small, there is a statistically significant chance of having a major collision in a large number of orbits. The hypothesis would also explain the selective nature of the evidence: most large animals died out, apparently at the same time; some smaller species survived. Finally the hypothesis leads to further testable conclusions in addition to the evidence it was postulated to explain. Layers of earth that can be dated as of this era should manifest relatively large amounts of iridium.

The alien pet hypothesis might also explain uncharacteristic behavior of some dogs and cats—it was introduced for that purpose. What intrinsic plausibility does it have? No plausible reason was presented, or even suggested, as to why aliens might want to seed the earth with pseudopets. Apart from the anomaly it is introduced to explain, there is no independent evidence offered to support the hypothesis of alien visitation. The article suggests no further testable consequences. Yet there should be some. Alien dogs and cats should, presumably, have some internal differences in their cells, in their DNA structure, in their inability to mate with nonalien forms. No such consequences are considered or tested. Finally, there is no account offered to explain why alien pets should have extremely charismatic personalities, extremely protective natures, very compelling eyes, and healing powers. There is, in other words, no *explanatory* relation between the hypothesis introduced and the data is is supposed to explain. The evidence supporting the alien-pet hypothesis is utterly worthless.

Let's consider another anomaly and the hypotheses introduced to explain it. On November 21, 1973, lawyers representing the White House informed Judge John Sirica, who was presiding over the 'Watergate' trial, that an eighteen-and-a-half minute segment was erased from the tape recording made in the President's Oval Office on June 20, 1972—a tape of a conversation between President Nixon and his chief of staff, H. R. Haldeman. Two months later a panel of technical experts reported to the Court that the tape gap was the result of at least five separate manual erasures. This implied that someone listened to the tape, went back and erased a section, listened some more and erased some more, and did this five times. The question was: Who did the erasing?[6]

Further investigation to determine when the tape was removed from storage indicated that the erasures must have been made one weekend when Nixon had the tapes at Camp David. Since only three people had access to the tapes that weekend, there seemed to be only four plausible hypotheses to account for the eighteen-and-a-half minute gap. The first hypothesis was that the gap was simply an accident. This was the explanation originally given by spokesmen for the White House and rejected by the technical experts hired by the Court. This left only three plausible hypotheses. H1: Rosemary Woods did it. H2: Stephen Bull did it. H3: Richard M. Nixon did it. Let's consider each.

H1 is initially the most plausible. Rosemary Woods was President Nixon's private secretary. She transcribed the tapes and typed them out. She also testified that she thought she was responsible for the erasures. She explained how she might have done this by accidently pushing a foot-control at the wrong time. However, it was later shown that she could not have reached the foot-control from her position in the chair at the time she was transcribing the tapes.

Stephen Bull was a technical expert hired by Nixon for assistance with the tapes. He worked with President Nixon on the tapes during the weekend stay at Camp David. There is, however, very little likelihood that a man who is a technical expert on tape recordings would make five successive accidental erasures. It is even less likely that a person hired as a technical expert would deliberately erase tapes of crucial conversations between the President and his top assistant on his own without authorization from the President.

This seems to leave only H3: Richard M. Nixon did it. He had the opportunity; he had the motive; no other hypothesis seems to fit the facts. Yet this cannot be considered conclusive proof. At issue here is a charge of criminal behavior. The issue of adequate proof should be settled in a court of law in accord with criteria of proof in criminal trials. On September 8, 1974, President Gerald Ford pardoned Richard Nixon for all federal crimes that he might have committed while serving as President. The issue of his guilt, which could definitively establish H3, was effectively blocked from settlement in any court.

These examples have considered evidence within a common-sense framework, one not requiring any specialized knowledge. This is the familiar framework we assimilate as part of growing up and learning a language. It functions well for the lived world of ordinary experience. Yet is has limitations. Consider a simple example. Suppose that you are walking forward at a brisk pace while holding a stone at shoulder level. What happens to the stone if you release it? First try to answer this and then test it by performing an experiment. Next suppose that the stone is tied to a string and that you whirl it round and round in a circle over your head. What kind of a path would the stone take if the string broke?

Surveys were taken among college students to determine the intuitive answers to these questions.[7] Those who had either not studied physics, or who did not relate the physics they studied to the world they experienced tended to give the intuitive common-sense answers. The stone the walker drops falls down in a straight line. The whirled stone travels in a curved path when the string breaks. These are the intuitive answers. Both are wrong. Actually, the stone dropped by the walker moves forward, while it falls, at the same rate the walker does. So, it travels in a curved path, a parabola. The stone whirled in a circle travels in a straight line when the string breaks. Both of these conclusions, which may be easily tested, are elementary applications of Newton's laws of motion.

Newtonian physics represents a major step beyond the common-sense framework. It has been followed by many more such steps, which represent successive and usually greater departures from the common-sense framework. A college education provides an introduction to some of these specialized fields. Our immediate concern, however, is not with assimilating such specialities, but with understanding the role they play in evaluating and using evidence. We will focus on the most straightforward use of specialized knowledge. One consults an expert, a person with specialized knowledge, and then relies on his or her evaluation.

8.3 EXPERTS

Relying on experts to evaluate evidence is a routine part of ordinary life. Sam Browne comes down with some peculiar ailment and doesn't know what to do about it. He consults a doctor. In addition to his own routine examination the doctor refers Sam to a hospital clinic for further tests. In the clinic, technicians take specimens of blood, urine, stool, and skin for further tests. The doctor also makes an appointment for Sam to have gastrointestinal tests requiring a barium enema and X-rays of the stomach and intestines. Sam is consulting an expert, the doctor, who in turn is consulting other experts, clinical diagnosticians, X-ray technicians, and others.

Reliance on experts is now a routine part of ordinary experience. We rely on the advice of experts when we have legal problems, when we have money to invest, when an automobile is not functioning properly, when we read reviews before deciding which movie to see, when we consult Dr. Spock's Baby Book, when we check weather reports before planning a picnic. In addition to the experts we consult on our own, we are barraged with expert advice in newspapers, TV ads, junk mail, and public lectures. "Scientific findings have shown that our product is best." Experts testify that one product corrects baldness, that contributing money to some cause will improve the condition of the atmosphere, or the survival of the bald eagle, or get pornography off TV.

The inference pattern we are expected to follow in all these cases is very simple and straightforward.

> Experts testify that X is true.
> Therefore, X is true.

In many cases, especially when we are seeking out expert advice, we simply follow this inference pattern. The doctor tells Sam Browne that tests reveal a peptic ulcer. So Sam accepts this as an established fact and follows the doctor's directions for treating an ulcer. The daily paper says that tomorrow will be clear and warm. So we decide on a picnic. A panel of experts agree that rocks found in Antarctica came from the Moon. So we accept that as true.

Yet, there are many cases where this line of reasoning is either doubtful or totally unreliable. When a defendant pleads innocent by virtue of insanity, his laywer usually produces a psychiatrist to testify that, in his expert opinion, the defendant was indeed insane at the time the crime was committed. But this expert usually testifies after the prosecution has produced its own psychiatrist to testify that, in her expert opinion the defendant was *not* insane at the time the crime was committed. Which expert should the jury believe? The simple inference formula given above does not settle this.

We can get conflicting advice from experts. We can also get untrustworthy advice from experts. When economists working for the oil companies testify before Congress that repeal of the windfall-profit tax is necessary for the economic well-being of the nation as well as of the oil companies, we have to evaluate their testimony in the light of our realization that the oil companies would not be likely to send an economist who gave any testimony in conflict with the interests of the oil companies. When an expert astrologer gives advice, the recipient has to consider the more general question of whether any astrological predictions have a claim to reasonable acceptance.

Before following any advice given by an expert we should evaluate the expert. It is often thought that an expert can only be evaluated by fellow experts. This is misleading. There are two different types of evaluations at issue here. The first is a test for professional competence. This does require people who are experts in the field. They generally have established methods for determining when some individual has achieved professional competence: passing the bar exam, getting an M.D. degree, going through a training program as an auto mechanic. The second is our evaluation of whether or not it is reasonable for us to accept the advice of an expert on some particular question. To get at this, the simple inference pattern given above should be expanded into a four-step inference pattern.[8]

1. An expert testified that X is true.
2. Therefore, the expert believes that X is true.

3. It is reasonable to accept this person as an expert on this question.
4. Therefore, it is reasonable for me to accept X as true.

Steps 1 and 4 summarize what is involved in *uncritical* acceptance of expert advice. Steps 2 and 3 concern the critical evaluation of this advice. These are the steps we will focus on.

An expert is, in general, a person with specialized knowledge or skill in some area. This expertise is usually the result of training, as one might become a computer expert by learning how to program in different computer languages, learning how to handle hardware as well as software, etc. Sometimes one becomes an expert on a particular issue just by virtue of circumstances. An eyewitness to an event is an expert on that particular event.

In addition to real experts we also have the phenomenon of apparent experts, people who look the way we expect experts to look. We are all familiar with commercials where a distinguished looking man wearing a white smock that makes him look like a doctor assures us that Bufferin works faster than aspirin. In fact, until there was a government crackdown, we regularly received assurances from apparent experts that aspirin works faster than Anacin and Bufferin, that Bufferin works faster than aspirin and Anacin, and that Anacin works faster than aspirin and Bufferin. In each case we were given the same evidence: "Laboratory tests have shown that . . . " The "trusted figure" plays the same role as the apparent expert. Celebrities with guaranteed audience acceptance are hired to endorse products because people trust them.

An expert is an expert because of specialized knowledge. If that knowledge is lacking, as with the apparent expert and the trusted figure, then the testimony has no special significance. There is no reason to believe that *they* believe what they are telling us. So there is no reason for us to believe it on the basis of their testimony. Until his retirement as anchorman, Walter Cronkite was, according to polls, the most trusted man in the United States. He refused to endorse any product; he took the people's trust seriously.

When we turn from apparent to real experts, the question of belief is still crucial. If an expert does not really believe what he or she is telling us, then the fact that the person is an expert has no significance. If the expert does not believe it, why should we believe it on the basis of the expert's testimony? But, how do we determine what the expert really believes? In most cases we can not crossexamine the expert or make an independent analysis of the evidence. If we could do that, then we would not need an expert.

Usually, the way around this impasse is a practical one. We are dealing with practical reasoning. The point at issue is not the inner mental state of some expert, but what it is reasonable for us to accept. Practical reasoning relies on presumptions. We presume that an expert really believes what she or he says, unless there is a *specific* reason for doubt. Rejection of expert advice on grounds such as "You can't trust anyone these days" gives us no basis for discriminating good advice from bad advice. A specific reason for doubt is some reason for believing that the expert may not really believe what he or she is telling us on this particular occasion.

This can be illustrated by considering two different types of reasons for doubting that an expert really believes what she or he is saying. The first and most obvious is when the expert has a motive for lying. A woman testifies before a jury that her son could not have committed the robbery because he was home with her on the evening in question. If he was home with her, she is, by virtue of these circumstance, an expert on his whereabouts that evening. Yet she has a motive for lying—the desire to keep her son out of jail. This is a specific reason for doubting that she really believes what she is saying. A specific reason for doubt is not usually an adequate reason for rejection. She may well be telling the truth. But a specific reason for doubt is adequate grounds for questioning, for trying to determine whether or not she is telling the truth. Anyone who has ever been on jury duty knows that the most difficult task most juries face is one of trying to determine which witnesses to believe.

Another situation that supplies specific ground for doubting that the expert really believes what he or she is saying is illustrated by the example of "the company spokesperson." Companies, political parties, government institutions, business associations, labor unions, and other types of institutions generally have official spokespeople whose task is to represent the institution to the public. The President's press secretary is an apt illustration. When the secretary informs the press that new economic measures are combatting inflation, that there is significant progress towards settling the Near-East crisis, or that there is hope for meaningful disarmament negotiations, he is telling them what he has been ordered to tell them. The announcement would be the same whether he believed what he is saying or not.

Just as there are specific reasons for doubting, so there may also be specific reasons for *not* doubting. When the label on a medicine bottle or a soup can list the ingredients inside, there is every reason to believe that the list is honest. Misrepresentation carries severe penalties. When an expert is hired as a consultant for a firm, she is not merely giving advice, she is often putting her professional reputation on the line. A reputation for giving bad advice can ruin a career. Under such circumstances an expert has strong motivation to testify only when she herself believes what she is saying.

Suppose that we pass the first two steps. An expert testifies that X is true and we judge that the expert really believes that X is true. This still may not be sufficient grounds for accepting the truth of X. We must evaluate the expert's *competence,* as well as his or her honesty. Is it reasonable for us to accept this expert's advice on the issue in question? There is, of course, no automatic way of answering such a question. It depends on the expert, the issue, the circumstances, and the cost of making a mistake. The best that can be done is to give some general guidelines.

The safest situation is when expert advice passes the 'all–any' test. If all experts in some field give the same advice, then it is usually reasonable to accept that advice. This may sound like an impossible standard. How can anyone check *all* the experts? It may not be necessary, if the expert can show that the advice given is standard advice. The tomatoes in the backyard garden always turn out small and withered. You take a soil sample to a nursery and it is sent out for an analysis. The report that comes back indicates the pH factor and other pertinent data. Then the nursery expert consults the standard guidebook to determine what sort of fertilizer is needed. All similar experts would give the same advice, because they would rely on the same guidebooks. In these circumstances it is generally reasonable to follow the expert's advice.

This is a common situation. Doctors, laywers, priests, plumbers, and electricians typify members of professions who are not licensed, or officially authorized to practice, until they meet certain minimum standards of competence. This generally involves mastering basic "state of the art" information. If they can show through standard reference works and precedents that the advice being given is standard, then it is reasonable to assume that any well-informed expert would give the same advice.

The weakened form of this criterion substitutes 'any' for 'all'. Thus, a doctor or a lawyer might give a client some advice with the comment that any other expert would give the same advice. This can be checked by getting a second opinion and seeing if the second expert also thinks the advice is standard. This is not necessary, however, if we take the doctor or lawyer's word for it that any other expert would give the same advice.

There is one obvious difficulty with this reliance on a consensus of expert opinion. It may be that they are all wrong, that the standard doctrine and methods relied on are quite inadequate. This is not as implausible as it sounds. There have been many times in the past when the standard expert opinion was simply wrong. At various times all the available experts believed that the earth is the center of the universe, that the world was created about 4,004 B.C., that epilepsy is caused by devil posession, and that scientific progress would inevitably lead to world peace. If the consensus of experts has been wrong in the past, it could be wrong now.

It could indeed. Yet if the consensus of the experts is wrong, this is only shown by further progress, a scientific breakthrough, the establishment of a better method. It is highly unlikely that a person who has to consult an expert for routine advice will be in a position to overturn the consensus of the experts. Again, we must remember that we are now concerned with practical reasoning. If the consensus of the experts is that something is true, that one policy works better than others, that some method will achieve the desired results, then the amateur who consults the expert is generally well advised to follow the advice based on the consensus that the expert gives.

The more difficult case occurs when there is no consensus of expert opinion, when experts disagree. This is not uncommon. Someone with money to invest might go to four different investment counselors and get quite a few different suggestions. How does one decide which one to accept?

Here again, there is no standard method. There are simply some plausible guidelines. Check the expert's track record; see how well her predictions and advice have fared in the past. Try to determine an expert's status within a field. Is he generally regarded as competent or erratic, as a leader or a follower? Ultimately, your judgment in such situations is often based on a very personal decision, the decision of whether or not to trust in another person's honesty and integrity.

EXERCISES

A. 1. What is the basic difference between deductive and inductive reasoning?
   2. What is the role of an hypothesis in explaining an anomaly?
   3. Explain the logic of hypothesis testing.
   4. Can one of several competing hypotheses ever be definitely established as the true hypothesis?
   5. How do practical and speculative reasoning interrelate in testing and accepting, or rejecting, hypotheses?
   6. Explain the role of the *conservative* principle in judging hypotheses.
   7. Explain the role of the *pragmatic* principle in judging hypotheses.
   8. Explain the four-step process of explaining anomalies.
   9. Why are there no strict rules for abduction?
  10. What role does plausibility play in judging hypotheses?
  11. What is the relation between deduction from an hypothesis and testing of an hypothesis?
  12. Why is an expert usually from some place else?
  13. What is the basic pattern of reasoning in arguments relying on expert evaluation?
  14. Does an expert always believe in the testimony he or she gives?
  15. What is the difference between general and specific reasons for doubting expert opinion?
  16. Is the consensus of expert opinion always true?
  17. Is it usually reasonable to accept the consensus of expert opinion on an issue?

B.   Most of the exercises given in this section concern the relation between puzzling facts and explanatory hypotheses or between claims and supporting evidence. In most cases there is no definitive answer. The point of these exercises is to learn to apply critical methods to puzzling cases.

   I. *Claims and Supporting Evidence.* Analyze the examples to determine how strongly the evidence given supports the claim in question. Might a different hypothesis explain the same evidence as well or better? If the claim is supported by an appeal to authority or testimony, then you should try to determine whether the testimony is adequately supported, is believable, and how strongly it supports the claim being made.

   1. Certain observations do seem to show that too great heat excites man to kill himself. During the Egyptian campaign [of Napoleon], the number of suicides in the French

army seems to have increased and this growth was attributed to the rise in temperature. In the tropics men are often seen to throw themselves abruptly into the ocean under the direct rays of the sun. Dr. Dietrich relates that in a trip around the world from 1844–87 by Count Charles de Gortz he noticed an irresistible impulse among the sailors, called by him *the horrors,* which he describes as follows: "The affliction usually appears in Winter when the sailors, landing after a long voyage, group themselves incautiously about a hot stove and, as is customary, indulge in all sorts of excesses. On returning on board the symptoms of the terrible *horrors* appear. Those stricken by it are irresistibly impelled to throw themselves into the water, whether overcome by dizziness in the midst of the work at the mast-tops, or during sleep, from which they start up violently with frightful cries." The *sirocco,* likewise, which produces a stifling heat, has been observed to have a similar effect on suicide.[9]

2. An advertisement for Dutch Boy paint shows two pictures of a house, first when it is painted in a blotchy faded green, secondly, when it is painted a sparkling yellow. The text is

When Dutch Boy Goes On, the Value Goes Up

Three professional appraisers carefully inspected this house. Its average value: $75,400. It was painted inside and out with quality Dutch Boy paint. And it was appraised again. Average value: $86,100.

3. The great danger which threatens the infant in our culture lies in the fact that the mother to whom it is confided in all its helplessness is almost always a discontented woman: sexually she is frigid or unsatisfied; socially she feels herself inferior to man; she has no independent grasp on the world or on the future. She will seek to compensate for all these frustrations through her child. When it is realized how difficult woman's present situation makes her full self-realization, how many desires, rebellious feelings, just claims she nurses in secret, one is frightened at the thought that defenseless infants are abandoned to her care. Just as when she coddled and tortured her dolls by turns, her behavior is symbolic; but symbols become grim reality for her child. A mother who whips her child is not beating the child alone; in a sense she is beating it all: she is taking her vengeance on a man, on the world, or on herself. Such a mother is often remorseful, and the child may not feel resentment, but it feels the blows.[10]

*4. **Discovery of a Strange Radiation**

. . . M. Niewenglowski has found that commercial phosphorescent calcium sulfide emits radiations which pass through opaque bodies. This action also occurs in several other phosphorescent bodies and in particular in the salts of uranium in which the phosphorescence is of very short duration. With the double sulfate of uranium and potassium of which I possess crystals in the form of a thin transparent crust I have made the following experiment:

A Lumière photgraphic plate with bromide emulsion was wrapped with two sheets of very thick black paper, such that the plate did not become clouded by exposure to the sun after a whole day.

A layer of the phosphorescent substance was placed on the outside of the paper and the combination exposed to the sun for several hours. When the photographic plate was developed, the silhouette of the phosphorescent substance appeared black on the negative. If one interposed a coin or a metal screen pierced by an openwork design between the phosphorescent substance and the paper the image of these objects appeared on the negative.

These same experiments may be repeated by interposing between the phosphorescent substance and the paper a thin glass sheet which excludes the possibility of chemical action resulting from vapors coming from the substance when heated by the sun's rays.

It is necessary to conclude from these experiments that the phosphorescent substance in question emits radiations that penetrate paper opaque to light and that reduce silver salts.[11]

5. In all that follows I adopt the standpoint, therefore, that the inclination to aggression is an original, self-subsisting instinctual disposition in man, and I return to my view that it constitutes the greatest impediment to civilization. At one point in the course of this enquiry I was led to the idea that civilization was a special process which mankind undergoes; and I am still under the influence of that idea. I may now add that civilization is a process in the service of Eros, whose purpose is to combine single human individuals, and after that families, then races, peoples, and nations, into one great unity, the unity of mankind. Why this has to happen, we do not know; the work of Eros is precisely this. These collections of men are to be libidinally bound to one another. Necessity alone, the advantages of work in common, will not hold them together. But man's natural aggressive instinct, the hostility of each against all and of all against each, opposes this programme of civilization. This aggressive instinct is the derivative and the main representative of the death instinct which we have found alongside of Eros and which shares world-dominion with it. And now, I think, the meaning of the evolution of civilization is no longer obscure to us. It must present a struggle between Eros and Death, between the instinct of life and the instinct of destruction, as it works itself out in the human species. This struggle is what all life essentially consists of, and the evolution of civilization may therefore be simply described as the struggle for life of the human species. And it is this battle of the giants that our nurse-maids try to appease with their lullaby about Heaven.[12]

II. Elementary, My Dear Watson

No character in literature is as famous for inferring facts from evidence as Sherlock Holmes. His assistant, Dr. Watson, learned from Holmes how to make the more obvious inferences from evidence. His mistakes on more subtle points served, by contrast, to bring out Holmes's brilliant powers of ''deduction.'' The inferences in question are, in fact, almost always inductive, rather than deductive. The classification as ''deductive'' comes from Dr. Watson, who regularly misinterprets Holmes.

Yet, one may wonder whether the inferences that work so unfailingly in the novels would always work as well in real life. Sir Arthur Conan Doyle, who created Holmes and Watson, pursued occult mysteries and arcane sciences. There is strong evidence to indicate that he was responsible for the scientific hoax known as the Piltdown man. These unorthodox scientific views and methods are sometimes reflected in the reasoning of Holmes and Watson. In analyzing the excerpts that follow, try to answer three questions:

a. How strong is the link between the evidence and the hypothesis introduced to explain it?
b. Might a different hypothesis explain the same evidence?
c. If many inferences link together to form a chain try to evaluate the strength of the chain.

This and the citations and summaries that follow are all from *The A. Conan Doyle Memorial Edition: The Complete Sherlock Holmes, Vol II.*[13] Reprinted by permission of the copyright owner.

*6. Holmes Confronting a New Client:

''You mentioned your name, as if I should recognize it but I assure you that, beyond the obvious facts that you are a bachelor, a solicitor, a Freemason, and an asthmatic, I know nothing whatever about you.''

Familiar as I was with my friend's methods, it was not difficult for me to follow his deductions, and to observe the untidiness of attire, the sheaf of legal papers, the watch-charm, and the breathing which had prompted them. Our client, however stared in amazement.

"Yes, I am all that, Mr. Holmes; and, in addition, I am the most unfortunate man at this moment in London."

7. **Dr. Watson (and Doyle) Interpret Faces.**

It was a tremendously virile and yet sinister face which was turned towards us. With the brow of a philosopher above and the jaw of a sensualist below, the man must have started with great capacities for good or for evil. But one could not look upon his cruel blue eyes, with their drooping, cynical lids, or upon the fierce, aggressive nose and the threatening, deep-lined brow, without reading Nature's plainest danger-signals. He took no heed of any of us, but his eyes were fixed upon Holmes's face with an expression in which hatred and amazement were equally blended. "You fiend!" he kept on muttering. "You clever, clever fiend!" [pp. 18–19].

8. **Holmes Interprets Toes, Fingers, and Faces.**

With a resigned air and a somewhat weary smile, Holmes begged the beautiful intruder to take a seat, and to inform us what it was that was troubling her.

"At least it cannot be your health," said he, as his keen eyes darted over her; "so ardent a bicyclist must be full of energy."

She glanced down in surprise at her own feet, and observed the slight roughening of the side of the sole cause by the friction of the edge of the pedal.

"Yes, I bicycle a good deal, Mr. Holmes, and that has something to do with my visit to you to-day."

My friend took the lady's ungloved hand, and examined it with as close an attention and as little sentiment as a scientist would show to a specimen.

"You will excuse me, I am sure. It is my business," said he, as he dropped it. "I nearly fell into the error of supposing that you were typewriting. Of course, it is obvious that it is music. You observe the spatulate finger-ends, Watson, which is common to both professions? There is a spirituality about the face, however"—she gently turned it towards the light—"which the typewriter does not generate. This lady is a musician."

"Yes, Mr. Holmes, I teach music." [pp. 84–85]

*9. **An Informative Walking Stick.**

. . . I stood upon the hearth-rug and picked up the stick which our visitor had left behind him the night before. It was a fine, thick piece of wood, bulbous-headed, of the sort which is known as a "Penang lawyer." Just under the head was a broad silver band, nearly an inch across. "To James Mortimer, M.R.C.S., from his friends of the C.C.H.," was engraved upon it, with the date "1884." It was just such a stick as the old-fashioned family practioner used to carry—dignified, solid, and reassuring.

"Well, Watson, what do you make of it?"

"I think," said I, following as far as I could the methods of my companion, "that Dr. Mortimer is a successful, elderly medical man, well-esteemed, since those who know him give him this mark of their appreciation . . . "

"Good!" said Holmes. "Excellent!"

"I think also that the probability is in favour of his being a country practicioner who does a good deal of his visiting on foot."

"Why so?"

"Because this stick, though originally a very handsome one, has been so knocked about that I can hardly imagine a town practioner carrying it. . . . The thick iron ferrule is worn down, so it is evident that he has done a great amount of walking with it."

"Perfectly sound!" said Holmes.

"And then again, there is the 'friends of the C.C.H.' I should guess that to be the

Something Hunt, the local hunt to whose members he has possibly given some surgical assistance, and which has made him a small presentation in return."

"Has anything escaped me?" I asked with some self-importance. "I trust that there is nothing of consequence which I have overlooked?"

"I am afraid, my dear Watson, that most of your conclusions were erroneous. . . . I would suggest, for example, that a presentation to a doctor is more likely to come from a hospital than from a hunt, and that when the initials 'C.C.' are placed before the hospital the words 'Charing Cross' very naturally suggest themselves."

"You may be right."

"The probability lies in that direction. And if we take this as a working hypothesis we have a fresh basis from which to start our construction of this unknown visitor." . . . When would his friends unite to give him a pledge of their good will? Obviously at the moment when Dr. Mortimer withdrew from the service of the hospital in order to start in practice for himself. . . . Now, you will observe that he could not have been on the staff of the hospital, since only a man well-established in London practice could hold such a position, and such a one would not drift into the country. What was he, then? If he was in the hospital and yet not on the staff he could only have been a house-surgeon or a house-physician — little more than a senior student. And he left five years ago — the date is on the stick. So your grave, middle-aged family practicioner vanishes into thin air, my dear Watson, and there emerges a young fellow under thirty, amiable, unambitious, absent-minded, and the possessor of a favourite dog, which I should describe roughly as being larger than a terrier and smaller than a mastiff."

I laughed incredulously as Sherlock Holmes leaned back in the settee and blew little wavering rings of smoke up to the ceiling. . . . I took down the Medical Dictionary and turned up the name.

"Mortimer, James, M. R. C. S., 1882, Grimpen, Dartmoor, Devon. House surgeon, from 1882 to 1884, at Charing Cross Hospital. Winner of the Jackson prize for Comparative Pathology, with essay entitled 'Is Disease a Reversion?'"

"No mention of that local hunt, Watson," said Holmes with a mischievous smile, "but a country doctor, as you astutely observed. I think that I am fairly justified in my inferences. As to the adjectives, I said, if I remember right, amiable, unambitious, and absent-minded. It is my experience that it is only an amiable man in this world who receives testimonials, only an unambitious one who abandons a London career for the country, and only an absent-minded one who leaves his stick and not his visiting-card after waiting an hour in your room."

"And the dog?"

"Has been in the habit of carrying this stick behind his master. Being a heavy stick the dog has held it tightly by the middle, and the marks of his teeth are very plainly visible. The dog's jaw, as shown in the space between marks, is too broad in my opinion for a terrier and not broad enough for a mastiff. It may have been — yes, by Jove, it *is* a curly-haired spaniel."

"My dear fellow, how can you possibly be sure of that?"

"For the very simple reason that I see the dog himself on our very door-step, and there is the ring of its owner" [pp. 137–41].

III. **Anomalies and Hypotheses**

The following examples involve anomalies and the hypotheses introduced to explain them. A critical appraisal should proceed on two levels. First, on the level of facts, one should ask if it is reasonable to believe that the descriptive account is correct. An affirmative answer to this question generally depends on accepting the honesty and competence of some source. Second, if the alleged facts are accepted as true, one should ask which explanatory hypothesis seems the most reasonable. To illustrate what is involved in critical appraisal the first example will be treated in some detail.

10. **The Destruction of Sodom and Gomorrah.**

Chapter 18 of the Book of Genesis relates that the Lord told Abraham that he would destroy Sodom and Gomorrah because they were full of sin. Chapter 19 describes two angels (strangers) visiting Lot in Sodom. That evening the men of the city came to Lot and said, "Where are the men who came to you tonight? Bring them out to us that we may know them" Lot replied, "I beg you, my brothers, do not act so wickedly. Behold, I have two daughters who have not known man; let me bring them out to you, and do to them as you please; only do nothing to these men, for they have come under the shelter of my roof."

The two visitors struck the mob at the door with blindness and then told Lot that they the Lord had sent them to destroy the city. The next morning they forced Lot and his family to flee and told them, "Flee for your life; do not look back or stop anywhere in the valley; flee to the hills, lest you be consumed." Then the Lord rained on Sodom and Gomorrah brimstone and fire from the Lord out of heaven; and he overthrew those cities, and all the valley, and all the inhabitants of the cities, and what grew on the ground. But Lot's wife behind him looked back, and she became a pillar of salt. The next morning Abraham came back to where the Lord had spoken to him and saw the smoke of the land going up like the smoke of a furnace.[14]

The first question is: Should this descriptive account be accepted as factually true? Three answers are possible. The first is that it must be accepted as true because everything in the Bible is true. The opposite answer is that the Bible has no more standing than any other ancient myth. However, archeological studies strongly support the position that the Biblical acount of the patriarchal era has a genuine historical core. Both historians specializing in the ancient Near East and nonfundamentalist Biblical scholars would interpret this as a folk history handed down by oral tradition, rather than a scientific historical presentation of objective facts. This would be compatible with the idea that after Sodom and Gomorrah were destroyed, perhaps by an earthquake, a moral explanation for the destruction was developed.

Those who take the description of the destruction more literally have developed some novel explanatory hypotheses. We will consider two. H1 is from Erik von Daniken's *Chariots of the Gods*. Within a few generations, his argument goes, we will have the ability to send a manned nuclear powered rocket ship to visit planets in another solar system. Suppose that these astronauts land on a planet with a civilization comparable to ours of 4,000 years ago, mine the planet for fissionable material to fuel their return trip home, and then leave after giving some instruction to friendly natives. These natives would surely think of them as the gods who came from and returned to the skies.

Early accounts from scattered parts of our globe tell of gods who came from the skies, did wonders, instructed some men, and then returned to the skies. If, with von Daniken, we were to assume that these accounts describe extraterrestrial astronauts quarrying the earth for nuclear fuel, then the account of the destruction of Sodom and Gomorrah becomes intelligible. The angels, or visitors from the heavens, became friends of Lot. So they warned him after they had begun the countdown for a nuclear explosion. They could easily produce temporary blindness in a mob by a weapon like a flaregun. They insisted that Lot and his wife go to the hills where the rocks would protect them from radiation. Lot's wife looked back and was killed by watching the atomic fireball. Abraham, too far away to witness the blast, saw the mushroom cloud ascending to the heavens.[15]

Before evaluating this we will consider a counterhypothesis, H2, developed by Clifford Wilson in an attack on von Daniken. Wilson's basic position is that the Bible is true in all that it teaches and that Biblical accounts can be substantiated by an acceptable reconstruction. After surveying archeological and geological information about the Dead Sea area he presents his reconstruction.

> Briefly then, it seems likely that at the time of this divine judgment an earthquake ground up rocks at the edge of the geological fault and natural gases from the underlying oil field carried many of these rocks, together with salt, sulphur and bitumen, high into the air. The natural gases ignited, and fire and bitumen literally rained from the sky.

> But the question might be asked, what about Lot's wife? Do you really believe the story about the pillar of salt? The answer, of course, is yes. If people in Pompeii could be overcome by volcanic lava, why could not a woman fleeing from Sodom be overcome by rock salt?[16]

One might reject Wilson's account on various grounds. One who believes in the literal truth of the Genesis account would not accept this ''scientific'' reconstruction. One who does not accept Genesis as anything more than an ancient document would think the effort at reconstruction to be a waste of time. The historians and Biblical scholars who accept this as a genuine historical document generally insist that Genesis has to be interpreted in terms of the literary forms proper to a primitive people. A folk history is a reconstruction of historical information transmitted through an oral tradition. The reconstruction is not intended to provide a more precise descriptive account, but to give the historical events a moral significance: God rewards the good and punishes the wicked. This does not necessarily imply that the descriptive details are wrong, merely that they were transmitted through a long oral tradition concerned more with significance than with historical accuracy. Thus, from the perspective of one who believes in the literal truth of Genesis, or of one who totally rejects the inspiration of the Bible, or of one who interprets the Bible by the criteria used in historical reconstruction, Wilson's attempt to provide a concordance of Biblical descriptive history and scientific explanation is essentially misguided.

The account given by von Daniken presupposes that the people behind the oral tradition were describing events that they witnessed but did not understand. It is similar to the situation most of us encounter witnessing, whether directly or through TV, frantic activity on the stock market. We can describe people rushing around, waving their arms, and yelling, but cannot really explain why they are doing the things they do. If ancient people had witnessed an atomic blast produced by extraterrestrial astronauts, they might make the same description.

It is instructive to compare von Daniken's account with the hypothesis that a meteor collision was responsible for the great dinosaur die-out. This hypothesis postulates that a meteor hit at a definite time and indicates what sorts of evidence would confirm or disconfirm the hypothesis. Von Daniken follows a grab-bag approach to evidence. His documentary support comes from scattered regions and from times ranging from 3,000 B.C. (the probable origin of the Gilgamesh epic he uses) to A.D. 1,600 (the approximate date of the Piri Reis map, a medieval Turkish map of the Atlantic ocean, which von Daniken interprets as based on photographs taken from above the stratosphere). If his hypothesis postulated a definite time for these ancient astronauts — the time of the destruction of Sodom, then much of his supporting evidence would really be disconfirming evidence. It can be interpreted as supporting evidence only by keeping both the hypothesis and the interpretation of the evidence as vague as possible.

Our purpose here is not to discuss the details of von Daniken's argument, but to indicate how arguments are evaluated. The conservative principle and the pragmatic principle discussed earlier serve as guides. An implausible hypothesis should generally not be accepted unless all the more plausible hypotheses have been eliminated. Even then it needs strong confirming evidence. The historical items von Daniken uses all admit of more plausible interpretations, which he never seriously considers. He produces no independent supporting evidence. There is no good reason for either accepting his hypothesis or taking it seriously.

11. **Napoleon Bonaparte Was Murdered.**

Napoleon, the most famous man of the nineteenth century, died at the age of fifty-one on the island of St. Helena, where he was exiled. A post-mortem examination led to the conclusion that he died of cancer of the stomach. Recently, a Swedish dentist, Dr. Sten Forsufvud, collected evidence that seems to indicate that Napoleon died of arsenic poisoning. Of the thirty known symptoms of arsenic poisoning, Napoleon exhibited twenty-four. Five locks that had been cut from Napoleon's hair while he was on St. Helena revealed high quantities of arsenic. It was known that some of the medicine that he was taking for stomach pains contained arsenic. The arsenic content could have been enhanced as a method of slow murder. There were many who hated and feared Napoleon.

Should the accepted history be revised?[17]

12. **The Cause of the Nile's Annual Flooding.**

[Herodotus was a Greek historian of the fifth century B.C. He gave one of the first clear examples of introducing hypotheses to explain a puzzling phenomenon and then judging the hypotheses by their plausibility and their consequences. What follows is taken from his text.]

I was particularly anxious to learn from them [the priests of Egypt] why the Nile, at the commencement of the summer solstice, begins to rise, and continues to increase for a hundred days — and why, as soon as that number is past, it forthwith retires and contracts its stream, continuing low during the whole of the winter until the summer solstice comes around again. On none of these points could I obtain any explanation from the inhabitants.

Some of the Greeks, however, wishing to get a reputation for cleverness, have offered explanations of the phenomena of the river, for which they have accounted in three different ways. One pretends that the Etesian winds cause the rise of the river by preventing the Nile water from running off into the sea. But in the first place it has often happened, when the Etesian winds did not blow, that the Nile has risen according to its usual wont; and further, if the Etesian winds produced the effect, the other rivers which flow in a direction opposite to those winds ought to present the same phenomenon as the Nile. But these rivers, of which there are many both in Syria and Lybia, are entirely unlike the Nile in this respect.

The second opinion is even more unscientific than the one just mentioned. It is that the Nile acts so strangely, becaues it flows from the ocean, and that the ocean flows all round the earth.

The third explanation, which is very much more plausible than either of the others, is positively the furthest from the truth; for there is really nothing in what it says, any more than in the other theories. It is, that the innundation of the Nile is caused by the melting of snows. Now, as the Nile flows out of Libia, through Ethiopia, into Egypt, how is it possible that it can be formed of melted snow, running as it does, from the hottest regions of the world into cooler countries?

I will proceed to explain what I think to be the reason of the Nile's swelling in the summer time. During the winter, the sun is driven out of his usual course by the storms, and removes to the upper parts of Libya. This is the whole secret in the fewest possible words; for it stands to reason that the country to which the Sun-god approaches the nearest, and which he passes most directly over, will be scantest of water, and that there the streams which feed the rivers will shrink the most.[18]

13. **The Bermuda Triangle.**

In 1609 a British ship, the *Sea Venture,* was wrecked off the coast of Bermuda. The long boat of the ship set out on a 500-mile journey to the West Coast of the U.S. It was never heard from again. This was the first of many disappearances in the Bermuda Triangle. The tringle covers an area between Bermuda, the southeast tip of Florida, and the Western tip of Puerto Rico. Well over a hundred disappearances have occurred in this area with a loss of more than 1,000 lives. Most of the disappearances are total. No bodies are found, nor are fragments of the lost boats and planes. Some pilots flying through this area have claimed to have had strange experiences, such as loss of control of the plane and strange glows from the wings. Ship captains have complained of loss of electrical power and malfunctioning of compasses in this triangle.

Various hypotheses have been introduced to account for these disappearances. One is the multiple-cause hypothesis. The region in question is one from which many hurricanes originate. It is also a region where the Gulf Stream, carrying warm water northward, encounters currents carrying cold waters southward. This can produce treacherous conditions. Also, the fast currents could remove bodies and debris. Finally, it is a busy region for air and sea transportation. These factors might account for a high accident rate. They do not seem to account for other puzzling phenomena such as glowing wings, malfunctioning compasses, loss of electrical power, and total absence of wreckage and bodies of victims.

More extreme hypotheses have been introduced to account both for the disappearances and for the other puzzling phenomena as well. One is that this is a region of *antigravity warp,* a region in which the normal gravitational laws do not operate in the accustomed fashion. Another hypothesis is that this is a region of *magnetic vortices* and that these vortices somehow produce these results. The proponents of these hypotheses do not explain how antigravity warps or magnetic vortices produce the mysterious effects. The basic contention is that, since neither gravity nor magnetism is adequately understood, they might well produce such effects.[19]

14. **The Dominant Male.**

The woman's rights movement began in 1848, when Elizabth Cady Stanton and Lucretia Mott, two leading abolitionists, organized a meeting in Seneca Falls, New York. The *Seneca Falls Declaration of Rights and Sentiments* insisted on the rights of women to vote, to hold office, to drop the term *obey* from the marriage contract, to hold property, to have opportunities for higher education and advancement in business, to receive equal pay for equal work, and to live under a uniform moral code, rather than a double standard. Most of these goals have been reached, though there are still inequalities in business opportunities and pay scales. Yet women have not achieved anything like equality with men as business leaders, in top government positions, in science, medicine, or higher education. Various hypotheses have been advanced to explain this inequality.

H1. It is due to a male plot. Men, whether consciously or not, form various old-boy networks that tend to favor males while suppressing females, and to inculcate standards that teach that this is the natural order.

H2. The difference is ultimately hormonal. Before puberty, boys and girls tend to be roughly equal, though different. Girls do better in language, manual dexterity, and speaking. Boys generally do better in problems involving visual–spatial orientation and in mathematics. After adolescence, boys generally pull ahead of girls, especially in mathematics, science, and leadership roles. The difference is due to the hormone testosterone, which is instrumental in the adolescent male's growth in muscles, aggressiveness, and competitiveness. These are the traits largely responsible for leadership.

H3. Acquired *social* characteristics are transmitted. During the long formative period of human history, males tended to be hunters, while females were food gatherers and rearers of children. According to sociobiologists, the behavioral characteristics that make for success at these occupations tend to be reinforced and transmitted over generations. Hunters need to be aggressive, competitive, and disciplined.

H4. Men and women have slightly different brain structures. The left brain controls verbal activity, while the right brain hemisphere is more visually oriented. On the whole, women appear to be more dominated by the left hemisphere, men by the right. What may be more significant is research indicating that men tend to have more functions under central control, while women have more diffuse mental controls.

H5. The status differences are only temporary. When women finally achieve truly equal treatment and equal opportunities, then they will also achieve equality with men in leadership roles.

M. I. Different sorts of accounts are judged by different criteria. The first step in deciding which criteria to apply is to categorize an account properly. Read the following brief excerpts and then categorize the main thrust of the account as:

A.   a descriptive account.
B.   a deductive argument.
C.   an inductive argument.
D.   an expression of an opinion, not an argument.
E.   an argument based on appeal to authority.

1. Jello is delicious and nourishing. Bill Cosby said so in a TV advertisement, and Cosby is an honest man.
2. Unemployment is continuing high. Though the overall unemployment figures are under 10 percent, the steel, automobile, and airline industries are well over 10 percent. There are also many regions of the country where the overall unemployment is over 10 percent.
3. Ellen turned me down when I asked her for a dance; so did Jennifer. Mary Ann headed for the ladies' room when she saw me coming across the dance floor. It certainly looks like I'm never going to get a chance to dance with anyone tonight.
4. ''Seek and ye shall find.'' That's what the Bible tells us. So, I can assure you that if you send $25 or more to our TV crusade, then your prayers will be answered.
5. There must be another planet outside the orbit of Pluto. I heard an astronomer discuss this and he says that there is no other way in which variations in the orbit of Neptune can be explained.
6. Most theorectical physicists do their best original work before they are thirty years old. Seymour is already over forty and he hasn't done anything really original. So, we shouldn't expect much from him.
7. I find Beethoven's odd-numbered symphonies to be much better than the even-numbered symphonies. I think that I have heard all of his symphonies at one time or another. The First Symphony is just so-so; the Seventh is very pleasant; the Third, Fifth, and Ninth are magnificent.
8. Of course you have to pay income taxes. You earn a salary and everyone who earns a salary has to pay income taxes.
9. I have a Honda and I find it a great car. Joe has had no trouble with his Honda in three years of driving. So there is no doubt about it; a Honda is a good car.
10. If the murderer had escaped through the back door, then it could not have been locked on the inside. But you can see that the inside bolt is still locked. So, whoever killed her could not have gone out the back door.
11. The gravestones were lined up in perfect rows. When you stood in the middle of the cemetery and looked in any direction you could see all the graves with their military markers radiating out like spokes from the center of a wheel. It's such an impressive sight.
12. If the cost of living keeps going up while my salary remains the same, then I'm falling

behind. The deal the company is offering gives a slight increase in salary, but a reduction in health benefits. Overall, there is really no net increase. So, if the union accepts it, it means that I will be falling behind.

13. A politician running for re-election hardly ever brings up the failures and shortcomings of his first term in office. So, you can bet your bottom dollar that Mayor Clement won't discuss the fact that grade school averages have been dropping since her austerity drive began.

II. Use the following code in answering questions 14 through 46;

   A.   expresses an anomaly, or puzzling fact.
   B.   expresses an hypothesis, or tentative explanation of some puzzling fact.
   C.   presents evidence confirming the hypothesis.
   D.   presents evidence disconfirming the hypothesis.
   E.   presents background information.

(1) The tomb had been undisturbed for over 3,000 years. (2) When it was opened, the contents were found to be almost perfectly preserved, because of the very dry climate. (3) Yet, there was a strange aura of mystery and fear among the explorers. (4) I think that the Pharaoh put a curse on anyone who disturbs his tomb. (5) Last week the Egyptian who led Sir Mortimer to the tomb died in an automobile accident. (6) Now Sir Mortimer has cancer of the pancreas. (7) The people who did the digging may all still be healthy. (8) But, if I were in their position, I would be worried.

14. Sentence (1) is
15. Sentence (2) is
16. Sentence (3) is
17. Sentence (4) is
18. Sentence (5) is
19. Sentence (6) is
20. Sentence (7) is

(1) Unemployment is up. (2) There is a freeze on wages and prices. (3) In the past, these factors usually reduced inflation. (4) Now, however, inflation is still high. (5) This is probably due to our bad international balance of payments. (6) Japan has a very favorable international balance of payments and very low inflation.

21. Sentence (1) is
22. Sentence (2) is
23. Sentence (3) is
24. Sentence (4) is
25. Sentence (5) is
26. Sentence (6) is

(1) In 1881 the British sailing vessel the *Ellen Austin* encountered a schooner drifting in the mid-Atlantic. (2) A boarding party found everything in order. (3) But there was no sign of the crew. (4) The boarding party sailed the ship parallel to the *Ellen Austin* until a storm blew them apart. (5) When the ship was found again, the boarding party was gone. (6) A second boarding party manned the ship and sailed for Newfoundland. (7) The ship was faster than the *Ellen Austin* and eventually pulled out of sight. (8) It never reached Newfoundland and was never seen again. (9) There seems to be some strange cosmic force making sailors disappear from ships. (10) This cosmic force might also explain similar mysterious disappearances of whole crews from the *Mary Celeste* in 1872 and from the *Joyita* in 1955.[20]

27. Sentence (1) is
28. Sentence (2) is
29. Sentence (3) is
30. Sentence (4) is
31. Sentence (5) is
32. Sentence (6) is
33. Sentence (7) is
34. Sentence (8) is
35. Sentence (9) is
36. Sentence (10) is

(1) Her body was found in a room in which the door and both windows were locked from the inside. (2) She had been shot through the head with a high-powered rifle bullet. (3) Yet, no rifle was found in the room. (4) It could be murder, disguised to look like suicide. (5) Tiny pin-holes near the door lock might indicate that a string tied to the pins first turned the lock and then pulled the pins out. (6) But if the murderer wanted to make it look like suicide he would have left the rifle in the room. (7) It could be suicide disguised to look like murder. (8) The combination of career failure and marriage break-up was a strong motive for suicide. (9) She had talked about committing suicide. (10) But, I can't think of any way she could have made the rifle disappear from a locked room.

37. Sentence (1) is
38. Sentence (2) is
39. Sentence (3) is
40. Sentence (4) is
41. Sentence (5) is
42. Sentence (6) is
43. Sentence (7) is
44. Sentence (8) is
45. Sentence (9) is
46. Sentence (10) is

REFERENCES

[1]The citations are all from B. W. Richardson, ed., *Snow on Cholera* (New York: Hafner, 1965). The general historical background is from Margaret Pelling's, *Cholera, Fever and English Medicine, 1825–1865* (Oxford: Oxford University Press, 1978).

[2]The ideas presented here were chiefly developed in the context of explaining scientific discoveries. Some of them are derived from the work of N. R. Hanson and T. Kuhn.

[3]This is a very simple summary of ideas that were developed in differing ways by the philosophers John Dewey and Martin Heidegger.

[4]The leading theory attempting to explain this anomaly—inflation theory—assumes that the observable universe is a small part of a much larger universe.

[5]*The National Enquirer,* May 3, 1983, p. 53.

[6]See *The Presidential Transcripts: In Conjunction with the Staff of the Washington Post* (New York: Dell, 1974).

[7]See Michael McCloskey, "Intuitive Physics," *Scientific American, 248* (April, 1983), 122–131.

[8]This four-stage analysis of expert advice was suggested by Larry Wright in his *Better Reasoning* (New York: Holt, Rinehart & Winston, 1982), pp. 110–121.

[9]Emile Durkheim, *Suicide,* trans. John Spaulding and George Simpson (Glencoe, Ill.: The Free Press, 1951, originally published in 1897), p. 110.

[10]Simone de Beauvoir, *The Second Sex,* trans. H. M. Parshley (New York: Knopf, 1953), p. 573.

[11]Henri Becquarel, "On Radiations Emitted with Phosphorescence," *Comptes Rendus,* 122 (1896), 420; in *The World of the Atom,* ed. H. Boorse and L. Motz (New York: Basic Books, 1966), Vol. I, p. 404.

[12]Sigmund Freud, *Civilization and its Discontents,* trans. James Strachey (New York: W. W. Norton, 1961), p. 69.

[13]*The A. Conan Doyle Memorial Edition: The Complete Sherlock Holmes, Vol. II* (New York: Doubleday, 1931).

[14]All citations from the Revised Standard Version of the Bible.

[15]For a fuller account of this argument see Erich von Daniken, *Chariots of the Gods? Unsolved Mysteries of the Past,* trans. Michael Heron (New York: G. B. Putnam's Sons, 1968).

[16]Clifford Wilson, *Crash Go the Chariots* (Victoria, Australia: Word of Truth Publications, 1972), pp. 56–57.

[17]See Ben Weider and David Hapgood, *The Murder of Napoleon* (New York: Congden and Lattes, 1982).

[18]Herodotus, *The Persian Wars,* trans. George Rawlinson (New York: Modern Library, 1942), p. 125. Reprinted by permission of Random House, Inc.

[19]See Colin Wilson, *Enigmas and Mysteries* (New York: Doubleday, 1976), pp. 51–59.

[20]This narration is based on Colin Wilson's, *Enigmas and Mysteries* (New York: Doubleday, 1976), chap 3.

Chapter 9

METHODS OF INDUCTIVE REASONING

In the previous chapter we considered the basic method of explaining anomalies or puzzling facts by introducing hypotheses and then testing the consequences of these hypotheses. This is the core of inductive reasoning. In some situations, however, inductive reasoning is improved by some systematic procedures. In this chapter we will study these procedures and the situations in which they should be employed. Before doing this we should briefly consider the rather notorious problem of justifying induction. We are not doing this in the hope of providing any new justification of induction. The only purpose for treating this is to situate the present treatment with respect to a long troubled history of discussions of induction and its problems. The conclusion drawn is that it is reasonable to rely on inductive reasoning. The practical problem to be faced is not one of justifying induction, but setting up standards for good inductive reasoning. One who accepts this conclusion as plausible may skip section 9.1 with little loss.

9.1 THE PROBLEM OF INDUCTION

Suppose that you examine an ear of corn and find that it has an even number of rows of kernels. Then you examine three more randomly selected ears of corn and find that each of them has an even number of rows. On this basis you formulate a general law: All ears of corn have an even number of rows of kernels. I will call this Jenny's law, since my daughter, Jennifer, formulated this law on the basis of these four observations. Is Jenny's law true?

Let's consider how you might try to settle this question. One method immediately suggests itself. Buy some more corn and count the number of rows of kernels. This might serve to *disprove* Jenny's law. Since the law has the form of a universal affirmative, or *A,* proposition, it is falsified by finding just one exception. But no number of observations could ever serve to *prove* Jenny's law. Even if you had examined every ear of corn that ever existed and found that each one had an even number of rows of kernels, it could still happen that the next one you examined would have an odd number of rows. A universal law covering a limited number of cases can be proved by examining them one by one. Thus I could use observation plus enumeration to settle the truth of the claim that all the coins in the piggy bank are pennies, or that claim that all the flowers in the garden behind my house are either daisies or petunias. But the method of observation and enumeration would never suffice to prove a general law that covers all possible as well as all actual cases.

A general law with an unlimited range of applications cannot be established by purely inductive means. Nor can it be established by purely deductive means. On this point there is widespread agreement. For the last two hundred years, however, there has been considerable disagreement about how induction is to be justified. For our purposes it is more helpful to focus on the practice of justification, rather than on disputes about justification, whether old[1] or new.[2]

Earlier, we used one basic criterion to distinguish deduction from induction. In a valid deductive argument the truth of the premises guarantees the truth of the conclusion. In an inductive argument the premises *support* but do not guarantee the truth of the conclusion. To see the problems this involves, let's consider some concrete examples.

Suppose that a scientist wants to make a precise measurement of the specific heat of mercury at room temperature. The specific heat is basically the ratio between the amount of heat required to raise one gram of water from 20° centigrade to 21° and the amount of heat required to raise one gram of mercury from 20° to 21°. Ordinarily a scientist would settle this by testing one pure sample of mercury and making careful measurements. Then she would announce her results in a statement like:

The specific heat of mercury at room temperature is 0.033.   (9.1)

Implicit in (9.1) is the claim that this is the specific heat of *all* pure mercury, not just of one sample. This general law is inductively established on the basis of one observation. Is our scientist thumbing her nose at the laws of logic?

No, she is merely behaving as a normal scientist. On the basis of a long tradition of successful practice, scientists make the assumption that all metals of the same kind have the same basic properties. As long as this works, they simply assume it. If they find some class of substances for which it does not work, then they seek some basis for dividing this into subclasses that are the same in their basic properties. With such an assumption our imaginary scientist's reasoning is perfectly good. It can be reconstructed in the form:

> All pure samples of mercury have the same specific heat.
> The specific heat of this pure sample is 0.033.
> _____
> The specific heat of all pure mercury is 0.033.   (9.2)

Within the context of scientific practice, argument (9.2) represents perfectly good reasoning. It is quite similar to the type of ordinary inductive reasoning we practice is such familiar arguments as:

> The eight-pound turkey has been baking at 350° for five hours. It must be done by now.   (9.3)

> He's been driving the truck for twelve hours without a break. He must be exhausted.   (9.4)

In each case we infer a conclusion from a premise, though in each case it is logically possible for the premise to be true and the conclusion to be false. When pushed, we can reconstruct any particular argument in a deductive form by restating the premise as a general rule and the conclusion as an instance of a rule. From a *descriptive* point of view, this is the way that inductive reasoning proceeds. Also, almost all would agree that practical reliance on such inductive reasoning is reasonable, because this reasoning works and there is no plausible alternative.

This descriptive account brings out three general features of inductive arguments that we will be considering in more detail in this chapter. We will list them now and explain them later.

1. *Induction rests on presuppositions.* Thus, the examples given above presuppose that all mercury has the same specific heat, that the turkey and oven are normal, that the truck driver's reactions to stress fall within the normal range.

2. *Inductive arguments have a kind of incompleteness.* Our earlier deductive argument from the premises that all Philadelphians are Pennsylvanians and that all Pennsylvanians are Americans to the conclusion that all Phila-

delphians are Americans is valid as it stands. Adding further propositions changes nothing. The inductive arguments given could all be strengthened or weakened by further propositions. If we can prove that our mercury sample is pure and normal, we strengthen (9.1). If we learn that the truck driver in question has extraordinary energy and never seems to be fatigued by long drives, then we weaken (9.4).

     3. Induction depends on acceptance.   This is an aspect of induction that relates to practical rather than speculative reasoning. Whether or not it is reasonable for us to accept the conclusion of an inductive argument may depend on our motives for acceptance or rejection as well as on the strength of the argument.

9.2 PRESUPPOSITIONS
OF INDUCTION

The practice of induction relies on presuppositions and policies of acceptance. In this section we wish to consider the presuppositions of induction. The method used here is basically an extension of the methods of plausible reasoning considered in the last chapter. A person confronted with an anomaly or puzzling phenomenon develops hypotheses which, if true, could explain the anomaly. Thus, the great dinosaur die-out might be explained by the impact of a meteor or by a change in world temperature. The transmission of cholera might be explained by some factor transmitted through water. One tries to test such hypotheses through their consequences and through the elimination of competing hypotheses.

     There are many cases in which there are no clear grounds for considering this definite a hypothesis. Instead one introduces, on a first level of plausibility, a *class* of hypotheses, often a class with fuzzy boundaries. On a particular afternoon 10 percent of the students in a particular high school complain of stomach cramps and digestive disturbances. The most plausible initial hypothesis is that it was probably due to something they had for lunch in the school cafeteria. It seems reasonable to presume that problems in the stomach are probably due to something put into the stomach. This is effectively a class of hypotheses. Either the hamburgers were responsible, or the french fries, or the potatoes, or the carrots, or something else.

     What is needed next is some systematic method for determining which factor is the culprit. The next section will treat such methods. For the present we will stick with more general considerations. Suppose that it could be determined that there was nothing wrong with any of the food served in the cafeteria. The most plausible class of hypotheses is eliminated. Then one retreats to classes of less likely hypotheses. One might consider the possibility that drugs are responsible. This again is really a class of hypotheses. The responsible factor is marijuana, or cocaine, or heroin, or amphetamines. If these are all eliminated, then one would try further hypotheses. Maybe, it's a student prank, or some gas transmitted through the heating system.

We mention these plausibility levels to situate inductive methods. There is nothing automatic about these methods, even when inductive methods employ complicated mathematics. Induction rests on hypotheses whose initial plausibility depends on how they fit into an already established network of relations. Inference is something we do. We should use the best tools available, realizing that the most basic tool of all, the one on which all others depend, is language.

Among the different types of presuppositions that shape and support inductive reasoning, there are two general classes that play a particularly important role. The first are connected with the ways in which we *categorize* objects. A category term, like 'bird' or 'metal' does not get its meaning just through the class of objects it may refer to. It also fits into a network of relations with other terms, laws, and rules. Most of the category terms we assimilate through the ordinary process of language learning are *resemblance class predicates.*[3] We learn to use 'tall' through clear cases of members: Doctor J is tall; Abraham Lincoln was tall; and clear cases of nonmembers: Mickey Rooney is not tall; jockies are not tall. This leaves fuzzy borders. Should a man who is 5′8″ be considered tall? 5′9″? How about 5′10″? The borders may be stipulated for a particular purpose. In many cities a man who measures less than 5′8″ is not tall enough to join the police force. Such stipulations, however, do not determine ordinary language usage.

Many resemblance class predicates depend on a cluster of concepts. Most X's have properties, A, B, C, D, . . . Suppose only some of these properties are present. Suppose that we find a substance that is hard, shiny, and dense, but does not conduct electricity. Should we call it a metal? Here again, there are fuzzy boundaries that can be fixed for particular purposes. The point in introducing this term is not to teach anyone how to introduce resemblance class predicates, but to characterize the terms we already use, the type of terms that are a functioning part of our language.

Putting an object in a category or attributing some property to it may suggest that it is also in some other category or has some other property. Here, for example, is a list of correlations that are suggested by the associations between terms in current American usage.

PROPERTY ONE suggests	PROPERTY TWO
liberal	for welfare
Republican	conservative
movie star	rich
theoretical physicist	good at mathematics
Sagittarian	lucky in gambling
waterwitch	able to find underground water

I am not, of course, claiming that all these correlations are true. They do, however, exemplify the type of correlations suggested by the language we speak and the more or less widely shared experiences that mould this usage. Such suggestions are often strong enough to merit testing, yet uncertain enough to require testing. Inductive methods build on such presuppositions.

The second general type of presupposition involves correlations between events. Here we deliberately use the vague term 'correlation', rather than the more specific terms *cause,* 'necessary condition', or 'sufficient condition'. We are still concerned with introducing plausible hypotheses, not with explaining results. There are many correlations that are so familiar that we take them for granted. We see a lightening bolt; we wait for a thunder clap. We see, on a TV set, a team win a World Series; we expect to see them pouring champagne over the heads of teammates. Some correlations are suggested on theoretical grounds. If crops are treated with fertilizer X, we expect increased growth. If the federal money supply is restricted, we expect interest rates to go down. In other cases we come to accept correlations on the ground of experience, though the reasons for the correlations are not well understood. If a child who is naturally left-handed is forced to act as a right-handed child, he is likely to become a stutterer. This correlation is clearer than any explanations of the correlation.

To say that language, or experience, or theory, or custom, or even prejudice suggests a correlation between events is not, of course, equivalent to settling the fact that there is such a correlation. This must be established. Inductive methods are often helpful in establishing such correlations. But the application of inductive methods presupposes plausible hypotheses that are tested by these methods. Accepted correlations often suggest tentative hypotheses and guide the initial assignment of degrees of plausibility to suggested hypotheses.

9.3 ARGUING FROM SAMPLES

The simplest and perhaps the most common inductive argument is from a sample to the whole the sample represents. Thus, the chemist considered earlier argues from the specific heat of one sample of mercury to the specific heat of all mercury. The Gallup Poll surveys the preferences of a small sample of voters and then predicts how the American people will vote. The Nielsen ratings people monitor the TV-viewing habits of some selected families and then tell the industry how many Americans are watching each major TV show. Stockbrokers check the standings of a few stocks and then predict the way the market will go.

The pattern is familiar and quite straightforward:

<u>X percent of the observed H's are K's.</u>
So, X percent of *all* H's are K's.   (9.5)

The crucial presupposition here is that the sample chosen is an adequate representation of the whole. In some cases this works quite well. The chemist assumes that any pure sample of mercury adequately represents the physical and chemical properties of all pure mercury. In some cases this presumption proves disastrous. In 1936 the now defunct *Literary Digest* conducted a telephone survey to predict whether Alfred Landon or Franklin Roosevelt would win the selection for presidency. On the basis of this sampling they confidently predicted *"Landon by a landslide."* Landon carried only the states of Maine and Vermont.

There are three basic means of selecting a sample that adequately represents a whole. They are: homogeneous groups, randomizing, and selecting. Though they are often mixed together, we will consider them separately. A homogeneous group is one in which all the members are, or are reasonably presumed to be, homogeneous with respect to the property in question. The chemist presumes that all pure samples of mercury have the same specific heat. In this respect the group of mercury samples is exactly homogeneous. John Snow assumed that different people have, by and large, the same susceptibility to cholera. If some groups, such as the poor or miners, have a much higher incidence of cholera, this is not due to greater susceptibility but to greater exposure. The presumption here is not a strict homogeneity, but a rough statistical homogeneity.

Suppose that you have a jar full of different-colored jellybeans. You wish to select a few and on the basis of the sample predict the percentage that are red. How would you do it? For most of us the first impulse would be to reach in and take out a fistfull. That becomes the sample. Suppose, however, that all the red jellybeans were put in first, then the green, the black, the yellow, the orange, the blue, and the pink. Since the red ones are on the bottom, the handful taken from the top would be chiefly pink and blue jellybeans. The sample does not adequately represent the whole with respect to the color of the jellybeans. To get a representative sample you should shake up the jar until the jellybeans are thoroughly mixed and then take out a fistfull. This should be representative.

This shaking is an example of a randomizing process, a way of making sure that the individuals selected are really randomly chosen. In particular cases it is important to pay careful attention to the method of randomization chosen, to see if it is really random or has a built-in bias. Dialing arbitrarily selected telephone numbers might seem to be a good example of a just such a randomizing process. Yet, it failed badly when the *Literary Digest* relied on it. It is not too difficult to understand why. In the year 1936 the Great Depression was at its peak. Only the relatively wealthy could afford the luxury of the new-fangled invention, the telephone. They were not the ones likely to support Roosevelt's policies of taxing the rich and supporting the poor. In arguing from a supposedly random selection it is always necessary to make sure that the method of selection does not have any built-in bias.

The final method is selection. Instead of choosing in a random way, one selects the members of a sample carefully. Political pollsters, for example, make detailed studies of the correlations between election results and characteristics of the voters such as age, occupation, religion, education, income level, residential area, sex, and marital status. Then they try to select a sample that is a crosssection of the whole. They might, for example, want 4 percent of their sample to be rural, married, Catholic women, with a high-school education, children, and no outside occupation. If they find a thousand people who meet these requirements, then they would make a random choice from this group.

Which characteristics count? There is no general or automatic way of determining this. There are, however, some methods that help to establish correlations between the factors on which a prediction is based and the results predicted. This is the topic we will consider next.

9.4 MILL'S METHODS

In a famous nineteenth-century treatise on logic, John Stuart Mill explained four methods of inductive reasoning. Few today would agree with his concluding evaluation: "The four methods which it has now been attempted to describe, are the only possible modes of experimental inquiry, of direct induction a *priori,* as distinguished from deduction."[4] Subsequent writers have found it more convenient to divide his methods into five (no real change). Neither Mill nor most who have adopted his methods have given an adequate account of the role presuppositions play an inductive reasoning. Such shortcomings notwithstanding, Mill's five methods supply a good framework for systematizing the methods of inductive reasoning.

We presuppose that there is some puzzling phenomenon to be explained and that plausibility considerations have led to the introduction of various hypotheses to explain the occurrence of the phenomenon. What we wish to consider now are some methods for deciding which hypotheses to accept or reject.

1. The method of agreement   Consider the simple example mentioned earlier, the high-school students who come down with stomach cramps and nausea in the afternoon. The most plausible assumption is that something served for lunch in the high-school cafeteria was responsible. But what? In an attempt to answer this, we collect a random sample of students. From the questions we ask them we construct the following table, where "+" signifies an affirmative answer to a question like, "Did you eat hamburger?," while "−" signifies a negative response.

STUDENT	HAMBURGER	FRIES	CARROTS	CAKE	JELLO	COLA	NAUSEA
Gillis	+	+	−	+	−	+	+
Munsler	−	−	−	+	+	+	−
Bacon	+	+	+	−	+	−	+
Ruis	−	+	−	−	+	+	+
Brossart	+	−	+	−	−	−	−
Marrow	+	+	+	+	+	+	+
Johnson	−	+	−	+	+	−	+
Hanrahan	+	−	−	+	−	+	−

(9.6)

What was responsible for the nausea? Let's try to correlate hamburgers and nausea. Gillis, Bacon, and Marrow had hamburgers and experienced nausea. But Brossart and Hanrahan had hamburger without nausea, while Ruis and Johnson did not have hamburger and did experience nausea. If we look at the next column in (9.6) we see that Gillis, Bacon, Ruis, Marrow, and Johnson all had fries and all experienced nausea. If we check the other columns we do not find a similar correlation with any other food item. Should we conclude that the fries caused the nausea?

J. S. Mill thought we should. His canon for the method of agreement was: If two or more instances of the phenomenon under investigation have only one circumstance in common, the circumstance in which alone all the instances agree is the cause (or effect) of the given phenomenon. This sort of dogmatic pronouncement, still repeated in some logic books, has brought Mill's methods into disfavor. Suppose that chart (9.6) is accurate but that Gillis, Bacon, Ruis, and Marrow and Johnson all spent the afternoon in a room where the heating system leaked carbon monoxide. That could be the cause and the fries could be innocent. Suppose that the fries had too much grease, but that this produced nausea only on an empty stomach. Then the fries might be a causal factor, but skipping breakfast would also be a contributing factor.

The method of agreement, as well as Mill's other methods should not be interpreted as *establishing* causal connections, but as a *guide* to inferences. To be clear on the type of inferences involved, we should briefly review some points developed in chapter 5. If A is a sufficient condition for B, as having four quarters is a *sufficient* condition for having a dollar, then two types of inferences are justified:

From the *presence* of A infer the *presence* of B
From the *absence* of B infer the *absence* of A

Suppose that X is a *necessary* condition for Y, as being a citizen is a necessary condition for being president. This also licenses two types of inferences:

From the *absence* of X infer the *absence* of Y
From the *presence* of Y infer the *presence* of X.

In inductive arguments we begin with an effect—a puzzling phenomenon—and seek the factors responsible. In the method of agreements we are attempting to determine what factors are always present whenever the effect is present. If the effect can occur while some particular factor, A, is absent, then A cannot be a necessary condition for the effect. If A is present whenever the effect occurs, then A could be a necessary condition. This necessary condition may well be a cause. Though Mill's methods by themselves do not supply an adequate basis for distinguishing between causes and conditions that are not causes, it is customary to use the term cause loosely and speak of Mill's method as a search for causes.

If we accept the presupposition that the food eaten in the school cafeteria was responsible for the nausea, then the method of agreements suggests that eating fries was a necessary condition (or part of a necessary condition) for getting nausea. Inductive reasoning is geared to policies of acceptance. Since acceptance is part of practical reasoning, it depends on motives for acceptance.

To make this more concrete, consider people with different motives looking at chart (9.6). The first is a student who is thinking of ordering fries. It is perfectly reasonable for this student to conclude "I won't order fries, because they might cause nausea." The second is the cook who prepares the fries. Chart (9.6) is certainly an adequate reason to investigate the fries and their preparation. The third person is the biology teacher who wants to determine the cause of the nausea. She would find chart (9.6) an initial guide in her search, but would not consider the search complete until she found the factor in the fries or their preparation responsible for the nausea. The fourth is a lawyer representing a group of students who want to sue the school for damages due to food poisoning. He too might find chart (9.6) a helpful guide. But no reasonable jury would consider that sufficient evidence to establish food poisoning due to fries as the cause of nausea.

The method of agreement is not a mechanical method of determining causal relations. Yet, it is helpful as a guide to inferences and practical decisions. Instead of the simplified artificial case of the sick students, consider a phenomenon that at present remains an outstanding puzzle. AIDS (Acquired Immune Deficiency Syndrome) is primarily found among homosexual men, addicts using drugs intravenously, hemophiliacs treated with blood transfusions, and Haitian refugees in the United States. It has spread to others, such as women in contact with infected men and babies receiving blood transfusions. Yet the primary group of victims are members of the four classes listed.

No one now knows what are the causes or conditions producing AIDS. People investigating this have been attempting to determine what factor members of these four groups have in common. Since none of the easy solutions worked, the investigation continues. Suppose that some factor could be found to be present in members of the four groups more strongly than in the general population, a factor such as susceptibility to some virus. This would not settle the issue of what causes AIDS. But it would guide further research. It could also guide practical decisions on methods of avoiding AIDS. This is similar to the situation considered in the last chapter. John Snow never really determined the cause of cholera. Yet, his inductive reasoning led to the conclusion that it was some factor transmitted through water and absorbed through the mouth into the digestive system. This guided such practical choices as how to get and treat the water supply for London.

2. The method of differences.   With this method we try to determine what factors are missing whenever the effect is absent. Since we are again arguing from the effect to the responsible factors, this is a search for a possible sufficient cause. Suppose, for example, that the workers at a chemical plant have an abnormally high incidence of skin cancer. It is plausible to assume that some factor in the working environment is responsible. But which factor? One might try to correlate particular factors in the plant with high correlations. But this would probably not be very effective if, for example, the smell of chemicals is circulated through the air-conditioning system so that everyone is exposed to it.

A typical experimental procedure to determine the responsible factor would involve exposing mice to concentrated doses of all the factors suspected of being the responsible agent. If the mice show a high incidence of skin cancer, then the experimenters would expose one group of mice to the same ingredients minus factor A, a second to the same ingredients minus factor B, etc. Suppose that every group shows a high incidence of skin cancer except the fourth group. These are exposed to all the plant chemicals except factor D. Then D would seem to be a cause, or sufficient condition, of the skin cancer, on the grounds that when D is absent the high incidence of skin cancer is also absent. It need not be a necessary condition, since factors other than D could also cause skin cancer.

Here again we will use the terms 'cause' and 'causal factor' loosely. Then the method of differences can be stated: *If the absence of antecedent factor, D, is always correlated with the absence of an effect, E, then D is a causal factor (or sufficient condition) for E.*

3. The method of agreement and disagreement.   This is a straightforward combination of the two methods just considered—so straightforward that Mills did not list it as a separate method. Chart (9.6) might seem to illustrate it. Whenever fries are present, nausea is present; whenever fries are absent, nausea is absent. This, however, does not really illustrate the use of a joint method; it simply indicates that (9.6) is a highly simplified chart.

Let's return to the previous example and the conclusion that factor D is responsible for the high incidence of skin cancer. The correlation established by the method of difference certainly supplies an adequate basis for drawing the conclusion that workers in the plant should not be exposed to this factor. It does not, however, supply an adequate basis for an article in a medical journal pinpointing D as a carcinogen. What most experimenters would do in this case is supplement the method of disagreement with the method of agreement. Isolate factor D. Shave some mice and then rub factor D on the mice's bare skin. If they contract skin cancer in the exposed area, then one has a strong basis for concluding that this factor is indeed a carcinogen. The method of agreement and the method of differences are used together as a check on each other.

Real experiments are more complicated than these simple examples in at least two ways. In the first place, in real experiments it is necessary to conduct double-blind experiments. Suppose that a researcher is attempting to determine whether some ingredient advertised as an appetite suppressor really does suppress appetites. In testing the ingredient's effectiveness, he must make sure that the well-known placebo effect does not affect his results. People who take a pill that they think will produce a certain effect are likely to experience that effect no matter what's in the pill. To counteract this, an experimenter needs a control group, people who get a pill that does not contain the ingredient being tested. The volunteers should not know whether they are in the test group or the control group. If the pill is really effective, results should be stronger in the test group than in the control group.

Patients are not the only ones influenced by their anticipations. A study of behavioral research led to the conclusion that if one group of experimenters has one hypothesis about what they expect to find, while another group of experimenters has the opposite hypothesis, then each group will obtain results that accord with the hypothesis it favors.[5] To counteract this, the people evaluating the results of the experiment should also be ignorant of which people are in which group. For this reason some random process is generally used to determine who is in the control group and who is in the test group.

This does not contradict the method of agreement and disagreement. It simply uses an extension of the method to eliminate extraneous factors. The other complicating factor in actual research is the need to rely on statistical correlations rather than the simple correlations presented here. Such considerations go beyond the scope of the present book. They do not, however, change the principles involved. One uses a statistical method to try to determine which factors are most likely to be present when the effect in question is present, and absent when the effect is absent.

With these qualifications, the Method of Agreement and Disagreement can be presented in summary form: *If the presence of a factor, A, is always correlated with the presence of an effect, E, and the absence of A is correlated with the absence of E then A is a cause (or necessary and sufficient condition) of E.*

    4. The method of concomitant variations.   The methods just considered are most effective when one is dealing with yes/no issues, rather than questions of degree. One tests to see what happens when some particular factor is present and what happens when it is absent. In many cases, however, we are concerned with the correlation between *degrees* of presence and absence. A farmer finds that his corn is not growing very tall and suspects that his soil is deficient in certain ingredients. As an experiment he, or researchers at an agricultural college, might divide a cornfield into sections and then give section one one dose of nutrient, section two two doses, etc. If he finds that within certain limits there is a clear correlation between the amount of the nutrient and the height of the corn, then he has learned how to produce better corn.

    This is an example of the method of concomitant variations. It may be summarized: *If a variation in an antecedent factor, D, is always correlated with a variation in the effect, E, then D and E are causally related.* Here again, the term 'cause' is being used loosely. This method *suggests* a causal connection, but further investigation is usually required to *establish* such a connection.

    One of the best examples of use of this method is a study initiated in the late 1950s by the American Cancer Society of the correlation of smoking with health problems. They took as their basis 187,000 men, some non-smokers, some light smokers, and some heavy smokers. Their study indicated that cigarette smokers died from heart attacks at a rate 70 percent higher than those who had never smoked, while deaths from lung cancer were ten times more frequent among cigarette smokers than among non-smokers. Their study was followed by the U.S. surgeon general's report of 1964 and by later reports showing a strong correlation between the number of cigarettes smoked and the incidence of lung cancer, heart disease, emphysema, cirrhosis of the liver, and other ailments. Such followup on preliminary studies illustrates the proper role of this method. The followup presented very strong evidence of a causal relation between cigarette smoking and serious health problems. It did not pinpoint the causal factors involved, but it did guide the search for such factors.

    Cigarette smoke contains more than 3,000 chemical substances. Four have been isolated as particularly harmful. Carbon monoxide interferes with the blood's ability to carry oxygen and thus contributes to heart problems and hardening of the arteries. Nicotine, the factor that makes smoking addictive, is a poison. Tars in cigarette smoke are known to be carcinogens. Finally, tiny smoke particles are absorbed in and damage the lining of the lungs.

This example illustrates the way inductive methods generally fit into an overall research program. These methods build on presuppositions, such as the presupposition that cigarette smoking is related to health problems. Inductive methods verified this presupposition and established clear correlations between the number of cigarettes smoked and the incidence of different health problems. These established correlations supplied a basis and a guide for further investigations aimed at determining which factors in cigarette smoke are responsible for individual health problems.

The method of concomitant variations is particularly helpful in analyzing situations that are *not* under a researcher's control, whether for physical or moral reasons. Astronomers, for example, cannot manipulate stars to test hypotheses, such as the recent hypothesis that stars that erupt in nova explosions are always superdense stars coupled to other stars in a binary system. They can only search for correlations between novas and binary systems. The World Health Organization is concerned with the relation between malnutrition and infant mortality rates. No responsible researcher would attempt to investigate this by depriving children of essential nutrients and then correlating the degree of deprivation with the number of deaths by starvation. In place of such a direct experiment, investigators collect the data available on nutritional deficiencies and infant mortality figures and examine the correlations between the two. This is quite similar to what John Snow did in looking for an area where he could investigate the correlation between the two different sources of drinking water and the incidence of cholera.

All of Mill's methods are open to abuse; none more than the method of concomitant variations. Because of the widespread use made of this method it is well to be aware of two prominent abuses: reliance on spurious correlations, and the misinterpretation of variations. The first is aptly illustrated by the attempts that have been made to find correlations between the Dow-Jones closing average and some other factor that might serve to predict this average or other stock market averages. People have bet on the height of hemlines, the standing of the New York Yankees, the water level in Lake Michigan, and astrological signs. Only one such correlation has strong inductive support. This is a correlation which we may call the SP–SB effect. The name is mine, but the discovery is not. I do not know who first noted the correlation. The effect is summarized in the table below.

The SB–SP Effect

SB	NFL TEAM	SCORE		AFL TEAM	SP 400
I	Green Bay Packers	35	10	Kansas City Chiefs	+23.3
II	Green Bay Packers	30	14	Oakland Raiders	+7.5
III	Baltimore Colts	7	16	New York Jets	−10.2
IV	Minnesota Vikings	7	23	Kansas City Chiefs	−0.6

The SB–SP Effect (*continued*)

SB	NFL TEAM	SCORE		AFL TEAM	SP 400
V	Dallas Cowboys	13	16	Baltimore Colts	+ 11.7
VI	Dallas Cowboys	24	3	Miami Dolphins	+ 17
VII	Washington Redskins	7	14	Miami Dolphins	− 17.4
VIII	Minnesota Vikings	7	24	Miami Dolphins	− 29.9
IX	Minnesota Vikings	6	16	Pittsburgh Steelers	+ 31.9
X	Dallas Cowboys	17	21	Pittsburgh Steelers	+ 18.4
XI	Minnesota Vikings	14	32	Oakland Raiders	− 12.3
XII	Dallas Cowboys	27	10	Denver Broncos	+ 2.4
XIII	Dallas Cowboys	31	35	Pittsburgh Steelers	+ 12.9
XIV	Los Angeles Rams	19	31	Pittsburgh Steelers	+ 27.6
XV	Philadelphia Eagles	10	27	Oakland Raiders	− 11.2
XVI	San Francisco 49ers	26	21	Cincinnati Bengals	+ 15
XVII	Washington Redskins	27	17	Miami Dolphins	− 23
XVIII	Washington Redskins	9	38	Los Angeles Raiders	??

SP 400 stands for the Standard and Poor's 400, a basic indicator of growth and decline on the stock market. The numbers in that column indicate the trend for that year. With five exceptions, there seems to be a definite trend. When an NFL team wins the Superbowl stocks go up, when an AFL team wins they go down. The Dow-Jones averages for the year show the same trend, but the correlation is not as precise. The figures for 1984 are not yet available. However, the day after the record Raiders (AFL) win the Dow-Jones dropped 14.6 points.

What makes this correlation truly remarkable is a consideration of the apparent exceptions, Superbowls V, IX, X, XIII, and XVII. The present division of teams stems from 1970 when the two leagues were reorganized into three Conferences: Eastern, Central, and Western. The NFL is the senior league, founded in 1925. The AFL was organized in 1959. It effectively superseded the All American Football Conference, organized in 1946. Baltimore became a member of this conference in 1947, when it took over a franchise that Miami had forfeited. The Colts joined the NFL in 1950. At that time the Pittsburgh Steelers belonged to the NFL. If one counts the Steelers as an *original* NFL team and the Colts as an *original* AFL team then Superbowls V, IX, X, and XIII fit the pattern. When an *original* NFL team wins, the SP 400 average for the year goes up; when an *original* AFL team wins, the SP 400 goes down.

Superbowl XVII seems to be the glaring exception to the SB–SP effect. The Washington Redskins are a long-time member of the NFL; they were NFL champions in 1937 and 1942. However, when the National American Football Conference was organized on March 4, 1950, the Redskins were in the NAFC. If this is counted as a predecessor of the AFL, then it can be

244 Methods of Inductive Reasoning

argued that the Redskins count as an *original* AFL team. If this dubious exception is allowed, then the SB–SP rule fits every case. If the first year is taken as a coincidence, then the chances of repeating the coincidence the next year are 1 in 2. The odds against repeating the coincidence seventeen years in a row are 1/65536.

The SB–SP effect has extremely strong empirical support. Should it be considered an established law or a mere coincidence? The answer to this question depends on one's interpretation of induction. The interpretation I have presented is that inductive evidence must be interpreted against a background of established laws and rules. Inductive arguments rest on plausible presuppositions of causal relations. The stock market aptly illustrates this. Individuals buy and sell stocks for a variety of reasons, including some irrational ones. Yet, the stock market has a *collective* rationality. When the economic indicators are good, the various stock market averages go up; when they are bad, the averages go down. There are plausible grounds for believing that a tightening or loosening of the money supply, a rise in the price of oil, or a crippling strike will have a causal effect on the Dow-Jones closing average or the SP yearly figures.

Of the various stock market indicators we have considered, the only one that has a supporting reason is the correlation with hemlines. The argument is that in times of recession people tend to be cautious and conservative, while in times of expansion they are more daring. Thus, miniskirts are an indication of self-confidence for the economy as well as for the women who wear them. This is a very weak argument. If it has any validity, it would indicate that the height of hemlines is an *effect* rather than a *predictor* of the stock market.

In the best of my knowledge, no one has presented any plausible reasons for the SB–SP effect. Without a supporting reason, the effect has to be considered a pure coincidence. I find the coincidence less striking than it appears to be on two grounds. First, the exceptions are interpreted away by dubious arguments (something philosophers call *ad hoc* hypotheses). If the SP average for 1983 had gone up 23 points, rather than down, then the Redskins would have been counted as an original NFL team. Second, if one searches long enough through enough data, some remarkable coincidences can always be found. On these grounds I conclude that the SB–SP effect is *not* an established law. If this interpretation is correct, then future figures should supply violations of the effect.

Astrology presents a more interesting case. Since its inception, around 300 B.C., astrologers have presented a variety of reasons to support their claims of a strong correlation between the planets in ascendency at the time of one's birth and one's future career. There have even been a few studies by nonastrologers that seem to supply statistical support for this contention.[6] Should this combination of astrological arguments and statistical evidence be interpreted as supporting the basic claims of astrology?

The influence that planets have through gravitational forces is well understood. The further forces postulated, at least implicitly, by astrologers, do not merely go beyond present physics and astronomy. They blatantly contradict well-established laws and theories. Established laws can be falsified. Accepted theories can eventually be rejected. But this happens when there is data contradicting established laws or a newer theory that replaces an established theory. Astrology does not fit into this pattern in any way. The laws of astrology do not correct or replace established scientific laws. What little theory astrology has bears no relation to any established scientific theory.

No inductive support for astrology could be considered as strong supporting evidence unless there were well-established and clearly defined correlations between astrological signs and randomly selected careers. Here the randomness is crucial. Astrologers can always find some careers that seem to fit their schemas. This is not a test, since evidence that does not support the theory is systematically ignored. If such random correlations were clearly established, then, as in the smoking studies, it would be important to take the next step and try to explain how astrological signs influence careers. At present the actual support for astrology rests on shoddy statistics and biased interpretations, without a trace of any real theory explaining how the postulated effects are produced. There is no rational ground for accepting astrology. The widespread inclusion of astrology columns in newspapers and magazines has to be interpreted as a commercially motivated capitulation of editors to the forces of irrationality.

The misinterpretation of correlations is generally done by those with a vested interest in supporting some conclusion. What makes this fairly easy is that, though an interpretation of correlations depends on a detailed analysis, a presentation of correlations is usually done by means of graphs or simple claims. Thus, it used to be claimed that Listerine helps prevent colds because Listerine kills more germs than any other mouthwash. The manufacturers failed to mention that there is no evidence that the germs that Listerine kills are responsible for colds.

Suppose an oil company makes a profit of $1,000,000,000. By various correlations this can be interpreted as a 2 percent return on sales, an 11 percent return on investments, a 2000 percent increase over the 1944–1946 average, or a 13 percent decrease compared to projected profits. The fact that this is a 4 percent increase over last year's profits could be presented to the general public as something relatively insignificant by a graph that only considers profits subsequent to the massive increases of the mid 1970s:

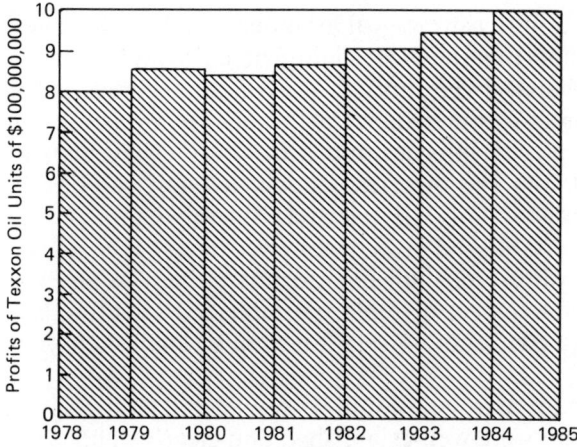

The same figures could be presented to investors as a significant increase in profits by a different graph,

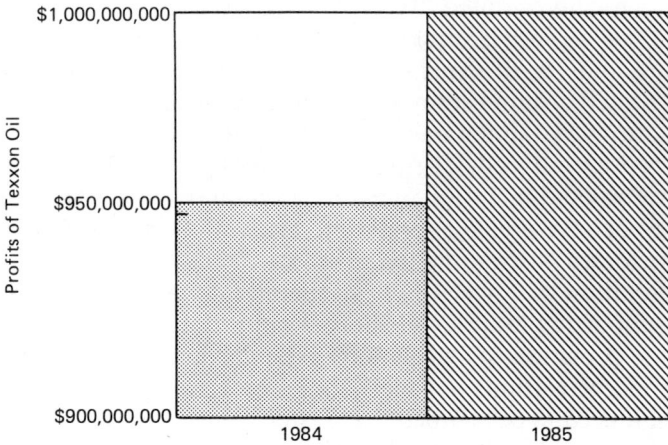

It is helpful to understand the method of concomitant variations not merely as a means of doing inductive reasoning, but also as a means of checking inductive arguments. Some awareness of its proper use and limitations should make us more critical of the spurious correlations and misleading inferences to which we are all regularly exposed.

5. *The method of residues.* To get sand for my daughter's sandbox I filled my car with empty boxes and then went to the local sand and gravel company. They weighed my car on the way in and weighed it again on the way out, when all the boxes were filled with sand. The difference between the two figures gave the amount of sand I had collected. This simple example is a model for the method of residues. Like the method of concomitant

variations, it is concerned with quantitative correspondences. Suppose that there is a certain effect, such as water decreasing in a storage tank, and that 90 percent of this effect can be explained by known causes. Then the residue must be explained by some other cause, perhaps one not yet known.

The now standard illustration of this method manifests both its strength and its limitations. In 1781 William Herschel discovered the planet Uranus. After there were enough good sightings to fix its orbit, it was possible to predict its future position on the basis of Newtonian mechanics. It travels in an ellipse governed by Kepler's law with perturbations due to the gravitational influences of Jupiter and Saturn. Later observations, over a period of sixty years, showed an increasing discrepancy between the observed and predicted values.

Independently, John Adams in England in 1845 and Urbain Leverrier in France argued that the residue in the effect must be due to a new cause, a planet outside Uranus's orbit that causes further perturbations. Each predicted, on the basis of Newtonian mechanics, where the postulated planet should be. Only Leverrier's claim was adequately implemented. He sent a letter, which was received by Johann Galle, a Berlin astronomer, on September 23, 1846. Within half an hour Galle found Neptune within 1° of the predicted position (but much bigger and much further out than anticipated). The method of residues had proved a resounding success.

Since 1842, Leverrier had been making detailed studies of the orbit of Mercury. By 1849 he concluded that the advance of the perihelion of Mercury (its closest approach to the sun) was not the 527 seconds of arc per century predicted on the basis of Newtonian mechanics but 527 seconds + 38 seconds. The problem he then faced was one of accounting for this 38 second residue. Not surprisingly, he repeated the method that had led to his greatest success. He postulated a tiny planet, Vulcan, between Mercury and the sun, which perturbed the orbit of Mercury as Neptune perturbed the orbit of Uranus.

Astronomers began a systematic search and quite a few reported sightings of Vulcan. Eventually it was realized that the sightings that were not pure fabrications were sightings of sunspots. The residue remained until 1916, when Einstein's general theory of relativity accounted precisely for the 43-second (an improvement over Leverrier's figures) advance of the perihelion of Mercury. Leverrier's reasoning presupposed the absolute validity of Newtonian mechanics. Einstein's general theory of relativity was an advance over and supplied corrections to Newtonian gravitational theory. The method of residues failed in this case. It failed, not because the method was wrong, but because the presuppositions it rested on were not adequate.[7]

After Neptune was discovered, astronomers began to track its orbit and compare observational data with theoretical predictions. By the early part of the present century it was clear that there was a significant discrepancy between the two. In 1915 the astronomer Percival Lowell published calculations predicting another planet outside the orbit of Neptune. This planet was discovered in 1930 by Clyde Tombaugh and named Pluto, so that the first two initials honored its predictor. The method of residues seemed to have another success.

A few years ago a tiny moon was discovered circuling Pluto. This enabled astronomers to determine Pluto's mass and to prove conclusively that Pluto was far too small to be the factor perturbing Neptune's orbit. At the present writing it is not known what this factor is. It could be a bigger planet a little further out, or a small dark star a lot further out. For technical reasons it seems clear that the discrepancy cannot be explained in this case by any inadequancy of Newtonian laws. So, the method of residues insists, there must be some presently unknown factor responsible for the as-yet-unexplained perturbation of Neptune's orbit.

9.5 THE PLACE OF INDUCTIVE REASONING

Now that we have surveyed the methods of inductive reasoning we are in a better position to consider the question: When are inductive methods appropriate? The standard answers to this question are those given by logicians who work in the field of inductive logic. They develop methods of inductive and probabilistic reasoning and then search for applications of these methods. They would generally answer that inductive methods are appropriate wherever they may be applied.

My answer to this question emerges from a different perspective, from a detailed historical examination of the way explanations function in the development of scientific thought.[8] Such historical studies indicate that inductive methods are basic at certain stages of development and tangential at others. By a rather gross oversimplification we may apply the lessons learned from the history of science to other fields. The typical development of a scientific theory can be broken down into three states: the initial stage, the formative period, and theoretical unification.

The initial stage occurs when some new domain is opened up to scientific investigation. In the late nineteenth century, for example, both anthropology and psychology emerged as new scientific disciplines. One might think that the activity proper to this stage is careful observation free from any theoretical preconceptions, a series of observations that gradually lead to articulation of empirical laws by the use of inductive methods. This never works. The rise of anthropology shows the pattern that is much more common.

The nineteenth-century founders of anthropology, L.H. Morgan, H. Spencer, E. Tylor, and others, began with theories about how any society *must* develop. It develops through stages of savagery, barbarism, and civilization. Each stage can be subdivided into substages characterized by tools and techniques. Thus, lower savagery is, in one scheme, characterized by fruit and nut subsistence; middle savagery by catching fish and building fires; upper savagery by the use of the bow and arrow. These stages were not derived from a study of primitive societies. They were derived from other sources, such as the writings of the French social theorist Montesquieu, and applied to the study of other societies. This approach implies that primitive societies in Africa, the South Pacific, the Pacific Northwest, or wherever, would, granted sufficient time, evolve in the direction of nineteenth-century European society—a highly implausible conjecture.

Plausible or not, such schematic outlines supplied a framework for knowing what sorts of data to collect and compare, such as the tools a society uses, its method of subsistence, its social organization. This led to extensive research and fact gathering. The facts eventually ruptured the framework that shaped their emergence and organization. Then fieldworkers began more inductive searches for general laws. They were guided in their search by some awareness of how observations and data clustered together in meaningful patterns. Something similar happened in the development of psychology. W. Wundt, the key figure in the transformation of psychology into a scientific discipline, thought of systematic introspection as *the* basic method of observation in psychology. This presupposition led to extensive fact gathering. Here again, the next generation abandoned this introspective approach. Unfortunately, there is still no agreement on proper methods or basic laws of psychology.

All of us are at times confronted by problems that we do not understand, situations where we have no clear idea of how to begin coming to an understanding. One is tempted to think that if one just collects enough facts a meaningful pattern will emerge. This almost never happens. Any hypothesis, no matter how implausible, is preferable to conceptual chaos. This is the time for daring, for wild conjectures, the "anything goes" stage of development. It is also the "easy come—easy go" stage of development. If a tentative conjecture cannot accommodate the data or a plan shows no sign of success, it should be abandoned and a new one should be tried.

Few in the history of science have put in the sustained effort at developing empirical generalizations that Johannes Kepler (1571–1630) put into the discovery of the three basic laws of planetary motion. Like many other discoverers, he began with a conjecture that ultimately proved untenable— that the orbits of the planets can be explained in terms of the five regular solids of Euclidean geometry. Even when the data would not fit his hypothesis he remained convinced that planetary orbits must be regular geometric figures and that there must be a regular correlation between such factors as position in an orbit and velocity, or between distance from the sun and period of revolution. Only the data, however, could supply a basis for determining what these correlations are. When the data did not fit his preconceptions, he kept trying other conjectures and adjustments until he finally found three laws that did fit. These were empirical laws with no theoretical justification.

This typifies the stage of development where inductive methods are most needed, when a body of knowledge has been sufficiently developed so that some sort of order has emerged. People know that correlations must obtain, but do not know what correlations obtain. Yet the science has not yet reached a stage of deductive unification that allows one to deduce factual conclusions from first principles.

Much of psychology, medicine, and the social sciences are at this stage of development. When a new disease appears, doctors know the sorts of entities that could be responsible, such as viruses or bacteria. They use inductive methods to determine which entities are actually involved. Psychologists plausibly assume that there must be a correlation between on-the-job stress and worker productivity. So, they use empirical methods to correlate different stress-producing factors with various aspects of productivity. The statistician's favorite model, a blindfolded person taking marbles out of an urn and then trying to determine what percentage are a certain color, bears little resemblance to most of the uses of inductive methods in science. These rest on presuppositions and on networks of established relations.

In such sciences as physics and chemistry, empirical generalizations are generally superseded by developed theories. Kepler's law (or the theoretical equivalent of these laws) can be deduced from Newtonian mechanics. Each atom emits characteristic spectral lines when heated. Thus, sodium, heated in a sodium vapor lamp, emits a distinctive yellow light due to spectral lines in the yellow part of the spectrum. Spectroscopists spent years developing and improving inductive laws about regularities in spectral lines. All of these can be deduced from quantum theory. Within such a science, inductive methods now play only a supplemental role, usually to determine relations that are too complicated to be deduced from first principles. One who wants to work in the field must either learn the theory or learn how to appraise the experts who already know the theory.

Most practical decisions are made on a quasi-inductive trial-and-error basis. A buyer for a department store relies on past experience to guess what dresses will sell next spring. A broker trying to find shrewd investments, a meteorologist trying to predict tomorrow's weather, a gambler trying to pick the winer of the next race, a pollster trying to predict the winner of an election all rely on inductive methods. These methods have an intermediate status. They have no use in a conceptual vacuum, in a chaos of random observations and unrelated facts. At the other extreme, inductive methods are generally a waste of time and effort when correlations can be determined theoretically. Even in the practical fields just considered, the growing use of computer programs drawing on large data banks provides the equivalent of a theory, a quasi-automatic way of determining correlations. The old-fashioned broker, who still believes in flying by the seat of his pants, is lumbering into extinction as computer networks and massive data banks guide newer brokers.

The intermediate range is one in which correlations are reasonably believed to exist, but their precise nature is unknown. Conditioning must influence behavior; social and economic conditions must correlate with voting patterns; high scores on I.Q. tests must have some relation to future success; the spread of a new form of influenza must be due to some new microorganism; unemployment rates and crime rates are surely related. In these and similar cases one uses inductive methods to try to fix precise correlations. If this succeeds, then the next step should be an attempt to understand why the correlation obtains, to seek causes and develop theories. Inductive methods also have an intermediate status as explanatory mechanisms. They lead from observations to empirical generalizations, and they prepare the ground for the theories or systematic accounts that explain why these regularities obtain.

EXERCISES

A. 1. What is wrong with a deductive justification of induction?
2. Is there anything wrong with using induction to justify the practice of induction?
3. What does the vindication of induction presuppose?
4. Can a limited generalization ever be established by simple enumeration?
5. What is wrong with attempting to establish an unlimited generalization by simple enumeration?
6. Is it ever reasonable to rely on induction?
7. What role do presuppositions play in inductive arguments?
8. What is meant by 'plausibility level'?
9. What is the relation between plausibility levels and classes of hypotheses?
10. Might inductive hypotheses be unreasonable on a first level of plausibility and yet be reasonably entertained on a higher level?
11. What is meant by 'resemblance class predicate'?
12. What is the difference between resemblance class predicates and the class predicates considered in logic?
13. How can a concept imply an empirical generalization?
14. What is meant by a necessary condition?
15. What is meant by a sufficient condition?
16. Is the cause of an event always a necessary condition for the occurrence of the event? Give an example that illustrates your answer.
17. What is Mill's method of agreement?
18. What is Mill's method of differences?
19. What sort of condtions are picked out by the joint method of agreement and differences?
20. What general difference is there between Mill's first three methods and the last two?
21. How does the method of concomitant variations work?
22. Might the method of concomitant variations work for negative as well as positive correlations?
23. What is the method of residues?
24. Can a fruitful investigation ever be based on an unreasonable or implausible hypothesis?
25. Can one use Mill's methods without relying on hypotheses?
26. Do scientific investigations always rely on inductive methods?

B. I. Relatively Simple Inductive Arguments
For the following (somewhat artificial) examples:

   a)   determine whether the argument is deductive or inductive;
   b)   if it is inductive, determine what method of induction is employed;
   c)   appraise the strength of the argument.

1. The evidence shows that the animal involved was cold-blooded and had a shell on its back. All cold-blooded animals with shells on their backs are turtles. So, the animal was a turtle.

*2. A sixth-grade teacher began a systematic study of pupils who performed poorly in spite of having high scores on aptitude tests. Some came from fairly wealthy families; a few from poor families; and the majority from middle-class families. About 60 percent of the underachievers were boys. Approximately 80 percent came from broken families. Almost 85 percent were interested in sports, and 95 percent watched television regularly. The teacher concluded that the broken-family situation was the chief cause of underachievement.

3. Harrison was elected president in 1840 and died in office. So did Lincoln, elected in 1860; Garfield, elected in 1880; McKinley, elected in 1900; Harding, elected in 1920; Roosevelt, elected in 1940; and Kennedy, elected in 1960. Anyone elected president in a year divisible by 20 is likely to die in office.

4. The manager of a factory decided that productivity was too low. So, she instituted a system of bonuses for those who were most productive. This had little effect on overall productivity. Next, with the consent of the union, she switched the workers from payment by the hour to piece work. This too had little effect, partially because of the union's insistence that the switchover was acceptable only if there was no decrease in the average pay check. Finally, she tried a ten-minute rest period every two hours. This increased productivity to acceptable levels. She concluded that regular rest periods improved productivity.

*5. Wee Willie spent Sunday evening drinking scotch and soda. On Monday morning he had an awful hangover. So he spent Monday night drinking bourbon and soda. Since this also produced a bad hangover, he switched to rye and soda Tuesday evening. One more hangover; so he spent Wednesday evening drinking vodka and soda. Another bad hangover. On Thursday evening he drank gin and soda. The Friday morning hangover was the worst of the week. So Wee Willie spent Friday evening drinking cognac and soda. Saturday morning was as bad as the rest. Then Wee Willie spent Saturday afternoon studying Mill's methods of induction and found the solution to his problem. "No more soda water for me," resolved Wee Willie.

*6. The greenskeeper saw that the grass on the fourth and sixth fairways was not growing well. He marked off a patch of the sixth fairway into six sections, each one foot square, and tried various experiments. In Section 1 he sprinkled a cup of fertilizer that had 10 percent nitrate-form nitrogen. This improved the growth. He sprinkled two cups of this fertilizer on section two and found that the grass grew better than in section 1. He sprinkled 3 cups on section three. The grass grew as profusely as in section 2, but much of it was burnt and withered. In section 4 he sprinkled one cup of a more expensive fertilizer containing 12 percent nitrate-form nitrogen. This grass seemed better than section 1, but not as good as section 2. In section 5 he tried 2 cups of the 12 percent fertilizer. This produced the best grass. In section 6 he tried 3 cups of the new fertilizer and found that the grass was badly burned. What method of treating the fourth and sixth fairways would represent the best combination of efficiency and economy?

7. In 1963 geneticist Baruch Blumberg found a new type of antigen (a special type of foreign substance that provokes the body's immune system) in blood serum taken

from an Australian Aborigine. He named it the Au-antigen. Blumberg began a systematic search of blood samples and learned that the Au-antigen was frequently found in blood serum taken from people living in Asia or Africa, but rarely found in blood serum taken from people living in North America or Western Europe. This paralleled the incidence of the infection known as hepatitis B. It was believed that hepatitis B was transmitted only by transfusion from a carrier of the infection or by innoculation involving a needle previously used on a hepatitis victim and not properly sterilized.

Students at the Willowbrook State School for retarded children in New York had an extremely high rate of hepatitis. A study conducted by Doctor Saul Krugman showed that a relatively high number of blood samples taken from Willowbrook students had Au-antigen. Some of the samples were from students not of Asian or African origin who had not received transfusion. Investigators concluded that Au-antigen was an indication of the presence of the virus responsible for one type of hepatitis and that hepatitis B could be transmitted by means other than injections and transfusions.

8. The suicide rate in the U.S. has been rising for the last twenty-five years. The official estimate is now 30,000 suicides a year. The actual number is probably considerably higher, since many coroners do not report a death as a suicide unless there is a suicide note. Suicidologists tend to link suicide with acute depression, which could be due to organic factors, or brought about by economic, social, or personal failure. Yet they regularly encounter cases of suicide where there are no indications of depression, failure, or lineliness. They conclude that some unknown factor must be responsible for these suicides.

9. Heavyweight boxing fights cause the U.S. murder rate to jump dramatically. Dr. David Phillips examined the homicide rates after eighteen heavyweight championship fights over a five year period and noted that the homicide rates shot up after the fights. The greatest jump, 12.46 percent came on the third day after a fight. It's as if the violence needed a couple of days to brew.[9]

10. The manager of a department store noted that the figures for sales during the year coupled to a detailed computer analysis of the ratio of sales to profits for the seven preceding years indicated that the store should have made a profit of $1,600,000. However, the actual profits were only $1,300,000. $150,000 of this profit gap was accounted for by expenses connected with store renovation. Another $50,000 was lost because a union contract forced the store to contribute more to worker health programs. Another $50,000 could be accounted for by the purchase of a new computer system. Yet, the manager could find no way to account for the $50,000 difference between his projected figures and actual profits. "They are stealing us blind," he concluded.

*11. The following law may be regarded as beyond dispute: *From the standpoint of suicide, marriage is more favorable to the wife the more widely practiced divorce is; and vice versa.*

Woman's sexual needs have less of a mental character because, generally speaking, her mental life is less developed. These needs are more closely related to the needs of the organism, following rather than leading them, and consequently find in them an efficient restraint. Being a more instinctive creature than man, woman has only to follow her instincts to find calmness and peace. She thus does not require so strict a social regulation as marriage, and particularly as monogamic marriage. Even when useful, such a discipline has its inconveniences. By fixing the conjugal state permanently, it prevents all retreat, regardless of consequence. By limiting the horizon, it closes all egress and forbids even legitimate hope. Man himself doubtless suffers from this immutability; but for him the evil is largely compensated by the advantages he gains in other respects. Custom, moreover, grants him certain privileges which allow him in some measure to lessen the strictness of the regime. There is no compensation or relief for the women. Monogamy is strictly obligatory for her, with no qualification of any sort, and, on the other hand, marriage is not in the same degree useful to her for limiting her desires, which are naturally limited, and for teaching her to be contented with her lot; but it prevents her from changing it if it becomes intolerable. Consequently, everything that makes it more flexible and lighter can only better the wife's situation. So divorce protects her and she has frequent recourse to it.[10]

II. More Complex Inductive Arguments
The following arguments are taken chiefly from scientific research. Few, if any, fit neatly into the patterns given by Mill's methods. In most cases it is necessary to reconstruct the argument. After that one should try to bring out:

a) the distinctive presuppositions;
b) the type of reasoning employed, such as reasoning from evidence, testing hypotheses, or using inductive methods;
c) and evaluate the strength of the argument.

C.1. *Transmission of Acquired Characteristics*
The frequent use of any organ, when confirmed by habit, increases the function of that organ, leads to its development and endows it with a size and power that it does not possess in animals that exercise it less.

The bird which is drawn to the water by its need of finding there the prey on which it lives, separates the digits of its feet in trying to strike the water and move about on the surface. The skin which unites these digits at their base acquires the habit of being stretched by these continually repeated separations of the digits, thus in course of time there are formed large webs which unite the digits of ducks, geese, etc., as we actually find them. In the same way efforts to swim, that is to push against the water so as to move about in it, have stretched the membranes between the digits of frogs, sea-tortoises, the otter, beaver, etc.

On the other hand, a bird which is accustomed to perch on trees and which springs from individuals all of whom had acquired this habit, necessarily has longer digits on its feet, and differently shaped from those of the aquatic animals that I have just named. Its claws in time become lengthened, sharpened, and curved into hooks, to clasp the branches on which the animal so often rests.

We find in the same way that the bird of the water-side which does not like swimming and yet is in need of going to the water's edge to secure its prey, is continually liable to sink in the mud. Now the bird tries to act in such a way that its body should not be immersed in the liquid, and hence makes its best efforts to stretch and lengthen its legs. The long-established habit acquired by this bird and all its race of continually stretching and lengthening its legs, results in the individuals of this race becoming raised as though on stilts, and gradually obtaining long bare legs, denuded of feathers up to the thighs and often further still.[11]

2. *Inductive Reasoning by Computers.*
Three researchers in artificial intelligence, Herbert Simon, Patrick Langley, and Gary Bradshaw, developed a program called Bacon.4 (named after the philosopher Francis Bacon, who stressed induction), which trains computers to do inductive reasoning. When given data about the outcomes of experiments, it has rediscovered scores of fundamental laws: Kepler's third law of planetary motion, Archimedes' principle for floating bodies, Boyle's law of gases, and many others. However, neither this, nor any other computer inductive program, has yet discovered a new scientific law. Critics contend that these programs work only on data that has been sufficiently cleaned of extraneous factors and formulated in appropriate concepts. In spite of this shortcoming, many researchers remain convinced that computer programs will eventually discover many new laws.[12]

3. *Kinsey on Female Reticence*

Whether a female decides to begin pre-marital coitus, or to continue it after she has once had it, must depend on a multiplicity of physical, situational, social, and other factors, on some of which we have specific information and on others of which we do not yet have sufficient data for analysis. Interestingly enough, the most significant correlation seems to have been with the presence or absence of experience. Among the unmarried females who had never had coital experience, 80 per cent insisted that they did not intend to have it before marriage; but among those who had already had such experience, only 30 per cent said that they did not intend to have more. A selective factor must have been involved; but it may be noted again that experience dispels many of the fears that gather about the unknown, especially when it is an unknown type of sexual activity.

In their own analyses of the factors which had restricted their pre-marital coitus, 89 per cent of the females in the sample said that moral considerations had been of primary importance. Some of these individuals had identified these factors as moral. However, some of them insisted that they were not accepting the traditional codes just because they were the codes, and believed that they had developed their attitudes as a result of their own rational analyses of what they considered to be expedient, decent, respectable, fine, sensible, right or wrong, better or best. . . .

Some 45 per cent of the females in the sample recognized that their lack of sexual responsiveness had been a factor in limiting their pre-marital activity; but it seems clear that a lack of responsiveness or an inability to respond was even more important than the females themselves understood.

These were the expressed reasons which the females gave for their lack of coitus, or for their decisions to limit their further coitus. In many cases these probably were the factors which had been involved; but in some cases these appeared to be nothing more than rationalizations of the real reasons. Taking all of our experience into account, we are inclined to list, in order of importance, the following as the primary factors which had limited the pre-marital activity of the females in the sample:

1.   The sexual unresponsiveness of many younger females
2.   The moral tradition of our American culture
3.   Lack of experience, and the individual's fear of engaging in any unfamiliar activity.[13]

4. *The Adjacency Principle in Perception*

[Psychologists test the way the perception of an object, such as a light point moving against a black background, is influenced by other objects, such as another light point moving in a perpendicular direction. The adjacency principle states that the relative weight that the perceptual system gives to such clues is inversely proportional to the apparent separation of the two objects.]

A more detailed test of the attention explanation was conducted with the three-dimensional display involving the vertically and horizontally oscillating points. Observers were asked to indicate the direction of the test point's apparent motion while they were attending to one pair of induction points and ignoring the other pair. We measured the ability of attention to account for adjacency effects by noting how the apparent direction changed as attention was directed to one or the other set of induction points. Attention accounted for about half of the total adjacency effect. . . .

Under some conditions, then, attention accounts for a substantial part—but not for all—of the adjacency effect. Its failure to account for all of the effect suggests that adjacency and attention are based on different processes. As for perceptual clarity, it may contribute to adjacency effects, but it cannot account for their magnitude. For example, depth-adjacency effects are present (in such situations as the oscillating point experiment) even when the separation between induction objects is less than the depth of focus of the eye, so that both induction objects are clearly seen. The experiments support the conclusion that although factors such as voluntary attention and visual clarity may contribute to adjacency phenomena, a core of adjacency effects remains that requires the postulation of some kind of unconscious weighing process determined by the perceived spatial separation of the objects.[14]

5. *Oliver Wendell Holmes on Puerperal Fever*

[At age 21, Holmes wrote "Old Ironsides." Later, in 1843, while teaching at Harvard Medical School, he wrote an anlysis of how puerperal, or childbirth, fever is transmitted.]

I am assured, on unquestionable authority, that "about three years since, a gentleman in extensive midwifery business, in a neighboring State, lost in the course of a few weeks eight patients in child-bed, seven of them being undoubted cases of puerperal fever. No other physician in town lost a single patient of this disease in the same period." And from what I have heard in conversation with some of our most experienced practitioners, I am inclined to think many cases of this kind might be brought to light by extensive inquiry.

This long catalogue of melancholy histories assumes a still darker aspect when we remember how kindly nature deals with the parturient female, when she is not immersed in the virulent atmosphere of an impure lying-in hospital, or poisoned in her chambers by the unsuspected breath of contagion. From all causes together not more than four deaths in a thousand births and miscarriages happened in England and Wales during the period embraced by the first Report of the Registrar-General. In the second Report the mortality was shown to be about five on one thousand. . . . In private practice, leaving out of view the cases that are to be acribed to the self-acting system of propagation, it would seem that the disease must be far from common. . . .

In the view of these facts it does appear a singular coincidence that one man or woman should have ten, twenty, thirty, or seventy cases of this rare disease following his or her footsteps with the keenness of a beagle, through the streets and lanes of a crowded city, while the scores that cross the same paths on the same errands know it only by name. It is a series of similar coincidences which has led us to consider the dagger, the musket, and certain innocent-looking white powders to be regarded as dangerous.

I shall now mention a few instances in which the disease appears to have been conveyed by the process of direct innoculation.

Dr. Campbell, of Edinburgh, states that in October, 1821, he assisted at the post-mortem examination of a patient who died with puerperal fever. He carried the pelvic viscera in his pocket to the class-room. The same evening he attended a woman in labor without previously changing his clothes; this patient died. The next morning he delivered a woman with the forceps; she died also, and of many others who were seized with the disease within a few weeks, three shared the same fate in succession. [This Dr. Campbell was a medical professor considered to be an expert on contagion. After listing many more cases Holmes draws some practical conclusions.]

1. A physician holding himself in readiness to attend cases of midwifery should never take an active part in the post-mortem examination of cases of puerperal fever.

2. If a physician is present at such autopsies, he should use thorough ablution, change every article of dress, and allow twenty-four hours or more to elapse before attending to any case of midwifery.

3. On the occurrence of a single case of puerperal fever in his practice, the physician is bound to consider the next female he attends in labor, unless some weeks at least have elapsed, as in danger of being infected by him, and it is his duty to take every precaution to diminish her risk of disease and death.

4. Whatever indulgence may be granted to those who have heretofore been the ignorant causes of so much misery, the time has come when the existence of a *private*

pestilence in the sphere of a single physician should be looked upon, not as a misfortune, but a crime; and in the knowledge of such occurrences the duties of the practitioner to his profession should give way to his paramount obligations to society.[15]

6. *A Lady in Distress — and her Stooges*
[This example was part of an experiment to test the influence of a role model in inducing helping behavior.]

The standard condition consisted of an undergraduate female stationed by a 1964 Ford Mustang (control car) with a flat left rear tire. An inflated tire was leaned upon the left side of the auto. The girl and the flat and the inflated tires were conspicuous to the passing traffic.

In the model condition, a 1965 Oldsmobile was located approximately a quarter of a mile from the control car. The car was raised by jack under the left rear bumper, and a girl was watching a male change the flat tire. Stooges played the same role throughout the experiment.

In the no-model condition, the model was absent; thus only the control car was visible to the passing traffic.

The cars were located in a predominantly residential section in Los Angeles, California. They were placed in such a manner that no intersection separated the model from the control car. No turnoffs were thus available to the passing traffic. Further, opposite flows of traffic were divided by a separator such that the first U turn available to the traffic going in the opposite direction of the control car would be after exposure to the model condition.

The experiment was conducted on two successive Saturdays between the hours of 1:45 and 5:50 P.M. Each treatment condition lasted for the time required for 1,000 vehicles to pass the control car. While private automobiles and trucks, motorscooters and motorcycles were tallied as vehicles, commercial trucks, taxis, and busses were not. Vehicle count was made by a fourth member of the experiment who stood approximately 100 feet from the control car hidden from the passing motorists. On the first Saturday, the model condition was run first and lasted from 1:45 to 3:15. In order to exploit changing traffic patterns and to keep the time intervals equal across treatment conditions, the control car was moved several blocks and placed on the opposite side of the street for the no-model condition. The time of the no-model treatment was 4:00 to 5:00 P.M. On the following Saturday, counterbalancing the order and the location of treatment condition was accomplished. That is, the no-model condition was run initially and the control car was placed in the same location that it had been placed on the previous Saturday during the model condition. The time of the no-model condition was 2:00 to 3:00 P.M. For the model condition, the control car was placed in that locale where it had been previously during the no-model condition. The time of the model condition was 4:30 to 5:30 P.M.

Individuals who had stopped to offer help were told by the young lady that she had already phoned an auto club and that help was imminent. Those who nevertheless insisted on helping her were told the nature of the experiment.

The dependent variable was the number of cars which stopped and from which at least one individual offered help to the stooge by the control car. Of the 4,000 passing vehicles, 93 stopped. With the model car being absent, 35 vehicles stopped; with the model present, 58 halted. The difference between the conditions was statistically significant. . . . The results of the present study support the hypothesis that helping behaviors can be significantly increased through the observation of others' helpfulness.[16]

M. 1. In attempting to reconstruct the ordinary arguments we encounter

    a) we should always attempt an inductive reconstruction.
    b) we should always attempt a deductive reconstruction.

    c)   we inevitably misrepresent the given argument.

    d)   we can generally use either an inductive or a deductive reconstruction.

    e)   we must rely on symbolic logic.

2. An inductive reconstruction is generally preferable

    a)   when we are dealing with facts.

    b)   whenever moral issues are involved.

    c)   only in scientific contexts.

    d)   when the crucial point is the relation of evidence to conclusion.

    e)   when we wish to clarify the overall logical form of the argument.

3. A deductive reconstruction is generally preferable

    a)   when we are dealing with facts.

    b)   whenever moral issues are involved.

    c)   only in scientific contexts.

    d)   when the crucial point is the relation of evidence to conclusion.

    e)   when we wish to clarify the overall logical form of the argument.

4. Inductive generalizations

    a)   are all disguised deductions.

    b)   are never justified in theory or in practice.

    c)   involve policies of acceptance as well as consideration of instances.

    d)   are only reasonably accepted when all possible cases are considered.

    e)   are unscientific.

*5. Most of our everyday inferences

    a)   are purely inductive.

    b)   are purely deductive.

    c)   rest on background presuppositions concerning normal beliefs, intentions, and desires.

    d)   are only reasonably accepted when purged of any influence of desires and intentions.

    e)   should be dismissed, because they are unscientific.

6. If p presupposes q, then

    a)   if q is true, then p must be true.

    b)   if q is false, then p must be false.

    c)   p cannot meaningfully be considered either true or false unless q is true.

    d)   p cannot meaningfully be considered either true or false unless q is false.

    e)   either both p and q are true, or both are false.

7. The number of cases sufficient to justify an inductive generalization as reasonable

    a)   must always be over 50 percent of the total cases.

    b)   is set by rules applicable to all inductions.

    c)   is the same regardless of whether one is dealing with homogeneous or heterogeneous cases.

    d)   is relatively low when considering heterogeneous cases.

    e)   is relatively low when considering homogeneous cases.

8. Generalizations concerning matters subject to human choice

   a) generally require a careful selection of individuals representing a crosssection of the whole group.
   b) can never be determined by inductive means.
   c) presuppose that free will is an illusion.
   d) are only valid within the sciences of psychology and sociology.
   e) are unintelligible unless the human will is truly free.

*9 Establishing an inductive relation between antecedent circumstances and the to-be-explained phenomena

   a) always requires the methods of experimental science.
   b) presupposes a suspension of belief in any previously held opinions.
   c) presupposes that any connection between antecedent circumstances and the phenomena is purely coincidental.
   d) invariably separates causes from mere coincidences.
   e) presupposes a prior understanding of the type of antecedent circumstances likely to influence the phenomena.

10. If p is a necessary condition for q, then

   a) if p is present, q must be present.
   b) either p and q are both present or both are absent.
   c) if p is absent, then q must be absent.
   d) q must be present regardless of whether p is present.
   e) p must be present regardless of whether q is present.

11. If p is a sufficient condition for q, then

   a) if p is present, q must be present.
   b) either p and q are both present or both are absent.
   c) if p is absent, then q must be absent.
   d) q must be present regardless of whether p is present.
   e) p must be present regardless of whether q is present.

12. If p is a necessary and sufficient condition for q, then

   a) if p is present, q must be present.
   b) either p and q are both present or both are absent.
   c) if p is absent, then q must be absent.
   d) q must be present regardless of whether p is present.
   e) p must be present regardless of whether q is present.

13. Mill's methods of induction

   a) are a guaranteed way of discovering causal connections.
   b) are used only to test already known causal connections.
   c) express some basic patterns used in attempts to establish hypotheses on the basis of evidence.
   d) do not require any hypotheses concerning the types of antecedents that may be introduced.
   e) have no role in contemporary scientific experimentation.

For questions 14 through 18 use the following choices:

A. helps to pick out a necessary condition among antecedent circumstances (hence-
    forth *antecedents*) thought to be causally related to the to-be-explained phenom-
    ena (henceforth *phenomena*).
B. correlates variations in the antecedents with variations in the phenomena.
C. helps pick out a sufficient condition among the antecedents thought to be causally
    related to the phenomena.
D. correlates an otherwise unexplained portion of the phenomena with a postulated
    additional antecedent.
E. helps to pick out a necessary and sufficient condition among the antecedents
    thought to be causally related to the phenomena.

14. Mill's method of agreement
15. Mill's method of differences
16. Mill's method of concomitant variations
*17. Mill's method of agreements and differences
18. Mill's method of residues

Alice, Bob, Carol, Dottie, and Ed have dinner in Ptomaine Tom's Bar and Grill. The
standard menu includes soup or salad, a choice of three entrees, a choice of domestic
or imported wine served by the glass, dessert, and coffee. Alice orders chicken and
imported wine. Bob has filet of sole and imported wine. Carol chooses steak medium
rare and domestic wine. Dottie has steak well done and imported wine. Ed has chicken
and domestic wine. All had hoped to get by without a big bill. Since all are students,
anything over $20 counts as a big bill. Yet Alice, Bob, and Dottie had big bills. A
couple of hours after the meal Alice and Ed experienced extreme nausea.
Before answering the following questions draw a chart and try Mill's methods.

19. The factor that seems to have caused the nausea was

    a) steak.
    b) chicken.
    c) filet of sole.
    d) imported wine.
    e) domestic wine.

20. The answer to question 19 was determined by

    a) the method of agreements.
    b) the method of differences.
    c) the method of agreement and differences.
    d) the method of concomitant variations.
    e) the method of residues.

21. One item that definitely contributed to producing a big bill was

    a) steak.
    b) chicken.
    c) filet of sole.
    d) imported wine.
    e) domestic wine.

22. The answer to question 22 was determined by

    a) the method of agreements.
    b) the method of differences.
    c) the method of agreement and differences.
    d) the method of concomitant variations.
    e) the method of residues.

Suppose that P is preceded by the following antecedents, which are presumed to be the only relevant ones. Before answering the following questions be sure that you are considering only the cases suggested.

CASE	A	B	C	D	P
1	+	+	+	+	+
2	+	−	+	−	+
3	−	+	+	−	+
4	−	−	−	+	−
5	−	+	−	+	−
6	+	−	−	−	−

$+$ = factor present
$-$ = factor missing

*23. Consider *only* cases 1 through 3. Then one should conclude

    a) that C is a necessary condition for P.
    b) that C is a sufficient condition for P.
    c) that C or A or both is a sufficient condition for P.
    d) that C is a necessary and sufficient condition for P.
    e) that C or A or both is a necessary condition for P.

*24. This conclusion to question 23 was reached by

    a) the method of agreements.
    b) the method of differences.
    c) the method of agreement and differences.
    d) the method of concomitant variations.
    e) the method of residues.

25. Consider all 6 cases. Then one should conclude

    a) that C is a necessary condition for P.
    b) that C is a sufficient condition for P.
    c) that C or A or both is a sufficient condition for P.
    d) that C is a necessary and sufficient condition for P.
    e) that C or A or both is a necessary condition for P.

26. The conclusion to question 25 was reached by

    a) the method of agreement.
    b) the method of differences.
    c) the method of agreement and differences.

    d)   the method of concomitant variations.
    e)   the method of residues.

27. Now consider only cases 4 and 5. Then one should conclude

    a)   that C is a necessary condition for P.
    b)   that C is a sufficient condition for P.
    c)   that C or A or both is a sufficient condition for P.
    d)   that C is a necessary and sufficient condition for P.
    e)   that C or A or both is a necessary condition for P.

28. The conclusion to question 27 was reached by

    a)   the method of agreement.
    b)   the method of differences.
    c)   the method of agreement and differences.
    d)   the method of concomitant variations.
    e)   the method of residues.

*29. The method of concomitant variations

    a)   depends on our ability to manipulate the antecedents.
    b)   requires some cases in which the effect is not present.
    c)   can be used even when it is not possible to eliminate some of the antecedents.
    d)   requires the introduction of a new antecedent.
    e)   requires cases in which different antecedents are present.

30. The method of residues

    a)   depends on our ability to manipulate the antecedents.
    b)   requires some cases in which the effect is not present.
    c)   can be used even when it is not possible to eliminate some of the antecedents.
    d)   requires the introduction of a new antecedent.
    e)   requires cases in which different antecedents are present.

SUMMARY

Inductive Arguments:

  may have true premises and a false conclusion.
  rest on *presuppositions*.
  may be strengthened or weakened by further premises.

The argument from a *sample* to a whole
has the general form

$$\frac{\text{X percent of all } observed \text{ H's are K's}}{\text{So, X percent of } all \text{ H's are K's.}}$$

depends on how well the sample represents the whole.
Mill's Methods of Inductive Reasoning:

are a guide to inference, not a guarantee of correctness.

We assume P, a to-be-explained phenomenon, and a class of explanatory
    hypotheses involving factors, A, B, C, D, E . . .

1. *Method of Agreement:* If two or more instances of P have only A in common,
   then A is a cause (or necessary condition) of P.
2. *Method of Differences:* If B is absent whenever P is absent, then B is a cause (or
   sufficient condition) of P.
3. *Method of Agreement and Disagreement:* If C is present whenever P occurs and
   absent whenever P is absent, then C is a cause (or necessary and sufficient condition) of P.
4. *Method of Concomitant Variations:* If a variation in D is always correlated with
   a variation in P, then D and P are causally related.
5. *Method of Residues:* If the known causal factors, A . . . D, cannot explain all of
   P, then there must be another causal factor, E, responsible for the residue in P.

REFERENCES

[1] See David Hume, *An Inquiry Concerning Human Understanding,* section IV. This is
reprinted in many introductions to philosophy. The position being presented in this chapter
was strongly influenced by the writings of Wilfrid Sellars, particularly his "Some Reflections
on Language Games," reprinted in *Science, Perception and Reality* (London: Routledge &
Kegan Paul, 1963), pp. 321–358; and "Induction as Vindication," reprinted in *Essays in Philosophy and its History* (Boston: Reidel, 1974), pp. 367–416. Both essays stress the interrelation
of speculative and practical reason in inductive reasoning. The idea that the ordinary development of human knowledge depends on accepting established positions as true rather than
probable is developed in Gilbert Harman's *Thought* (Princeton: Princeton University Press,
1973), and in some of his other writings on this subject. The position presented here bears
resemblances to that developed by Karl Popper.

[2] Nelson Goodman, *Fact, Fiction, and Forecast* (Cambridge: Harvard University Press,
1955), chap. 3.

[3] The term 'resemblance class predicates' is taken from Stephan Korner, *Experience and
Theory: An Essay in the Philosophy of Science* (New York: Humanities Press, 1966). Many
others have developed the same idea in different terms.

[4] J. S. Mill, *A System of Logic* (New York: Harper & Brothers, 1881, original published
in 1843), pp. 222–237. A good modern treatment of Mill's method may be found in Brian
Skyrms, *Choice and Chance,* 2nd ed. (Encino, Calif.: Dickenson, 1975), chap. 4.

[5] This is a conclusion drawn in R. Rosenthal, *Experimental Effects in Behavioral
Research* (New York: Appleton-Century-Crofts, 1966).

[6] A summary of such data may be found in H. J. Eysenck and D. K. B. Nais, *Astrology:
Science or Superstition* (London: Maurice Temple Smith, Ltd., 1982). One point not sufficiently
stressed here is that a large percentage of popular astronomers, including those with syndicated
columns, rely on astronomical data that is simply incorrect. In determining which planets were
in ascendancy at the time of a person's birth they rely on ancient charts and planetary guides,
which do not take account of the precession of the equinox. This is a small wobble of the earth's
axis that takes about 25,000 years. Though this was discovered by Hipparchos of Rhodes, who
died around 120 B.C., and explained by Isaac Newton, who died in 1727, many astrologers seem
to be quite unaware of it.

[7] This history is drawn from N.R. Hanson's, "Leverier: The Zenith and Nadir of Newtonian Mechanics," in the posthumous collection, *What I Do Not Believe, and Other Essays,*
eds. S. Toulmin and H. Woolf (Boston: D. Reidel, 1971), pp. 103–126.

[8] The historical research behind this claim is chiefly presented in my *Scientific Explanation and Atomic Physics* (Chicago: The University of Chicago Press, 1982). A summary
account related to the present problem was presented in my article, "The Discovery of a New

Quantum Theory," in T. Nickles, ed., *Scientific Discovery: Case Studies* (Boston: Reidel, 1980), pp. 261–272.

[9]From *The National Enquirer,* Sept. 27, 1983, p. 5

[10]Emile Durkheim, *Suicide*, trans. John Spaulding and George Simpson (Glencoe, Ill.: The Free Press, 1951), p. 272.

[11]J. B. Lamarck, *Zoological Philosophy,* trans., Hugh Eliot (New York: Hafner, 1963, originally published in 1809), p. 119–120.

[12]Martin Gardner, "The Computer as Scientist," *Discover* (June 1983), p. 871. Copyright © 1983 *Discover* Magazine, Time Inc. Reprinted by permission.

[13]Alfred Kinsey, et al., *Sexual Behavior in the Human Female* (Philadelphia: W. B. Saunders, 1953), pp. 314–316. Reprinted by permission of The Kinsey Institute for Research in Sex, Gender, and Reproduction, Inc., Indiana University, Bloomington, Indiana.

[14]Walter C. Gogel, "The Adjacency Principle in Visual Perception," *Scientific American, 238* (May, 1978), p. 136. Reprinted by permission of W. H. Freeman & Co. for *Scientific American.*

[15]This essay appeared in 1843 in a short-lived periodical and was reprinted in *Medical Essays* (Boston: Houghton, Mifflin & Co., 1855).

[16]James H. Bryan and Mary A. Test, "Models and Helping: Naturalistic Studies in Aiding Behavior," *Journal of Personality and Social Psychology 6* (1967), pp. 400–407.

FALLACIES
AND FAILINGS
IN REASONING

10.1 WHAT ARE FALLACIES?

Before discussing fallacies we should briefly review the basic notions involved. 'True' and 'false' are predicates that apply to propositions, not to arguments. Arguments are classified as valid or invalid, strong or weak, persuasive or nonpersuasive, depending on the type of argument and the way it is used. *'Fallacy'* is a term that applies to arguments. A fallacy is an argument that *looks* like a valid argument, or a strong argument or a persuasive argument, but is not. The premises do not really support the conclusion. The appearance of validity is deceptive. We can best bring this out by recalling a fallacy we have already treated.

The fallacy of *affirming the consequent:*

If he is a communist, then he is an athiest.
He is an atheist.
Therefore, he is communist.   (10.1)

This looks like direct inference, but it is not. Both premises could be true and the conclusion could be false. This is an example of a *formal* fallacy. The form of inference used is wrong. In considering formal fallacies we can ignore the content of the argument and just consider the form of the inference. Since almost any violation of the rules given in chapters 5, 6, and 7 leads to a formal fallacy, we have been exposed to many formal fallacies.

In addition to formal fallacies there are also *informal* fallacies. These depend on the content, rather than merely the form, of the argument. Consider the following argument:

> All power belongs to the people.
> We are the people.
> Therefore, all power belongs to us.   (10.2)

There is nothing wrong with the form of this argument. Yet, if we heard this at a political rally, we would reasonably reject it. In the first premise the term 'people' refers to all the people. In the second it refers to a particular group of people. This change in reference vitiates the argument, since there is no good reason for believing that all power belongs to some particular group of people.

We have deferred a treatment of fallacies to the concluding chapter for two reasons. The first is a practical one. Effort is better spent in learning how to reason correctly than in examining the various and sundry ways in which reasoning can go wrong. Until one has basic standards for valid arguments and reasonable inferences, there is no nonarbitrary way to decide which forms of reasoning should be considered fallacies.

The second reason for postponing a treatment of fallacies is that there is no developed theory of fallacies. There are various catalogs, some listing more than seventy different types of fallacies, but there is no developed theory underlying these classifications. Part of the difficulty here is inherent in the very nature of the subject. The number of ways of going wrong is unlimited. They cannot be predetermined by any schematism, since they generally depend on the content, rather than the form of an argument. Another part of the difficulty lies in the fact that any attempt to classify a given argument as a fallacy generally involves a reconstruction of the argument given. A given argument may be considered invalid on one reconstruction, but valid on another. Consider the simple argument that a woodsman might use:

> She's a mother bear with cubs.
> So, she's dangerous.   (10.3)

A straightforward reconstruction of this argument would be:

> All mother bears with cubs are dangerous.
> She's a mother bear with cubs.
> So, she's dangerous.   (10.4)

Argument (10.4) would have to be rejected as unsound, since the major premise is not true. However, (10.3) could be reconstructed as an inductive argument:

> Most mother bears with cubs are dangerous.
> She's a mother bear with cubs.
> So, she's probably dangerous.   (10.5)

This would be a good inductive argument, since the premises do support the conclusion. Finally (10.3) could be reconstructed as a practical argument (woodsmen tend to be practical people):

> * I intend to avoid trouble.
> Most mother bears with cubs are dangerous.
> She's a mother bear with cubs.
> So, I better avoid her.   (10.6)

This is a perfectly reasonable argument.

Though a study of fallacies cannot be considered central to a study of reasoning, it is helpful to consider some common fallacies for at least two reasons. First, it may help in avoiding them in our own practice. Second, many people use fallacious arguments, even when they realize that the arguments are fallacious. Since we are inevitably exposed to such arguments, a familiarity with some common fallacies is a help in spotting them. The only practical way of doing this is to classify informal fallacies into different types.

There is a long and rather muddled tradition of classifying informal fallacies. The classification that will be used here is purely pedagogical. It lists the fallacies that seem to cause the most trouble, but it makes no pretension to being complete. We have, in fact, deliberately omitted some of the more esoteric types discussed by logicians. In the text of this chapter we will concentrate on the problems underlying the fallacies treated here. The summary at the end of the chapter lists the fallacies treated and some that have not been treated. The grouping of the fallacies treated grows out of the four topics that have played the most important role in the earlier sections of this book: language, deduction, induction, and practical reasoning. In this way the treatment of fallacies will also serve as something of a review.

10.2 VERBAL VEXATIONS

When arguments fail because of verbal problems, the failure is often due to ambiguity or vagueness of some key terms. The solution seems obvious.

One should resolve the ambiguity, or replace a vague expression by a more precise expression. The complication here is not with the practice but with the theory. Any attempt to explain how ambiguity or vagueness is resolved inevitably involves discussions of how terms get meaning and how terms refer. Meaning and reference are two of the most disputed issues in modern philosophy.

We do not intend to enter into, much less resolve, these theoretical disputes. I will simply present a position that reflects the main stream of modern Anglo-American philosophy and use this as a basis for my treatment.[1] The basic point is that the meaning of a term is set by the way the term is used in language. Definitions found in dictionaries do not *set* meanings; they report the meaning, or variety of meanings, that terms already have. This is even truer of definitions we may give in a talk or a paper. We cannot set the meanings of terms. This would involve changing the English language, something that is not under our direct control. There are, however, two sorts of things we can do to resolve verbal vexations. We can handle vagueness by a more careful choice of expressions, and we can handle ambiguity by distinguishing different meanings a term may have and then selecting one. In treating each verbal problem we will work from simpler cases towards more disputed ones.

Many of the basic concepts we use are fuzzy concepts, concepts that have no precise boundaries. This is particularly true of the resemblance class predicates mentioned earlier. We learn to use terms like 'tall', 'rich', 'heavy', 'truck', or 'boat' by associating these terms with standard members (Abraham Lincoln was tall; many baseball superstars are rich) and with standard nonmembers (cork is not heavy; a Thunderbird is not a truck). This leaves a fuzzy border. Is a man who is six one tall? Is a hovercraft a boat?

This is not a defect of our language. A language with fuzzy concepts is far more flexible than a language in which fuzzy concepts are replaced by more precise one. Fuzzy concepts can function in different ways in different contexts. At the time of this writing, for example, Gary Hart, who is 47, is being called young, while Pete Rose, who is 41, is being called old. A presidential campaign supplies a context that differs significantly from a baseball dugout. Instead of learning a battery of terms proper to different contexts, we can use one term like 'tall' plus some intensifiers, like 'very' or 'quite', and some deintensifiers, like 'somewhat' or 'kind of' to supply more precision when needed.

When vagueness is a problem, the difficulty usually lies, not with the English language, but with our usage of the language. There can be vagueness in meaning or vagueness in reference. Let's consider some examples. An advertisement in a newspaper claims:

> During our storewide sale you can buy dresses at a fraction of their regular cost.

(10.7)

What does 'fraction' mean in this context: $\frac{1}{10}$, $\frac{1}{2}$, or $\frac{999}{1000}$? All are fractions. The advertisement is deliberately vague, attempting to persuade through the suggestive power of the term 'fraction'. Suppose that a term paper summarizes Isaac Newton's place in the history of science this way.

> Newton was a great scientist. He made fundamental discoveries that had a lasting significance. His achievements inspired the work of later scientists.

$$(10.8)$$

Most instructors correcting this paper would write something like "Too vague" in the margin. We need more details on what Newton discovered, what contributions he made. (10.8) could be applied to an indefinite number of people.

There can be vagueness in reference as well as vagueness in meaning. Consider such notoriously fuzzy terms as 'liberal', 'conservative', 'realist', and 'idealist'. The term 'liberal' has different connotations in political, economic, educational, moral, sexual, or theological contexts. This does not mean that there is anything wrong with the term. In some cases the very fuzziness of the term gives it much of its inferential force. A person tends to think of herself or himself as being either liberal or conservative. Thus, a self-proclaimed political liberal who moves to a new state will generally get his initial orientation to local political issues through something like the following argument:

> The liberals are supporting these people and these issues.
> I'm a liberal.
> _____
> So, these are the people and issues I'll support.

$$(10.9)$$

Any later changes in support would usually be due to better knowledge of local politicians or issues, not to any distinction in the term 'liberal'.

Suppose that a politician in the same district argues

> The liberals will support me.
> Their support will give me 53 percent of the vote.
> _____
> Therefore, I'll win the election.

$$(10.10)$$

The premise that 53 percent of the people in a district are liberal could vitiate the argument. If one were to use a nonfuzzy concept, then one could say that a fixed percentage of the people in some district are of Italian origin, or are steel-workers, or are people who voted for the Democratic candidate in the last election. But the fact that some poll indicated that 53 percent of the people in some district consider themselves liberal does not mean that all of them will vote for the candidate who calls himself a liberal. The class that the term refers to is not fixed.

We might summarize the general point by saying that the usage of a term is vague, in a bad sense, if it does not supply an adequate basis for deciding whether or not a case in question comes under the term. One resolves the problem by supplying such a basis. This may be done by stipulating the meaning that a vague term has in a particular context. Thus I might clarify my use of the term 'good student' by saying that I am not discussing anyone's morals, but am referring to students who have a grade-point average of 3.5 or better. Or the resolution may be essentially a practical decision. Parents, for example, who do not want their children to see pornographic movies might implement this by decreeing: No R-rated movies for our kids. Yet the same parents might strongly object to having R-rated movies *they* want to see labeled 'pornographic'. This does not settle the general issue of which movies come under the vague term 'pornographic'. But it does settle the particular problem of deciding which movies the children can see.

Ambiguity presents a more complex problem. The usage of a term is ambiguous when the term has more than one meaning and an argument conflates different meanings. The complication here is that there is no automatic way of specifying how many meanings a term has. There is a range from terms that have clearly distinct meanings to terms that seem to have only one meaning until we analyze them more critically. There are many terms that have several totally different meanings. A *bank* is the side of a river or a business that handles money. A *cause* is something that produces an effect or a goal to be achieved by some group, such as the cause of freedom. For a young couple 'love' might seem to mean everything. In a tennis game 'love' means nothing. Most of us have been familiar with examples of homonyms since grammar school. Few serious errors in argumentation ever hinge on such clear-cut differences of meaning. If they do, one dissolves the error by distinguishing the ambiguity, as in the argument considered in an earlier chapter

> Only men are rational animals.
> Women are not men.
> ———————————————————————
> Therefore, women are not rational animals.   (10.11)

Here the problem is not vagueness of meaning, but two distinct meanings, neither of which is vague. In the first premise of (10.11) 'man' refers to the species. In the minor premise it refers to male members of the species.

In (10.11) the distinction was obvious. The difficult cases are those involving distinctions that are not obvious, because they are only needed in special contexts. Consider the argument

> If my salary is doubled, then I'll have twice as much money. If anyone else has her salary doubled, then she too will have twice as much money. The basic

cause of poverty in this country is that there is not enough money. So, the way to solve the problem of poverty is to have the government print twice as much money as it now does and to double everyone's salary.

'Money' is an ambiguous term in this argument. It can refer to currency or to purchasing power. When we are discussing the finances of one or more individuals, the distinction is not crucial. If my salary is doubled I have twice the purchasing power. However, if we double everyone's salary by printing twice as much money, then we double the currency, but we do not double the purchasing power.

Consider the following claim, a paraphrase of one found in a food advertisement:

Our vegetable oil is very low in cholesterols.
Cholesterol in veins and arteries is a leading cause of heart attacks.

So, using our vegetable oil helps to prevent heart attacks.   (10.12)

Should this be accepted as a sound argument?

The argument presupposes that cholesterol in food becomes cholesterol in the blood stream. The situation is not that simple. Cholesterol in food is broken down by enzymes in the digestive system into simpler molecules. The cholesterol in the blood stream is manufactured by the body itself. Accordingly, to clarify the issues involved in (10.12) it is necessary to make a distinction between food cholesterol and serum cholesterol. This distinction is not a part of ordinary usage and will probably not become a part of ordinary usage. The term 'cholesterol' already has a very precise meaning. It is the name of a complex organic molecule with the formula, $C_{27}H_{45}OH$. The distinction is needed, however, to clarify the issues involved in (10.12). After this distinction has been made, the argument of (10.12) is seen to be unsound as it stands. To make it into a sound argument one would have to argue that the intake of food cholesterol leads to the increased production of serum cholesterol.

A considerable amount of philosophical argumentation hinges on making precise distinctions and then justifying these distinctions through illustrative examples. Philosophers since Socrates have presented arguments whose validity depended on distinguishing different senses of 'know', 'true', 'good', 'justice', 'beautiful', and other disputed philosophical terms. The practice, however, is not confined to philosophers.

Evolutionary biologists, for example, are not merely faced with opposition from science-creationists. Recently, defenders of evolution have been accusing each other of relying on unsound arguments. K.S. Thomson showed that much of the confusion stemmed from the fact that the term 'evolution' was being used in three somewhat different senses.[2] In sense-1 'evolution' means 'change over time'. In sense-2 'evolution' means 'organisms are related by descent through common ancestry'. In sense-3 'evolution' refers to particular explanatory mechanisms for the pattern and process of sense-1 and sense-2.

Has evolution been proved? Proof depends on arguments and arguments hinge on the meaning of terms. If one is using 'evolution' in sense-1, then the argument is inductive and the evidence is overwhelming. A claim for sense-2 evolution is really a hypothesis. Most evolutionists accept the hypothesis in a general form and then look for evidence to support particular lines of descent. Evolution in sense-3 involves a collection of hypotheses, each requiring its own supporting evidence.

These considerations do not lead to any clear-cut list of fallacies together with semiautomatic criteria for detecting and avoiding them. They suggest, rather, methods of improving our practices of argumentation. When one suspects that error or confusion hinges on ambiguities in the use of key terms, then one should examine the way in which these terms are used in typical cases and differing contexts. This may suggest distinctions that reduce confusion and obviate failings in argumentation due to confusions.

Reasoning may go awry because of linguistic problems other than ambiguity. We will consider two—complex questions and loaded language. In these cases the same general advice applies. Pay careful attention to usage in different contexts and distinguish usages that are significantly different in the context of the argument.

A *complex question* is a question of the form, "Have you stopped beating your wife?" Either a "Yes" or "No" answer would seem to affirm the presupposition of the question, that the man has been beating his wife. The solution to this is rather obvious. Distinguish the question from the presupposition. In proper parliamentary procedure a call to distinguish the question is considered a point of order and, as such, takes precedence over a point of fact. The fallacy of the complex question seems to be effective as a fallacy only when the questioner is in such a position of authority that the person being questioned is not allowed to introduce such distinctions. Thus, a mother asking her son, "Will you be a good boy and go to bed?" might disallow any answer of the form, "Why can't I stay up and be a good boy?"

By *loaded language* we mean language that effectively presupposes a value judgment. The classical example is Bertrand Russell's rules for conjugation: "I am firm; you are stubborn; he is pig-headed." Here again, the obvious examples are easily spotted and handled by replacing loaded terms with more neutral terms. Thus, 'traitor' is replaced by 'convert'; welfare chiseler' by 'welfare recipient'; 'pinko' by 'liberal'.

The more difficult cases of loaded language as an obstacle to clear argumentation are cases of different subgroups with somewhat different ways of using key terms. This is aptly illustrated by the problems of the ecumenical movement. In the 1950s Catholic, Protestant, and Orthodox religious leaders began to meet regularly for serious constructive dialogs aimed at overcoming, or at least reducing, the theological barriers that had so long served to separate them. They discovered that constructive dialog could not really begin until some linguistic barriers were overcome. Should, for example, historical figures like Martin Luther and John Calvin be referred to as 'reformers' or as 'heretics'? The obvious answer here was to drop the loaded terms proper to each tradition and to substitute a neutral term like 'religious leader'. The same technique could be used to defuse such controversial or controverted terms as 'veneration of saints' vs. 'idolatry', 'mariology' vs. 'mariolatry', 'private interpretation of scripture' vs. 'rejection of tradition', 'papist' vs. 'Catholic'; and to clarify terms that were used differently in different traditions. In some cases this involved distinguishing differences in meaning. Terms such as: 'indulgence', 'grace', 'sacrament', 'faith', 'authority', and 'tradition' had somewhat different meanings within the Catholic and Protestant traditions. In some cases this involved differences in reference. Catholics and Orthodox agreed on the basic meaning of 'Ecumenical Council'. But the Orthodox tradition used this term only to refer to councils held before A.D. 1,000, while Catholics used it to refer to these and to later conciliar meetings.

The linguistic differences between the different traditions extended beyond meanings for key terms to more subtle differences in usage. As the Lutheran theologian, Karl Barth, put it: 'alone' is a protestant term; 'and' is a Catholic term. Thus where Catholics speak of God and man, faith and good works, scripture and tradition, nature and grace; Lutherans emphasize God alone, faith alone, scripture alone, grace alone. Dialog on these points required more subtle changes in usage until some shared common usage was developed. This shared usage did not solve the theological differences, but it did help the participants to understand each other's arguments.

Some Christian communities, most notably Fundamentalists, chose not to participate in the ecumenical movement. This choice is inevitably reflected in linguistic usage characterizing these separated traditions. Thus, one may regularly hear TV evangelists make statements of the form: "If you are a Christian, then you will do X." By indirect inference, this would imply that those who do not do X should not be counted as Christians. In practice the values substituted for X often exclude the majority of Catholics, Protestants, and Orthodox. Any use of the term 'Christian' that excludes the majority of Christians certainly represents a departure from normal usage. If interfaith dialog were desired, then the chances of a successful dialog would be distinctly improved by introducing qualifications such as "Christians who believe in the literal interpretation of scripture," or "Southern Baptist Christians." If, on the other hand, fundamentalist leaders wish to *exclude* interfaith dialogs, then the use of loaded language serves as an effective tool blocking any theological give and take. Here, as elsewhere, the use of language is part of a complex situation involving goals and intentions as well as meanings and classes.

10.3 DEDUCTIVE DIFFICULTIES

A *formal* fallacy in deduction is a deductive argument that does not meet the rules for deductive validity. We have indirectly treated these in treating the rules for validity. Thus a syllogism in standard form with two negative premises or two particular premises is an invalid argument form. The fallacy of denying the antecedent and the fallacy of affirming the consequent are also formal fallacies.

An *informal* deductive fallacy involves an argument that looks convincing, yet is not valid because the truth of the premises does not *guarantee* the truth of the conclusion. Though the idea is simple its application is not always a straightforward matter of relating the premises to the conclusion. Consider an argument that might be presented to a jury by a lawyer defending a woman accused of shoplifting.

> Ladies and gentlemen of the jury, could my client be guilty of shoplifting, a woman without a job, a woman who is the sole support of four young children? No, not her! So, you should return a verdict of *Not Guilty*.

(10.13)

This looks like a very simple example of the fallacy called *An Appeal to Pity*. It certainly is, if (10.13) is reconstructed as:

> My client is a woman without a job.
> She is the sole support of four young children.
> _____
> So, she did not commit the crime of shoplifting.

(10.14)

In this reconstruction the original argument, (10.13) is interpreted as being a speculative argument, one in which the truth of the premises supports the truth of the conclusion. In this reconstruction the argument is certainly fallacious. The truth of the premises in (10.14) are irrelevant to the truth of the conclusion. They would constitute, if anything, a motive for shoplifting. Suppose, however, that the lawyer's argument is reconstructed as:

> My client is a woman without a job.
> She is the sole support for four young children.
> _____
> So, you should return a verdict of not guilty.

(10.15)

The central point at issue in (10.15) is not the truth of the statement that the woman stole some mechandise. It is the practical decision that the jury has to make. Should they return a verdict of guilty or not guilty? The judge will undoubtedly instruct them that considerations of pity should play no role. An experienced lawyer knows that such considerations often do play a crucial role in reaching a verdict. The original argument may achieve its purpose of convincing and persuading. Regardless of what we label it, it might make sense for a lawyer to use it.

There are some standard argument forms that are labelled as fallacies of irrelevance. This means that if the argument is interpreted, or reconstructed, as an argument affirming the truth of the conclusion on the grounds of the truth of the premises, then it is not valid. It is invalid precisely because the conclusion might be false though the premises are true. A listing is of some help in spotting the principle.

Fallacies of Irrelevance

1. The appeal to pity.   This is a fallacy when one is expected to accept the truth of a conclusion out of pity for someone who would suffer if the conclusion were not accepted as true.

2. The appeal to force.   This is similar to (1) except that the motive involved is fear. This is a common argument. Every lobbyist, for example, puts pressure on legislators by hinting of distasteful consequences that might follow if the legislator does not vote the way the lobbyist wants. Yet this is rarely a fallacy. Ordinarily, the point at issue is not the truth of the conclusion but some practical decision, such as which way to vote on an issue. In making a practical decision, it is reasonable to consider the consequences of alternative choices.

3. Personal attack (a.k.a. the ad hominem *argument).*   This is not usually used as part of a direct argument, but as part of a refutation. Instead of showing that an opponent's reasons do not support his or her conclusion, one attacks the character of the opponent. In some circumstances this is justified and even necessary. If the opposing argument is an argument from authority, then one should investigate how competent and trustworthy the authority is. If a person presents herself as a candidate for public office, then she is asking voters to trust her integrity, competence, and reliability. Her character and competence are legitimate topics for analysis and discussion.

This character attack becomes a fallacy only when the point at issue is the truth of a conclusion, not the character of the person presenting it. In the mid1950s, for example, the publicly debated argument that fluoridation of drinking water would help prevent tooth decay was sometimes countered by alleging that the supporters of fluoridation were communists. Few are fooled by so blatant an irrelevancy. The people who were influenced by this character attack were usually influenced because they related it to other premises and arguments they already accepted. If the communists are behind it, they felt, there must be further harmful consequences that they know about and we don't. Thus, for reasons that utterly lack scientific support, some thought that fluoridation would lead to impotence and that this, in turn, would damage the virility needed to fight the Russians. In this case the basic difficulty is misinformation, rather than an informal fallacy.

   4. Appeal to ignorance.   In its crudest form this is the argument that some conclusion should be accepted as true, because its truth can not be disproven. Arguments of this form, or at least suggestions of such arguments, are often found in books and TV shows suggesting the reality of extrasensory perception, of alien astronauts visiting the early earth, of flying saucers, and of psychokinetic powers. In the TV shows it is often difficult to draw a sharp dividing line between argumentation and entertainment. When an argument of this form is found to be persuasive, it is usually not because people accept the fallacy as a valid argument, but because the argument fits into a background of assumptions, beliefs, and prejudices.

   In our country and elsewhere there is an undercurrent of suspicion of the scientific establishment. This is somewhat inevitable when people feel that their lives are being controlled directly or indirectly by distant experts on the basis of reasons that only the experts understand. Any priestly caste tends to generate anticlericalism. The scientist has emerged as the high priest of our culture, the person whose pronouncements are accepted as true even when, perhaps especially when, they are not understood. Reaction against these authoritarian figures often takes the form of looking for cases where scientists were proved wrong, where their prejudices led them to neglect or deny facts that did not fit these preconceptions. The literature on ancient astronauts, flying saucers, ESP, biorhythm, the Bermuda triangle, parapsychology, pyramid power, science-creationism, and astrology are the most likely sources in which the fallacy of the argument from ignorance may be found. Yet here such arguments do not become persuasive because of their functioning as isolated fallacies. This literature derives much of what persuasive force it has from its implicit but sustained attack on the scientific establishment and its values.

   Real-life arguments, as opposed to textbook examples, function in contexts involving people, their presuppositions, goals, values, intentions, and desires. These, rather than obvious fallacies, are usually the sources of sustained disagreement in ongoing arguments. This is aptly illustrated by a speech that the former Russian leader, Leonid Brezhnev, delivered to the Indian Parliament in New Delhi, India, on December 10, 1980. This was shortly after the Russian invasion of India's near-neighbor Afghanistan. Brezhnev was attempting to convince the Indian leaders that it was the West, particularly the U.S., that represented a threat to peace in the area, rather than the U.S.S.R.[3]

When we get by the obvious differences in the use of such terms as 'forces of imperalism' and 'people's government', then Brezhnev's basic argument is clear. Only the Russians are fully cooperating with the leaders of the Afghan government in seeking to implement the goals that these leaders set. Western leaders are attempting to block the implementation of these goals and to frustrate the functioning of the government of Afghanistan and are supporting those attempting to overthrow this government. If they would cease such efforts, then Russia would gladly withdraw all Soviet troops from Afghanistan. Therefore, it is the West, not Russia, that represents a threat to peace in Asia.

Our initial reaction, when confronted with such a speech, is to think of it as involving at least two fallacies. There is an appeal to force—Russia represents a distinct threat to her near neighbors. One might also reconstruct this as involving an appeal to ignorance, an assumption that his hearers were unaware of what was really going on in Afghanistan. These, however, are *our* logical reconstructions. From Brezhnev's perspective there is no logical flaw or fallacy in this argument. Nor is there any factual error. The claim that the Russian forces were supporting the established government and that Western forces were opposing this government was certainly true at the time Brezhnev's speech was delivered. The problem is with the presupposition that the government of Afghanistan is a legitimate government. In the Declaration of Independence Thomas Jefferson gave the classical Western formulation of the criteria that should be used to decide whether the *de facto* rulers of a country should be considered legitimate governors to be obeyed or tyrants to be opposed. The 1980 leader of Afghanistan was imposed by Russian troops after they had arranged the execution of the incumbent president. The new leader took his orders directly from Russian leaders. By our criteria he is not a legitimate leader, but a tyrant who should be opposed. The Russian leaders do not accept these criteria of legitimacy. They would insist on the legitimacy of the leader they imposed. The barriers between Russia and the West cannot be removed simply by appealing to fallacies in argumentation.

10.4 INDUCTIVE INFELICITIES

Inductive arguments and arguments based on analogy do not admit of any neat division into valid and invalid, or sound and unsound. In such arguments the premises give reasons for accepting the conclusion. Whether or not one accepts the conclusion depends both on the strength of the arguments offered and on reasons for acceptance, which may differ from the arguments offered. Both factors admit of degrees. Instead of cataloging fallacies, accordingly, we will indicate the ways in which inductive arguments are most likely to be deficient. It is sometimes convenient to use traditional fallacy titles as pegs, provided we realize that such classifications are matters of degrees and circumstances. They are not absolutes.

The first source of difficulty in inductive arguments lies in *presuppositions.* As we have repeatedly indicated, every type of argument involves presuppositions and can be flawed or invalidated when the presuppositions are faulty. The distinctive presuppositions that require special consideration in examining inductive infelicities are the hypotheses involved in classifying things or events as similar in the relevant respects. Perhaps the most important point here is to realize that what is at issue is a tentative hypothesis subject to revision or rejection in the face of contrary evidence.

We may briefly consider how three different types of inductive bases may lead to errors. The first is the classification of things into types. If this involves strict classes in the technical sense, then one is generally dealing with deductive arguments. Thus, if everyone who is a junior is obliged to take SAT tests and I am a junior, then I am obliged to take these tests. Inductive arguments are generally based on classification through resemblance class predicates, or through classification where the criteria for membership are not the same for the property in question.

More concretely, consider the person, typified by TV's Archie Bunker, who thinks in terms of racial stereotypes. The classifications may be beyond dispute in most cases. The people involved would classify themselves as Catholic, Protestant, Jewish, Italian, Polish, Chinese, etc. Archie assumes that such classifications supply a good basis for inductive arguments concerning behavioral traits. If the Italians he has met prefer spaghetti and meatballs to corned beef and cabbage, then all Italians prefer spaghetti and meatballs to corned beef and cabbage. Here is an induction based on resemblance class predicates. One learns a class by learning what count as prototypical class members and then decides whether other candidates should count as members by their degree of resemblance to these prototypes. Archie is assuming that members of the same race or nationality are essentially homogeneous with respect to their tastes in food.

When there are specific reasons for doubting such correlations in a particular case, then two sorts of considerations are appropriate. The first is linguistic. Does the categorization imply or suggest that the items so classified should have a certain property? To classify something as a vegetable is to imply that it is edible. To call someone a movie star is to imply that she is rich and famous. The suggestions may be false in both cases. In ordinary reasoning, however, they are generally accepted unless there are specific reasons for doubting them. The second sort of consideration is empirical. We learn that a neighbor is an accountant and assume that he is Republican. Nothing in the term 'accountant' implies being a Republican. Whether or not most accountants are Republicans is a question for empirical investigation.

The second type of common inductive base is the classification of events as similar. In routine cases this is unproblematic. Turning on the hair dryer or the vacuum cleaner today is essentially the same as turning them on yesterday or last week. The same results may be expected in each case. In some cases there is no sharp dividing line between shared classifications and the use of analogies. Consider an argument that is not uncommon in political disucssions. Chamberlain and Daladier appeased Hitler on the dismemberment of Czechoslovakia in 1938 and this appeasement led to World War II. If we appease Russia in some political takeover, then this could lead to World War III. This could be interpreted either as an inductive argument from one case to the general conclusion: "All appeasement leads to war" or as an argument based on an analogy between the political situation in the Europe of 1938 and some contemporary situation. In either case the argument needs much stronger support.

The third common type of inductive base involves arguing from a sample to a total population. The important point here is to make sure that the sample is representative of the total population with respect to the characteristics in question. Professional pollsters have developed detailed techniques for selecting samples that reflect whole groups on political issues. In physical situations some process of randomization is usually employed to ensure that a sample is a fair representation of a group. We shake up the bottle of jelly beans, shuffle the deck of cards, or use a random number sequence as a basis for selecting names before picking a sample to represent the whole. The details of such methods are not our present concern. The only point that now concerns us is the logical one. Unless there is good reason for believing that the sample is representative of the whole in the relevant respects, there is no good reason to accept inductive generalizations based on samples. When a TV commercial shows three women in a row saying that the margarine they just sampled tastes like butter, there is no basis for accepting them as representing anything more than part of an advertisement.

With this brief background we may discuss three fairly common types of failings in inductive reasoning: *hasty generalization, the slippery slope,* and *false analogy.* A hasty generalization is a generalization drawn from too weak a base. This may apply to any one of the three types of bases considered. Whether or not a generalization from an inadequate basis should be considered a fallacy or a failing really depends on how the generalization is used and affirmed.

If the class is based on some categorization, then an inductive argument has the form

Most observed A's are B's.
So, most A's are B's.   (10.16)

Whether or not this is a hasty generalization generally depends on whether there is some good reason for believing that things that are A's are also B's. The weaker the reason, the stronger the evidence required to justify (10.16). One may easily go from the assertion, "All the observed conductors of heat are conductors of electricity," to the assertion, "All conductors of heat are conductors of electricity" on the plausible assumption that both depend on the same process—here, flow of electrons. How about going from "All the Libras I know are lucky in love" to the assertion "All Libras are lucky in love"? Here it is impossible to establish any causal connection between the two categorizations. Between these two extremes lie correlations between categories that are more or less plausible: being a banker—being a Republican; being a truck driver—being a fan of country music.

The same type of considerations apply to the other two inductive bases. Arguments based on them can be cast in the form (10.16). If we have good reason to believe that there is a definite correlation between event A and event B, then less inductive evidence is needed. This applies, for example, to the correlation between an AFL team winning the Superbowl and a decline in the Standard and Poor's Index. With samples as our inductive basis, the crucial issue is the reasonableness of believing that a sample is representative of the whole.

We have already discussed the fallacy of the slippery slope. This is usually a refutation of the form: If a certain conclusion is drawn or a practice allowed in case A, then it would also have to be allowed in case B, C, D. . . . If this extension is seen as a disaster, we should also disallow case A. What we wish to consider now is when and why this way of reasoning is a fallacy. This depends on the type of link that is thought to connect A with the subsequent cases, B, C, D. . . . Three different types of links may be considered.

The first is the case where A, B, C, D . . . are essentially the same in the relevant respects. Consider the Golden Rule: Do unto others as you would have others do unto you. This entails that the principles I use in judging my own case (A), should be extended indefinitely to other cases (B, C, D . . .). This is ultimately seen as a principle of fairness: cases that are essentially similar in the relevant respects should be judged similarly. In such cases the slippery slope refutation (or the "if the camel gets his nose in the tent the rest will follow" argument) is usually a means of evasion of responsibility. Thus, executives of automobile companies have argued: "If we admit that *this* fatal accident was due to a manufacturing defect, then we would be liable for damages for an indefinite number of further accidents involving the same car. We can't afford that. So we can't admit that the accident was due to a manufacturing defect." Defenders of segregation and apartheid regularly rely on such arguments.

This fallacy is often invoked in controversies. If you grant our opponents A, then you will have to grant them B, C, D . . . as well. Here, two rather different types of links may be involved. The first is the claim or presumption that this is what our opponents intend. If you give them control of handguns, then they will try to control rifles, then shotguns, then knives. The second type of link is the assumption that, human nature being what it is, if A is granted, then B, C, D . . . will inevitably follow. When I was a student I attended a lecture by the police officer in charge of the Boston Vice squad. He was arguing very strongly that if pornography were allowed, widespread rape would inevitably follow. The pornography he had in mind—in those distant days—was the type of nude photographs that can now be found in magazines available in most newsstands and drug stores. Any red-blooded man, seeing such pictures, would become so excited, that he would be likely to attack the first girl he meets. At the end of the lecture the officer invited the members of the all-male audience to examine the supporting evidence he had collected! The basic point is the same in both cases. If the link between A and the rest of the series is not clear or automatic, then it must be settled by argument rather than presumption. This is a fallacy when the presumption that the precedent of case A would also extend to cases B, C, D . . . is not supported.

Something similar must be said about the fallacy of the false analogy. To label this a fallacy seems to presuppose that there are some established criteria for determining which analogies are good ones and which are misleading. There are not. Analogies are suggestive tools for reasoning about the relatively unknown in terms of the relatively better known. Sometimes wild analogies help. The organic chemist, Kekulé, struggled unsuccessfully to explain the structure of benzene. He awoke from a half-sleep dreaming of a snake biting his tail. Maybe, he reasoned, benzene is like this snake. This led to the model of the benzene molecule as a ring, the first successful model of a complex organic molecule. Historians of science have shown that many scientific breakthroughs were suggested by fanciful or farfetched analogies.

Models and analogies are particularly helpful in two types of situations. The first is when one is groping for hypotheses that might serve to explain some puzzling anomaly. The second is when one is trying to explain a technical issue to people who lack the background needed to understand a technical account. Analogies tend to become false when they are either pushed beyond these limits, or when they are treated as definitive explanations rather than as tentative hypotheses or popular accounts.

The analogies that are the most pervasive sources of faulty reasoning and the most difficult to deal with are not the wild or fanciful analogies. They are, rather, those that are so much a part of our habitual thinking that we no longer recognize them as analogies. They are submerged metaphors. The man is the head of the house, the woman is the heart of the house. The king is the head of the country; his ministers are his strong right arm; his messengers are his feet. The comparison between the human body and such social organizations as the family and the state is not merely an analogy. It has so structured the language traditionally used to speak of these social institutions that certain conclusions follow automatically. The body can only have one head. The head has authority over the members. It is unnatural to reverse this ordering.

Consider some other embedded metaphors.[4] The analogy between argument and warfare structures the way we speak of and experience arguments. Your claims are indefensible. He attacked the weak points in my argument. His refutation demolished the opposing position. Her argument advanced her position. Her refutation wiped out the opposition. This structuring actually determines the way we experience arguments and the truth values of claims concerning them. The statement "He won the argument" can be judged true or false on the basis of evidence. What evidence could one bring to bear to judge the truth of the claim, "He won the discussion," or "She lost the conversation"?

A theory is like a building. It requires a secure foundation. It must be carefully built so that the foundations support the higher levels. It can be shaken by criticism, yet continue to stand if the criticism is superficial. It may be toppled by an opposing theory or demolished by discoveries that contradict the foundational assumptions. The early twentieth century witnessed a sustained and ultimately frustrating effort to find the foundations of mathematics. In spite of these failures, many logicians and mathematicians were shocked by Wittgenstein's idea that perhaps mathematics requires no foundation. An organized body of knowledge *has* to have a foundation. Why must it have a foundation? In many cases people did not really ask this question. They presupposed that there must be a foundation for mathematics, or even for all reliable knowledge, and then asked the question: What is the foundation?

Time is a commodity, like money. We should not waste valuable time, especially the time we invest in training or the time we spend getting experience. We have to budget our time, use methods that save time so we have spare time to spend with our families. Love is a journey. We meet along the way, travel together until we come to a crossroads, and then go our separate ways. Many embedded analogies structure the way we experience and think about reality without our being consciously aware that we are using analogies.

Wild analogies are readily, almost automatically, recognized as analogies. They are so obvious that they rarely induce serious failures in reasoning. The analogies that are more likely to generate misleading conclusions are the types of embedded metaphors just considered. Many of these invisible metaphors reflect, to adapt Foucault's apt phrase, the archaeology of human experience.[5] Our distant ancestors adapted language proper to one realm of experience and used it to structure some other realm. We use this embedded archaeological residue as a structure guiding patterns of inference.

Ideas are food. We chew on them, digest them, absorb the ones we can assimilate and spit out the others. I describe someone else's paper as containing nothing but raw data, half-baked ideas, and warmed-over theories. It leaves a bad taste in my mouth. A good paper, on the other hand, contains real food for thought, something I can really sink my teeth into. I devour papers like this vorciously, especially the meaty parts. This implicit metaphor, however, does not extend beyond primitive methods of cooking. Does it make sense to speak of a paper with parboiled data, sautéed laws, gourmet theories, and microwaved examples?

Not only do these implicit metaphors structure inferences. They structure the way we experience reality and the way we discuss the reality experienced as well. In this sense they are much like presuppositions and can generate similar difficulties. Consider an implicit analogy, or buried metaphor, that developed in early Greek thought and has bedeviled philosophy ever since Plato presented his doctrine of ideas.[6] Understanding is seeing with the eyes of the mind. We have to see problems in proper perspective, see how the parts fit together, throw more light on obscure areas, view difficult problems from a different perspective, learn how others see a situation, or persuade them to see it our way. This all seems harmless until philosophers use such language to structure the questions they ask about the nature, limits, and validity of human knowledge. Thus, the understanding-is-mental-seeing analogy, when pushed to the limit, leads to an "I am a camera" type of epistemology. Our knowledge, to be true, must be a faithful picture of reality. If it is not, then skepticism is the easy way out. However, the two embedded metaphors—ideas are food, understanding is seeing—slight the constructive aspect of human reasoning and the fact that claims whose truth we are considering are only meaningful in the context of other claims, presuppositions, and linguistic conventions.

One cannot solve such problems by the facile means of labeling opposing arguments as fallacies. One must pay careful attention to the language used, see how it functions in its natural environment, examine the aspects that are extended to other environments, try to uncover the metaphorical structures that are used to describe experiences and channel inferences. Such considerations go far beyond our present purposes. Yet, it is helpful in understanding the limits of what we have treated to glimpse what is over the horizon.

10.5 PRACTICAL PROBLEMS

Practical reasoning, treated in chapter 4, is concerned with choices and decisions, rather than with the truth of the conclusion. Since practical reasoning shares many of the basic features of speculative reasoning, it inevitably shares many of the same possibilities of failure. Practical reasoning, for example, relies on presuppositions and can be vitiated by faulty presuppositions. However, we have already had a sufficient discussion of these shared features. Here, accordingly, we will concentrate on the problems and potential failings peculiar to practical reasoning.

Practical reasoning involves reasons for or against a decision. Making a decision, however, is not merely a matter of analyzing reasons and evaluating arguments. It also depends on intentions and goals. The distinctive sources of error that we wish to consider in practical reasoning are those that concern choices and those that concern goals.

CHOOSE COHEN OR CHOOSE CHAOS

Suppose that you encounter this as a slogan in a mayoral election. A simplistic response would be: I'm against chaos; therefore I'll vote for Cohen. But, is chaos inevitable if Cohen loses? What we are presented with here is a *misleading choice*. The choice the voters actually encounter is Cohen, or Symthe, or Gonzales, or Baltassare, or McDougal. The supporters of Cohen are suggesting that only Cohen can prevent chaos. But, this is a claim that needs more than a slogan to back it up.

A variant of the misleading choice strategy is the *straw man fallacy*. The idea behind the metaphor is that one replaces one's actual opponent with a straw man and then demolishes the straw man. This is surprisingly common in TV advertisements. An ad for a leading muffler company shows a man with a burnt-out muffler visiting a different muffler repairshop. There the repairs are being made by chimpanzees with baseball bats. Other shops the poor victim visits promise five-year waits and give no guarantees. Finally, as the background music reaches a climax, he comes to the right muffler shop where he receives quick courteous service from smiling competent mechanics and a guarantee good for the life of the car. Where should you, the TV viewer, go to have your muffler repaired?

In discussing other fallacies I have frequently expressed the opinion, not a very common one, that people are generally not deceived by the fallacious aspects of an inference. To understand why arguments that we construe as fallacies are accepted as persuasive by others we must attempt to reconstruct the arguments in the context of the presuppositions, intentions, and values of those who accept them. It seems to me that the same can*not* be said of the straw man fallacy. It is simpler than most of the other fallacies we have considered. It involves distorting an opponent's position, something that can easily be checked by comparing the straw man with the real opponent. Yet, judging by its extreme prevalence in such varied sources as political speeches, sermons by TV evangelists, and even syndicated columns, this fallacy seems to be quite effective. Why?

Most political speeches are delivered to a candidate's supporters. Sermons are, for the most part, just preached to believers. Syndicated columns are read chiefly by those who share the columnist's views. True followers often know the opposition positions only through the reconstructions given by their side. They do not compare what they are told with the actual opposition in any direct fashion. On a personal basis this shortcoming can be best overcome by studying the opposing position directly, rather than at second hand. On a public basis it is best overcome by such public forums as TV confrontations with competent reporters (but not celebrity interviews), or by publicly staged debates.

The final problem in practical reasoning we wish to consider could be dubbed the *"quick fix fallacy."* Most of us, for example, are barraged with letters of the form: If you want to save the whale, suppress pornography, preserve Indian reservations, help starving orphans, turn the rascals out of office, protest international violations of human rights, or convert the heathens, then *Send Us Money*. We share the goal; so we make the contribution. In many cases most of the money sent in is used to prepare, print, and mail further soliciting letters and to pay the salaries of those whose time is spent in this activity.

Ultimate goals in practical reasoning are anlaogous to the starting premises in a chain of deductive inferences. Neither are valid unless there are steps leading from the beginning to the end. Practical reasoning involves choosing a means in the hope of reaching a goal. We should be able to show how the choice in question can or might lead to the goal desired. The quick fix fallacy skips or skims the intervening steps. Sometimes others use this to trick us. Do you want to be popular?—Then take this six-month course in ballroom dancing? Do you want to make it big in the world of computers?—Then take our six-week course. Sometimes we deceive ourselves, substituting wishful thinking for realistic planning. One way to overcome this is to apply, in a deliberate and systematic way, the techniques of basic reasoning to the problems we encounter and the goals we aspire to.

EXERCISES

A. 1. Could an argument be interpreted as a fallacy on one reconstruction but not on another? If so, are we justified in claiming that the original argument was fallacious?
  2. What is the difference between a fallacy and a falsity?
  3. Does a dictionary set the meanings of terms or reflect the meanings that terms have?
  4. How is the meaning of a term determined?
  5. What is the difference between defining a term and stipulating a meaning?
  6. How can one distinguish different meanings that a term may have?
  7. Can you present an example of an argument that hinges on distinguishing different meanings of one term?
  8. What is meant by a 'fuzzy concept'?
  9. Should we always strive to avoid fuzzy concepts? Give a reason for your answer.
  10. What is a complex question?
  11. What is the basic method of handling complex questions?
  12. When should the use of loaded language be considered a fallacy?
  13. Is an appeal to pity in an argument always a fallacy?
  14. When should an appeal to force be considered a fallacy?
  15. Can class concepts play a role in inductive as well as deductive logic?
  16. List some cases in which a generalization could be considered a hasty generalization.
  17. Should all analogies that lead to false conclusions be considered false analogies?
  18. What is meant by an 'implicit analogy,' or 'buried metaphor'?
  19. What is meant by the 'fallacy of the quick fix'?

B.   The following selections usually involve, or can be reconstructed as involving, fallacies. Indicate the type of fallacy involved, and discuss its significance. Since the attribution of fallacious reasoning to an individual generally depends on the intentions attributed to the individual, we will generally avoid citing particular individuals.
  1. Comment on the following (from an anonymous source)

     a) He's dynamic; she's aggressive.
     b) he's good on details; she's picky.
     c) He's critical; she's bitchy.
     d) He's a two-fisted drinker; she's a lush.
     e) He's a man of the world; she's a tramp.
     f) He's talkative; she never knows when to shut up.

  2. The Pacific Gas and Electric Company included the following printed message with its monthly bills. What does the message say?

     This message in inserted in your bill
     by order of
     the California Public Utilities Commission:

     One item of expense included in the rate increase recently granted to PG&E by the Public Utilities Commission, amounting to $177.4 million, was attributable to President Reagan's Economic Recovery Tax Act of 1981, which requires the Public Utilities Commission to charge ratepayers for the expenses of taxes which are not now being paid to the Federal Government and which may never be paid. This expense may increase in the future.
  3. The Veterans Administration repeatedly insisted that there is absolutely no evidence to support the claim that soldiers' exposure to agent orange in Vietnam was responsible for any subsequent health problems. The same administration steadfastly refused to investigate such claims or to consider any evidence in their support.

4. If special benefits are accorded to the handicapped, then they will have to be accorded to women and minorities. Everyone will end up getting special benefits.

*5. Will you people be reasonable and accept this very generous offer that management has made?

6. There is no point in listening to anything she has to say on this subject. We all know that she is one of the leaders of the radical feminists.

7. All loyal Americans will support the passage of this arms-appropriation bill.

*8. Rome tolerated, and even praised, homosexuality. This led to the collapse of the Roman Empire. Now America is beginning to tolerate homosexuality; in San Francisco, it's a regular way of life. If we continue in this path, it will surely lead to the collapse of our country.

9. There is no way that scientists will ever be able to examine all the planets around all the stars in billions of galaxies. It is simply impossible to show that there are no intelligent beings existing elsewhere. So it seems altogether clear that there are intelligent beings in the universe besides us.

*10. I think that all of you members of the City Council will have to agree that this plan is best for our city. If you vote against it, the downtown business interests are sure to cease investing in further office buildings and housing. The unemployment rate will go up, so labor will also turn against you. Your political futures will be in jeopardy.

11. What's a nice girl like you doing in a place like this?

12. Newton made his fundamental contributions in physics when he was twenty-six years old. Einstein's great papers on the photoelectric effect, special relativity, and Brownian motion were written when he was twenty-six. Heisenberg, Pauli, Dirac, Lee, and Yang all received Nobel prizes in physics for work done in their early twenties. You have to be young to do creative work in theoretical physics.

13. Do you want to major in philosophy and learn something about everything, or do you want to major in a subject that is so specialized and so narrow that you end up learning everything about nothing?

14.   GOVERNMENTS
                                         INVITED
                          TO SOLVE THEIR PROBLEMS

THE WORLD GOVERNMENT OF THE AGE OF ENLIGHTENMENT ANNOUNCES its readiness to solve the problems of any government regardless of the magnitude and nature of the problem — political, economic, social, or religious; and irrespective of its system — capitalism, communism, socialism, democracy, or dictatorship. Governments are invited to contract with the World Government of the Age of Enlightenment to solve their problems on the basis of cost reimbursement after the target is reached.[7]

*15. Would you like a high-paying job as a specialist in computer programming? If you would, then sign up for our thirty-day course, *Computer Programming for Beginners.*

16. When our family exceeds its budget, everyone in the family practices a little austerity. We go without the extras, and even make sacrifices. Within a couple of months our family finances are back in the black. The federal government has been exceeding its budget by a few hundreds of billions of dollars. We all should practice a little austerity and get the bureaucrats to make some sacrifices. If we do, then pretty soon the government will be back in the black.

17. How could she be an expert cook? She never went to college; she didn't even graduate from high school.

18. If we increase the income tax on cooperate profits, then we will decrease the net profits that companies actually make. If their net profits go down then their investments will go down, especially investments in expansion of the industrial base. This

will mean fewer jobs and less buying power. This is the combination of factors that will trigger a new recession.

19. It is our children that they are educationg. It's our money that built the schools. It's our tax dollars that pay the teacher's salaries. So, the decision on what books our children should be assigned in our schools by our teachers should be ours and ours alone.

20. Anyone who is a Communist or a Communist sympathizer always opposes any expansion of American military might. Senator Cortez has consistently voted against every weapons system the Pentagon has requested. So, he must be either a Communist or a Communist sympathizer.

21. We live in a democracy. Everyone in a democracy is supposed to have an equal vote. So, when it comes to setting school policy, a student's vote should count just as much as a teacher's or a principal's.

22. Our party is the "People's Party." All power belongs to the people. So, all power belongs to us.

*23. I'm on probation this term. If I don't get a passing mark in this course, I'll be dropped from the school. So, I certainly deserve at least a C for the course.

24.   THE BIBLE: FACT OR FALLACY
                          YOU BE THE JUDGE

M.   Use the following code to answer questions 1 through 6:

   A.   a misleading choice.
   B.   the fallacy of affirming the consequent.
   C.   a sound argument.
   D.   a fallacious complex question.
   E.   a fallacious appeal to authority.

1. How do you as a scientist explain the existence of the Abominable Snowman? This is an instance of _____.

2. If the tight-money policy is eased, then the prime rate will begin to go down. As a matter of fact the prime has already begun to decline. So, it seems clear that the tight-money policy has been eased. This is an instance of _____.

*3. Either you major in one of the liberal arts or you remain a cultural ignoramus for the rest of your life. The choice is yours. This is an instance of _____.

4. If she is a Methodist, then she is a Protestant. However, when we were discussing religious positions she insisted that she is not a Protestant. So, she's not a Methodist. This is an instance of _____.

*5. Sigmund Freud claimed that Hamlet was unable to take revenge on his uncle because of his Oedipus complex. Hamlet subconsciously wanted to kill his father and marry his mother. When his uncle did that, he identified with him. Freud was one of the most influential psychologists of the twentieth century. So, this must have been what Shakespeare intended when he wrote the play. This is an instance of _____.

6. Have you finally decided to start paying attention to what is going on in class? This is an instance of _____.

Use the following code to answer questons 7 through 13:

   A.   ambiguous or equivocal language.
   B.   a fallacious appeal to pity.
   C.   the straw man fallacy.

    D.   a fallacious character attack.

    E.   a sound argument.

7. The choice is yours. Do you want to vote for me or to vote for a candidate who always favors policies of appeasing our enemies and alienating our friends? This is an instance of _____.

8. This witness is wearing a miniskirt in court. Her hair is obviously bleached. She's decked out with cheap perfume and junk jewelry. So, there is certainly no good reason to believe her account of how the accident happened.
This is an instance of _____.

*9. If my opponent claims that I voted for an increase in the tax rate, then she's a liar. You've all seen the campaign ad on TV where she makes precisely that claim. So I say to you that my opponent is a liar. This is an instance of _____.

10. Basically, what distinguishes religious persons from nonreligious persons is faith. The Secretary of the Treasury insists that he has faith in the President's plan for economic recovery. So, the Secretary must be a religious person. This is an instance of _____.

11. There is no point in listening to her account of the issues. Everyone knows that she is a radical feminist. So, we can't trust her accounts of any feminist issues. This is an instance of _____.

12. I certainly deserve a passing mark in this course, because if I don't get a passing mark then I'll lose my scholarship. I can't afford to continue here if I lose my scholarship. This is an instance of _____.

13. If you don't mind looking like a guy who sleeps in his suit or like someone who's auditioning for the Charlie Chaplin role in *The Little Tramp,* then you can buy one of their suits. Otherwise, you had better buy one of ours. This is an instance of _____.

Use the following code to answer questions 14 through 25:

    A.   the fallacy of denying the antecedent.

    B.   the fallacy of the slippery slope.

    C.   a fallacious appeal to force.

    D.   an appeal to ignorance.

    E.   a sound argument.

14. If she does not have an ulcer, then the X-rays will not show any distinctive blotches. The X-rays did show these distinctive blotches. Therefore, I think that she does have an ulcer. This is an instance of _____.

*15. You, as the Congressman representing the Seventh Congressional District, should vote against the Coastal Protection Plan and the other bills that these environmentalists keep pushing. Your predecessor supported the environmentalists. I lined up the other oil companies that want offshore drilling rights. Cyrus lined up the leaders of the fishing fleet and the markets they sell their fish to. Together, we succeeded in getting McCluskey defeated. If you reflect on this, I think you'll see that you owe it to your constituents to vote against the Coastal Protection Plan. This is an instance of _____.

16. Almost all the students I have known who have completed graduate degrees in computer mathematics have been offered high-paying jobs. All that she has left to do is pass the comprehensive examination and finish her dissertation. Her track record is good; she generally completes anything she sets out to do. So, I think that she has a

very good chance of being offered a high-paying job. This is an instance of _____.

17. All the attempts to find a virus, a bacillus, or a staph germ responsible for Legionnaire's Disease have failed. Scientists admit that they are as much in the dark as they ever were about the real cause of the disease and the manner of its transmission. So, it must be due to a virus much smaller than yet detected even with an electron microscope. This is an instance of _____.

18. If we can keep pulling that mousetrap play against the middle linebacker, then the safeties won't know whether to fill in the hole or to stay downfield. Their coach will be confused and the team's morale will be shot. No doubt about it, if we can get that mousetrap lay to work just one more time, the whole team will collapse. This is an instance of _____.

*19. If my period starts within two days of the regular cycle, then I'm sure I'm not pregnant. I'm already three days overdue and there's no sign of my period starting. So, I must be pregnant. This is an instance of _____.

20. If I don't get some coverage on national television, then I'll never be offered an NBA contract. But last week the ABC sports roundup showed the winning slam dunk I made against Villanova. I figure that I'm due to get an NBA contract any day now. This is an instance of _____.

21. If abortion is allowed, then euthanasia will certainly come next. Eventually the government will execute anyone that the leaders dislike. This is an instance of _____.

22. The Bible tells us that we will always have the poor with us, right till the end of the world. If these left-wing plans for welfare reform were in effect everywhere, there wouldn't really be any poor poeple any more. The end of the world would be at hand. If you don't want the world to end soon, then you better not support the socialist plans for a welfare state. This is an instance of _____.

*23. That medicine has not been adequately tested. Even the pharmaceutical company that produces it admits that there may be side effects that they haven't yet discovered. So, I'm not going to take it, even if the doctor prescribes it. If I did, it would make my condition much worse. This is an instance of _____.

24. Even if you think that one joint won't do any damage and could produce a pleasant high, you shouldn't take it. If you try it, it's just a question of time till you're hooked on it. Then you'll go to hashish and then heroin. Eventually, you'll be a hopeless drug addict. This is an instance of _____.

25. No computer with a hard disk drive included is in that price range. So, none of those new Korean computers can have hard disk drives included, because all of them are in the price range that you mentioned. This is an instance of _____.

Use the following code to answer questions 26 through 33:

A. a hasty generalization.
B. a reasonable inductive generalization.
C. a false analogy.
D. a fallacious reliance on loaded language.
E. the quick fix fallacy.

*26. Keats, Shelley, and Byron all produced great poetry as young men. Coleridge, Wordsworth, and Matthew Arnold kept producing when they were middle aged. But their later works were not as good as their earlier poetry. For all practical purposes, both Coleridge and Arnold eventually gave up poetry in favor of literary criticism. Even when the Romantic movement faded away, later poets like Swinburne, Whitman, and even Tennyson wrote their best lyric poetry when they were young. It seems clear that most poeple writing lyric poetry can expect to do their best work when they are young. This is an instance of _____ .

27. Do you want to become popular with all the girls in your high school? Would you like to have the most beautiful girl in the senior class invite you to the prom? Would you like to be the envy of all the other boys in the graduating class? If you would, then fill out this form and send it with a check for fifty dollars to *Correspondence Class in Ballroom Dancing.* This is an instance of _____ .

28. When a cat feels sick, it finds a hole to crawl into, some place where it feels protected. A lot of dogs do the same thing. That hamster usually runs around the cage all night. It stayed underneath the little roof all last night. So, it must be feeling sick. This is an instance of _____ .

29. He appeals to the readers because he's a liberal intellectual. But a liberal intellectual is just a person educated beyond his intelligence. So, I don't see why I should pay any attention to those pseudoscientific arguments he spins out. This is an instance of ___ .

30. Rats in theree different laboratories had their fur shaved off and had concentrated doses of this chemical rubbed in to their skin every day for six months. The rate of skin cancer was 17 percent higher in the exposed skin than in the skin that had not been treated. I conclude that this substance could be a carcinogen and should not be an ingredient in any acceptable antidandruff shampoo. This is an instance of

_____ .

31. There are seven days of the week, seven sacraments, seven parts of speech, seven ages of man, and seven seas girdling our globe. Seven is a natural number, an indication of harmony with nature. So, we should restrict the U.N. Security Council to seven members if we want it to be an agency for world peace. This is an instance of

_____ .

*32. The last three times that jockey had the post position he won the race. He'll have the post position in the feature race tomorrow, so he's a good bet to win again. This is an instance of _____ .

33. She has the same sort of fresh wholesome good looks that Grace Kelly and Cheryl Tiegs had when they started off. She is a good actress. She works hard, and she is willing to make whatever sacrifices she has to get ahead. Her chances of becoming a success are good. This is an instance of _____ .

SUMMARY

1. *Vagueness:* A term in an argument may be harmfully vague if it is used in such a way that we cannot be sure which instances come under the term.

2. *Ambiguity:* An argument involves ambiguity when different instances of a key term have somewhat different meanings and the force of the argument depends on confusing these differences.

3. *Complex Question:* A question is complex in the pejorative sense when either an affirmative or a negative answer implicitly affirms a debatable presupposition of the question.

4. *Loaded Language:* Language is loaded when the terms used suggest a value judgment about the point being argued.

5. *Begging the Question:* An argument is question begging when a premise presupposes or depends on the conclusion. For example the argument "Our leader says that he always tells the truth; so, whatever he tells us is true," would be

valid if the premise is true. This premise, however, depends on the conclusion being true.

6. *Appeal to Pity; Appeal to Force;* and *Appeal to Prejudice:*
   These three are similar in that one is expected to accept a conclusion because of prejudice or because of the consequences of not accepting it, rather than because of the support of the premises.

7. *Appeal to Ignorance:* If a conclusion cannot be shown to be false, then it should be accepted as true.

8. *Appeal to Authority:* This is fallacious if the expert is not an authority on the point at issue.

9. *Personal Attack:* This usually occurs when one attempts to refute an opponent by attacking his or her character rather than his or her arguments.

10. *Missing the Point:* An argument in which the premises are not relevant to the conclusion. For example: Today is Friday the thirteenth. So, if I play poker I'm bound to lose.

11. *Hasty Generalization:* A generalization based on a sample that does not adequately represent the whole.

12. *Slippery Slope:* This occurs chiefly in refutations of arguments supporting a decision and takes the form: Doing A will inevitably lead to doing B; doing B will lead to doing C, etc. If we do not want C then we should reject A.

13. *False Analogy:* An argument based on analogy is misleading when the similarity between two things or events does not supply a sufficient basis for a conclusion. For example: The last time I had a cold I took orange pills and they helped. These new pills are orange. So they should help cure my flu.

14. *False Cause:* This occurs when one interprets as a cause either a coincidence or common effects of the same cause. For example: Every time the bell goes off the slot machine pays a bonus. So the bell produces the bonus.

15. *Misleading Choice:* this occurs when the alternatives presented (Candidate A or chaos) do not adequately represent the choices available (Candidates A, B, C, and D).

16. *Straw Man:* This occurs when one refutes a distorted or grossly oversimplified version of an opposing argument rather than the real argument.

17. *Quick Fix.* This is an unjustified leap from proximate principles to an ultimate conclusion.

REFERENCES

[1] I take the analytic tradition as the main stream of contemporary Anglo-American philosophy. Many philosophers would disagree with this evaluation.

[2] Keith Stewart Thomson, "Marginalia," *American Scientist,* 70 (1982), 529–531.

[3] A translation of this talk may be found in *Vital Speeches,* (1981), pp. 228–230.

[4] Most of these examples are drawn from George Lakoff and Mark Johnson, "Conceptual Metaphors in Everyday Language," *Journal of Philosophy,* 77 (1980), 453–86; and George Lakoff and Mark Johnson, *Metaphors We Live By* (Chicago: The University of Chicago Press, 1980).

[5] Michel Foucault introduces this phrase in his, *The Order of Things: An Archeology of the Human Sciences* (New York: Vintage Books, 1970). The most influential account of the ways in which early people might have adapted linguistic structures to new domains is given

in Claude Levi-Strauss, *The Savage Mind,* trans. George Weidenfeld and Nicolson Ltd. (Chicago, The University of Chicago Press, 1966).

[6]The means by which these metaphors came to structure Greek ways of speaking is traced in Bruno Snell's *The Discovery of Mind,* trans. T. G. Rosenmayer (Cambridge, MA: Harvard University Press, 1953).

[7]An advertisement by His Holiness Maharishi Mahesh Yogi, Founder of the Science of Creative Intelligence and the Technology of the United Field, Founder of the World Government of the Age of Enlightenment.

ANSWERS
TO SELECTED QUESTIONS

CHAPTER 1

B

1. **a)** It is a description of an ideal driving experience.
   b) The Porsche fulfills this ideal.
   c) The only support is the ad's claim that the Porsche does fulfill this ideal.
   d) The description brings out the idea that the Porsche is a prestige car. One who owns and drives such an expensive car announces to the world that he or she is a success. This claim, in turn, is subordinated to selling Porsches.

3. **a)** This is an argument.
   b) What really contributes to sexual fulfillment is excitement of the mind and body, not just of the sex organs.
   c) This is developed by contrasting women's reactions to men's and by attaching the idea that a woman can find satisfaction through purely mechanical stimulation.
   d) She is trying to inform people, especially men, about women's distinctive needs and by so doing to improve sexual behavior.

6. **a)** It is an argument.
   b) Uncritical acceptance of technological progress is a trap that underdeveloped nations should avoid.
   c) By suggesting that technological advances have had a dehumanizing effect in the rich white West.
   d) Roszak is criticizing the standards operative in our technological society and attempting to replace them by more humane ones.

8.   **a)** It is an argument.
   b) Forbidding some species is one way of stressing their significance in a particular culture.
   c) He rejects other interpretations of this practice, such as the claims that some species are forbidden because of their psychical or mystical properties. He argues, though supporting details are not given here, that apparently opposed commands, forbidding or commanding the eating of some species, can produce the same effect of emphasizing a species.
   d) This is a small section of a book in which Levi-Strauss argues that the same mental structures are operative in the savage and the civilized mind.

CHAPTER 2

B (exercises following section 2.3)

2.   (1) ⟨The Shing could not be surprised;⟩ (2) ⟨they were too self-absorbed, too egocentric.⟩

   $2 \rightarrow 1$

4.   (1) ⟨It . . . asymmetry.⟩ (Hence) (2) ⟨gravitation . . . nature.⟩ (3) ⟨From it . . . emerge.⟩ (Therefore) (4) ⟨There is . . . nature.⟩

   $1 \rightarrow 2 \rightarrow 3 \rightarrow 4$

9.   (1) ⟨If the motion . . . forwards.⟩ (2) ⟨The retarded . . . carriage.⟩ (3) ⟨The mechanical . . . considered,⟩ (and for this reason) (4) ⟨it would appear . . . motion.⟩

$$\begin{array}{c} 1 \rightarrow 2 \\ + \rightarrow 4 \\ 3 \end{array}$$

13.   (WHEREAS) (1) ⟨it is common . . . affection"); ⟩
(and WHEREAS) (2) ⟨the marriage contract . . . functions;⟩
(and WHEREAS) (3) ⟨the marriage contract . . . contract⟩
(THEREFORE) (4) ⟨WE, . . . women of this city.⟩

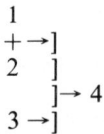

$$\begin{array}{c} 1 \\ + \rightarrow] \\ 2 \quad] \\ \quad\quad] \rightarrow 4 \\ 3 \rightarrow] \end{array}$$

M

4. D	**10.** C
7. B	**15.** D

B (exercises at the end of chapter 2)

3.   **b)** (1) ⟨No businessman will refuse my offer of: Cooperate or be murdered.⟩ (2) ⟨He is a businessman.⟩ (Therefore) (3) ⟨he will not refuse my offer.⟩

$$\begin{array}{c} 1 \\ + \rightarrow 3 \\ 2 \end{array}$$

d) (1) ⟨Wrong as we think slavery is we can yet afford to let it alone where it is⟩, (because) (2) ⟨that much is due to the necessity arising from its actual presence in the nation.⟩ (3) ⟨We cannot allow it to spread into the national Territories.⟩ (and) (4) ⟨We cannot allow slavery to overrun us here in these free States.⟩ (5) ⟨If our sense of duty forbids (3 + 4) ⟨this⟩ then⟩ (6) ⟨let us stand by our duty fearlessly and effectively.⟩ (6) ⟨Let us be directed by none ... true men do care.⟩

Sentences 1 and 2 are not a direct part of the argument, but a concession to the opponent's argument that any attempt to outlaw slavery would never work. It has the form 2 → 1. The final sentence is a rhetorical restatement of (6). This gives the overall form

$$5 \to 6 \to \begin{matrix} 2 \\ + \\ 3. \end{matrix}$$

i) (1) ⟨Some commit crimes just to be sent to hard labor.⟩ (And thus) ⟨they escape from the liberty that is more painful than confinement.⟩ (3) ⟨A man's life is miserable.⟩ (4) ⟨He has probably never been able to satisfy his hunger.⟩ (5) ⟨He worked to death in order to enrich his master.⟩ (6) ⟨In the convict prison his work will be less severe.⟩ (7) ⟨He will eat more and better food.⟩ (8) ⟨He will have an opportunity to earn extra money.⟩ (9) ⟨He will have better companionship than he has ever known.⟩

```
4 →]
    ] → 3 →]
5 →]   6 →]
       7 →] → 1 → 2
       8 →]
       9 →]
```

CHAPTER 3

B (exercises following section 3.2)

1.   (1) ⟨For the foreseeable future the U.S. will have to rely on surface ships to transport large quantities of goods and raw materials.⟩
(2) ⟨These ships require protection in time of war.⟩
(3) ⟨Other means of protection are insufficient.⟩
(4) ⟨Submarines are useless against airplanes.⟩
(5) ⟨Land based aircraft cannot be used at great distances from their base.⟩
(6) Therefore, ⟨the U.S. cannot dispense with surface ships like aircraft carriers, amphibious assault ships, and destroyers.⟩

```
         1
         +
         2
4 →]→ + → 6
   ]→ 3
5 →]
```

4.   This is a practical argument with the conclusion—directed to members of Common Cause—that the effort of the New Right to curtail the courts merits opposition. This is supported by two coupled premises. The first, that the New Right effort is a politically expedient attempt to assume power that traditionally belongs to the courts, summarizes the narrative parts of the argument. The second, that such an assumption of power would produce disastrous effects, summarizes the more argumentative parts of the article. Here the distinction between narration and argumentation is not at all strict for two reasons. First, the narration is couched in argumentative terms—the leaders of the New Right would hardly describe their efforts as an unprincipled attack. Second, in legal reasoning historical precedents have an argumentative force. To put this argument into a simplified form, accordingly, requires a considerable amount of reconstruction.

(1) ⟨The New Right and related groups are attacking the Supreme Court and the whole court system.⟩

(2) ⟨Their "blueprint for judicial reform" would prevent the courts from hearing suits on such issues as abortion, busing, and prayer in public schools.⟩

(3) ⟨Such a restriction severely curtails the power of the Supreme Court to pass judgment on constitutional issues.⟩

(4) ⟨They are bypassing acceptable means of reforming bad decisions.⟩

(5) ⟨The proposed reforms would have disastrous effects.⟩

(6) ⟨It would limit a citizen's right to appeal to the Supreme Court in cases relating to basic rights.⟩

(7) ⟨It would upset the balance of powers established by the Constitution.⟩
Therefore, (8) ⟨the proposed judicial reform merits determined opposition.⟩

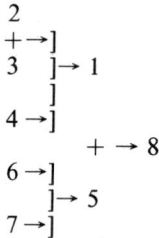

```
  2
  + →]
  3   ]→ 1
      ]
  4 →]
          + → 8
  6 →]
      ]→ 5
  7 →]
```

6.   To put the argument in our own terms, we should replace some nineteenth century usages with those common in the twentieth century, such as 'humor' for 'comic' and 'psychological' for 'metaphysical'. Though the last two do not have the same meaning, we are accustomed to discussing character traits in psychological, rather than metaphysical, terms.

(1) ⟨If the essence of humor consists in the contrast between professed ideals and false performances, then a sense of humor serves a useful purpose.⟩

(2) ⟨An awareness of this contrast helps to preserve personal integrity.⟩

(3) ⟨It also contributes to a psychological balance.⟩

(4) ⟨This is an aid to sympathy and sanity.⟩

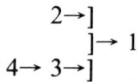

```
   2→]
       ]→ 1
 4→ 3→]
```

B (exercises at the end of chapter 3)

2.   c) This is a difficult example because it presupposes some familiarity with Freudian terminology. By the time Freud wrote *The Ego and the Id* (1923), he had established a distinction between *the latent,* items that are not in

consciousness but could easily be recalled (such as names of neighborhood streets), and the *unconscious,* items that are not in consciousness because of an internal repression. The citation involves two rather different types of presuppositions. The first, a psychological one, is that the mind can be understood as an arena of conflicting forces. In this case the crucial conflict is between a force of repression and a force striving to bring the repressed item to consciousness. The second presupposition is methodological. He claims that the fact that the methods of psychoanalysis allow unconscious ideas to be expressed renders the theory of psychoanalysis irrefutable. In making such a claim Freud seems to be presupposing that a hypothesis that works must be true. As will be seen later, this is an extremely dubious presuppostion, so dubious that Freud is best interpreted here as indulging in rhetorical exaggeration.

e) The author of this letter presupposes that Picasso's failure to depict a woman's legs realistically was due to a lack of anatomical knowledge on Picasso's part. He also presupposes that Michelangelo drew women's legs more realistically. Michelangelo's women always looked masculine and had big, muscular legs. Since Picasso had painted women realistically before 1910, it is not reasonable to presume that later departures from realism were due to a lack of anatomical knowledge.

3.   b) The perspective here is that actions that are otherwise immoral (a father killing his son) is moral when done out of obedience to a divine command. There is a further presupposition that whatever the Bible teaches is true. If the Bible states that God commanded Abraham to kill his son, Isaac, then God did indeed command this and Abraham knew that God had so commanded.

e) St. Thomas Aquinas, the most brilliant of the medieval theologians, worked out a synthesis of the Christian tradition and Aristotelian philosophy. From St. Paul's Epistle to the Romans, chap. 8, he accepts the idea that all of creation will find its fulfillment, and its freedom from decay, through the completion of Christian redemption. From Book 4 of Aristotle's physics he accepts the idea that all physical motion on earth depends on the transmission of motion from the celestial bodies that revolve around the earth, the moon, the planets, the sun, and the stars. If men are to be free from change, then the heavenly bodies must cease rotating. Since time is, in Aristotle's phrase, the measure of motion, a cessation of all motion means an end of time.

CHAPTER 4

B

5.   Both justices agree on the *grounds:* the State of Georgia has banned film distributors from showing a particular movie even to audiences limited to consenting adults. They also agreed that the crucial issue was not the merits of the particular movie but the conflict between freedom of speech and the right of a state to protect its citizens from harm.

Justice Burger

Warrant: The state has a right to regulate obscene materials.
Qualification: provided this prohibition does not run afoul of specific constitutional prohibitions.
Conclusion: The state of Georgia was justified in banning distribution of the film.

Justice Brennan

Warrant: The state should not prohibit what its citizens can read or see.

Qualification: provided they are consenting adults.

Conclusion: The state is not justified in banning the movie.

When the two positions are compared in this way, it becomes clear that the real point of disagreement is the warrant. The crucial point, accordingly, is an evaluation of the argument supporting the warrant as more important than the qualification, which in each case is the opposing warrant. The reasons are:

Justice Burger

1.   It has long been recognized that the state has such rights.
2.   The state has a need to do this:
      in the interest of public safety;
      in the interest of the quality of life;
      to regulate the tone of commerce;
      and to protect public safety.

Justice Brennan

1.   Such a prohibition would lead to further undesirable regimentation.
2.   Such a prohibition violates constitutional rights to free speech.
6.   The two speakers agree on the basic facts that (in the first half of 1981) there was an economic recession. The principal factors involved in the depression were high unemployment rates, a high inflation rate, and a large budget deficit. They also agreed that the chief tool for improving the economy is the government budget. They disagreed on their priorities and on their interpretation of the facts.

Speech by Cornish

Grounds:

1.   There is a high debt load.
2.   There is high unemployment. Cornish inteprets this as due chiefly to worker's laziness and unwillingness to make sacrifices.
      Warrant: To achieve a healthy economy we must find other means of doing the work that a depression does. This work is one of reducing the high debt load and disciplining the work force.
      Claim: We can achieve these results without a depression. Some means suggested are eliminating the debt load by massive defaults and by government inflation, and disciplining the work force by putting the unemployed in very demanding and difficult work camps.

Speech by Jordan

Grounds:

1.   The poor or near poor suffer serious hardships.
2.   The black community suffers great disadvantages, especially in unemployment and inadequate training.
3.   The safety net program in the federal budget does not provide for the needs of the really poor.
4.   The federal budget does not provide the marginally employed with incentives to work, rather than go on welfare.

Warrant: The federal budget should meet the needs of the nation while providing poor people with opportunities to join the mainstream of economic growth.

Claim: The federal budget for the year 1981 does not meet the requirements proper to a federal budget.

B *(exercises following section 4.5)*

3.   Before applying any sort of utility theory to this problem it is necessary to determine the goals and values proper to each situation. In Situation I the primary value for most people is security. Investing the money in an insured bank account guarantees a modest return and leaves the $100,000 intact as a nest egg. If economic security is the highest goal, then *a* is the most reasonable choice.

In Situation II the primary value is presumably getting the best overall return on investment. A simple nontechnical utility chart can easily be constructed.

CHOICE	VALUE	CHANCE	UTILITY	NET UTILITY
Investment	8,000/yr	1.0	8,000/yr	8,000/yr
Stocks	−20,000	0.5	−10,000	
	+40,000	0.5	+20,000	+10,000
Oil	−100,000	0.8	−80,000	
Exploration	+1,000,000	0.2	+200,000	+120,000

The risky oil exploration represents the best investment for the investor who can absorb a loss. It might be the best investment for the retired couple if they value a chance for a final fling higher than economic security.

M

2. b   **11.** b
6. f   **12.** b
8. e   **17.** a

CHAPTER 5

B *(exercises following section 5.1)*

3.   Partial inclusion

4.   **b)** All persons over thirty are persons I don't trust.

M

1. A   6. E

B *(exercises following section 5.3)*

I,4.

Given:

Some tumors are not malignant.	O	T	F	Assumed
All tumors are malignant.	A	F	T	
No tumors are malignant	E	U	F	
Some tumors are malignant.	I	U	T	

M

15. B	**19.** D
16. A	**20.** D
17. D	**38.** D
18. B	

CHAPTER 6

B (exercises following section 6.2)

I.2

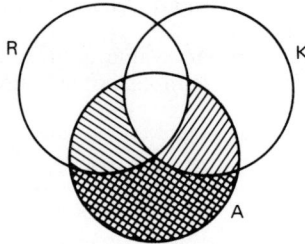

Some rocky formations are in Keplerian orbits. This is valid on the existential presupposition that there are asteroids.

II.2

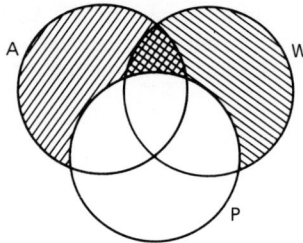

Invalid

III.3   All mammals are warm-blooded creatures.
        All mammals are sentient creatures.
        ───────────────────────────────
        All sentient creatures are warm-blooded creatures.

(Snakes and other reptiles are sentient but not warm-blooded.)

M

1. d	**13.** C
4. b	**16.** E
8. c	**20.** A
10. E	

B (exercises following section 6.3)

2.   The first figure has a valid EI form. Both the E and I forms retain their truth
            values if subject and predicate are interchanged. If "Some M is L" is true,
            so is "Some L is M." Both are represented by the same Venn diagram. So
            the EI form must be valid in all figures, since the other figures are obtained
            from figures one forms by switching subject and predicate. The IE form
            would have the same conclusion as the EI form, but with subject and pred-
            icate interchanged. Since this is convertible, both forms are equivalent.
            Only one needs to be listed.

3.   c) Fig. 1, AAA, valid.
       e) Fig. 3, EOO, invalid.
       j) Fig. 3, EAO, valid on the assumption that there are switchhitters.

4.   e) F–U   A   h) M–U   E
          N–U   A   S–M   A
          N–F   A Fig. 1, valid   S–U   E Fig. 1, valid

M

26. C   30. C
28. A   35. E

CHAPTER 7

B (exercises following section 7.5)

2.   Invalid; fallacy of denying antecedent.
4.   Valid; indirect inference.
8.   Invalid; fallacy of affirming the consequent.
13.   Valid; a series of hypothetical syllogisms.
15.   Valid; hypothetical syllogism plus indirect inference.

M

1. B   9. E
3. A

B (exercises following section 7.6)

1.   Invalid; fallacy of affirming the consequent.
2.   Valid; direct inference using the 'only if' connection.
5.   Invalid.

M

11. E   14. C
12. D   19. E

B (exercises following section 7.7)

1.   Invalid; neither disjunct affirmed.
5.   Valid; disjunctive argument.
10.   Valid; disjunctive argument.

M

22. E   **29.** A
25. A

CHAPTER 8

B

4.   This records the beginning of the work for which Becquerel was awarded (along with Pierre and Marie Curie) the 1903 Nobel prize. Like many scientific discoveries, it begins with confusion. After the discovery of X-rays, penetrating radiation was associated with phosphorescence. Becquerel worked with uranium salts, which phosphoresced. Since phosphorescence is in the range of visible light, Becquerel wished to test the relation of the mysterious penetrating radiation to visible light.
Anomaly: Invisible radiation
H1. Penetrating radiation is like visible light.
H2. Penetrating radiation is not like visible light.
If H1 is true, then the radiation associated with phosphorescent salts should not be able to penetrate two layers of thick black paper and darken a photographic plate. Sunlight, which was known to contain infrared and ultraviolet radiation, could not do this.
Since the phosphorescent salt of uranium darkened the photographic plate, H1 is eliminated, leaving H2. However, it was not clear that the darkening of the photographic plate was due to radiation, rather than to something else like chemical activity. The second part of the experiment tested this. Radiation travels in straight lines. The fact that a wire mesh between the salts and the plate left its image on the plate indicated that whatever the salts gave off travelled in a straight line.
Through further experiments Becquerel learned that uranium salts that did not phosphoresce produced the same effect. After that he associated the penetrating radiation with uranium rather than with phosphorescence.

6.   Since Holmes's inferences are labeled 'deductions', we will test their validity by transforming them into deductions.
  a) Only bachelors are sloppy men.
        (Or: All sloppy men are bachelors.)
        The visitor is sloppy.

      Therefore, the visitor is a bachelor.
  b) Only freemasons wear watchchains with a masonic symbol.
        The visitor is wearing a watch chain with a masonic symbol.

      Therefore, the visitor is a freemason.
  c) The visitor's breathing indicates an asthmatic condition.
        Therefore, the visitor has asthma.
        The major of the first argument was more plausible at the turn of the century than now. Without synthetic fabrics, most clothes needed regular ironing. Generally, only women did ironing. A bachelor living alone might wear unpressed clothes. However, servants were cheap, so that even the moderately well-to-do could afford maid service. As the story develops, the visitor is a prosperous builder, who lives with his parents. The first argument, accordingly, is valid as reconstructed, but not sound. There is no good reason for believing the major to be true.

The second argument seems sound since the major is generally true.

The third argument is not deductive, but an inference from symptoms to a cause. Since Sir Arthur Conan Doyle was a physician himself, he, and presumably Dr. Watson as well, realized that no competent physician relied on such a snap diagnosis.

9. Hunt clubs, and similar voluntary associations, do give awards to members at regular occasions. What hospital gives an expensive award to an intern (our equivalent of the medical status Holmes is discussing) simply because the intern completed his term? An expensive award is more likely to be given to a retiring staff physician. Holmes rules this out on the grounds that no successful physician would retire from a London hospital to take up a country practice. The inference from a walking stick as an award to a young man is very dubious.

The further inferences could easily be put in deductive form with such majors as: Only amiable people get awards; only unambitious doctors leave London for country practice; only absent-minded people leave a walking stick behind. Are these true? Awards are generally given by institutions for outstanding achievements (the leading salesperson) or for length of service (the gold watch after fifty years). What institution grants awards to its members just for being amiable? Holmes deduced that the doctor is unambitious. Yet, Watson's medical dictionary indicated that, while still an intern, the doctor won the Jackson prize for comparative pathology. Absent-mindedness is a trait. Can any character trait be established on the basis of one indirect observation?

The reasoning about the dog is best approached backwards. Suppose that the dog did leave teeth marks on the walking stick from which his jaw size could be estimated. Then two further implications seem to follow. First, when the doctor goes for a walk with his prized walking stick, he has his dog carry it. If he does not want it for walking, why not leave it behind? Second, if the dog who habitually carries the walking stick were to bite the stick in slightly different places, or move it around in his mouth while walking, then the teeth marks would show a spread. If there were such a spread, then the inference from teeth marks to jaw size to dog size would not hold. What dog always picks up a walking stick in exactly the middle every time and then holds it rigidly for a long walk? The "deductions" always work in the stories simply because Doyle wrote the stories and made them work.

CHAPTER 9

B

2. a) The argument is inductive.
   b) She is using the method of concomitant variations.
   c) Any evaluation of the strength of the argument depends on an appraisal of the operative presuppositions. If the teacher assumes that approximately 95 percent of *all* students in the sixth grade watch TV regularly and that roughly 85 percent are interested in sports, but that less than half come from broken families, then she has some justification for assuming a correlation between broken families and scholastic underachievement. This would be an adequate argument if her purpose was one of spotting potential underachievers. If, however, she intended to write a study correlating underachievement with broken homes, then she would need a much more systematic study.

5.   **a)** The argument is inductive.
     b) He is relying on the method of agreement.
     c) Again, an appraisal depends on an evaluation of the operative presupposi-
     tions. On the extremely unlikely presupposition that Wee Willie would buy
     scotch, bourbon, and other liquors without knowing that they contain alco-
     hol, then his inductive argument does support the conclusion that soda
     water is the only factor present in all the cases considered. The inevitable
     further experiment of spending an evening drinking scotch or bourbon
     without soda would soon produce disconfirming evidence.

6.   **a)** The argument is inductive.
     b) He is using the method of concomitant variations.
     c) If the greenskeeper assumes that the nitrate is the active ingredient respon-
     sible for increased growth and that two cups of the more expensive fertilizer
     per square foot gives the best result, then he can also conclude that 2.4 cups
     of the fertilizer with 10 percent nitrate have the same amount of nitrate as
     2 cups of the fertilizer with 12 percent nitrate. If 2.4 cups of the cheaper
     fertilizer cost less than 2 cups of the more expensive fertilizer, then it is the
     better buy.

M

5. C	**23.** B
9. E	**24.** A
17. E	**29.** C

CHAPTER 10

B

5.   Complex question. It suggests that it is not possible to be reasonable and
     reject management's offer.

8.   The analogy is misleading on at least two grounds. First, there is no evi-
     dence to suggest that homosexuality was causally responsible for the decline
     of Rome. Second, homosexuality was tolerated during the era of pagan
     Rome, when the empire was strong. It was widely condemned during the
     Christian era, and this was when the western Roman empire collapsed.

10. On a standard reconstruction this is an appeal to force. The reasons offered
     might support the claim that members of the city council who vote against
     the plan will suffer adverse consequences. They do not support the conclu-
     sion that the plan is best for the city.

15. This is an example of the quick fix fallacy. A thirty day computer program
     is just an introduction to computing. It cannot produce computer
     specialists.

23. An appeal to pity. The reason given might support a request for consider-
     ation, but not the claim that the student *deserves* a passing mark.

M

3. A	**19.** A
5. E	**23.** D

9. E   26. B

15. C

32.   **B.** This is a weak argument. Yet it is often the type of argument that gamblers use to supplement the standard information that the other bettors have in order to get a slight competitive edge. A professional gambler banks on a slight competitive edge, not on guaranteed conclusions.

INDEX